Age Estimation in the Living

Age Estimation in the Living
The Practitioners Guide

Sue Black, Anil Aggrawal and Jason Payne-James

A John Wiley & Sons, Ltd, Publication

Library of Congress Cataloging-in-Publication Data
Black, Sue M.
   Age estimation in the living : the practitioners guide / Sue Black, Anil Aggrawal and Jason Payne-James.
      p. cm.
   Includes index.
   ISBN 978-0-470-51967-7 (cloth)
   1. Physical anthropology.   2. Anthropometry.   3. Human growth.   4. Human body–Composition–Age factors.   5. Forensic anthropology.   6. Dental anthropology.   I. Aggrawal, Anil.   II. Payne-James, Jason.   III. Title.
   GN51.B555 2011
   599.9–dc22
                                                                          2010024536

ISBN: 978-0-470-51967-7

A catalogue record for this book is available from the British Library.

Set in 10/12 Sabon by Aptara Inc., New Delhi, India.
Printed and Bound in Singapore by Markono Print Media Pte Ltd.

Impression   2010

Professor Anil Aggrawal wishes to dedicate this text to – my son Tarun, nephew Nitin and niece Khushboo for believing in me.

Contents

Foreword

Most people in the developed world, if asked, would be able to say how old they are. This would be hearsay information, of course, as none of us can speak to this from our own knowledge. We have to depend on others to tell us when we were born. But family tradition, supported by information carefully recorded in the appropriate public register, enables us to fill this gap and, when this is needed, to satisfy the relevant authorities.

But there are a surprisingly large number of situations where people are either unable to tell the authorities when they were born or wish to persuade them that they are older or younger than they in fact are. For much of ordinary day-to-day living this does not matter. But time and time again the complex legal systems in which we live require this information to be given and require that the information provided is accurate. Age is a significant factor as to the way people are treated by the criminal law, by the social services and by asylum and immigration law, to take just some examples. Many asylum seekers arrive in this country without documentary evidence of their age and identity. An increasing number of them are claiming to be under the age of 18. No doubt this is because they have been advised to seek the special treatment, including the provision of accommodation by a local authority, that our legal system gives to persons under that age. Local authorities are under a statutory duty to provide accommodation for any child in need within their area. The statute says that a child for this purpose means a person under the age of 18.

As this book shows however, there is a significant difference between the assumption about information as to a person's age on which legislation of this kind is based and what can actually be achieved in practice where there are no records or where the recorded information cannot be relied upon. In a recent case[1] the UK Supreme Court held that, in enacting provisions of this kind, Parliament intended that the question of a person's age was for determination ultimately by a court. This was because age, for the purpose of these provisions, is a question of objective fact. The statute proceeds on the basis that it will be possible to determine precisely when a person moves from one age group to another. That can readily be done, of course, in cases where the information can be supplied by the production of a birth certificate. Providing the answer with that degree of precision where, because reliable information of that kind is lacking, professional opinion has to be relied upon instead is much more difficult.

---

[1] *R(A) v Croydon London Borough Council* [2009] UKSC 8, [2009] 1 WLR 2557.

The value of this book lies as much in the advice that it gives as to what ought not to be done in that situation as in the guidance that it gives as to what can. It warns that formal age evaluation must never be put in the hands of the inexperienced practitioner. The expertise of a forensic specialist is essential and, as various methods may have to be used in what is often a multi-disciplinary exercise, it may be necessary for specialists with the relevant expertise to consult with one another before an answer is reached. It aims to be authoritative and comprehensive. By raising awareness as to the limitations of the main approaches to age estimation, it encourages an approach which is careful and well-grounded in a proper understanding of the relevant disciplines. It may not be possible to achieve the precision that can be found by examining a person's birth certificate. But in the right hands, and with an informed understanding the methods that can be used to achieve this, age estimation can get very close to it.

The editors and their contributors are to be congratulated on producing such a fascinating and well-researched textbook. It deserves to be in every practitioner's library.

By
The Rt Hon Lord Hope of Craighead KT

Preface

Most healthcare practitioners are inexperienced in even the most approximate estimation of the age of living individuals – and may rely on little more than simple guesswork. Whilst this approach may be appropriate in situations where accuracy may have little relevance, there are situations where a 'rough estimate of age' may have far-reaching implications on the manner and nature of the response of the state or judicial system to that individual. In particular, minor differences in age may represent the difference between classification as an adult or a child and can result in major implications for the rights of the individual, such as in relation to accommodation and care and also in the tariffs for criminal offences.

Individuals may have lost, or never had, documentary evidence of their age, or may be genuinely unaware of their chronological age, or they may wish to conceal their true age for a variety of reasons. It therefore becomes incumbent upon the court or other bodies to obtain a formal estimation of their age.

In recent years, with increasing movement of individuals between countries – perhaps as a result of refugee movement, migration or even human trafficking the need to determine the age of a living individual has gained increasing medico-legal importance and cases requiring mediation or investigation occur with increasing frequency. Different jurisdictions approach the concept of estimation of age in varying ways. In addition to *inter*-jurisdictional differences there may also be substantial *intra*-jurisdictional differences, many of which may be tested by legal process. For those professionals called upon to provide an estimation of age in the living individual it is right that those requesting such estimations should be provided with as far as possible, valid, reproducible and interpretable estimates.

The available analytical expertise includes odontology, radiology, anthropology, psychology and clinical assessment which require input from a number of specialist practitioners and it is important that all those involved are aware not only of the appropriate techniques and their inherent strengths and weaknesses, but also the ethical and legal frameworks in which they must operate. Age-estimation requires a multi-professional skill set and all those involved should understand and respect how these frameworks may sometimes appear to conflict.

This book is intended to identify and explain the main approaches to age estimation in the living – and to define when a parameter may be of value and to raise awareness of its limitations. There is no simple test for age estimation, and the best available options for each assessment should be used. Each of the key approaches to age estimation is allotted a single chapter written by those with particular skills and expertise in that field. It is in the interests of all parties and in the interests of justice that practitioners aim to estimate age reliably and realistically whilst ensuring that the best interests and rights of both the individual and the needs of the court are served. It is hoped that this book brings together a corpus of knowledge that will assist both those seeking age estimations and those called upon to provide age estimations in the living individual. We are particularly grateful to Fiona Woods and Nicky McGirr from Wiley for their support, patience and enthusiasm for this project. We hope it achieves its aims in ensuring that this complex issue is approached in an independent, scientific and evidence-based manner.

Sue Black Dundee
Jason Payne-James London
Anil Aggrawal New Delhi July 2010

Glossary of Abbreviations

AGFAD	Arbeitsgemeinshaf fur Forensische Altersdiagnostik (Study Group on Forensic Age Diagnostics)
BASW	British Association of Social Workers
BMI	Body Mass Index
CDC	Centers for Disease Control
CRL	Crown–Rump Length
CT	Computerized Tomography
EDC	Endocrine Disrupting Chemicals
FSH	Follicle Stimulating Hormone
GH	Growth Hormone
GMC	General Medical Council
GnRH	Gonadotrophic Releasing Hormone
HPG	Hypothalamic Pituitary Gonadal axis
ID	Identification
IDP	Internally Displaced Persons
LBW	Low Birth Weight
LMP	Last Menstrual Period
MRI	Magnetic Resonance Imaging
PP	Precocious Puberty
PR	Parental Responsibility
PROS	Pediatric Research in Office Settings
RCPCH	Royal College of Paediatrics and Child Health
SES	Socio-Economic Status
SGA	Small for Gestational Age
UASC	Unaccompanied Asylum Seeking Children
UKBA	UK Border Agency
UNHCR	United Nations High Commissioner for Refugees
UNODC	United Nations Office on Drugs and Crime
WHO	World Health Organization

1

An Introduction to the History of Age Estimation in the Living

Andreas Schmeling[1] and Sue Black[2]
[1]*Universitätsklinikum Münster, Institut für Rechtsmedizin, Röntgenstraße 23, 48149 Münster, Germany*
[2]*Centre for Anatomy and Human Identification, University of Dundee, Dundee DD1 5EH, UK*

1.1   Introduction

Despite the alleged use of the eruption of second molars by the ancient Romans to evaluate readiness for military service (Müller, 1990), age estimation (sometimes known as age evaluation, age determination, age diagnostics or age assessment) in living individuals is a relatively recent area of applied research within the forensic sciences. Its value and importance as an assessment tool has risen exponentially as the needs for an informed opinion on the age of an individual have assumed increasing importance for the assessment of both criminal culpability and legal/social categorization. Age is an important classifier in most cultural and judicial hierarchies, and the absence of credible legal documentation often demands that authorities must seek the expertise of the scientist and the clinician for guidance and assistance in this regard.

There are many areas in which the evaluation of age in the living has become relevant but the most prevalent concern issues pertaining to refugee and asylum seekers, criminals and their victims, human trafficking and child pornography (UNHCR, 2004; Lee, 2007; O'Donnell and Milner, 2007; Cattaneo *et al.*, 2009). Age evaluation is also required for adoptive children from countries without birth registration (Crossner and Mansfeld, 1983; Melsen *et al.*, 1986; Fleischer-Peters, 1987). An additional category is age evaluation in competitive sports to ensure that athletes are competing within an age appropriate banding for the sake of both fairness

Age Estimation in the Living: The Practitioners Guide   Sue Black, Anil Aggrawal and Jason Payne-James
© 2010 John Wiley & Sons, Ltd

and health protection (Braude, Henning and Lambert, 2007; Dvorak *et al.*, 2007a, 2007b; Houlihan, 2007). Parents have also been known to falsify the ages of their children, particularly of their sons, to obtain preferential educational opportunities (Chagula, 1960). While it is undeniable that the majority of issues raised concerning age evaluation are predominantly within the juvenile aspect of the human age range, there are issues of legality in relation to the elderly, for example those which relate to matters of eligibility for state-funded pension support or retirement law (Ritz-Timme *et al.*, 2002).

The assignment of age to address appropriate and fair processing of asylum and refugee seekers is influenced heavily by issues pertaining to international human rights. These issues are largely governed by the UN Convention on the Rights of the Child (1989) and the UNHCR Guidelines on Policies and Procedures in Dealing with Unaccompanied Children Seeking Asylum (1997). Both documents follow the guiding principles that the best interests of the child take precedence and that the child should be given the benefit of the doubt if their chronological age remains uncertain (UNHCR, 1997). For most countries that recognize the 1989 United Nations Convention on the Rights of the Child, the legal age of maturity is accepted as 18 years of age and this is largely supported by the modern legal framework of most nations. If an individual claims to be younger than 18 years of age, and there is some doubt, then there may be a statutory obligation that the receiving nation is required to offer asylum and support to that minor until age is established to the satisfaction of the authorities. Therefore, the demarcation between 17 and 18 years is a key milestone with regards to both legal and social responsibility – from the perspective of both the state and the individual.

Human trafficking is concerned with the recruitment, movement and sale of people for exploitative purposes. Trafficking has been recognized and in some respects tolerated if not indeed condoned by many countries throughout history. While slave labour, prostitution and organized crime are the trademarks of human trafficking, it shares a blurred boundary with the crime of human smuggling, which seeks to extort money from criminalizing migrants (UN, 2000). Each of these crimes trespasses into the juvenile age spectrum and does so particularly boldly in the areas of slave labour and prostitution, as witnessed by the increasing prevalence of juvenile sex tourism, particularly in the Far East (Singh, 2002; Lindstrom, 2004).

The introduction of the Internet has unquestionably played a significant role in the incidence of child pornography and the sharing of illegal images by increasingly large and sophisticated paedophile rings (Lanning and Burgess, 1989; Jones and Skogrand, 2005; O'Donnell and Milner, 2007). In addition to the taking, holding and sharing of illegal images, is the nature of the content of those images and whether there is any degree of physical sexual interaction with the child as this will impact significantly on the severity of the criminal sentence. Under Irish statute, the Child Trafficking and Pornography Act 1998, child pornography is defined in relation to images as 'the depiction for a sexual purpose, of the genital or anal region of a child'. The definition of that 'child' or 'minor' is important for prosecutorial purposes as it is not illegal to take, hold or share indecent images of consenting adults as long as they do not include a minor. Irish law reverses the burden of proof, which is placed on the accused to prove that the image is *not* that of an underage individual – as this is accepted as being almost impossible to enforce, this poses a potential human rights issue in its own regard. As if to openly challenge the legal boundary, there is an active Internet 'barely legal' teen genre which purports to take pornographic photographs of individuals within hours of their eighteenth birthday and therefore exploits the sexual frisson of the now 'technically' legal images which would have been illegal only hours previously (Lane, 2001).

A description of the (relatively short) history of forensic age estimation in living individuals must take full cognizance of the early research undertaken in age evaluation (frequently not on the living) and must therefore concentrate on the three major components of this process:

1. assessment of dental development,

2. evaluation of skeletal maturation and

3. expression of secondary sexual characteristics.

Emphasis will obviously be given to those methods that are directly relevant and applicable to forensic age estimation in living individuals. It is recognized that there are other techniques that are not directly relevant to the subject matter of this chapter and these will not be discussed in this text.

1.2   Dental Development

Teeth are the only hard tissue structures of the human body that are visible to the naked eye and so it is not surprising that the study of tooth development was linked to the chronological age of the individual from early times (Scheuer and Black, 2000). One of the first documented uses of teeth as an indicator of age for legal requirements dates to the first half of the nineteenth century. The British Factory Act of 1833 attempted to improve the working environment of the child and prevent exploitation. Clauses included:

- Outlawing the employment of children younger than 9 years of age in the textile industry.

- Children aged between 9 and 13 years could not work for more than 8 hours and were required to have a 1 hour lunch break.

- Children aged between 9 and 13 years had to receive 2 hours of education per day.

- Children aged between 14 and 18 years could not work for more than 12 hours a day and had to have a 1 hour lunch break.

- Children under 18 years could not work at night.

In 1837, Saunders presented a publication 'The Teeth, a Test of Age, Considered with Reference to the Factory Children, Addressed to the Members of Both Houses of Parliament', in which he expounded upon the value of dental emergence for age estimation. His studies were performed on 1000 children and he stated that with the aid of his tables and a little 'industrious application', the assessment of age for Factory Act purposes could be conducted by 'relatively untrained people'. One year earlier, Thomson (1936) reported that 'if the third molar [first permanent molar] hath not protruded, you can have no hesitation in affirming that the culprit has not passed his seventh year' and this prevented a significant number of young children from being subjected to the harsh penal code of the time.

Since then, several hundred other studies of dental growth have focused on eruption, which incorporates the entire journey of the tooth from its formation in the alveolar crypts to full occlusion. However, the vast majority of studies which refer to 'eruption' actually relate to 'emergence', which is restricted to the time when any part of the tooth finally clears the gingival margin and becomes visible in the mouth (Demirjian, 1986; Scheuer and Black, 2000) until the stage when the tooth finally comes into occlusion with its partner tooth from the opposing jaw.

Mineralization has also been addressed in many studies and this refers to the development of both the crown and the root while still confined within the alveolar crypt. Early information on tooth development was established via techniques of dissection, histological sectioning and staining (Schour and Massler, 1941). One of the earliest such studies was performed by Legros and Magitot in 1873 and using their data, Peirce (1877) created one of the first dental mapping schemes, which was reproduced in many textbooks for several decades thereafter. The total number of teeth present in the mouth was first used to assess age by Cattell (1928), but this was a rather crude approach, which received limited scientific support. Very shortly after this date the utilization of radiographs opened up new avenues for visualization of direct dental development in the living and the deceased, and Bustin, Leist and Priesel (1929) and Hess, Lewis and Roman (1932) were among the first to perform dental radiological examinations on children.

The examination most commonly quoted in secondary literature sources was performed by Logan and Kronfeld (1933). These authors used 25 anatomical preparations of children, most of whom had died of tuberculosis, associated diseases or enteritis. In 1940, Schour and Massler created dental mapping schemes based on Logan and Kronfeld's data. However these studies were all cross-sectional and gave no appreciation of how the dentition developed within an individual in direct relation to chronological age, and it was not until the 1950s that the benefits of longitudinal radiographic studies were to be appreciated, and of course, never again repeated for very justifiable health and safety reasons (Liversidge and Molleson, 1999).

Gleiser and Hunt (1955) examined 25 male and 25 female white children aged 1.5 to 10 years who lived in the Boston area. They restricted their observations to the first mandibular molars, for which they established 15 mineralization stages. Further stage classifications for the determination of dental mineralization were subsequently recommended by others (Nolla, 1960; Haavikko, 1970; Liliequist and Lundberg, 1971; Demirjian, Goldstein and Tanner, 1973; Gustafson and Koch, 1974; van der Linden and Duterloo, 1976; Nortje, 1983; Harris and Nortje, 1984; Kullman, Johanson and Akesson, 1992; Köhler et al., 1994). Frequently used reference studies on the time frame of third molars which are particularly relevant to age estimation in living individuals were published by Anderson, Thompson and Popovich (1976), Kahl and Schwarze (1988), Mincer, Harris and Berryman (1993), Köhler *et al.* (1994), Gunst *et al.* (2003) and Olze *et al.* (2003, 2004).

Such a plethora of scientific reporting and publication does not assist the process of single case evaluation and there is a preference for the use of single source standardized charts or atlases. However, these are dangerous precepts as the methodology of data collection, statistical representation and the data source are unlikely to be either time or group specific and can engender a false sense of security in the application of the results and reliance upon the outcome.

In adults, where all teeth are fully formed, other criteria must be used for estimating the age of the individual. Regressive tooth changes, which progress in severity with the age of the individual, have been described by early authors (Bodecker, 1925). However, a more systematic and statistical approach to dental age estimation was not presented until 1947, when Gustafson published a scoring system with the use of a regression model. Six age-associated parameters (attrition, periodontal recession, cementum apposition, root resorption, secondary dentine formation and root translucency) were evaluated in longitudinal sections of teeth cut through the central area. The small sample size and subsequent statistical shortcomings exposed Gustafson's method to some criticism (Maples and Rice, 1979). Later investigations by Dalitz (1962), Johanson (1971), Maples (1978) and Solheim (1993), however, resulted in considerable improvements with regards to both material and statistical evaluation. Matsikidis and Schulz (1982) evaluated Gustafson's criteria with the help of X-ray analysis, making this more applicable for the living. The radiological technique developed by Kvaal *et al.* (1995) is based on only one of Gustafson's criteria: the secondary dentine formation. As technology advanced, full use was made of these opportunities, and more recent studies have utilized orthopantomograms (Cameriere, Ferrante and Cingolani, 2004; Paewinsky, Pfeiffer and Brinkmann, 2004; Bosmans *et al.*, 2005; Landa *et al.*, 2009) and cone-beam computerized tomography (CT) (Yang, Jacobs and Willems, 2006). Ever mindful of the need to determine age in the living, other authors, including Solheim (1995), have devised techniques that are non-destructive and based on visually identifiable characteristics including attrition, colour and recession of the periodontal attachment.

The evaluation of cementum annulation (Stott, Sis and Levy, 1981; Condon *et al.*, 1986; Wittwer-Backofen, Gampe and Vaupel, 2004) and the degree of racemization of aspartic acid in the dentine (Ogino, Ogino and Nagy, 1985; Ritz, Schütz and Peper, 1993; Mörnstad, Pfeiffer and Teivens, 1994) are applicable to age estimation in older living individuals. However, these approaches necessitate tooth extraction and this is not a process which is advocated, or indeed permitted, by most countries (Ritz-Timme *et al.*, 2002). Chapter 10 in this text considers the current status of age estimation in the living from dental evidence.

1.3 Skeletal Maturation

Parallel to the establishment of methods for dental age estimation, methods for the evaluation of skeletal maturation were developed. In this context, thanks to the discovery of X-rays, methods that had originally been developed using dry skeletal material could now be applied to living individuals as well.

At a conference of the Munich Medical Society on 1 April 1896, only one year after the discovery of X-rays, von Ranke proposed that the age of children could also be examined with the help of an X-ray of the hand. Around the beginning of the twentieth century, the Polish court pianist Raoul Koczalski, who is said to have already given public concerts when he was only four years old and who had caused a sensation in Munich as a wunderkind, gave a performance in Munich. Von Ranke mistrusted the young court pianist and suspected that he was older than he portrayed. However, it is not known if von Ranke verified his suspicion with an X-ray examination – but it is an interesting potential application of a science occurring at the leading edge of a technology's development.

In order to establish the chronological age of an individual from their skeletal development, at least one of the three phases of osseous development must be assessed:

- The age of appearance (i.e. ossification) of the different parts of the bone.

- The morphological appearance and/or size of the bone and its constituent parts.

- The timing of fusion of different parts of a bone.

The assessment of these three phases can occur either via direct observance of the bone or via radiographic images of the living individual, and the research literature is rather evenly peppered with this dual origin of source material (Ubelaker, 1978). A significant proportion of the work undertaken on dry bone analysis arises through archaeological sources and much of the material is subsequently not of known, that is chronological, age. There are a few skeletal collections that hold documented information about the deceased individuals but there is a very low proportion of juvenile material within these resources (Scheuer and Black, 2000). Therefore age related information that has been derived from archaeological sources must be viewed with some caution as they have adopted a circular argument where the age has been assigned by various other existing techniques before the new methodology is tested. In this situation, the distribution of the sample will always mimic the parent profile upon which the method was derived (Bocquet-Apel and Masset, 1982, 1985) and the circular argument so developed will not withstand forensic scrutiny.

Much of the clinical data is sourced from systematic, non-repeatable, longitudinal radiological growth studies of children carried out between 1930 and 1960. Large groups of children, mostly white and middle class, were radiographed repeatedly throughout their growing years and the data compiled for clinical purposes to assess the normal pattern of growth in relation to maturation so that abnormalities of pattern could be identified. There were five noteworthy longitudinal surveys that were published at this time in the United States and the United Kingdom, which are discussed in more detail in Chapter 6:

- The University of Colorado study reported on by Maresh and Hansman.

- The Brush Foundation, Case Western Reserve study, which was reported on by Todd, Greulich, Hoerr and Pyle.

- The Fels Institute, Ohio study reported on by Garn and colleagues.

- The Harpenden Growth Study reported on by Tanner and colleagues.

- The Oxford Child Health Survey reported on by Hewitt, Acheson and colleagues.

With advances in awareness of the health issues associated with repeated exposure to radiation, these studies are consigned to the past and most recent work relies on data that is not specifically collected for the purpose of research into ageing or evaluation of maturational status and is of course cross-sectional. With the development of non radio-imaging, for example magnetic resonance imaging (MRI) or ultrasound, the opportunities to continue to accumulate data safely has seen resurgence.

One of the first images associated with radiography is that of the hand of Wilhelm Conrad Röntgen's wife, complete with rings, which was taken on 22 December 1895 and presented to the University of Freiburg on 1 January 1896. The hand is an easy and readily accessible part of the body for imaging and so it is not surprising that much early information concentrated on the hand and of course also on the foot. A study of the ossification of the human hand published by Behrendsen in 1897 was followed in 1909 by a publication from the American paediatrician Rotch, who believed that it was possible to estimate a child's readiness for school using roentgenographic skeletal age assessment. Carter (1926) and Baldwin, Busby and Garside (1928) performed direct measurements of the bone area on X-rays for skeletal age assessment via an approach known as planimetry, and later this method was simplified by measuring only the length and/or the width (Schmid and Moll, 1960). That this approach is still viable is evidenced by the method recently published by Cameriere et al. (2006), which is fundamentally a further development of the planimetric approach where the ratio of the area of the ossified part of the hand skeleton and the total area of the hand is determined.

Numerical methods count the number of ossification centres present and compare the sum of those with values from normal healthy children. This method was first recommended by Sontag, Snell and Anderson (1939), while Elgenmark (1946) improved and expanded the method. This required X-rays to be taken of an entire half of the body or multiple images of several body regions. However, due to the high expenditure of time and considerable radiation exposure, it is not surprising that this method did not gain widespread acceptance in practice.

Skeletal age assessment according to 'age-of-appearance lists' needs to be differentiated from Elgenmark's method as in this approach, bone age is assessed according to the ossification centre(s) which appeared last, thereby giving a demarking guide. Garn, Rohmann and Silverman (1967) put together the most appropriate instructions on this approach in relation to evaluation of the hand but summaries are available in Scheuer and Black (2004) and Schaefer, Black and Scheuer (2009).

Unquestionably, the most favoured approach to evaluation of age or maturity from the skeletal system has been to utilize a skeletal atlas. This approach identifies a 'standard' for each age group (usually segregated on the basis of sex) where a match can be selected that most closely resembles that of the comparison image. The first hand/wrist atlas was published in 1898 (Poland, 1898). However, it did not take account of sex differences and not every age was represented by an image. A further atlas of normal hand ossification was published by Siegert in 1935, closely followed by the better known atlas of Todd (1937). The atlas by Greulich and Pyle, the first edition of which was published in 1950, and the second improved edition in 1959, is an extension of Todd's work and probably remains one of the most utilized approaches to skeletal evaluation of maturity. There are several further atlases of radiographic anatomy available depending upon the body segment under investigation (e.g. Hoerr, Pyle and Francis, 1962; Pyle and Hoerr, 1969; Pyle, Waterhouse and Greulich, 1971; de Roo and Schröder, 1976; Brodeur, Silberstein and Gravis, 1981; Gilsanz and Ratib, 2005; Thiemann, Nitz and Schmeling, 2006) and new data are forthcoming on a regular basis.

The 'Oxford method' was proposed by Acheson (1954) and allocates point values related to corresponding developmental stages to single bones in different body regions, and indeed the three versions of score methods for the hand skeleton by Tanner, Whitehouse and Healy (1962) and Tanner et al. (1975, 2001) are similar to this approach. While the allocation of point values to the individual developmental stages by Tanner et al. was at random, the Fels single-bone-method (Roche, Chumlea and Thissen, 1988) was based on statistically confirmed weightings.

Age evaluation in the living requires careful consideration of the areas of the body to be examined and while some regions are known to be more reliable than others, they cannot always be accessed for both health and safety reasons and for reasons of accessibility to view (Thodberg, 2009). Therefore it is not surprising that the atlas methods have concentrated on major joint areas of the appendicular skeleton (i.e. elbow, wrist, hand, knee, ankle and foot). However, as the most frequent age cohort to be addressed is that between 17 and 18 years of age, most of these joints have ceased to show significant and predictable signs of age alteration by this age. It is well known by osteologists that the fusion of the medial epiphysis of the clavicle, the iliac crest and the junction between the bodies of the first and second sacral vertebrae are probably the most useful in this regard but they are all axial body segments and therefore not ethically amenable to radiographic interpretation, particularly the latter two. Therefore the medial region of the clavicle offers an intriguing opportunity. Although several older roentgenologic or dry bone studies are available on the time frame of clavicular maturation (Flecker, 1933; Galstaun, 1937; Jit and Kullkarni, 1976; Black and Scheuer, 1996), Kreitner et al. (1997, 1998) deserve the credit for applying this to forensic age diagnostics in the living. The first pilot studies with MRI (Schmidt et al., 2007) and ultrasound (Schulz et al., 2008; Quirmbach, Ramsthaler and Verhoff, 2009) showed that the stage of clavicular ossification can also be assessed by means of radiation-free procedures, leaving the way open for true validation of this research field in the modern world and access to the other late maturing regions of the skeleton. More detailed discussion on the value of skeletal maturation for age estimation can be found in Chapter 11.

1.4   Secondary Sexual Development

The process of maturation at puberty is a multidimensional set of events that can, and has been, utilized for age related evaluation. Documentation of the progress of events during this process has generally been undertaken by clinical paediatricians to assess normal versus abnormal development and therefore the outcomes have not been specifically evaluated for the purposes of age estimation. Puberty is a complex sequence of events that will ultimately lead to sexual maturity and requires both gonadal and adrenal stimulation (Reyes, Winter and Faiman, 1973). Female maturation within this process is generally assessed on the age of onset of menses, degree of breast development and degree of axillary and pubic hair. Male maturation is generally assessed on the basis of testicular and penile enlargement and also on the degree of hair development, mainly pubic but also axillary and facial (Marshall, 1975; Sizonenko, 1987; Wheeler, 1991).

While the age of commencement of menstruation is a timed event remembered by most females, and recognized by society as an important indicator of maturity, it relies on a verbal account by the individual as to whether this event has yet occurred and when it did commence as it is an internal maturational event (Cameron and Kuhrt, 1983; Brown, 1989). Therefore the method cannot be objectively assessed by the biological investigator and therefore it has a limited confirmatory value in age estimation. The development of the external genitalia lends itself more readily to both visual and metric evaluation although the ethical and social issues that surround collecting this data are not insignificant. Two age groups are the focus for external genital development – the fetus and neonate for the purposes of identifying abnormalities early in life (Feldman and Smith, 1975; Sutan-Assin, Rukman and Dahlan, 1989; Phillip et al., 1996; Tuladhar et al., 1998; Zalel et al., 2001) and the developing child prior to puberty for the purposes of diagnosing either precocious or delayed sexual maturation (Stolz and Stolz, 1951; Falkner, 1962a; Zachmann et al., 1974; Karlberg and Taranger, 1976; Faust, 1977; Sorensen et al., 1979; Lall et al., 1980; Takihara et al., 1983; Kaplowitz and Oberfield, 1999).

In the past, various stage classifications of sexual maturation were introduced (Stratz, 1904; Reich, 1924; Greulich et al., 1938, 1942; Reynolds and Wines, 1948, 1951; Hansen and With, 1951; Stolz and Stolz, 1951; Quaade, 1955; Falkner, 1962b); however, there is no doubting that the increase on research in this area was greatest after 1969/70 as two papers were core to the development of this topic – Marshall and Tanner (1969, 1970). This work was longitudinal in nature (as well as cross-sectional) and laid the groundwork for clinical evaluation of secondary sexual characteristics (Tanner and Whitehouse, 1976; Tanner, 1978; Euling et al., 2009). Almost all work after this time refers to the 'Tanner stages of secondary sexual development' and in summary these are generally regarded as:

Pubic Hair (Both Male and Female)

Stage I: no pubic hair.

Stage II: small amount of long, downy hair with slight pigmentation at the base of the penis and scrotum (males) or on the labia majora (females).

Stage III: hair becomes more coarse and curly, and begins to extend laterally.

Stage IV: adult-like hair quality, extending across pubis but sparse on the medial aspect of the thigh.

Stage V: hair extends to medial surface of the thighs.

Genitals (Male)

Stage I: testicular volume less than 1.5 ml; penis of 3 cm or less.

Stage II – testicular volume between 1.6 and 6 ml; skin on scrotum thins, reddens and enlarges; penis length unchanged.

Stage III – testicular volume between 6 and 12 ml; scrotum enlarges further; penis begins to lengthen to about 6 cm.

Stage IV – testicular volume between 12 and 20 ml; scrotum enlarges further and darkens; penis increases in circumference and length to 10 cm.

Stage V – testicular volume greater than 20 ml; adult scrotum and penis of approx. 15 cm in length.

Breasts (Female)

Stage I: no glandular tissue; areola follows the skin contours of the chest.

Stage II: breast bud forms, with small area of surrounding glandular tissue; areola begins to widen.

Stage III: breast begins to become more elevated, and extends beyond the borders of the areola, which continues to widen but remains in contour with surrounding breast.

Stage IV: increased breast size and elevation; areola and papilla form a secondary mound projecting from the contour of the surrounding breast.

Stage V: breast reaches final adult size; areola returns to contour of the surrounding breast, with a projecting central papilla.

An age diagnosis on the basis of sexual maturation should be performed very cautiously due to the wide range of scatter. However, a physical examination in the course of age estimation is crucial, because it is essential to determine whether the physical development is congruent with the other age characteristics and whether there are indications of diseases that might affect the development. A more detailed discussion of soft tissue maturation can be found in Chapter 9.

1.5 Conclusion

A professional opinion on the age of a living person, whether from an image or from direct interaction with the individual in question, is an increasingly common request placed before scientists, clinicians, pathologists and anthropologists. However, the estimation of age in the living is a hybrid discipline which utilizes techniques and data that were not primarily designed for this purpose. This throws the validation of their use in the forensic context into some debate. Further, there are no universally agreed minimum standards with relation to data collection and no universally accepted data upon which to base these age estimation conclusions. Therefore this is an area of scientific and medical investigation that must rely heavily on a realistic understanding of variability and error and must not succumb to a cookbook approach of providing a definitive age. However, conflict arises as unfortunately this is often the ultimate desired outcome of investigators and the courts. It is generally appreciated that age estimation from the living as a forensic tool has yet to be truly validated and until such time as an objective and reliable methodology is devised, it must be treated with caution and never placed in the hands of a single inexperienced practitioner. The courts must act as the alert gatekeepers for the unscrupulous or naive 'expert' whose potentially flawed opinions may do little to serve justice. It is broadly agreed that for the most reliable age estimation to be realized in living juveniles and adolescents, realistic and experienced collaboration is essential between professionals, including forensic pathologists, paediatricians, social workers, radiologists and forensic anthropologists.

There is no doubt that Germany leads with regard to the research and implementation of data in this area. A survey by means of a questionnaire on the state of forensic age diagnostics in the German-speaking area revealed a tripling of age reports by forensic pathologists, dentists and forensic anthropologists between 1990 and 1998, with most of the expert opinions prepared within the framework of criminal proceedings. The main countries and regions of origin of the individuals to be examined were Africa, Turkey, Romania, the Balkans, Lebanon and Vietnam (Geserick and Schmeling, 2001; Schmeling *et al.*, 2001a).

The first transregional scientific analysis of forensic age diagnostics in living individuals was conducted on the occasion of the tenth Lübeck Meeting of German Forensic Physicians in December 1999. At this meeting, it was suggested that a study group be set up which would include forensic pathologists, dentists, radiologists and anthropologists. They were tasked with producing recommendations for the issuing of expert opinions in order to standardize the hitherto common and partly varying procedure and to achieve quality assurance for expert opinions.

The international and interdisciplinary 'Study Group on Forensic Age Diagnostics' (http://rechtsmedizin.klinikum.uni-muenster.de/agfad/index) was established in Berlin, Germany, on 10 March 2000. This study group has given recommendations for forensic age estimation in living individuals in criminal proceedings (Schmeling *et al.*, 2001b, 2008), in civil and asylum procedures (Lockemann *et al.*, 2004) as well as in pension procedures (Ritz-Timme *et al.*, 2002). As an external quality control measure, the Study Group on Forensic Age Diagnostics annually organizes proficiency tests in which participants are sent the X-rays and physical examination results for a set of subjects and asked to estimate their ages.

This text comes at a time when the multidisciplinary approach to age evaluation in the living has largely been accepted and there is a strong awareness that standardization of data and methodologies is essential.

References

Acheson, R.M. (1954) A method of assessing skeletal maturity from radiographs: a report from the Oxford Child Health Survey. *Journal of Anatomy*, **88**, 498–508.

Anderson, D.L., Thompson, G.W. and Popovich, F. (1976) Age of attainment of mineralization stages of the permanent dentition. *Journal of Forensic Sciences*, **21**, 191–200.

Baldwin, B.T., Busby, L.M. and Garside, H.V. (1928) Anatomic growth of children; a study of some bones of the hand, wrist, and lower forearm by means of roentgenograms. *University of Iowa Studies in Child Welfare*, **14**, 1–88.

Behrendsen, E. (1897) Studien über die Ossification der menschlichen Hand vermittels des Roentgenschen Verfahrens. *Deutsche Medizinische Wochenschrift*, **23**, 433–435.

Black, S.M. and Scheuer, J.L. (1996) Age changes in the human clavicle: from the early neonatal period to skeletal maturity. *International Journal of Osteoarchaeology*, **6**, 425–434.

Bocquet-Apel, J.-P. and Masset, C. (1982) Farewell to palaeodemography. *Journal of Human Evolution*, **11**, 321–333.

Bocquet-Apel, J.-P. and Masset, C. (1985) Matters of moment. *Journal of Human Evolution*, **14**, 107–111.

Bodecker, C.F. (1925) A consideration of some of the changes in the teeth from young to old age. *Dental Cosmos*, **67**, 543–549.

Bosmans, N., Ann, P., Medhat, A. and Willems, G. (2005) The application of Kvaal's dental age calculation technique on panoramic dental radiographs. *Forensic Science International*, **153**, 208–212.

Braude, S.C., Henning, L.M. and Lambert, M.I. (2007) Accuracy of bone assessments for verifying age in adolescents – application in sport. *South African Journal of Radiology*, **11** (2), 4–7.

Brodeur, A.E., Silberstein, M.J. and Gravis, E.R. (1981) *Radiology of the Pediatric Elbow*, G.K. Hall, London.

Brown, J.E. (1989) *The Sacred Pipe – Black Elk's Account of the Seven Rites of the Oglala Sioux*, University of Oklahoma Press, Norman, OK.

Bustin, E., Leist, M. and Priesel, R. (1929) Röntgenologische Studien am kindlichen Gebiß. *Fortschritte auf dem Gebiete der Röntgenstrahlen*, **40**, 80–88.

Cameriere, R., Ferrante, L. and Cingolani, M. (2004) Precision and reliability of pulp/tooth area ratio (RA) of second molar as indicator of adult age. *Journal of Forensic Sciences*, **49**, 1319–1323.

Cameriere, R., Ferrante, L., Mirtella, D. and Cingolani, M. (2006) Carpals and epiphyses of radius and ulna as age indicators. *International Journal of Legal Medicine*, **120**, 143–146.

Cameron, A. and Kuhrt, A. (1983) *Images of Women in Antiquity*, Wayne State University Press, Detroit, MI.

Carter, T.M. (1926) Technique and devices used in radiography study of the wrist bones of children. *Journal of Educational Psychology*, **17**, 237–247.

Cattaneo, C., Ritz-Timme, S., Gabriel, P. *et al.* (2009) The difficult issue of age assessment on pedo-pornographic material. *Forensic Science International*, **183**, e21–e24.

Cattell, P. (1928) The eruption and growth of the permanent teeth. *Journal of Dental Research*, **8**, 279–287.

Chagula, W.K. (1960) The age at eruption of third permanent molars in male East Africans. *American Journal of Physical Anthropology*, **18**, 77–82.

Condon, K., Charles, D.K., Cheverud, J.M. and Buikstra, J.E. (1986) Cementum annulation and age determination in *Homo sapiens*. II. Estimates and accuracy. *American Journal of Physical Anthropology*, **71**, 321–330.

Crossner, C.G. and Mansfeld, L. (1983) Determination of dental age in adopted non-European children. *Swedish Dental Journal*, 7, 1–10.

Dalitz, G.D. (1962) Age determination of human remains by teeth examination. *Journal of the Forensic Science Society*, 3, 11–21.

Demirjian, A. (1986) Dentition, in *Human Growth, Postnatal Growth*, 2nd edn, vol. 2 (eds F. Falkner and J.M. Tanner), Plenum Press, New York, pp. 269–298.

Demirjian, A., Goldstein, H. and Tanner, J.M. (1973) A new system of dental age assessment. *Human Biology*, 45, 221–227.

de Roo, T. and Schröder, H.J. (1976) *Pocket Atlas of Skeletal Age*, Martinus Nijhoff, The Hague.

Dvorak, J., George, J., Junge, A. and Hodler, J. (2007a) Age determination by magnetic resonance imaging of the wrist in adolescent male football players. *British Journal of Sports Medicine*, 41, 45–52.

Dvorak, J., George, J., Junge, A. and Hodler, J. (2007b) Application of MRI of the wrist for age determination in international U-17 soccer competitions. *British Journal of Sports Medicine*, 41, 497–500.

Elgenmark, O. (1946) The normal development of the ossific centers during infancy and childhood: clinical, roentgenologic, and statistical study. *Acta Paediatrica*, 33 (Suppl 1), 1–79.

Euling, S.Y., Herman-Giddens, M.E., Lee, P.A. *et al.* (2009) Examination of US puberty-timing data from 1940 to 1994 for secular trends: panel findings. *Pediatrics*, 121, S172–S191.

Falkner, F. (1962a) Some physical growth standards for white North American children. *Peds*, 29 (3), 467–474.

Falkner, F. (1962b) The physical development of children. A guide to interpretation of growth-charts and development assessments; and a commentary on contemporary and future problems. *Pediatrics*, 29, 448–466.

Faust, M.S. (1977) Somatic development of adolescent girls. *Monographs for Research in Child Development*, 169 (42), 1–90.

Feldman, K.W. and Smith, D.W. (1975) Fetal phallic growth and penile standards for newborn male infants. *Journal of Paediatrics*, 86, 395–398.

Flecker, H. (1933) Roentgenographic observations of the times of appearance of epiphyses and their fusion with the diaphyses. *Journal of Anatomy*, 67, 118–164.

Fleischer-Peters, A. (1987) Die Bedeutung der Zähne für die Altersschätzung von Findelkindern. *Deutsche Zahnärztliche Zeitschrift*, 42, 712–718.

Galstaun, G. (1937) A study of ossification as observed in Indian subjects. *Indian Journal of Medical Research*, 25, 267–324.

Garn, S.M., Rohmann, C.G. and Silverman, F.N. (1967) Radiographic standards for post-natal ossification and tooth calcification. *Medical Radiography and Photography*, 43, 45–66.

Geserick, G. and Schmeling, A. (2001) Übersicht zum gegenwärtigen Stand der Altersschätzung Lebender im deutschsprachigen Raum, in *Osteologische Identifikation und Altersschätzung* (eds M. Oehmichen and G. Geserick), Schmidt-Römhild, Lübeck, pp. 255–261.

Gilsanz, V. and Ratib, O. (2005) *Hand Bone Age. A Digital Atlas of Skeletal Maturity*, Springer, Berlin.

Gleiser, I. and Hunt, E.E. (1955) The permanent mandibular first molar; its calcification, eruption and decay. *American Journal of Physical Anthropology*, 13, 253–284.

Greulich, W.W. and Pyle, S.I. (1950, 1959) *Radiographic Atlas of Skeletal Development of the Hand and Wrist*, Stanford University Press, Stanford, CA.

Greulich, W.W., Day, H.G., Lachmann, S.E. *et al.* (1938) A handbook of methods for the study of adolescent children. *Monographs of the Society for Research in Child Development*, **3** (2).

Greulich, W.W., Dorfman, R.I., Catchpole, H.R. *et al.* (1942) Somatic and endocrine studies of pubertal and adolescent boys. *Monographs of the Society for Research in Child Development*, **7** (3).

Gunst, K., Mesotten, K., Carbonez, A. and Willems, G. (2003) Third molar root development in relation to chronological age: a large sample sized retrospective study. *Forensic Science International*, **136**, 52–57.

Gustafson, G. (1947) Aldersbestämningar pa tänder. *Odontologisk Tidskrift*, **55**, 556–568.

Gustafson, G. and Koch, G. (1974) Age estimation up to 16 years of age based on dental development. *Odontologisk Revy*, **25**, 297–306.

Haavikko, K. (1970) The formation and the alveolar and clinical eruption of the permanent teeth. *Suomen Hammaslaakariseuran Toimituksia*, **66**, 103–170.

Hansen, F. P and With, T.K. (1951) Clinical measurements of the testes in boys and men. *Acta Medica Scandinavica*, **142** (Suppl 266), 457–465.

Harris, M.J.P. and Nortje, C.J. (1984) The mesial root of the third mandibular molar. A possible indicator of age. *Journal of Forensic Odontostomatology*, **2**, 39–43.

Hess, A.F., Lewis, J.M. and Roman, B. (1932) A radiographic study of calcification of the teeth from birth to adolescence. *Dental Cosmos*, **74**, 1053–1061.

Hoerr, N.L., Pyle, S.I. and Francis, C.C. (1962) *Radiographic Atlas of Skeletal Development of the Foot and Ankle*, Charles C. Thomas, Springfield, IL.

Houlihan, B. (2007) *Sport and Society*, 2nd edn, Sage, London.

Jit, I. and Kulkarni, M. (1976) Times of appearance and fusion of epiphysis at the medial end of the clavicle. *Indian Journal of Medical Research*, **64**, 773–782.

Johanson, G. (1971) Age determination from human teeth. A critical evaluation with special consideration of changes after fourteen years of age. *Odontologisk Revy*, **22** (Suppl), 1–126.

Jones, V. and Skogrand, E. (2005) Position paper regarding online images of sexual abuse and other internet-related sexual exploitation of children, Save the Children, Copenhagen.

Kahl, B. and Schwarze, C.W. (1988) Aktualisierung der Dentitionstabelle von I Schour und M Massler von 1941. *Fortschritte der Kieferorthopädie*, **49**, 432–443.

Kaplowitz, P.B. and Oberfield, S.E. (1999) Re-examination of the age limit for defining when puberty is precocious in girls of the United States. *Pediatrics*, **104** (4), 936–941.

Karlberg, P. and Taranger, J. (1976) The somatic development of children in a Swedish urban community. *Acta Paediatrica Scandinavica Supplement*, **258**, 1–148.

Köhler, S., Schmelzle, R., Loitz, C. and Püschel, K. (1994) Die Entwicklung des Weisheitszahnes als Kriterium der Lebensalterbestimmung. *Annals of Anatomy*, **176**, 339–345.

Kreitner, K.-F., Schweden, F., Schild, H.H. *et al.* (1997) Die computertomographisch bestimmte Ausreifung der medialen Klavikulaepiphyse – Eine additive Methode zur Altersbestimmung im Adoleszentenalter und in der dritten Lebensdekade? *Fortschritte auf dem Gebiete der Röntgenstrahlen und der Nuklearmedizin*, **166**, 481–486.

Kreitner, K.-F., Schweden, F.J., Riepert, T. *et al.* (1998) Bone age determination based on the study of the medial extremity of the clavicle. *European Radiology*, **8**, 1116–1122.

Kullman, L., Johanson, G. and Akesson, L. (1992) Root development of the lower third molar and its relation to chronological age. *Swedish Dental Journal*, **16**, 161–167.

Kvaal, S.I., Kolltveit, K.M., Thompsen, I.O. and Solheim, T. (1995) Age determination of adults from radiographs. *Forensic Science International*, **74**, 175–185.

Lall, K.B., Singh, S., Gurhani, M. *et al.* (1980) Normal testicular volume in school children. *Indian Journal of Pediatrics*, **47** (5), 389–393.

Landa, M.I., Garamendi, P.M., Botella, M.C. and Alemán, I. (2009) Application of the method of Kvaal et al. to digital orthopantomograms. *International Journal of Legal Medicine* **123** (2), 123–128.

Lane, F.S. (2001) *Obscene Profits: The Entrepreneurs of Pornography in the Cyber Age*, Routledge, London.

Lanning, K.V. and Burgess, A.W. (1989) Child pornography and sex rings, in *Pornography: Research Advances and Policy Considerations* (eds D. Zillmann and J. Bryant), Lawrence Erlbaum Associates, Hillsdale, NJ, pp. 235–255.

Lee, M. (2007) *Human Trafficking*, Willan Publishing, Portland, OR.

Legros, C. and Magitot, E. (1873) Origine et formation du follicule dentaire chez les mammifères. *Journal de l'Anatomie et de la Physiologie*, **9**, 449–503.

Liliequist, B. and Lundberg, M. (1971) Skeletal and tooth development: a methodologic investigation. *Acta Radiologica: Diagnosis*, **11**, 97–112.

Lindstrom, N. (2004) Regional sex trafficking in the Balkans: transnational networks in an enlarged Europe. *Problems of Post-Communism*, **51** (3), 45–52.

Liversidge, H.M. and Molleson, T.I. (1999) Developing permanent tooth length as an estimate of age. *Journal of Forensic Sciences*, **44**, 917–920.

Lockemann, U., Fuhrmann, A., Püschel, K. *et al.* (2004) Empfehlungen für die Altersdiagnostik bei Jugendlichen und jungen Erwachsenen außerhalb des Strafverfahrens. *Rechtsmedizin*, **14**, 123–125.

Logan, W.H.G. and Kronfeld, R. (1933) Development of human jaws and surrounding structures from birth to the age of fifteen years. *Journal of the American Dental Association*, **20**, 379–429.

Maples, W.R. (1978) An improved technique using dental histology for estimation of adult age. *Journal of Forensic Sciences*, **23**, 764–770.

Maples, W.R. and Rice, P.M. (1979) Some difficulties in the Gustafson dental age estimations. *Journal of Forensic Sciences*, **24**, 168–172.

Marshall, W.A. (1975) Growth and sexual maturation in normal puberty. *Clinics in Endocrinology and Metabolism*, **4** (1), 3–25.

Marshall, W.A. and Tanner, J.M. (1969) Variations in pattern of pubertal changes in girls. *Archives of Diseases in Childhood*, **44**, 291–303.

Marshall, W.A. and Tanner, J.M. (1970) Variations in the pattern of pubertal changes in boys. *Archives of Diseases in Childhood*, **45**, 13–23.

Matsikidis, G. and Schulz, P. (1982) Altersbestimmung nach dem Gebiss mit Hilfe des Zahnfilms. *Zahnärztliche Mitteilungen*, **72**, 2524–2528.

Melsen, B., Wenzel, A., Miletic, T. *et al.* (1986) Dental and skeletal maturity in adoptive children: assessments at arrival and after one year in the admitting country. *Annals of Human Biology*, **13**, 153–159.

Mincer, H.H., Harris, E.F. and Berryman, H.E. (1993) The ABFO study of third molar development and its use as an estimator of chronological age. *Journal of Forensic Sciences*, **38**, 379–390.

Mörnstad, H., Pfeiffer, H. and Teivens, A. (1994) Estimation of dental age using HPLC-technique to determine the degree of aspartic acid racemization. *Journal of Forensic Sciences*, **39**, 1425–1431.

Müller, N. (1990) Zur Altersbestimmung beim Menschen unter besonderer Berücksichtigung der Weisheitszähne, MD Thesis, University of Erlangen-Nürnberg.

Nolla, C.M. (1960) The development of the permanent teeth. *Journal of Dentistry for Children*, **27**, 254–266.

Nortje, C.J. (1983) The permanent mandibular third molar. *Journal of Forensic Odontostomatology*, **1**, 27–31.

O'Donnell, I. and Milner, C. (2007) *Child Pornography: Crime, Computers and Society*, Willan Publishing, Portland, OR.

Ogino, T., Ogino, H. and Nagy, B. (1985) Application of aspartic acid racimization to forensic odontology: post mortem designation of age of death. *Forensic Science International*, **29**, 259–267.

Olze, A., Schmeling, A., Rieger, K. *et al.* (2003) Untersuchungen zum zeitlichen Verlauf der Weisheitszahnmineralisation bei einer deutschen Population. *Rechtsmedizin*, **13**, 5–10.

Olze, A., Schmeling, A., Taniguchi, M. *et al.* (2004) Forensic age estimation in living subjects: the ethnic factor in wisdom tooth mineralization. *International Journal of Legal Medicine*, **118**, 170–173.

Paewinsky, E., Pfeiffer, H. and Brinkmann, B. (2004) Quantification of secondary dentine formation from orthopantomograms – a contribution to forensic age estimation in adults. *International Journal of Legal Medicine*, **119**, 27–30.

Peirce, C.N. (1877) The development of the teeth as recognized by the authorities of today. *Dental Cosmos*, **26**, 399–407.

Phillip, M., de Boer, C., Pilpel, D. *et al.* (1996) Clitoral and penile sizes of full term newborns in two different ethnic groups. *Journal of Pediatric Endocrinology and Metabolism*, **9** (2), 175–179.

Poland, J. (1898) *Skiagraphic Atlas Showing the Development of the Bones of the Wrist and Hand*, Smith, Elder & Co., London.

Pyle, S.I. and Hoerr, N.L. (1969) *A Radiographic Standard of Reference for the Growing Knee*, Charles C. Thomas, Springfield, IL.

Pyle, S.I., Waterhouse, A.M. and Greulich, W.W. (1971) *A Radiographic Standard of Reference for the Growing Hand and Wrist*, The Press of Case Western Reserve University, Cleveland, OH.

Quaade, F. (1955) *Obese Children, Anthropology and Environment*, Danish Science Press, Copenhagen.

Quirmbach, F., Ramsthaler, F. and Verhoff, M.A. (2009) Evaluation of the ossification of the medial clavicular epiphysis with a digital ultrasonic system to determine the age threshold of 21 years. *International Journal of Legal Medicine*, **123**, 241–245.

Reich, H. (1924) Klinische Testikelmessungen bei Kindern. *Jahrbuch für Kinderheilkunde*, **105**, 290–300.

Reyes, F.I., Winter, J.S.D. and Faiman, C. (1973) Studies on human sexual development. 1. Fetal gonadal and adrenal sex steroids. *Journal of Clinical Endocrinology and Metabolism*, **37**, 74–78.

Reynolds, E.L. and Wines, J.V. (1948) Individual differences in physical changes associated with adolescence in girls. *American Journal of Diseases of Children*, **75**, 329–350.

Reynolds, E.L. and Wines, J.V. (1951) Physical changes associated with adolescence in boys. *American Journal of Diseases of Children*, **82**, 529–547.

Ritz, S., Schütz, H.W. and Peper, C. (1993) Postmortem estimation of age at death based on aspartic acid racemization in dentin: its applicability for root dentin. *International Journal of Legal Medicine*, **105**, 289–293.

Ritz-Timme, S., Kaatsch, H.-J., Marré, B. *et al.* (2002) Empfehlungen für die Altersdiagnostik bei Lebenden im Rentenverfahren. *Rechtsmedizin*, **12**, 193–194.

Roche, A.F., Chumlea, W.C. and Thissen, D. (1988) *Assessing the Skeletal Maturity of the Hand-Wrist: Fels method*, Charles C. Thomas, Springfield, IL.

Rotch, T.M. (1909) A study of the development of the bones in childhood by the Roentgen method with the view of establishing a developmental index for the grading of and the protection of early life. *Transactions of the Association of American Physicians*, **124**, 603–630.

Saunders, E. (1837) *The Teeth, a Test of Age, Considered with Reference to the Factory Children, Addressed to the Members of Both Houses of Parliament*, Renshaw, London.

Schaefer, M., Black, S.M. and Scheuer, L. (2009) *Juvenile Osteology: A Laboratory and Field Manual*, Elsevier, London.

Scheuer, L. and Black, S. (2000) *Developmental Juvenile Osteology*, Academic Press, London.

Scheuer, J.L. and Black, S.M. (2004) *The Juvenile Skeleton*, Academic Press, London.

Schmeling, A., Olze, A., Reisinger, W. and Geserick, G. (2001a) Age estimation of living people undergoing criminal proceedings. *Lancet*, **358**, 89–90.

Schmeling, A., Kaatsch, H.-J., Marré, B. *et al.* (2001b) Empfehlungen für die Altersdiagnostik bei Lebenden im Strafverfahren. *Rechtsmedizin*, **11**, 1–3.

Schmeling, A., Grundmann, C., Fuhrmann, A. *et al.* (2008) Criteria for age estimation in living individuals. *International Journal of Legal Medicine*, **122**, 457–460.

Schmid, F. and Moll, H. (1960) *Atlas der normalen und pathologischen Handskelettentwicklung*, Springer, Berlin.

Schmidt, S., Mühler, M., Schmeling, A. *et al.* (2007) Magnetic resonance imaging of the clavicular ossification. *International Journal of Legal Medicine*, **121**, 321–324.

Schour, I. and Massler, M. (1940) Studies in tooth development: Part I: The growth of human teeth. *Journal of the American Dental Association*, **27**, 1778–1793.

Schour, I. and Massler, M. (1941) The development of the human dentition. *Journal of the American Dental Association*, **28**, 1153–1160.

Schulz, R., Zwiesigk, P., Schiborr, M. *et al.* (2008) Ultrasound studies on the time course of clavicular ossification. *International Journal of Legal Medicine*, **122**, 163–167.

Siegert, F. (1935) *Atlas der normalen Ossifikation der menschlichen Hand*, Thieme, Leipzig.

Singh, S.P. (2002) Transnational organized crime: the Indian perspective, in Annual Report for 2000 and Resource Material Series, No. 59, Tokyo, Unafei, pp. 570–587, www.unafei.or.jp/english/pdf/PDF_rms/no59/ch29.pdf (accessed 29 June 2009).

Sizonenko, P.C. (1987) Normal sexual maturation. *Pediatrician*, **14** (4), 191–201.

Solheim, T. (1993) A new method for dental age estimation in adults. *Forensic Science International*, **59**, 137–147.

Solheim, T. (1995) En ny metode for a beregne alderen hos voksne basert pa ikke-ekstraherte tenner, in *XII Nordiske Møte i Rettsmedisin: Kongressrapport* (eds B. Olaisen and B. Teige), University of Oslo, Oslo, pp. 72–76.

Sontag, L.W., Snell, D. and Anderson, M. (1939) Rate of appearance of ossification centers from birth to the age of five years. *American Journal of Diseases of Children*, **58**, 949–956.

Sorensen, K., Nielsen, J., Busch, P. *et al.* (1979) Measurement of testicular volume within Prader's orchiometer in 1389 boys. *Ugeskrift for laeger*, **141** (14), 915–918.

Stolz, H.R. and Stolz, L.M. (1951) *Somatic Development of Adolescent Boys: A Study of the Growth of Boys during the Second Decade of Life*, Macmillan, New York.

Stott, G.G., Sis, R.F. and Levy, B.M. (1981) Cementum annulation as an age criterion in forensic dentistry. *Journal of Dental Research*, **61**, 814–817.

Stratz, C.H. (1904) *Der Körper des Kindes*, Enke, Stuttgart.

Sutan-Assin, M., Rukman, J. and Dahlan, A. (1989) Penile dimensions of newborn infants. *Paediatrica Indonesiana*, **29** (7–8), 146–150.

Takihara, H., Sakatoku, J., Fuji, M. *et al.* (1983) Significance of testicular size measurement in andrology. 1. A new orchiometer and its clinical application. *Fertility and Sterility*, **39** (6), 836–840.

Tanner, J.M. (1978) *Foetus into Man: Physical Growth from Conception to Maturity*, Open Books, London.

Tanner, J.M., Whitehouse, R.H. and Healy, M.J.R. (1962) *A New System for Estimating Skeletal Maturity from the Hand and Wrist, with Standards Derived from a Study of 2,600 Healthy British Children*, Centre International de l'Enfance, Paris.

Tanner, J.M., Whitehouse, R.H., Marshall, W.A. *et al.* (1975) *Assessment of Skeletal Maturity and Prediction of Adult Height (TW2 Method)*, Academic Press, London.

Tanner, J.M., Healy, M.J.R., Goldstein, H. and Cameron, N. (2001) *Assessment of Skeletal Maturity and Prediction of Adult Height (TW3 Method)*, W.B. Saunders, London.

Tanner, J.M. and Whitehouse, R.H. (1976) Clinical longitudinal standards for height, weight, height velocity, weight velocity and stages of puberty. *Archives of Diseases in Childhood*, **51**, 170–179.

Thiemann, H.H., Nitz, I. and Schmeling, A. (2006) *Röntgenatlas der normalen Hand im Kindesalter*, Thieme, Stuttgart.

Thodberg, H.H. (2009) An automated method for determination of bone age. *Journal of Clinical Endocrinology and Metabolism*, **94** (7), 2239–2244.

Thomson, A.T. (1936) Lectures on medical jurisprudence now in course of delivery at London University. *Lancet*, **1**, 281–286.

Todd, T.W. (1937) *Atlas of Skeletal Maturation*, C.V. Mosby, St Louis, MO.

Tuladhar, R., Davis, P.G., Batcha, J. and Doyle, L.W. (1998) Establishment of a normal range of penile length in preterm infants. *Journal of Paediatrics and Child Health*, **34** (5), 471–473.

Ubelaker, D.H. (1978) *Human Skeletal Remains: Excavation, Analysis and Interpretation*, Smithsonian Institute Press, Washington, DC.

UN (2000) United Nations Convention against Transnational Organized Crime, Trafficking Protocol, www.unodc.org/documents/treaties/UNTOC/Publications/TOC%20Convention/TOCebook-e.pdf (accessed 23 June 2009).

UNHCR (1997) Guidelines on Policies and Procedures in Dealing with Unaccompanied Children Seeking Asylum, www.unhcr.org/refworld/docid/3ae6b3360.html (accessed 23 June 2009).

UNHCR (2004) Trends in Unaccompanied and Separated Children Seeking Asylum in Industrialized Countries, 2001–2003, www.unhcr.org/40f646444.pdf (accessed 23 June 2009).

van der Linden, F.P.G.M. and Duterloo, H.S. (1976) *The Development of the Human Dentition: An Atlas*, Harper and Row, Hagerstown, MD.

von Ranke, H. (1896) Die Ossification der Hand unter Röntgenbeleuchtung. *Münchner Medizinische Wochenschrift*, **45**, 1365–1369.

Wheeler, M.D. (1991) Physical changes of puberty. *Endocrinology and Metabolism Clinics of North America*, **20** (1), 1–14.

Wittwer-Backofen, U., Gampe, J. and Vaupel, J.W. (2004) Tooth cementum annulation for age estimation: results from a large known-age validation study. *American Journal of Physical Anthropology*, **123**, 119–129.

Yang, F., Jacobs, R. and Willems, G. (2006) Dental age estimation through volume matching of teeth imaged by cone-beam CT. *Forensic Science International*, **159S**, S78–S83.

Zachmann, M., Prader, A., Kind, H.P. *et al.* (1974) Testicular volume during adolescence. Cross sectional and longitudinal studies. *Helvetica Paediatrica Acta*, **29** (1), 61–72.

Zalel, Y., Pinhas-Hamid, O., Lipitz, S. *et al.* (2001) The development of the fetal penis: an *in utero* sonographic evaluation. *Ultrasound in Obstetrics and Gynecology*, **17** (2), 129–131.

2

Immigration, Asylum Seekers and Undocumented Identity

Heather Law[1], Lorraine Mensah[2], Sue Bailey[3] and Julia Nelki[4]
[1]*Greater Manchester West Mental Health NHS Foundation Trust, Bury New Road, Prestwich, Manchester M25 3BL, UK*
[2]*India Buildings Chambers, 8th Floor, India Buildings, Water Street, Liverpool, L2 0XG, UK*
[3]*University of Central Lancashire, Preston, Lancashire PR1 2HE, UK*
[4]*Alder Hey Children's NHS Foundation Trust, Eaton Road, West Derby, Liverpool L12 2AP, UK*

Over the course of the twentieth century every country has been affected by international migration and as such, the latter part of the twentieth century has been dubbed 'the age of migration' (Castles and Miller, 1996). This pattern of increased movement of individuals was influenced by various policy changes and world events, including the liberalization of admission policies in several countries beginning in the 1960s; the 1965 Immigration and Nationality Act in the US; the formation of the European Community after the Merger Treaty in 1967; the European 'oil crisis' and consequent Arabian 'oil boom' in 1973; the collapse of the Soviet Union beginning in 1985; and the creation of the European Union in 1993.

Current estimates suggest that, globally, there are over 185 million international migrants and statistical trends show that immigration is heavily biased towards the developed world. As can be seen in Figure 2.1, the key areas for immigration (shown in blue) are North America, the European Union, South Africa, Australia and the Russian Federation. Patterns of emigration are generally away from Central America and Mexico, South America, Northern Africa, Eastern Europe and South East Asia (shown in brown).

It is perhaps not surprising that the European Union has been the focus of immigration for centuries. The wealth of Europe and its historical links with the rest

Age Estimation in the Living: The Practitioners Guide   Sue Black, Anil Aggrawal and Jason Payne-James
© 2010 John Wiley & Sons, Ltd

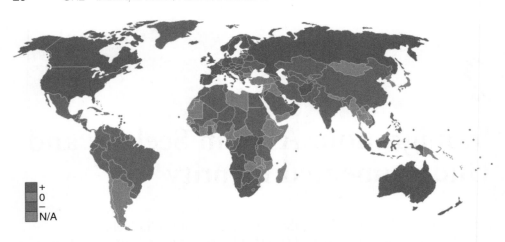

Figure 2.1   Net migration rate based on data from https://www.cia.gov/library/publications/the-world-factbook/fields/2112.html (accessed 1 June 2009).

of the world are deeply embedded into the psychological fabric of many poorer or less well-developed societies. The history of the United Kingdom (UK) as a former colonial power is such that it is common to hear those who first migrate talk of the UK as a wealthy country with strong and well-established community links to many African, Asian and Far Eastern countries.

The influx of immigrants is therefore not a new thing in Europe or in the UK, but what has changed is the fact that most countries in Europe now wish to control the influx of immigrants through tighter legal controls and stronger physical control of their borders.

Well-educated and wealthy migrants who can contribute to the economic dynamic of the country's might are filtered through one set of ideals, while those forced to flee civil conflict and wars are managed through a separate route. The development of laws to govern those who were forced out of their home countries and abroad, encapsulated a desire to bring about order to displaced migration, which often occurs as a chaotic and sudden movement of large numbers of people. The key principles that have shaped refugee status today stem from the *1951 Convention Relating to the Status of Refugees*. The mandate of the Convention states:

> that the term "refugee" should be applied to any individual who owing to a well-founded fear of being persecuted for reasons of race, religion, nationality, membership of a particular social group or political opinion, is outside the country of his nationality and is unable or, owing to such a fear, unwilling to avail himself of the protection of that country; or who, not having a nationality and being outside the country of his former habitual residence as a result of such events, is unable or, owing to such a fear, is unwilling to return to it.

This mandate contains the key terms that have, over the course of over 50 years, shaped refugee law today. The ease of world travel and the well-developed market in forged documentation has allowed individuals from all over the world to gain entry into the UK and other European countries. Those who wish to enter for economic purposes normally apply to enter in any one of the Embassies or Consulates abroad. Those who claim they are refugees cannot normally apply to enter the UK through an Embassy abroad, although it is permissible for family members of those who have established themselves as refugees in the UK to do so. Instead, refugees will generally only have their claims to fear of serious harm abroad considered if they are already in the UK. The result is that many of those seeking asylum use false documents to enter the UK or enter hidden in the back of commercial lorries or via a variety of other means. Obviously the mechanism for entry to the UK is country specific and the processes for other countries should be consulted.

A recent report from the Office of the United Nations High Commissioner for Refugees (UNHCR) (2009a) identifies seven groups of migrants to be included as 'persons of concern'. These are: refugees, asylum seekers, internally displaced persons (IDPs), returned refugees, returned internally displaced persons, stateless persons and 'other' groups of concern. As described earlier, a refugee is defined as someone who flees to escape conflict, persecution or natural disaster, and an asylum seeker is an individual whose application for refugee status is pending a final decision. IDPs are those who have fled to escape conflict, persecution or natural disaster but have not crossed an international border. The terms 'returned refugees' and 're-turned internally displaced persons' refer to those who have been returned to their country or residence of origin. 'Stateless' persons include people with undetermined nationality and those who are not nationals of a recognized State. Based on human-itarian or other special grounds, the UNHCR also provides protection and services to individuals who may not fall into any of the above categories. These individuals fall into the 'other' groups of concern category.

The UNHCR report (2009a) also states that in 2007, there were an estimated 25 million refugees and IDPs falling under UNHCRs responsibility. However, the report suggests that the likely global total for 'forcibly displaced people' is more likely to approach 67 million. This includes 16 million refugees worldwide and it is estimated that there are also 12 million stateless people worldwide.

The report estimates that almost half of the world's refugees are children while only 27% of asylum seekers are children. In a recent report compiled by UNHCR (2003) the proportion of child refugees was found to vary according to region. For example, only one fifth of Central and Eastern European refugees are under 18, while the majority (57%) of Central African refugees are children.

While the UNHCR are able to provide estimated statistics for refugees and IDPs falling under their responsibility, the UK and other countries around the world find it inherently difficult to provide figures for the illegal immigrant population residing in their homelands. Various different methodologies have been employed around the world based on hypothetical calculations and extrapolations from indicative data sources. However, the very nature of illegal immigration makes any form of registra-tion or statistical coverage virtually impossible, and there is continuous fluctuation in the illegally resident population. This results in the actual scale of illegal immigration only being 'roughly estimated' (Futo and Tass, 2001).

As an example, the data available relating to the UK is discussed further. The most recent official estimate of illegal immigrants residing in the UK was provided by the Home Office in 2005. This estimate was produced using the 'residual method', which involves deducting an estimate of the lawfully resident foreign born population from the total foreign-born population based on the 2001 census. This remaining difference is an estimate of the number of unauthorized migrants living in the UK. Using this method, the central estimate for illegal immigrants living in the UK on census day in 2001 was 430 000, with the overall estimate ranging from 310 000 to 570 000 (Home Office, 2005).

These figures were later challenged by Migration Watch (2005), which pointed out that they do not include the UK-born children of immigrants. Migration Watch recommended that an allowance of between 5% and 15% should be made to cover this omission. This would potentially inflate the estimate by between 15 000 and 85 000. Taking the central figure, this would increase the Home Office estimate to 473 000 illegal immigrants residing in the UK. Migration Watch also noted that the estimate is based on the 2001 census data and was therefore four years out of date at the time of publication.

In a more recent study by the London School of Economics (2009), the Home Office figures from 2005 again came into question. This report advised that the estimate of illegal immigrants living in the UK should be raised to between 417 000 and 863 000 with a central estimate being 618 000. This figure used the Home Office 2005 estimate of 430 000 plus an allowance for the change in numbers of resident failed asylum seekers and overstayers/illegal entrants between 2001 and 2007, deductions for regularized migrants between 2003 and 2007, and inclusion of an estimated 85 000 UK-born children of illegal immigrants.

The trends in nationalities of illegal immigrants entering the UK and other countries are often mapped by world events. It is perhaps not surprising that in October 1998 with the continuing Kosovo conflict, the largest number of asylum seekers came from Yugoslavia with 1160 people claiming asylum (Home Office, 1999). In the first quarter of 2008, the largest numbers were more widespread, with 830 people from Afghanistan, 700 people from Iraq, 640 people from Zimbabwe and 580 people from Iran (Home Office, 2008). There are some countries whose long-standing civil conflicts have put them in the top 10 nationalities of asylum seekers in the UK for a significant period of time. Since the outbreak of full-scale civil war in Somalia in 1991, the United Kingdom has consistently received an influx of asylum seekers, and Somalia has remained consistently in the top 10.

Globally, by the end of 2007, Afghanistan continued to be the top source country for those seeking asylum in industrialized countries (see Figure 2.2). Iraqis were the second largest group, followed by Columbians, Sudanese and Somalis (UNHCR, 2009a). The top four host countries of asylum seekers and refugees were Pakistan, Syria, Iran and Germany.

The most recent data on trends of asylum seeking include the first six months of 2009. The top five source countries for those seeking asylum in industrialized countries in 2009 were Iraq, Afghanistan, Somalia, China and Serbia (UNHCR, 2009b). Iraq again featured in the top five source countries, with 13 200 claims. Over the past decade, Iraq has been the main country of origin for asylum seekers in 2000, 2002, 2006 and again for the first half of 2009. The latest figures indicate a decrease for the second quarter of 2009 to 5400 applications for asylum, which is the

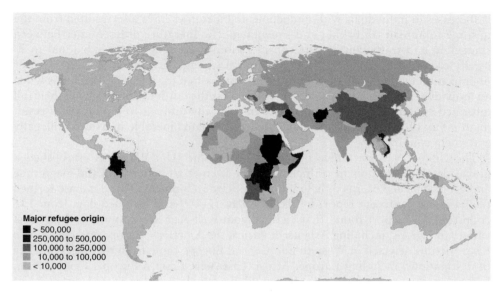

Major refugee origin
- > 500,000
- 250,000 to 500,000
- 100,000 to 250,000
- 10,000 to 100,000
- < 10,000

Figure 2.2   Major source countries of refugees, end 2007.
Source: UNHCR, 2008.

lowest since 2006. Applications from Iraqi asylum seekers were mainly submitted to Germany, Turkey, Sweden and the Netherlands. The recent decrease may be attributed to a change in policy in Sweden, which declared that Iraq was no longer subject to 'armed conflict'.

Afghanistan also continued to feature in the top five countries of origin although it dropped to the second largest source country for the first half of 2009. Despite Iraq becoming the main country of origin for 2009, Afghan asylum seekers submitted 12 000 applications, which was double the figure for the same period in 2008. One in three of the applications were submitted in the UK or Norway. The number of applications submitted in Norway was six times the number submitted in the same period for 2008.

Somalia was the third largest source country for asylum seekers in the first half of 2009, with 11 100 applications registered. The majority of these requests were made to the Netherlands, Sweden and Italy. The fourth and fifth largest source countries were China and Serbia, with both increasing in their numbers of applications to their highest since 2005.

With such high numbers of asylum seekers from a range of countries, it is perhaps not surprising that many are unable to produce any documentary evidence of their identity or to prove their claimed history is true. The fact that an individual is undocumented does not mean that they cannot claim asylum, and it is usually consideration of their story as a whole and how it compares with the known facts that is relied upon by the decision maker. The relevance of documentation is, however, more important in certain types of claims, for example when individuals claim that they are stateless and have no place to which they can be repatriated with safety.

Increases in individuals with undocumented identities have also resulted from the upsurge in human trafficking and smuggling. The literature differentiates between smuggling and trafficking by the consideration of consent of the individual to illegally cross the border of a country. Human smuggling is when an individual or organization facilitates an illegal border crossing, often for a fee. Trafficking is when an individual is coerced or forced to illegally cross the border without giving their full informed consent. Both phenomena are intrinsically difficult to monitor and result in an influx of undetected, undocumented and often vulnerable individuals illegally entering a country.

The United Nations Office on Drugs and Crime (UNODC) has established a global database on human trafficking in an attempt to understand the magnitude and geographical patterns to help inform policy development. This database formed the basis for the recent report by the UNODC (2009) and included data from 155 countries. The report found that victims from East Asia were found in the widest variety of regions, including Asia itself, Africa, the Americas, Europe and the Middle East. Victims detected in Western and Central Europe came from the widest variety of destinations, including Europe, Africa, East Asia, Eastern Europe, Central Asia, Latin America and South Asia. It should be noted that due to the difficulty of detecting trafficked victims, these findings are not representative of the problem as a whole and only represent detected cases and are therefore likely to be a significant underestimate of the magnitude of the situation.

In the preliminary analysis of this international database, Kangaspunta (2003) found that as many as 150 countries were cited in the database as destination countries for human trafficking, with the top three destination regions being the United States of America, the European Union and Japan. The top three countries of origin for victims of trafficking were the Russian Federation, Ukraine and Nigeria. Unsurprisingly, as with other forms of immigration, developed countries were the favoured destinations. However, it is also worthy of note that 96 countries were mentioned as 'transit' countries and that these were most commonly in the developed countries of Central and Eastern Europe. It is highly likely that many individuals ultimately remain in these transit countries and do not reach their intended destinations, although the scale of this phenomenon would be inherently difficult to quantify and there are currently no local or global estimates for immigrants who reside in intended 'transit' countries.

Refugees, asylum seekers and those with undocumented identities face a range of legal, political and social barriers upon arrival in their destination countries. In a working paper from the Centre on Migration, Policy and Society (see Crawley, 2005), the beliefs and attitudes of the general public towards asylum and immigration are explored. Across the UK and indeed throughout Europe, the evidence suggests an increasingly negative and often intolerant attitude towards asylum and immigration issues (Saggar and Drean, 2001). This report also explores the factors that influence these attitudes, including individual demographic characteristics, national culture and policy, and socio-economic variables.

Individual socio-demographic factors, including age, gender, ethnic origin or background, education and employment, are all related to attitudes towards immigrants and asylum seekers. Some evidence suggests that women are more likely to have more positive opinions towards immigration and asylum issues than men (Stonewall, 2003) and that younger people have more negative attitudes towards immigration and asylum (MORI, 2002), although both these concepts have been disputed elsewhere (Amnesty International, 2004; Finney, 2005). Similarly, although a theory of cultural affinity would suggest those from ethnic minorities would have more positive attitudes towards immigration and asylum issues than their white peers, recent surveys suggest there is a surprising level of hostility among ethnic minorities towards asylum and migration (YouGov, 2004).

One reason for such divergence in survey and opinion poll results is the considerable impact of the current political and economic climate on attitudes and opinions. For instance, negative attitudes towards immigrants are often associated with downturns in the labour market, and theories suggest that hostility towards immigrants results from economic deprivation and the fear of further financial decline. In addition to the belief that immigrants will reduce the number of available jobs and/or reduce wages, there is also the perception that immigrants abuse the welfare system and do not contribute economically to society. It is often the combination of these factors alongside a perceived unfairness of government policy in general which impacts upon public attitudes towards immigrants.

Another significant influence on the views and attitude of the general public towards immigrants is that of the media. There has been a considerable increase in recent years in the number of negative stories in the national press relating to immigration and asylum issues. Research suggests that, while stories in the media could be seen to spark useful public debate, often the material presented is far from accurate and may sensationalize the scale and impact of immigration and asylum issues (Buchanan, Grillo and Threadgold, 2003). This material then forms the basis for the public's opinions and is frequently used to justify prejudices. While some of the material in the national press is controlled by the use of timely releases of government statistics and policy, the national media is still heavily biased towards anti-immigration views and this directly impacts upon the way in which immigrants and asylum seekers are viewed and treated by the native inhabitants.

In order to gain control of the flow of people entering the country, the government in England and Wales has established a set of what are commonly referred to as 'Immigration Rules' and which are formally known as the *Immigration Rules, HC 395 of 1994 (as amended)*. These rules are designed to reflect the government's changing views on economic entry into and stay in the UK. The power to make such rules stems from the *Immigration Act 1971* and in particular Section 3(2), which gives the Secretary of State the power to create statements of rules, or of any changes in the rules, laid down by him/her as to the practice to be followed in the administration of the 1971 Act. Over the years, the rules have developed from general guidance for Immigration officials to a complex and detailed set of instructions on who can legally enter or stay in the UK, and what evidence they need to provide to establish that they meet the requirements. The rules also run alongside various Acts such as the *Human Rights Act 1998* and the *Nationality, Immigration and Asylum Act 2002* and various procedural rules. *The Human Rights Act 1998* incorporated the *European Convention for the Protection of Human Rights and Fundamental*

Freedoms into national law. The regulations now incorporate rules about who is a refugee and when they should be granted refugee status.

In England and Wales the government has set up a specialist tribunal system to deal with and process those who wish to enter or remain in the UK. The title of the tribunal has changed over the years, but it is currently called the Asylum and Immigration Tribunal. The Tribunal hears cases of those who have been refused a right to enter or remain in the UK by the government in England and Wales. The tribunal hearings are adversarial and heard by Immigration Judges. The Secretary of State will normally be represented by an advocate known as a Home Office Presenting Officer and the person wishing to enter or stay in the UK will commonly be represented by a legal representative or sponsor or can, if practical, attend in person. The decision of the Immigration Judge is only open to challenge where the Judge has erred in his or her legal analysis. The procedure of the Tribunal is governed by *The Asylum and Immigration Tribunal (Procedure) Rules* 2005.

2.1   Asylum Seeker to Refugee

There is no simple way to gain illegal entry into the UK; the journey can often be dangerous and the use of false documents can result in criminal prosecution. However, thousands travel halfway across the world to attempt to gain entry into the UK. Some enter via air and sea ports with false passports, while some hide in the back of lorries and employ other inventive means to allow them to then claim asylum due to events they claim occurred while they were abroad.

Those who manage to gain entry into the UK and claim they are refugees are referred to as asylum seekers. They remain asylum seekers until either their claims have been rejected and any appeal rights exhausted or they have been recognized as refugees. On arrival in the UK an asylum seeker is expected to declare their presence to the authorities immediately and to attend a series of interviews. The interviews allow the immigration officials to consider the asylum seeker's evidence before making a decision to grant refugee status or reject the claim. If refused, the asylum seeker can appeal and his or her case will be considered by the Immigration and Asylum Chamber.

The result of long-standing conflicts around the world is that those recognized as refugees wish to be reunited with their families, who are often left behind in the home countries or in refugee camps in host countries. In recognition of the right to family life, the UK allows those individuals who were existing family members and formed part of the family unit before the refugee fled to apply abroad to join their family member in the UK. This is most commonly spouses and children but can include elderly parents or children over 18 if there are compelling and com-passionate circumstances. Originally, consideration of such applications was made under a policy document drafted on behalf of the Secretary of State as guidance for officials considering such applications. Since 18 September 2002 the policy has been incorporated into the Immigration Rules. The result is that families can be reunited in the UK.

There is a separate category of asylum seeker who is allowed to stay in the UK. If individuals prove that they cannot return to their home country or the place where they were habitually or legally able to reside but fail to demonstrate they have a conventional reason, they can be granted a form of inferior status known as 'discretionary leave' and previously called 'exceptional leave'. The status is inferior because those granted discretionary leave do not have a right to bring their family members to the UK immediately. The rationale for this is summed up in the comments of the Minister of State, Home Office (Mrs Barbara Roche) in the House of Commons on 1 March 2000, Column 84 WH.

As my hon. Friend rightly said, although the families of those recognised as refugees in the United Kingdom are eligible to join them in this country immediately, the families of those who have been refused asylum but granted exceptional leave to remain must normally wait until they have completed four years in that category before their families are eligible to join them. My hon. Friend has covered the reasons for that, but it is worth my mentioning them briefly.

As I am sure hon. Members appreciate, exceptional leave to remain may be granted for a variety of reasons. As my hon. Friend conceded, a person who is granted exceptional leave does not have to meet the strict criteria required of someone recognised as a refugee under the 1951 United Nations convention relating to the status of refugees. Therefore, there is a considerable distinction between the two groups.

People who have been granted exceptional leave to remain have considerable entitlements in the United Kingdom, but I am not persuaded that it would be appropriate to offer them the full range of benefits currently available to refugees. Under the 1951 convention and the way in which it is applied by countries that are signatories to it, that is a special status and carries with it special entitlements. It is right to maintain those special entitlements.

The result is that those with this inferior form of status are legally resident in the UK but can remain estranged from their families for many years. It is open to debate whether this approach will continue for the long term, with the development and recognition of family life expanding through judicial analysis to include the need to recognize the impact of such decisions on the family as a whole rather than just the individual.

One area of concern faced by UK officials is the increasing number of unaccompanied minors. It may be surprising to know that asylum seekers are not always adults, and children as young as six are sometimes brought into the UK and left in the hands of the authorities. The increase in the numbers of those either claiming to be under the age of 18 or who are under 18 has created a need for special procedures and policies. Clearly children cannot necessarily be put through the same rigorous asylum process as adults, and deporting or removing a child to another country is fraught with difficulties for the officials involved. While those unaccompanied minors who are accepted as such are often granted temporary status until they are 18 years old, there are a large number who are not accepted as minors and find they have to prove their age through the asylum process. While the standard of proof is low in asylum appeals, it is often difficult for a claimant to gain access to documentation such as a birth certificate, which is often left behind, and medical evidence is only accessible if the individual manages to obtain legal representation.

Countries around the world have invested substantial funds in tightening their borders to prevent entry of those wishing to enter illegally for either economic advantage or asylum. While the fences are built ever higher it is yet to be seen whether those whose aim it is to gain entry will be prevented from doing so. The fact of persecution and serious harm of civilians and the global failure to prevent international displacement means there will always be mass migration, and the need to deal with those individuals who are displaced by conflict is yet to be adequately resolved (see Chapter 5). Until there is an answer, it is difficult to see how any wall, no matter how high, will keep people out.

References

Amnesty International (2004) *Refugees and Asylum Seekers: Northern Ireland Youth Attitudes Survey*, www.amnesty.org.uk/images/ul/a/attitudes.pdf (accessed 14 December 2009).

Asylum and Immigration Tribunal (Procedure) Rules (2005), www.ait.gov.uk/Documents/2005_ProcedureRules.pdf (accessed 19 October 2009).

Buchanan, S., Grillo, B. and Threadgold, T. (2003) What's the story? Results from research into media coverage of refugees and asylum seekers in the UK, ARTICLE 19, London, www.article19.org/pdfs/publications/refugees-what-s-the-story-.pdf (accessed 14 December 2009).

Castles, S. and Miller, M. (1996) *The Age of Migration: International Population Movements in the Modern World*, Macmillan, London.

Crawley, H. (2005) Evidence on attitudes to asylum and immigration: What we know, don't know and need to know, Centre on Migration, Policy and Society Working Paper No. 23, University of Oxford, Oxford, www.compas.ox.ac.uk/fileadmin/files/pdfs/Heaven%20Crawley%20WP0523.pdf (accessed 19 October 2009).

Finney, N. (2005) Key issues: public opinion on asylum and refugee issues, Information Centre about Asylum and Refugees (ICAR), London, www.icar.org.uk/9551/briefings/public-attitudes.html (accessed 14 December 2009).

Futo, P. and Tass, T. (2001) Apprehension from border guards of Central and Eastern Europe – a resource for measuring illegal migration? Working Group, Chisinau, 18–19 September.

Home Office (1999) Asylum statistics, October 1998, United Kingdom, Home Office, London, www.homeoffice.gov.uk/rds/pdfs/asy-oct98.pdf (accessed 19 October 2009).

Home Office (2005) Sizing the unauthorised (illegal) migrant population in the United Kingdom in 2001, Home Office Online Report 29/05, www.homeoffice.gov.uk/rds/pdfs05/rdsolr2905.pdf (accessed 9 November 2009).

Home Office (2008) Asylum statistics, 1st quarter 2008, United Kingdom, Research Development Statistics, Home Office, London, www.homeoffice.gov.uk/rds/pdfs08/asylumq108.pdf (accessed 10 October 2009).

Kangaspunta, K. (2003) Mapping the inhuman trade: preliminary findings of the database on trafficking in human beings, *Forum on Crime and Society*, 3 (1 and 2), 82–102, www.unodc.org/pdf/crime/forum/forum3.pdf (accessed 19 October 2009).

Migration Watch UK (2005) The illegal migrant population in the UK, Briefing Paper, Migration Watch UK, London, www.migrationwatchuk.org/dynPdf/briefingPaper_11.6_109_20050728.pdf (accessed 9 November 2009).

MORI (2002) Attitudes to asylum seekers for 'Refugee Week', www.ipsos-mori.com/researchpublications/researcharchive/poll.aspx?oItemId=1061 (accessed 19 October 2009).

Saggar, S. and Drean, J. (2001) British public attitudes and ethnic minorities, Cabinet Office Performance and Innovation Unit, London, www.cabinetoffice.gov.uk/media/cabinetoffice/strategy/assets/british.pdf (accessed 19 October 2009).

Stonewall (2003) Profiles of prejudice: the nature of prejudice in England: in-depth findings, Stonewall, London, www.stonewall.org.uk/documents/profiles.doc (accessed 19 October 2009).

UN General Assembly (1951) Convention relating to the status of refugees, 28th July 1951, United Nations, Treaty Series, vol. 189, p. 137, www.unhcr.org/refworld/docid/3be01b964.html (accessed 19 October 2009).

UNHCR (2003) World refugee day 2003: information kit, www.unhcr.org/3ee8b0f04.pdf (accessed 19 October 2009).

UNHCR (2009a) 2008 Global trends: refugees, asylum-seekers, returnees, internally displaced and stateless persons, www.unhcr.org/4a375c426.html (accessed 19 October 2009).

UNHCR (2009b) Asylum levels and trends in industrialized countries, first half 2009, www.unhcr.org/4adebca49.html (accessed 9 November 2009).

United Nations Office on Drugs and Crime (UNODC) (2009) Global report on trafficking in persons, www.unodc.org/documents/Global_Report_on_TIP.pdf (accessed 19 October 2009).

YouGov (2004) Survey on racial equality, www.yougov.co.uk/extranets/ygarchives/content/pdf/RCF040101001_1.pdf (accessed 19 October 2009).

3

Clinical and Legal Requirements for Age Determination in the Living

Philip Beh[1] and Jason Payne-James[2]

[1] Department of Pathology, University of Hong Kong, Queen Mary Hospital, Pokfulam Road, Hong Kong

[2] Cameron Forensic Medical Sciences, Barts and London School of Medicine and Dentistry, London EC1M 6BQ, UK

3.1   Introduction

Throughout the world, principles of assessment of individuals in the healthcare setting are the same. For doctors, an assessment of anyone with a medical problem involves taking a relevant history, undertaking an appropriate physical examination, determining possible diagnoses and devising a management plan to confirm or exclude a diagnosis. There are certain common questions in any assessment. 'How old are you?' or, more precisely, 'what is your date of birth?' These are questions that doctors and other healthcare professionals ask all the time and rarely stop to think about reasons for the question or the truth of the response. Indeed, why should they? In 'normal' healthcare settings, there would be no reason to question the accuracy of an answer provided by the patient. This of course also follows the assumption that the individual knows their date of birth and their age. Variation or apparent inaccuracies may be present because of the use of different calendars (e.g. Ethiopia) where years may be substantially different. Birthdays and birth dates may not be celebrated and there are believed to be tens of millions of individuals who do not know their birth date or their place of birth.

There are however many settings in which healthcare professionals may, on reflection, realize that such questions may provide answers that are incorrect. This

---

Age Estimation in the Living: The Practitioners Guide   Sue Black, Anil Aggrawal and Jason Payne-James

will not necessarily be a surprise to those who work within the criminal setting, where false names, false addresses and false dates of birth may be given for a number of reasons. That person may already be wanted by the police or other agencies or they may have escaped from custody and thus wish to avoid identification. In such cases, individuals are unlikely to provide dates of birth that are vastly different from their true date of birth but sufficiently different to obfuscate the truth. However, if difference in age of just a year or two can alter how a person is, or could be, treated by government or judicial authorities, then the substitution of a single digit at the end of a year of birth may completely alter that person's status within that jurisdiction.

This chapter explores the medical and legal issues surrounding this very difficult yet neglected area of medical practice. Many doctors will be asked to estimate or evaluate the age of an individual – most will quite rightly indicate that they do not have the expert knowledge or skills to undertake this. A small number will attempt to provide an estimate, without being aware of the means of assessing age or the limitations, even when undertaken correctly. A small number will have the necessary skills to undertake an estimation of age and provide responses appropriate to the respective degrees of certainty required in criminal or civil proceedings. Forensic pathologists, odontologists and anthropologists are often required to estimate the age of human remains or of a deceased person. Of those healthcare professionals asked to undertake age estimations in the living, forensic physicians, paediatricians and radiologists are the medical specialists most commonly requested to perform such estimates. Forensic odontologists are probably the healthcare professionals most frequently called upon to undertake age estimations although other sciences such as forensic anthropology may also be called upon to assist with age estimations in the living. Details of the variety of techniques available can be found in the chapters of this book.

3.2 Contrasts between Age Assessment in the Living and the Deceased

Although techniques of age investigation may be the same in both the living and the deceased, the reasons for the determinations of age may differ widely. In addition to the different reasons for age estimation, the issues of consent, confidentiality, retention of tissue, health and safety, human rights and application of law vary between the living and the deceased, and moreover vary dependent on the jurisdiction in which the age estimation is sought. This chapter addresses the general principles of age estimation and its application, and Chapter 4 will concentrate on the professional legal and ethical issues that have relevance when required to undertake age estimation. Examples predominantly from within the English and Welsh, or Scottish jurisdictions will be used but the principles identified apply in any country in the world although the details may vary. In general, the legal and medical issues for estimating the age in a living person compared to those for the deceased are markedly different and considerably more complex.

3.3 Reasons for Age Estimation of Bodies and Human Remains

In most jurisdictions where the identity of a body or human remains is unknown, a forensic pathologist will be the first contact who will (on behalf of a court – in England and Wales, the Coroner) be required to establish an age estimate. Dependent on the condition of the body or human remains, the pathologist may seek the opinion of a forensic anthropologist or odontologist. The process by which the findings are sought and recorded will be covered by the appropriate death investigation or death registration legislations pertinent to the country of their practice.

In England and Wales, when a Coroner is informed that a body is lying in his/her district and there is reasonable cause to suspect that the deceased: (i) has died a violent or unnatural death, (ii) has died a sudden death of unknown cause or (iii) has died in prison or in circumstances as to require an inquest under any other Act, then whether the cause of death arose within his/her district or not, the Coroner shall as soon as practicable hold an inquest (Coroners Act 1988). In England and Wales, the body does not belong to the Coroner (Procurator Fiscal in Scotland), but the Coroner has lawful control of that body. Thus if tissue is required for age estimation (e.g. tooth extraction for assessment of degree of racemisation of aspartic acid) then the Coroner can direct the removal of that tissue. So far as identification is concerned, the legal position is that when the police are dealing with a suspicious death they work on behalf of the Coroner because he/she has both the responsibility for identification and the right to possession of the body until all coronial functions have been fulfilled.

In many countries, all deaths have to be registered and the medical practitioner (doctor) responsible for the issue of the death certificate is also responsible for establishing not just the cause of death but also the accuracy of all the other registration details such as name, sex, age and occupation. Many doctors are unaware of, or neglect this legal burden and generally accept it without challenge or supporting information from family members. In the vast majority of instances, such information is true, but it is wise to consider whether any documentation (e.g. birth certificate, passport) can support the information given.

3.4 Reasons for Age Estimation of Living Individuals

Age can confer certain rights and also penalties upon individuals. In very broad terms, a younger age is more likely to allow state support of that individual, and a younger age is more likely to result in lesser punishments in relation to criminal issues. A child is entitled to a suite of protections, services and support that are not available to adults, including health, accommodation and education, and, if applicable, also to progress through the asylum process as a child.

As discussed below with some examples, and dependent on jurisdiction, a day or two difference in age may place someone in the category for that jurisdiction of being

Table 3.1   Examples of reasons for age estimation in the living when age is unknown (does not apply to all jurisdictions).

Age of criminal responsibility
To determine whether a child
To determine whether an adult
Refugee and asylum seeker status
Stateless individuals
Human trafficking
Human smuggling
Sex workers
Competency and legal capacity
Consent for medical treatment or procedures
Guardianship orders
Consent for marriage
Employment recruitment
Retirement benefits
Pensions claims
Consent for medical treatment
Age of marriage
Complainant of sexual offence
Pornographic images

below the age of criminal responsibility, or in a position to receive different care or management plans (Children Act 1989).

With greater movement of individuals between countries and where there is movement from a country where date of birth is not regularly or formerly recorded to one where it is (and upon which a legal framework may be based), problems may obviously arise if the chronological age of that individual is not known. Of course, this is a simplistic approach, as so many factors may affect an individual's maturity and behaviour, but a reliable estimate of chronological age provides an appropriate base from which decisions can be made. In the UK in 2005 ~45% of all asylum applicants who presented as separated children were age disputed and treated as adults (Crawley, 2007).

Table 3.1 lists examples where age estimation may be required for social and legal (criminal or civil) proceedings. Table 3.2 lists examples of legal ages of criminal responsibility and Table 3.3 lists legal ages for marriage. These tables are used to illustrate the diversity of need for knowledge of age in many communities, and these ages may change as cultures and societies develop or evolve.

The volume of international migration in recent years has in many respects acted as an international driver for recognition of the need for robust age estimation techniques (UNHCR, 2008). It is also recognized that for many valid reasons (e.g. destruction of home, loss of records, flight from country etc.) documentary evidence of identity and age may be absent. The emphasis must be that the age estimation takes into account as many factors as possible. However, problems may arise even when an age estimation has been undertaken. Internal conflicts within a country at

Table 3.2 Ages of criminal responsibility.

Age (years)	Jurisdictions
6	North Carolina (US)
7	Thailand, Singapore, India, Pakistan, South Africa
8	Scotland[a]
10	England, Wales, Northern Ireland, Australia
11	Turkey
12	Canada, Netherlands
14	China, Austria, Germany, Japan, New Zealand
15	Sweden, Norway, Finland
16	Portugal
17	France
18	International Criminal Court, Belgium

[a] The age will be raised to 12 if the Criminal Justice and Licensing (Scotland) Bill is passed in Parliament.

administrative level may result in different bodies relying on different evidence of age and thus the individual who has been assessed may become involved in situations beyond their control.

It is of interest to look at age assessment in asylum seekers within the England and Wales jurisdiction by reference to recent decided cases. It is likely that similar cases are extant in other jurisdictions and highlight the complexity of the issue and the need for an appropriate and recognized understanding of age assessment and estimation.

In England a male from Pakistan, seeking asylum and claiming to be 15 was assessed at his point of entry in Liverpool and found to be 18. He was removed to a detention centre elsewhere and in his asylum appeal the judge held him to be 15 – which brought him under the remit of the Children Act 1989. However, on his release he transferred back to Liverpool where he was held to be an adult again (EWHC 1702). This kind of action may be prevented if a more robust age estimation had been undertaken that was less likely to be challenged.

In a similar case (EWHC 2921) it was found that an expert report had been produced in accordance with guidelines from the Royal College of Paediatrics and Child Health (1999), and the local authority was not entitled *not* to consider the expert's report because of a general objection to such reports. To some extent this identifies the reluctance or misunderstanding of non-healthcare professionals and non-scientists in the interpretation of such findings.

This approach in England and Wales was related to findings in another case (EWHC 1753), where it was determined *inter alia* that 'whilst it is not necessary for the local authority to obtain a medical report, a medical opinion will always be helpful ... reliable medical opinion can only be got from one of the few paediatricians with experience in the area, but they may be of limited help ... when conducting or reviewing an age assessment, the local authority is under a duty to consider any medical report submitted ... where a local authority decides not to follow the views

Table 3.3 Legal age for marriage.

Age (years)	Gender	Jurisdiction
12	Traditional marriages for females	South Africa, Tanzania
14	Traditional marriages for males	South Africa
	Female	Paraguay
14 (with judicial consent)	Male and female	Canada, Mexico
14 (with parental consent)	Female	Venezuela
15 (with parental consent)	Male and female	Estonia
16	Male and female	Kenya, Scotland
	Male	Paraguay
	Female	Tanzania
16 (with parental consent)	Male and female	Hong Kong, Belgium, Hungary, Netherlands, Portugal, Ireland, Canada, Mexico, US
	Male	Venezuela, Argentina
	Female	Pakistan, Japan
16 (with special licence)	Female	Malaysia
17	Female	Armenia, Israel
17 (with parental consent)	Male and female	Thailand, Turkey
18	Male and female	South Africa, Belgium, Philippines, Turkey, France, England, Wales, Northern Ireland, Canada, Mexico, US
	Male	Tanzania, Armenia, Israel
	Female	Algeria, India, Vietnam
18 (with parental consent)	Male and female	Malaysia, South Korea
	Male	Pakistan, Japan
20	Male and female	Japan, South Korea
	Male	Vietnam
	Female	China
21	Male and female	Hong Kong, Malaysia, Singapore, Argentina
	Male	Algeria, India
22	Male	China

in a medical report, it is under a duty to give reasons why for not following those views'.

The robustness of age assessments remains one that is readily open to challenge and review in England and Wales (EWHC 1993). It is perhaps encouraging that some courts recognize that the process of age estimation is variable to say the least – for example, one assessment (of a young Chinese asylum seeker) that was said to be based on 'appearance and demeanour' was held by the judge to be wholly inadequate (EWHC 928). However two other recent cases resulted in rejection of a challenge to the local authority's age assessment by social workers, which overrode paediatric evidence. The judge accepted the local authority's position that assessment of age undertaken by trained and experienced social workers is as reliable as that of paediatricians and that he could not interfere unless their decisions 'verged on absurdity' (EWHC 939). This has resulted in a recent call to produce clearer guidance that will strengthen the evidence base and reliability of assessments and develop appropriate training. However, this focuses simply on the use of social workers and paediatricians without any reference to other professionals who may also have the specific skills to undertake this task (Tyler and Vickers, 2009).

More recently, the Supreme Court has looked at this issue (UKSC, 2009). The ruling addressed squarely the problem of who is to determine a child's age in the absence of documentary evidence. In this case the local authority, supported by the Home Office, maintained that where there is a dispute about a child's age, the local authority should decide the matter. This issue is one of real importance for an unaccompanied child. A child will be looked after by a local authority children's services department under Section 20 of the Children Act 1989, rather than by the UK Border Agency (UKBA), an executive agency of the Home Office, while their claim is decided.

If age is undocumented, the UKBA will assess the age of a newly arrived asylum seeker who claims to be a child, based on appearance, and classify them as either child, adult or age-disputed (when the applicant claims to be a child but their appearance or demeanour suggests they are 18 years or older). It is the policy of the UKBA to refer age-disputed cases for assessment by local authorities and then subsequently to accept that assessment.

Previously, applicants were only able to question the process undertaken by the local authority when making an age assessment, rather than the findings and decision of the local authority. The procedure followed could only be challenged by means of judicial review. The appeals to the Supreme Court challenged the view that only the local authority could decide on the age of the child, and the Supreme Court held unanimously that the question of whether a person was a child was an issue of fact, and the court should decide this issue where it is in dispute.

These matters are further considered in Chapter 5.

One other area where age assessment is increasing sought by investigative agencies is ageing of images used in online pornography or child sex abuse. Many states have rightly taken the view that such practices cannot be tolerated, and possession and/or distribution of such images amounts to a serious criminal offence. Age evaluations may be asked for during the examination of these images to attempt an opinion on the age of the individuals depicted in the photographs, as (dependent on juris-diction) both age and activity depicted may impact on the severity of the offence. Investigating authorities must be made aware of the difficulties and lack of data with regard to making estimations from photographs. The authenticity of images may also be questioned. The ethnic origin of the subject may be unknown. The assessor must emphasize that their advice may merely be limited to assessing the degree of sexual maturity, and in many cases even that is not possible. In the absence of any evident secondary sexual characteristics, it may be appropriate to indicate that the individual portrayed is likely to be under the age of 16 years, but no certainty can be offered.

3.5   Assessment Techniques

Assessment techniques are explored in detail in other chapters. In general, age at death can be determined with some degree of accuracy, certainly in younger age groups, by assessment of biological maturity including osteology and odontology (Schmeling *et al.* 2005, 2007). Such techniques are obviously applicable in the living but the degree to which such techniques may be used may be far more extensive in the deceased, subject to local application of retention of tissue statute. Invasive techniques, tissue sampling and radiological exposure are far more limited in the living. In some countries even low dose exposure to radiological imaging for age determination for radiological purposes may be considered inappropriate (Royal College of Paediatrics and Child Health, 1999; Benson and Williams, 2008).

3.6   How Age May Be Specifically Documented

Unlike the deceased where a number of features may be used to identify an individual and thus their age (using identification features including visual appearance, personal effects, facial features, other physical attributes, scars, prostheses, teeth, fingerprints, DNA etc.), many of these are unlikely to assist in determination of age in the living. However, an external physical examination may identify features (e.g. a tattoo with a style, a name, a place or a date, or a scar) that itself may act as a clue, either to corroborate or disprove the claims of an individual. A physical examination may also identify physical disease or deformity that may act as a unique identifier when taking all other aspects into account. Physical examination may also identify clinical conditions (e.g. malnutrition or chronic illness) or conditions which may affect bone maturity and skeletal or dental development, which may cause inappropriate interpretation of odontological, radiological or osteological data if not considered. Pubertal retardation, precocity or socio-economic factors may be identified which impact on maturity. The external physical examination is essential in determining the status of secondary sexual development, which must be documented in detail. Medical examination may also identify signs or risk factors of emotional, sexual or physical abuse, which may impact on development. Anthropometric measurements may be undertaken. These in isolation are of little value in age estimation but may, in the developing child, allow a determination as to whether the development is consistent with published growth centile curves (Martille and Baccino, 2005). The appropriateness of such examination may include visualization and palpation of genitalia, and this in itself results in a number of cultural, human rights, ethical and consent issues. It must, however, be emphasized that an appropriate age assessment may confer considerable benefit upon an individual and that age evaluations should not be considered a process that can only benefit the state or the requesting authority.

Many documents are issued and are available for use in establishing some degree of confidence about details of the individual, provided of course that such documents are authentic and not forgeries. Some documents carry legal weight and some simply provide information. All can be forged relatively easy, often for very little cost.

Detection of such forgeries is beyond the scope and expertise of healthcare personnel and is best left to law enforcement authorities. Sometimes, however, tampering or fraud may be obvious and if observed should be brought to the attention of relevant authorities, subject to the appropriateness and requirements of confidentiality.

3.7   Birth Certificates

In developed countries with healthcare and civil systems that are in place and functional, the most common form of legal documentation of age is the birth certificate. This is an official certificate issued by the authorities documenting the fact that a child was born at a specific time and date with information supported by appropriate medical or midwifery personnel. The birth certificate also states the sex of the child, the name that the child was given and the name of the mother and often the father. Such documentation when available is invaluable and reliable, and its authenticity can be checked relatively quickly.

A problem arises in that many families throughout the world keep this important document in a 'safe place'. Unfortunately, even 'safe places' such as safes or bank vaults may be destroyed in attacks or natural disasters. In situations of civil unrest or war, families often have to flee quickly and these documents are not retrieved or available. It is situations like these, which are not uncommon, that can give some credence to the need for virtual databases keeping individuals' identifiable characteristics from an early age.

3.8   Identity Cards

Countries including Singapore, Malaysia and Hong Kong require all citizens to have a government-issued identity card. These cards usually contain not only a frontal photograph of the individual but fingerprint information, date of birth, sex and a variety of other personal details. In these jurisdictions this document is accepted as the only required proof of identity until proven otherwise. The authorities also place considerable resources into maintaining the integrity of these documents and preventing their forgery. In this digital age, some of these identity cards come with a smart chip that can be read by frontline police officers, for example, when needed and information such as unpaid fines can be accessed instantly. There are generally two types of ID cards, one for children who have reached 12 years of age and another for individuals who have reached 18 or 21 years, whichever age is used to indicate adulthood in the jurisdiction concerned. An example of an identity card can be seen in Figure 3.1.

3.9   Driving Licence

In the industrialized countries, particularly the US, a driving licence is often accepted as proof of identity. Not only does it identify an individual, it enables some estimation

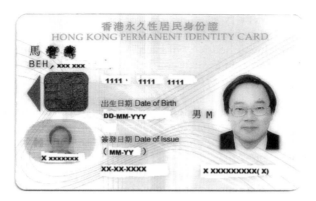

Figure 3.1 An identity card.

of age, as driving licences are only issued to those who have reached a certain age. This, however, varies from 16 to 18 and also varies between whether the licence is for a car or for a motorcycle. Many examples of the different driving licences can be found on the Internet.

3.10 Passports

Passports are documents issued to nationals of a country that testify to the identity and details of an individual and are supported and verified by the issuing authority. Such documents confer some degree of guarantee from the issuing authority on the authenticity of the details recorded on the document and often also provide some information on the date and route of travel of the individual. However, there are governments or passport issuing authorities around the world where such guarantees are non-existent. These passports can be easily purchased and the dilemma is whether they are authentic documents. There is of course also a lucrative trade in stolen and forged passports, and such documents can be worth substantial amounts of money on the black market. One of the chapter authors was offered a UK passport outside the Gare du Nord in Paris.

Passports are not compulsory and many individuals who do not travel beyond the borders of their own country would not need one and it is common in many countries that individuals will never possess a passport. A large proportion of citizens of the US do not hold passports and although it is not an official statistic it is generally accepted that only some 20% of the North American population own a passport. There are of course individuals who hold more than one passport. Increasingly biometric passports are used around the world (all recent issue UK passports are now biometric). The chip inside the passport contains information about the holder's face, such as the distances between eyes, nose, mouth and ears. These details are taken from the passport photograph supplied. They can then be used to identify the passport holder. The chip also holds the information that is printed on the personal details page of the passport, which includes date of birth.

In general, all document types stated above provide a high degree of proof of the details of the said individual, including their age. However, the doctor is in no position to determine the authenticity of such documents and would require the law enforcement agencies to provide such confirmation. However, when available they are adequate for the purposes of the doctor to establish the name, sex and age of an individual.

From time to time, however, despite the authenticity of presented documents, the patient confesses to the doctor that the information provided is incorrect and was done so knowingly by the individual for a variety of reasons, including a mistaken belief that a younger age or an older age was favourable to them at the time of their registration for the document. Care should be exercised when an individual is producing a document that is not from their country of birth.

3.11   Age Verification Cards

Age verification cards are used increasingly in some countries with legal requirements for such things as buying of alcohol, weapons or knives and a simple Web search will reveal numerous sources through which fabricated age verification cards can be bought relatively cheaply.

3.12   Other Documents

These are for intent and purposes not formal identification documents but have been found to be helpful in informing on the likely age of an individual when available. Documents such as immunization cards provide a good clue as to the likely age of the individual, particularly as the sequence and timing of national immunization programmes are available from the World Health Organization (WHO) and can help provide an indication of the likely age of the child, provided the document is not borrowed or stolen.

School student cards or library cards are documents that are often applied for during times of civility when there is little reason to provide false information. Many libraries include a photo of the individual and allow a young reader to apply for the document without adult help. Hence, in their innocence, such documents are often very helpful. The same can be said for club membership cards, credit cards, and so on.

3.13   Medical Issues

3.13.1   Duties to Examinee

This will be covered in detail in other chapters of this book; however, the healthcare professional must be aware of his or her own professional duties with regard to any contact with an individual in relation to age estimation. For all healthcare professionals, duties of consent and confidentiality apply to a greater or lesser degree. It is absolutely essential that a healthcare professional undertaking an assessment is aware of the professional framework regarding his or her duties to the examinee, and the local jurisdictional legal framework under which the request for assessment is undertaken.

Available methods for estimating age in a living individual are discussed at length in other chapters. Some of these methods (e.g. exposure to irradiation) may be safe, in medical terms, but considered inappropriate by local professional standards. Others involve actual physical harm such as the extraction or removal of a specimen of tooth. In jurisdictions where such techniques are accepted, the healthcare professional must be in a position to inform the individual of the benefits, limitations and disadvantages of such examinations and the limitations in accuracy as well as the likely consequences of the process.

3.14 Communication

The above requires an adequate communication with the individual and it is imperative that the healthcare professional insists on the provision of a competent interpreter service. It would be an injustice to all concerned if such an important communication between doctor and patient is incorrect because of a misunderstanding due to poor language interpretation. Regional variations may lose nuances of language that may have great relevance in estimating age.

There is never a rush with such examinations and the doctor should never allow him/herself to be pressured to do anything unless he or she is totally comfortable that the medical and legal requirements are met and satisfied.

In the unlikely case of an emergency medical condition, the doctor need only consider the issues in relation to serving the best benefit and interest of the patient and nothing else. Such actions should, however, be communicated clearly and directly to all concerned, taking into consideration careful explanation where cultural, religious or racial differences exist.

The German Study Group on Forensic Age Diagnostics (Arbeitsgruppe Forensische Altersdiagnostik, AGFAD) has issued guidelines whereby individuals should not be subjected to X-ray skeletal examination to estimate age unless such acts are sanctioned by the courts. It will be interesting to see whether the recent Supreme Court judgment in the UK results in any judicially directed radiological imaging being performed for age assessment. The German approach is laudable and assists individual practitioners by providing a professional platform of support. In jurisdictions where such support is not forthcoming, healthcare professionals should reflect and seek help from professional bodies and colleagues where appropriate.

3.15 Summary and Conclusions

It is not possible to review such a subject as age estimation in the living without accepting that the need for such assessments places a financial burden on either the state or the individual. The individual may not be eligible for, or have access to, legal advice for many reasons (e.g. because of presumed age, lack of funds, language difficulties, fear of authorities etc.) and thus no access to appropriate age assessment facilities that may support their case.

It is in most states' interest to minimize the possible burden of care for children or young people and the cynic might consider that it is therefore in the state's best interest to err on the side of assuming an individual to be adult.

Whatever the case, it is essential that in any legal, clinical or medical setting where age may impact on care, treatment, autonomy or human rights that everyone should have access to an appropriate means of age estimation that can be robustly presented to a court.

No healthcare or other professional should undertake the estimation of age in the living without adequate training and understanding of the available methods and their limitations and without the support of a multidisciplinary team of colleagues who can assist to make evaluations from a variety of means to produce the best age estimate that current knowledge will allow.

References

A vs. *London Borough of Croydon and Secretary of State for the Home Department; WK vs. Secretary of State for the Home Department and Kent County Council* [2009] EWHC 939 (Admin).

A by his litigation friend Mejzninin vs. *Croydon London, Borough Council* [2008] EWHC 2921 (Admin).

Benson, J. and Williams, J. (2008) Age determination in refugee children. *Australian Family Physician*, **32** (10), 821–824.

Crawley, H. (2007) *When Is a Child Not a Child? Asylum, Age Disputes and the Process of Age Assessment*, Immigration Law Practitioners' Association, London.

Liverpool City Council (R, on the application of) vs. *London Borough of Hillingdon* [2008] EWHC 1702 (Admin).

Martrille, L. and Baccino, E. (2005) Age estimation in the living, in *Encyclopedia of Forensic and Legal Medicine* (eds J.J. Payne-James, R. Byard, T. Corey and C. Henderson), Elsevier, London.

P *(R, on the application of)* vs. *London Borough of Croydon* [2009] EWHC 1993 (Admin).

R *(on the application of A) (FC)* vs. *London Borough of Croydon; R (on the application of M (FC)* vs. *London Borough of Lambeth* (2009) UKSC 8.

R *(on the application of HBH)* vs. *Secretary of State* [2009] EWHC 928 (Admin).

R *(C)* vs. *London Borough of Merton* [2005] EWHC 1753 (Admin).

Royal College of Paediatrics and Child Health (1999) The health of refugee children: Guidelines for paediatricians. Royal College of Paediatrics and Child Health, London.

Schmeling, A., Reisinger, W., Geserick, G. and Olze, A. (2005) The current state of forensic age estimation of live subjects for the purpose of criminal prosecution. *Forensic Science, Medicine, and Pathology*, **1** (4), 239–246.

Schmeling, A., Reisinger, W., Geserick, G. and Olze, A. (2007) Age estimation. *Forensic Science International*, **165**, 178–181.

Tyler, L. and Vickers, D. (2009) Age assessment of asylum seekers. *British Medical Journal*, **338**, 2056.

UNHCR (2009) 2008 Global trends: refugees, asylum-seekers, returnees, internally displaced and stateless persons, www.unhcr.org/4a375c426.html (accessed 26 January 2010).

4

Legal Implications of Age Determination: Consent and Other Issues

George Fernie[1] and Jason Payne-James[2]
[1] *The Faculty of Forensic and Legal Medicine, 3rd Floor, 116 Great Portland Street, London W1W 6PJ, UK*
[2] *Cameron Forensic Medical Sciences, Barts and London School of Medicine and Dentistry, London EC1M 6BQ, UK*

4.1   Introduction

The assessment of age estimation in the living is one that touches on a number of key professional duties. This chapter will address these issues by reference to practice in the United Kingdom (UK), and more specifically the English and Welsh and Scottish jurisdictions within the UK. Most healthcare professionals and those other non-healthcare professionals working around the world will operate within professional guidelines or codes of practice. For most, serious breaches of such codes or guidelines could result in sanctions such as withdrawal of the right to work in that field. It is therefore crucial that anyone working in areas that may involve either the examination or interpretation of healthcare data as applied to an individual is fully aware of their own professional duties to the examinee, as applied to the setting and jurisdiction within which they work.

Medical practitioners (doctors), the perspective from which the authors of this chapter write, are considered to be at risk of 'multiple medical jeopardy' if they breach their duties, by virtue of risk of not only sanction from their own medical professional body, but also from civil and criminal courts.

Jurisdictional issues can be complex. For example, the professional guidelines under which doctors work in England apply throughout the UK, but doctors are

Age Estimation in the Living: The Practitioners Guide   Sue Black, Anil Aggrawal and Jason Payne-James
© 2010 John Wiley & Sons, Ltd

subject to the laws of England and Wales, while those working in Scotland are subject to Scottish law. Individuals who are being age assessed may be transferred from one jurisdiction to another so all professionals involved should be aware that the legal process applied to a person may change, while professional duties will not.

Although the information being sought is the chronological age of that individual, the presumptive age at the time of assessment is generally the one to which the relative statute applies at that time (although it may be altered by the age estimation itself). The key division is between adult and child. In general the child (or a minor) is defined as 'a person under the age of 18 years'.

4.2   Principles of Practice

In the UK the General Medical Council (GMC) registers doctors to practice medicine. Its declared purpose is to protect, promote and maintain the health and safety of the public by ensuring proper standards in the practice of medicine. Table 4.1 summarizes the duties of doctors as determined by the GMC (2006). The term 'patient' is used and it is wise for doctors to consider that anyone for whom they are undertaking an age estimation is still a patient (although not perhaps in the conventional sense) and they must still adhere to those duties.

Table 4.1   General Medical Council: duties of a doctor.

Patients must be able to trust doctors with their lives and health. To justify that trust the practitioner must show respect for human life and must:

- Make the care of the patient their first concern.
- Protect and promote the health of patients and the public.
- Provide a good standard of practice and care:
  - Keep professional knowledge and skills up to date.
  - Recognize and work within the limits of their competence.
  - Work with colleagues in the ways that best serve patients' interests.
- Treat patients as individuals and respect their dignity:
  - Treat patients politely and considerately.
  - Respect patients' right to confidentiality.
- Work in partnership with patients:
  - Listen to patients and respond to their concerns and preferences.
  - Give patients the information they want or need in a way they can understand.
  - Respect patients' right to reach decisions about their treatment and care.
  - Support patients in caring for themselves to improve and maintain their health.
- Be honest and open and act with integrity:
  - Act without delay if there is good reason to believe that they or a colleague may be putting patients at risk.
  - Never discriminate unfairly against patients or colleagues.
  - Never abuse patients' trust in the practitioner or the public's trust in the profession.

Source: General Medical Council (2006).

Table 4.2 British Association of Social Workers code of ethics: key principles.

Human dignity and worth:

- Respect human dignity and individual and cultural diversity.
- Value every human being, their beliefs, goals, preferences and needs.
- Respect human rights and self determination.
- Partnership and empowerment with users of services and with carers.
- Ensuring protection for vulnerable people.

Social justice:

- Promoting fair access to resources.
- Equal treatment without prejudice or discrimination.
- Reducing disadvantage and exclusion.
- Challenging the abuse of power.

Service:

- Helping with personal and social needs.
- Enabling people to develop their potential.
- Contributing to creating a fairer society.

Integrity:

- Honesty, reliability and confidentiality.

Competence:

- Maintaining and expanding competence to provide a quality service.

Source: British Association of Social Workers (2010).

Similarly, within the UK, social workers have considerable involvement in age estimations. The British Association of Social Workers (BASW) is the largest association representing social work and social workers in the UK and publishes a code of ethics shown in Table 4.2 (BASW, 2010). It is important that all professionals involved in age estimation procedures work from an appropriate and approved ethical framework.

Age estimation in the living, unlike in the deceased, requires the consent of that individual for whom the determination is required. Consent is often thought to be an imprecise and ill-defined concept, but in both healthcare and legal settings this is far from correct. Absence of consent to a process may have results that adversely affect not only the person from whom the consent has either not been sought or has been refused, but also for the individual seeking such consent.

Although the ethical precept of informed consent has attracted attention in a variety of legal jurisdictions, it was not until the twenty-first century that the GMC acknowledged this concept when advising medical practitioners on the issue of consent. This evolution occurred with a developing respect for autonomy or 'self-rule' and 'self-determination'.

The other main specific duty for the doctor (and most healthcare professionals) is to observe confidentiality. This is of increasing relevance when one considers the issues at play for age estimation in the living but, necessarily, may also extend beyond life. The medical profession owes the deceased that same duty of confidentiality where if that person in life indicated by way of an advance directive that certain matters were not to be imparted to another then this should be considered binding. That being said, the regulatory body helpfully describes a balancing act between the deceased's right to confidentiality and the possible benefit or harm to the living. As a result of this approach, it is necessary to be mindful of the implications that the wishes of the living have once they have died.

Therefore, one can readily see that it is appropriate that the practitioner has a requirement to obtain informed consent to any assessment and also ensure that the ethical duty of confidentiality, first established in the fifth century BC and espoused in the Hippocratic Oath, is not breached.

In considering the legal and ethical implications affecting age determination, it is necessary to establish the reasons why such a procedure might be required. Age estimation in the living covers a range of individuals (and in some cases the individual may be involved in more than one legal process).

These individuals may require age estimation for criminal process (e.g. legal age for sex), immigration issues (e.g. unaccompanied asylum seeking children and age disputes) and civil issues (e.g. child protection, family proceedings). Here, although there is an increasing acceptance that a mature minor may elect to have sex without a doctor breaching confidentiality on that disclosure (save in an abusive relationship), there can be issues with paedophilic pornography where the court wishes an opinion on the age of the child based solely on the recovered images. With separated parents, the courts acknowledge that relationships break down and expect that both parties to such an arrangement who have produced a child should have a role in the child's upbringing. Legal issues will revolve around whether that individual has parental responsibility unless, of course, their involvement was contrary to the child's best interests, this being the underpinning principle.

Refugee and asylum seeker issues are particularly problematic in that there must be a degree of coercion in the relationship between the asylum seeker and the healthcare professional whereby they do not enjoy the same degree of autonomy that typically exists between, for example, a primary care physician and her/his patient. Serious thought must be given to how 'informed' consent will be in this scenario where the person concerned will be anxious to do all they can to achieve residency in a particular country. These issues will also be influenced by many other factors, including language, emotional maturity and awareness of legal process in a different country.

Uniquely, the refugee and asylum seeker element of age estimation is one that is easiest to quantify (see also Chapter 2). UK figures for 2007 (Home Office, 2008) show that 3525 unaccompanied asylum seeking children (UASCs) aged 17 or under applied for asylum in the UK. Current Home Office policy is that when an asylum applicant claims to be a minor but his/her appearance strongly suggests that he/she is over 18, the applicant is treated as an adult until there is credible documentary or other persuasive evidence to demonstrate the age claimed. This is an age disputed application.

In 2007, 1915 applications were lodged with the Home Office for which the age was disputed. However, the most recent figures for 2008 (Home Office, 2009) show a total of >31 000 asylum applications (including dependents), with an 18% increase to 4285 UASCs, but with a reduction in age disputed applications to 1400. By May 2009 this figure was reduced to 785 as a result of either withdrawal of claim or presentation of credible evidence that the applicant was the age claimed.

It appears that most age disputes arise when the asylum seeker first applies for asylum, and there is no formal age estimation (i.e. using some of the physical techniques described in this book), but a judgement will be made on the basis of physical appearance, demeanour and any documentation produced.

It is at this stage that the individual may be at their most vulnerable and most subject to coercion. It is possible, but unknown, that withdrawals of claim may result from either lack of informed consent about their rights, or possible lack of appropriate legal advice. This is an area where those professionals involved must recognize their duties to the individual, as well as to the organizations which employ them, which may put pressure on employees to find outcomes that are perhaps more beneficial to the organization than to the individual being assessed. This may be reflected by the observation that local authorities and social services (in the UK) may decide to dispute a child's age even though it has not been disputed by the Home Office (Crawley, 2007).

4.3   Duties of the Examining Practitioner

Who makes the request for formal age estimation to be undertaken? Prosecuting authorities, defence teams, immigration lawyers, asylum tribunals or the individuals themselves? The answer is – all of the above, but probably the individual is the one who most rarely seeks such an assessment, because of lack of awareness of the benefits or otherwise of moving from adult to child, or child to adult by virtue of confirmation of chronological age. There are a variety of sources from which a request for a report might emanate and it is incumbent upon registered medical practitioners to satisfy themselves as to the legitimacy of such an approach. In the UK with an adversarial legal system, experienced forensic practitioners are able to declare and assert their independence and will accept instruction from either the prosecuting team or the defence, recognizing that their duty is to the court as a whole and not their instructing body. Clearly, there is no contractual obligation to agree to do this work. Once agreed, duties apply. For doctors in the UK, they must be aware of and adhere to the GMC guidance contained within 'Good Medical Practice' whereby in writing reports, providing curriculum vitae, giving evidence and signing documents, 'You must be honest and trustworthy when writing reports, and when completing or signing forms, reports and other documents'. Further, 'You must do your best to make sure that any documents you write or sign are not false or misleading'. Earlier in the same publication, the GMC reminds practitioners that in providing care one must 'recognize and work within the limits of your competence'. In the view of the authors, the provision of care is likely to be synonymous with agreeing to provide an opinion on age estimation in the living.

This means that one must take reasonable steps to verify the information in the documents and cannot omit to record relevant information deliberately. In particular, if one has agreed to prepare a report, complete or sign a document or provide evidence, then this must be achieved without unreasonable delay. What constitutes an 'unreasonable delay' is not entirely clear but the regulator has certainly dealt with complaints of such a nature.

Consent, whatever the jurisdiction, should be fully informed and valid where the doctor should take steps to ascertain that the individual is aware of what is proposed by way of an assessment and to whom this report will be divulged. An informed consent can be said to have been given based upon a clear appreciation and understanding of the facts, implications and future consequences of an action. In order to give informed consent, the individual concerned must have adequate reasoning faculties and be in possession of all relevant facts at the time consent is given. The GMC has also expressed the view that the patient should be informed of the likely consequences of a disclosure and this may not be so easy to do as the examiner cannot know the outcome in advance of the consenting process, or its possible legal implications. As identified above, it is not always clear whether the person upon whom the age estimation will be performed is a 'patient' in the true sense of the word but it would appear entirely appropriate to adhere to the same ethical principles one would expect to apply in such circumstances. An additional issue with age estimation is that the person may well be a minor and although there is clear guidance based on the doctrine of necessity in treating patients in this category, where the measures are therapeutic in nature, based on their understanding of what is proposed and the likely consequences, we are now talking about a legal process that may or may not be beneficial to their well-being.

There is an expectation that doctors will not divulge information gleaned by them in the course of their clinical practice – the duty of confidentiality – dating back to one of the first medical codes promulgated, the Hippocratic Oath. The historical concept is succinctly explained by the GMC in its publication 'Confidentiality: protecting and providing information' (2009), where it comments that good medical practice makes clear that patients have a right to expect that information about them will be held in confidence by their doctors. This guidance sets out the principles of confidentiality and respect for patients' privacy that one is expected to understand and follow (Table 4.3).

Access to other records in most jurisdictions is governed by statute where the pervasive influence of enlightened European law has resulted in a number of Acts of Parliament affecting access to health records, with the most recent being by way of the Data Protection Act 1998, which gives living individuals the right to know what information is held about them, to mandate that information to a third party, to have inaccuracies corrected and to claim compensation through the courts from a data controller for any breach of that Act.

The Data Protection Act sets out the basis for making a subject access request by an individual person for disclosure of documentation with this applying to written and computerized records along with images stored within a 'relevant filing system' to enable an appropriate clinician to give a view on their estimated age.

4.4   Criminal Issues in Age Determination in the Living

The age of criminal responsibility will be raised in Scotland from 8 to 12 years by the Criminal Justice and Licensing (Scotland) Bill (going through Parliament at the time of writing) to bring this into line with most other European countries albeit elsewhere in the UK a child can be charged and brought before the courts aged

Table 4.3 General Medical Council: principles of confidentiality.

- Confidentiality is central to trust between doctors and patients. Without assurances about confidentiality, patients may be reluctant to seek medical attention or to give doctors the information they need in order to provide good care. But appropriate information sharing is essential to the efficient provision of safe, effective care, both for the individual patient and for the wider community of patients.
- The practitioner should make sure that information is readily available to patients explaining that, unless they object, their personal information may be disclosed for the sake of their own care and for local clinical audit. Patients usually understand that information about them has to be shared within the healthcare team to provide their care. But it is not always clear to patients that others who support the provision of care might also need to have access to their personal information. And patients may not be aware of disclosures to others for purposes other than their care, such as service planning or medical research. The practitioner must inform patients about disclosures for purposes they would not reasonably expect, or check that they have already received information about such disclosures.
- Confidentiality is an important duty, but it is not absolute. One can disclose personal information if:
  - (a) it is required by law;
  - (b) the patient consents – either implicitly for the sake of their own care or expressly for other purposes;
  - (c) it is justified in the public interest.
- When disclosing information about a patient, one must:
  - (a) use anonymised or coded information if practicable and if it will serve the purpose;
  - (b) be satisfied that the patient:
    - (i) has ready access to information that explains that their personal information might be disclosed for the sake of their own care, or for local clinical audit, and that they can object and
    - (ii) has not objected.
  - (c) get the patient's express consent if identifiable information is to be disclosed for purposes other than their care or local clinical audit, unless the disclosure is required by law or can be justified in the public interest;
  - (d) keep disclosures to the minimum necessary and
  - (e) keep up to date with, and observe, all relevant legal requirements, including the common law and data protection legislation.
- When the practitioner is satisfied that information should be disclosed, he/she should act promptly to disclose all relevant information.
- The practitioner should respect, and help patients to exercise, their legal rights to:
  - (a) be informed about how their information will be used and
  - (b) have access to, or copies of, their health records.

Source: General Medical Council (2009).

10 years. In contrast to this, in the United States the age varies from 6 to 12 years depending upon the location.

Statute or law may confer checks or balances; for example, civil law varies depending on the jurisdictional location, with either case law or statute indicating what decisions a person is lawfully able to make. The Age of Legal Capacity (Scotland) Act 1991 specifies that a person under the age of 16 years shall have legal capacity to consent on his/her own behalf to any surgical, medical or dental procedure or treatment where, in the opinion of a qualified attending medical practitioner, he/she is capable of understanding the nature and possible consequences of the procedure or treatment.

In England, the Gillick (1985) case and Lord Fraser's judgment remain a useful basis and the leading authority under which to determine a mature minor's capacity, bearing in mind that consent is not an all or nothing phenomenon and there will be certain procedures, depending on the implications arising to which, a young person may never be able to agree to have undertaken.[1]

Although this approach is quoted and accepted in many other jurisdictions, because of the reasoning process set out therein, many observers believe the statute based law in neighbouring Scotland goes somewhat beyond this with specific reference to a variety of circumstances affecting the mature minor going further than simply consent to medical treatment but also embracing the issues of transactions, testamentary capacity, instruction of a solicitor and adoption.

It is clear that there is significant variation throughout the world in judicial systems with both age of responsibility for criminal acts and the capacity to agree to medical procedures or taking responsibility for consequences in civil law applying at different ages. Until 2009, the age of criminal responsibility in Scotland was 8 years in contrast to elsewhere in Europe where the age was 12 years with the Lord Advocate criticizing the current age at the time as being 'extremely low' and criminalizing children. For a country that prides itself on an enlightened approach to protecting minors through the Children's Panel system, it was a somewhat curious anomaly that required to be addressed.

One also has to be aware that penalties for certain offences may change depending on the age of the individual. Within the Sexual Offences Act 2003 applying in England and Wales it is an offence to sexually penetrate a child under 13 years of age irrespective of whether they consented to that act or not but there is recognition under Section 22 that a lower penalty should be applicable for a person under the age of 18 years who is the perpetrator. There is a public interest requirement involving a realistic prospect test here that must be taken into account by the prosecutor.

It is certainly recognized by practitioners in this area of practice that there is a marked difference in approach required between the treatment of medical conditions where a minor is gradually able to assume responsibility allowing them to consent

---

[1] *'Gillick competence'* is a term used to decide whether a child (16 years or younger) is able to consent to his or her own medical treatment, without the need for parental permission or knowledge.

'Fraser competent' is a term used to describe a child under 16 who is considered to be of sufficient age and understanding to be competent to receive contraceptive advice without parental knowledge or consent.

to progressively more complicated procedures, albeit the clinician will typically be protected with the doctrine of necessity where the preservation of life is at stake, and the scenario where the decision in question may affect their future liberty.

The GMC specifically identifies this issue and addresses such matters in its publication '0–18 years: guidance for all doctors' (General Medical Council, 2007), acknowledging the complexity of the law in this area.

The underpinning principle of 'the best interests of the child' is stated, with this applying as much to age estimation as to other areas of practice involving a medical practitioner.

There is a necessity to ensure children or parents understand the key points affecting any decision making. The GMC specifies that parents cannot override the competent consent of a young person to treatment that the doctor considers to be in their best interests. However, 'you can rely on parental consent when a child lacks the capacity to consent'.

Where the investigation concerned requires a court order, although the doctor may theoretically lawfully proceed without that person's consent, the various professional bodies advise against this because of the likely ethical breach that will result.

4.5 Practical Implications

Specific techniques used in age estimation in the living may require procedures that have a perceived health risk (e.g. radiology) or may constitute some form of technical assault (in England and Wales, contrary to the Offence Against the Persons Act 1861). Such issues may be considered differently in different jurisdictions. For example, radiological examinations for age estimation have been shown persuasively to have a very low health risk (Schmeling *et al.*, 2000) (and see Chapter 8). However despite this, in the UK, the Royal College of Paediatrics and Child Health (RCPCH) (1999) makes the following comments:

> In 1996, The Royal College of Radiologists (1996) gave useful advice to its members about the use of X-rays in the assessment of age. They advised that if an immigration official requests an applicant to have a radiograph obtained to confirm their alleged chronological age, the College would regard it as unjustified. They argue strongly that ionising radiation should be used only in cases of clinical need. However, if an individual seeking entry wishes to support their case, an X-ray of the hand presents negligible risk of radiation. However, they add that the accuracy of estimation of age from hand radiography amongst groups that have not been studied in detail remains in doubt. The Board of Faculty expressed reservations about advising on bone age for other than personal health issues or research projects approved by appropriate ethics committees.

The RCPCH (1999) further quotes from the (then) Department of Immigration and Nationality (1999):

> Medical assessments of age . . . It is inappropriate for X-rays to be used merely to assist in age determination for immigration purposes. Under no circumstances should a caseworker suggest that an applicant should have X-rays taken for this purpose.

Table 4.4   General Medical Council: determining 'best interests' for 0–18 year olds.

- An assessment of best interests will include what is clinically indicated in a particular case. One should also consider:
  a) the views of the child or young person, so far as they can express them, including any previously expressed preferences;
  b) the views of parents;
  c) the views of others close to the child or young person;
  d) the cultural, religious or other beliefs and values of the child or parents;
  e) the views of other healthcare professionals involved in providing care to the child or young person, and of any other professionals who have an interest in their welfare;
  f) which choice, if there is more than one, will least restrict the child or young person's future options.
- This list is not exhaustive. The weight attached to each point will depend on the circumstances, and the practitioner should consider any other relevant information. Unjustified assumptions must not be made about a child or young person's best interests based on irrelevant or discriminatory factors which include their behaviour, appearance or disability.

Source: General Medical Council (2007).

This latter reference is instructing caseworkers, not medical doctors, although the RCPCH is providing guidelines for doctors.

Recent GMC guidance (2007) regarding children states that 'Both the GMC and the law permit doctors to undertake procedures that do not offer immediate or obvious therapeutic benefits for children or young people, so long as they are in their best interests and performed with consent'. Table 4.4 lists the factors that may be taken into account regarding 'best interests'. It is therefore possible that with an individual able to provide fully informed consent that this may address the problem. Further problems will still arise if, for example, the person is a minor and does not have the required mental capacity determined by case law or statute in legislation such as the Age of Legal Capacity (Scotland) Act 1991 to give their legal consent.

Increasingly there has been recognition that patients are entitled to view their medical and dental records including images contained therein as part of the move to respect their autonomy. The purpose of this is so they might ascertain if the material held is accurate and afford them the opportunity of seeking to have this corrected by the medical or dental practitioner who holds this data.

Legislation relating to the gaining of access to personal information has generally been derived from the European Data Protection Directive (Directive 95/46/EC). In UK law this resulted in the original Data Protection Act (1984), which applied only to computerized data held but was later widened to the Access to Medical Reports Act (1988) before the Access to Health Records Act (1990) came into force for all medical records. This is still the relevant statute for deceased persons albeit it has now been superseded by the Data Protection Act for living persons (1998).

There is a requirement for all data processors to be registered under the Act, allowing patients to make a subject access request and obtain the information they seek under these provisions. The same statute applies to all these records and a breach of the Act is a potential criminal offence.

As well as the statutory basis for accessing the deceased's records, the GMC (2009) describes a helpful balancing act between the right to privacy of the deceased, which is a well-established ethical precept, and any possible benefit or harm to the patient's partner or family. As for the living, the position has been reaffirmed that apart from exceptional situations such as those meriting a public interest disclosure, the 'norm' will be that either that person's consent or a court order is required before data will be released.

It is essential that documentation is safeguarded and, when needed, appropriate and valid disclosure is ensured. Doctors have a duty to look after the sensitive records they hold on patients and take reasonable steps to ensure security and comply with statutory requirements such as registration under the Data Protection Act (1998). It also necessary that patients understand what will be disclosed, to whom the information will be released and the likely consequences thereof. Clearly, if that practitioner is not working within her/his expertise in that scenario then they should refer to an appropriate colleague who has the ability to advise the person accordingly.

4.6   Summary

The examples above highlight the duties of professionals involved in age estimation, for adults and children (or, more correctly, presumptive adults and children), whatever their professional background and country or location of work. Every practitioner must be aware of their professional duties and respect the duties of others, which may conflict or overlap with their own. Every practitioner must be aware of the legal principles and laws that encompass the element of age estimation in the jurisdiction within which they must operate.

On every occasion the practitioner should consider the following three key questions, which will enable them to undertake an appropriate robust assessment that will provide the individual and the relevant court or tribunal the appropriate information on which they may base any subsequent action or judgement:

- Do I have informed consent?

- Am I acting in the individual's best interests?

- What information should I keep confidential and what can I disclose?

References

British Association of Social Workers (2010) Code of ethics. www.basw.co.uk/about/codeofethics (accessed 30 January 2010).

Crawley, H. (2007) *When Is a Child Not a Child? Asylum, Age Disputes and the Process of Age Assessment*, Immigration Law Practitioners' Association, London.

General Medical Council (2006) *Duties of a doctor*, General Medical Council, London.

General Medical Council (2007) 0–18: Guidance for all doctors, General Medical Council, London.

General Medical Council (2009) Confidentiality: protecting and providing information, General Medical Council, London.

Gillick vs. *West Norfolk and Wisbech Area Health Authority* [1985] 3 All ER 402 (HL).

Home Office (2008) Asylum statistics – United Kingdom 2007, Home Office Statistical Bulletin, London.

Home Office (2009) Control of immigration statistics – United Kingdom 2008, Home Office Statistical Bulletin, London.

Home Office (1999) Asylum casework instructions, Immigration and Nationality, Department, London.

Royal College of Paediatrics and Child Health (1999) The health of refugee children: Guidelines for paediatricians. Royal College of Paediatrics and Child Health, London.

Royal College of Radiologists (1996) [at that time of publication a Faculty]. Letter ref. BFCR (96) 9 to all Home Clinical radiology Fellows and Members from Dr Iain Watt, Dean, Faculty of Clinical Radiology.

Schmeling, A., Reisenger, W., Wormanns, D. and Geserick, G. (2000) Strahlenexposition bei Rontgenuntersuchungen zur forensischen Altersschatzung Lebender. *Rechtsmedizin*, **10**, 135–137.

5

The Challenges of Psychological Assessments of Maturity

Julia Nelki[1], Pete Grady[2], Sue Bailey[3], and Heather Law[4]
[1] *Alder Hey Children's NHS Foundation Trust, Eaton Road, West Derby, Liverpool L12 2AP, UK*
[2] *Honorary Lecturer, Liverpool John Moores University, Roscoe Court, 4 Rodney Street, Liverpool L1 2TZ, UK*
[3] *University of Central Lancashire, Preston, Lancashire PR1 2HE, UK*
[4] *Greater Manchester West Mental Health NHS Foundation Trust, Bury New Road, Prestwich, Manchester M25 3BL, UK*

"Character is timeless. Ageless. We live back and forth in the past or in the present or in the future.... We do not grow absolutely, chronologically. We grow sometimes in one dimension, and not in another; unevenly. We grow partially. We are relative. We are mature in one realm, childish in another. The past, present, and future mingle and pull us backward, forward, or fix us in the present. We are made up of layers, cells, constellations." (Nin 1971, 4 :142)

5.1   Introduction

Maturity is a cultural, as well as a relative, concept. How we define maturity depends very much on context; on family and community values of the society one is raised in, as well as genetic and ethnic factors. Assessing the developmental stage and maturity of a child is challenging, even in children indigenous to the United Kingdom (UK), where comparative data and idealized norms exist and the assessment can be done within the child's social and family context. The consideration of children from different countries, cultures and societies adds levels of complexity to this process. As an example, this chapter considers the current position, predominantly from a UK perspective, in relation to the psychological assessment of maturity for children

Age Estimation in the Living: The Practitioners Guide   Sue Black, Anil Aggrawal and Jason Payne-James
© 2010 John Wiley & Sons, Ltd

and young people who are subject to immigration control by social work assessment teams and for whom there may be concerns about the legitimacy of their claims to be a certain age. It will explore the current context of these assessments and how the absence of the usual contextual markers may limit the reliability and validity of such assessments. Finally, an alternative model will be proposed with an ethical framework that shifts the focus more clearly towards needs and places less emphasis on age as the exclusive and defining category for practice.

The current experiences of children and young people who are subject to immigration control can be considered as confusing and potentially dehumanizing (11 Million, 2009). Immigration control requires a distinctive approach to working with all potential asylum seekers, which sets a high priority on evidence and proof at the expense of welfare (Hayes, 2004). For children and young people these concerns may overshadow paying attention to their needs and require welfare to be subsumed into bureaucratic processes (Crawley, 2007). This tension is most evident in the case of young people who arrive in the UK as Unaccompanied Asylum Seeking Children (UASC) or Separated Children, and whose age is not accepted, or is disputed, by the port of entry screening officers. Such disputed children are required to prove their age through the process of an assessment that is also designed to assess their needs and by implication their maturity. This is a relatively new area of practice, which is characterized by the absence of real facts and little documentation and can lead to a desire for certainty and simplicity in order to make the job possible. Currently there is little standardization and equity of practice across the UK (Crawley, 2007; 11 Million, 2009). Additionally there is a relatively recent increase in movement of people throughout the world claiming asylum (Unicef, 2009) and a greater number of younger children are travelling on their own: 'The UN's refugee agency warned today that children as young as three are among the migrants attempting to reach Britain and that the number of unaccompanied refugee children is on the increase ... The warning came three days after the French government destroyed a makeshift refugee camp known as the "jungle" near Calais' (Topping, 2009).

Often as a result of political sensitivities, asylum and immigration systems have been set up quickly, and at times roles, responsibilities and tasks appear unclear (Davies, 2008). The current requirement for social work teams in the UK to undertake assessments with separated children to determine their entitlement to services is a difficult one, which necessitates a clear focus on the needs of a particularly vulnerable child or young person. For a small group of young people the addition of the assessment of their age requires an even more focused approach and brings with it layers of uncertainty and concern. These are heightened when one considers that this is not a traditional part of the social worker's role or training, is an area fraught with uncertainty, yet it is taken on independently of other agencies and is increasingly described in the immigration literature as an appropriate and professionally specific task (Crawley, 2007).

It is clear that a new framework that prioritizes the assessment of need in terms of maturity and puts together, as accurately as possible, all the available appropriate evidence while recognizing but perhaps deprioritizing age, is very much needed. The need for a multi-agency response with the roles and responsibilities of each being clearly specified as well as highlighting similarities to other established assessments will be explored.

5.1.1 Current Status in the UK

Recent concern about immigration in the UK has arisen in the context of a fear of encroachment and overpopulation (ICAR, 2004) although the number of people entering the UK and claiming refugee status is relatively small. In 2007, 23 450 claims were lodged. This number is the third highest in Europe after France and Sweden in absolute terms; however, proportionately viewed (per 1000 head of population), it is the eleventh highest total for Europe (Home Office, 2009). This figure does not include children who were dependents of adults claiming for a family group. It does, however, include all children who made a claim in their own right. UASC, also referred to as separated children, are 'young people under the age of 18, applying for asylum in their own right, separated from both parents and not being cared for by an adult' (UKBA, 2007). In 2007 there were 3525 UASC (Crawley, 2007). There is, however, no guarantee of the accuracy of this figure as it does not include those claimants who were age disputed and therefore deemed to be adults at the point of claim. It is estimated that up to 40% of claims are disputed at the point of initial claim by the UK Border Agency (UKBA) staff so there may have been up to 5000 children claiming asylum in 2007. A significant number is reassessed as children, possibly 1000 (Home Office, 2009). It is reasonable to assume that there is a similar figure for 2008 as the statistics available suggest that the number of claims have remained relatively stable over the past 5 years (Crawley, 2007).

Separated children are required to claim asylum in their own right and are processed by Border Agency staff. An initial assessment of the legitimacy of their claim is made, including an assessment of their age based on their physical appearance and demeanour by the screening officer (Crawley, 2007; Home Office, 2009). Those deemed not to be children are then disputed and treated as adults until an assessment of their age has been made by the local authority social services department.

There is growing concern surrounding the process by which such decisions are made and the systems that are in place to protect such potentially vulnerable children and young people (Ayotte, 1998; Crawley, 2007, UKBA, 2007). It has been suggested that asylum seeking children in general have lower levels of protection in relation to a range of rights that are unrelated to their immigration status (JCHR, 2006) and until recently the UK had registered a reservation against adopting the UN Convention on the Rights of the Child to enable it to treat asylum seeking children differently (Grady, 2004; Gillen, 2008). There is mounting concern about the lack of safeguards for this vulnerable group (Lorek, Ehntholt and Wey, 2009; Robjant and Robbins, 2009).

The provision of social care services for children and young people is generally governed by the Children Act 1989, which places a duty on Local Authorities to determine who are the children in need in their area. Section 17 of the Children Act 1989 states, 'It shall be the general duty of every local authority to safeguard and promote the welfare of children within their area who are in need'. This duty is routinely met by assessing children who may be in need, to determine the extent to which they require assistance and to provide appropriate services to them in partnership with a wide range of other agencies. Recent developments in this area have seen the establishment of the Common Assessment Framework (DCSF, 2007), which is designed to facilitate integrated practices and ensure that children, young people and their families are provided with appropriate services from all of the agencies that may be working with them. The assessment of separated children falls within the general duty described by Section 17 of the Act, particularly as they are considered to be 'abandoned', having no one who is able to exercise Parental Responsibility (PR) for them, and the local authority is, therefore, empowered to make routine decisions in their best interests. The exercise of PR is key in English law to the protection of children and young people, with the 1989 Act describing the key responsibilities that parents must undertake in respect of their children in conjunction with the actions of the state (Section 2 Children Act).

For a separated child there is no one to supply the additional contextual information, which, coupled with a lack of any documentation, means that a satisfactory outcome is frequently difficult to achieve.

5.2   Need for Determination of Maturity

An additional challenge to the social work teams who are involved in age determination is that of assessing the level of maturity of the young person, independent of their age. This assessment is designed to account for their physical, social, emotional and psychological needs and of the internal and ecological resources that they can deploy in order to achieve them, with little consideration of age beyond the notion of what a 'normal' child of a certain age may be expected to do. Indeed, the ability to conceptualize and deploy strategies may be independent of age, being more dependent upon experience, resilience and coping behaviours rather than any direct link to the chronological passage of time. The whole purpose of a 'needs led' assessment is to determine whether a young person has the psychological maturity to look after his/her self safely.

The absence of family and ecological familiarity and the requirement to conduct an assessment in an unfamiliar and time constrained setting, as in the asylum and immigration context, may have an impact on potential outcomes. The potential for the context to interfere with the process, the need for speed and the lack of essential tools means that ethical principles need to be prioritized and clearly guide any assessment of maturity in order to achieve as much safety and neutrality as possible. Clarity of purpose for conducting such assessments of unaccompanied young people is essential in order that they fulfil their task to the best of their ability.

Currently, the main reason for assessing psychological maturity is in the area of age disputes in young people claiming asylum. The context, which allows some people to access services and not others, is age dependent, political and an area of high emotional stress and polarization. The political context, resource implications, public attitudes and the potential for abuse on both sides leads to confusion as to whether the primary purpose of such an assessment is to determine age or is driven by the need to control/limit immigration (Barkham, 2008).

The implications of all of these considerations for separated young people is that there are additional layers of concern about defining age that may not pay sufficient attention to their needs or there may not be the professional tools available to facilitate an accurate understanding of. It is essential that we consider the methods that are engaged to explore with separated young people their current and future needs and the impact that their age may have on this process.

For age disputed young people, attempts to find a reliable, valid and accurate system for estimating age across cultures and environments has been challenging (EWHC 1025; EWHC 939). Whichever measures are used, the accepted conclusion is that an approximate figure with a margin of error of plus or minus 2 years is the best that can be expected and this has largely been supported by all investigators across Europe (Save the Children, 2004). Such an assessment can never be exact and whatever is done will still likely be perceived as unfair by some, especially when the young people are from countries where certification does not have the same priority as in the West, where they may have fled leaving documents behind and where those seeking asylum may be acting in desperation and be prepared to do almost anything to survive.

5.3 Psychological Maturity as a Concept

Childhood itself is a social construction and is constructed in the context of the culture and geographical location within which it occurs. From the work of Aries (1962) until the present date, many authors have paid attention to the mechanisms that surround the construction process. James, Jenks and Prout (1998) identified the process of development of childhood in Britain from the seventeenth century and of the significance of the cultural and sociological processes that accompany it. The transition from childhood to mini-adulthood is inextricably linked to an understanding of various stages in the development of society, with one of the most significant being the contribution of Victorian policy makers to the recognition of the child in law as having distinct rights and expectations separate from adults, including their parents. In this context 'child' and 'childhood' can only be defined in terms of the cultural spaces in which they are developed.

Maturity is defined as 'deliberateness of action, mature consideration, due development, ripe, the state of being complete' (*Oxford English Dictionary*, 2009). This literary definition is easier to examine in physical development since physical growth is measurable and visible and generally stops at a particular point, unlike psychological maturity, which is culturally defined and a state of mental maturity that may come at different ages and in uneven ways, depending on life experiences, genetics, environment and other factors. There is no set cut-off point; no age at which we are psychologically mature; and we must ensure an understanding that different situations may bring out different levels of maturity in each of us.

Erikson (1977) describes maturity as linked to psychosocial well-being and defines adulthood 'in terms of taking care of those to whom one finds oneself committed as one emerges from the identity-forming period of adolescence'. It has been described as an ability to balance emotion and reason with awareness of long-term consequences of one's actions; an ability to understand another's point of view; to shift perspectives, to be able to be in the 'here and now' and to think ahead (Ben-Shahar, 2009). Rayner (1972) defines maturity as a time when a person's mental organization of skill, concern, guilt and foresight has developed to the point where he or she is aware of responsibility in a variety of situations.

There is a correlation between age and maturity but it is not an automatic one, although for certain legal purposes a person may not be considered sufficiently psychologically mature to perform certain tasks. The age of consent and the age at which one can marry vary from country to country. In the UK this is 16 years for all young people. However, in Egypt the age of majority to enter into marriage is 18 years, whereas in Afghanistan it is 12 years for males and 14 for females (Melchiore, 2004).

Age is also, therefore, both a biological and social concept. Although chronological age refers to the period that has elapsed since an individual's birth and extending to any given point in time, this apparently definitive point, which is used to predict stages of development, entitlement to particular services, permission to do certain activities and so on, may not always be helpful or indeed possible to define with any degree of exactitude. For example, the longer survival of premature babies means that gestational age may also need to be considered if age is to be used as an indicator of 'maturity' to assess, for example, readiness to go to school.

In the West, age since birth is a definite, 'a quantity legally measurable to within a few hours' (Aries, 1962) and of immense importance in our civic society, where most things we do depend on our knowing this and having the paper that proves it. This is very different from a few hundred years ago, when age was far less precise, as is still the case in many countries, including the African bush, the deserts of Somalia, the mountains of Afghanistan and many others, where the notion of age is not of great importance and no birth documents are kept. In fact, many people cannot read or write and so it would be meaningless to ask for, or therefore possess, such superfluous documentation (Davies, 2008).

5.3.1   Child Development

Development does not happen in isolation from a child's environment, and qualities that define maturity may differ depending on context. As physical, cognitive, emotional and psychosocial aspects of development interact and influence each other, so all the external factors in a child's life, from the family, to the community and to the wider society, contribute towards the development of that person and help form an understanding of what being 'grown up' means. The concept of milestones, whereby children go through similar stages in the same order but at different ages can be helpful in assessing child attainment, although some areas, and psychological development would be one of them, do not develop in discrete leaps but are more continuous and gradual and different depending on a particular environment. Vygotsky (1978) sees cognitive functions, even those carried out alone, as affected by the beliefs, values and tools of the culture in which a person develops. Both Piaget (1972) and Vygotsky (1962) believed that young children are curious and actively involved in their own learning though Vygotsky placed more emphasis on the importance of social support in that learning.

A developmental ecological model (Jones and Ramchandani, 1999) allows for the complexity of interactions between individual, family and environmental factors and reinforces the idea that simple unilateral views of psychological assessment of maturity will be very limited in accuracy or usefulness. The developmental strand describes the child as becoming more organized, integrated and complex as he or she grows up, influenced by genetic, physical, psychological, family and community factors. The ecological aspect considers the complexity of the environmental influences, school, neighbourhood, family and culture that increase as the child develops, allowing for development to be viewed as a complex interactive continuum.

Aldgate and Jones (2006) present the view that some aspects of development, for example attachment, whereby children reach out to parents for security and protection, are universal, but different expectations of social development across cultures influence expression and outcome of development. The complexity of the term 'culture' itself needs to be understood when thinking about development. Emde (2006) summarized some key features, saying, 'It refers to meaning that is shared by a group of people; occurs in a particular setting and is dynamic, depending on events and other developments'. It 'operates silently and with voices' and much is implicit, things we imbue from what is around us without necessarily being able to articulate what that is. Culture brings expectations of social development so, for example, Western culture emphasizes individuality whereas Eastern cultures may place greater emphasis on social connectedness. Culture also 'influences expressions of distress' and 'is mediated through the parenting relationship' (Emde, 2006) so any assessment of age or maturity that is undertaken in the absence of these or when in a heightened state of distress will require these factors to be taken into account.

Erikson (1977) described psychological development from a psychoanalytic perspective in terms of key conflicts at different stages that roughly correlate with age and physical development and that if resolved lead towards maturity. Being part of a war; witnessing and experiencing violence; fleeing one's country and loss of one's family are all factors that will have an effect on one's development and maturity, especially when coming from another country and culture. This chapter will now review some aspects of development into adulthood in more detail.

5.3.2 Middle Childhood

Middle childhood is the period when a child enters a more social world, often with the starting of school (though this differs from culture to culture) and more separateness from parents and close family. It brings new challenges and is a time of advanced learning in terms of social skills, peer group relationships, relationship to authority, play and learning the rules of the outside world. Children become better able to think logically and to work things out for themselves. Piaget (1952) called this time the 'concrete operational period'. The child learns strategies for remembering and problem solving and the capacity to think about their own minds. Vygotsky (1978) introduced the idea of children being active explorers of their environment and able to learn more within a social context. Their world is now more complex and the environment can affect how this capacity to strategise develops and how well they learn that their environment is predictable, or not. This is the time when they develop a greater understanding of self in relation to the outside world. They learn to manage their emotions better by using internal representations and their capacity to think and reflect rather than act immediately. Their sense of morality and spirituality develops from initially being very bound by rules to their own internal sense of what is right and wrong, believing it is very important to do the right thing at this age (Schofield, 2006).

5.3.3   Adolescence

A key task of adolescence is the development of a separate identity and capacity to form intimate relationships and the end of it is when one is seen to be fully mature though there is no clear cut-off point. The development of ethnic identity is a key challenge during this time (Phinney, 2001).

For Erikson (1968), identity is a subjective sense of wholeness achieved during adolescence through an identity crisis and is a crucial time in terms of what peer groups one forms and how this period, which can be a time of great upheaval, is managed. There is a strong relationship between physical, mental and social health during this time (Bailey, 2006), with pubertal changes and sexual awareness developing together. Abstract thought and moral development progress alongside each other (Kohlberg and Turiel, 1971). Identity and culture are two of the building blocks of ethnicity (Nagel, 1994), and Phinney and Chavira (1992) describe a three-stage model whereby an individual initially has a crisis or awakening which leads to a period of experimentation or exploration and then a commitment or integration of ethnic identity.

According to Winefield and Harvey (1996), an important component of psychological maturity is the capacity to experience and recognize intimacy in social relationships and a sense of identity. Although this is a Western idea, these capacities do develop further in this stage.

With asylum seekers, and especially young ones, the formation of identity is likely to be highly affected by their experiences of loss, separation and arrival in a new country. Loss of identity is often mentioned as a key area of difficulty (Burnett and Peel, 2001) and it is to be expected that this stage of development will likely be quite confusing. Asylum seekers are often rejected by their country because of their ethnicity, for example Tamil Muslims or Hutu Rwandans, and may be placed in areas without established communities or may not want contact with their community. They may lack a peer group or parental, family and community context. Separated adolescents, whose parents may have been killed because of their ethnicity, may find it difficult to accept or integrate their ethnicity or be quite confused about where they belong. Equally, they may reject or fiercely identify with their ethnic group.

Psychological maturity implies more than being able to care for oneself in terms of simply being able, for example, to feed and clothe oneself. There are no clear tests, no obvious cut-off points and no age at which psychological maturity is reached. Any assessment needs to include a measure of the capacity to keep oneself safe; make responsible decisions; have a sense of one's self in relation to others; be able to form relationships; look after others; think logically; use facts, reason and experience rather than simply react to emotion; become a parent and be able to fulfil parental responsibility. Many other factors may apply.

5.3.4 Ethical Framework

The process of assessment of children and young people has always attracted ethical consideration, whether that is child protection, access to services or assessment of needs. In the area of age determination and the assessment of unaccompanied young people there are, however, additional factors that need to be taken into account to ensure that practice falls within the ethical guidelines of the professionals undertaking the assessment. One of the most important is the consideration of the ability of the young person to provide informed consent to the process. As noted, the lack of the safety net of PR acting in the child's best interests means that all practitioners working with separated children must be mindful of the need to put in place appropriate checks and balances in order that they receive the full protection of the welfare system. A clear example of this is the principle of giving 'the benefit of the doubt' when making decisions about age. According to Crawley (2007), it is not used as often as it should and needs to be given higher priority. This is clearly articulated in the proforma currently used for estimating age (K. Goodman, personal communication, 2009).

The lack of a binding code of ethics for social workers may mean that decisions such as when to give the benefit of the doubt or when consent to an assessment can or cannot be given become less clear cut. The only point of reference available to social workers in any detail is that of the BASW code of ethics (BASW, 2002), which is not binding but should act as a basis for good practice. Examining the concept of social justice as formulated within the code leads us to identify areas of potential conflict between current practice and the underlying ethical considerations. The code identifies the values that underpin the assumption of social justice as a key element of social work ethics; BASW suggests that this include:

> Fair access to public services and benefits, to achieve human potential . . .
> EQUAL treatment and protection under the law

BASW goes on to suggest that this can be achieved by considering a number of principles for practice, which include the duty to:

(a) Bring to the attention of those in power and the general public, and where appropriate challenge ways in which the policies or activities of government, organisations or society create or contribute to structural disadvantage, hardship and suffering, or militate against their relief.

(b) Promote policies, practices and social conditions which uphold human rights and which seek to ensure access, equity and participation for all.

c) Challenge the abuse of power for suppression and for excluding people from decisions which affect them.

Pragmatically, it is suggested that social workers should consider the potential for age determination processes conducted without clear consent and the protection of the law to pose an ethical dilemma for practice. There is little evidence in practice of these concerns coming to the fore (Crawley, 2007) and no need for social workers to adhere to this code as it is not mandatory, which is of some concern (see Chapter 4).

The current arrangements for practice might usefully consider the impact of a more rigorous and well-supported framework for ethical practice. If the contribution of the codes of ethics or professional practice of other professions are considered, guidance may be provided that would enable the social work teams engaged in age estimation to develop a more focused approach to their practice (see Chapter 4). It is suggested that two particular aspects of the code of ethics for the medical profession may be particularly useful: beneficence and non-maleficence (Gopfert and McLelland, 2010).

The requirement of beneficence, which is to do the best for the individual, is not necessarily captured particularly well in the BASW code of ethics. A clear commitment to the individual beyond the restraints of resources and environment means that the practitioner must always bear them in mind; as such, we would suggest that this would mean that the onus of assessment would be to ensure that as accurate a judgement can be made as possible, supporting the young person to be able to tell their story in an open way while helping them to fully understand the consequences of what they say. Such an approach would ensure that any assessment is truly person-centred and supportive of the individual and would place the social worker as an independent agent in the context of immigration control, rather than as potentially part of the system. This would challenge the dilemma of the current code of ethics to address the deficiencies of the system from within, something which is always a difficult position to hold.

A clear statement of non-maleficence, which relates to the obligation not to harm others, and in an extended sense also covers obligations not to allow others to come to harm, would also be useful to social workers and those undertaking age estimation. In this context, it would be important to not place an adult with children, for the protection of the children, but this needs balancing with the risk of placing someone who may be a child with adults. This dilemma is one that is constantly referred to in the practice arena, with the concern for children rightly being paramount; however, the utilitarian resolution of protecting the many from the few (that is, not placing an adult with children) does not resolve the potential harm that may accrue to a child who is deemed to be an adult. The lack of certainty within the age determination process means that often a conclusion based on the balance of probabilities is relied upon, which would meet the test in law; however, this decision needs to acknowledge that occasionally this requires a 'benefit of the doubt' application in practice. Such a decision making process needs to be considered as an ethical judgement which can be grounded in the principle of non-maleficence.

These principles could open up a debate about the ethics of age estimation for a profession that may seek, through its practice, to uphold and promote social justice and to challenge injustice actively, at all levels. There is an obvious disjunction between the ethical statements and the practice reality as the engagement with age determination denies the fundamental right of social workers to challenge policies or activities of government and prevents the challenge of the potential abuse of power with which they are complicit.

5.4   Current Practice

Crawley (2007) studied practice in relation to age determination at screening centres in the UK and highlighted a number of concerns. These included the screening of 'adults' out of the process via a reliance on physical appearance as a determining factor in the process of assessment and the lack of openness of the process to external scrutiny and challenge in the event of dispute. Concerns were also raised about the co-location of social work assessment teams within the context of the Home Office screening unit (Crawley, 2007; 11 Million, 2008).

The process for the estimation of age is currently governed by the Age Assessment Proforma (K. Goodman, personal communication, 2009). This document has status in law (the Merton judgment) (EWHC 1689) although it does not originate in any statutory guidance. It arose out of the need for some structure within which to locate the emerging requirement for age estimation in the 1990s. It describes assessment as a process and provides some guidance on the areas that might be considered, although it does not claim to be accurate or comprehensive but is rather a guide for practice. As it currently stands, this is the only guidance available to practitioners from which to conduct an age estimation in the case of dispute (Home Office, 2009). The conduct and outcomes of age assessments have been subject to scrutiny from many different quarters. Legally, cases such as Merton have acknowledged the need for any assessment process to be fair, and the terms of the Merton judgment identify a framework within which any assessment must be conducted. Even with this scrutiny, concerns persist about the nature of the assessment process and the need to challenge any decision through the courts, which is a lengthy and expensive process and one that any child would find daunting. Put in the context of immigration, it suggests that access to this system will be limited and dependent upon the quality of legal advice and support that any young person can access through the system.

Other concerns include a perceived lack of experience and expertise among those undertaking the assessments, who are mainly social workers with little formal or assessed training in the assessment of age as a distinct and specialist area of practice. Consequently the standard of age estimations in this setting can be called into question as there is little research evidence available based on this guidance and certainly no evidence of a uniform standard of practice across geographical and regional boundaries (Crawley, 2007).

There are also a range of criticisms of the process of assessment: many are conducted by one or two social workers, using an interpreter (sometimes via a telephone interpretation service). In the case of co-located teams they may be completed in one session or in one day (97% in Liverpool: Nelki, personal communication). How this is perceived by the young people involved is not clear. However, it would be reasonable to assume that any young person born in the UK let alone a foreign country would find it difficult to engage with an assessment of their needs in one day. The complexity of immigration status, language, comprehension and translation can only add to these difficulties, as can the issues of trauma and separation, which are often not accounted for in the process.

Due to the lack of detailed research evidence in this area and the secretive nature of the assessment process, which is not readily open to external scrutiny, sitting as it does firmly within immigration control rather than welfare services, it is hard to make a judgement about the fairness of the process. The little research that has been conducted (Crawley, 2007; 11 Million, 2009) has questioned the fairness of the process and the potential for it to increase the trauma experienced by potentially vulnerable young people. The process has not been tested for effectiveness or even accuracy of outcomes and has acquired a status as the best way to undertake age estimations when in reality it is currently *the only way* in the UK to undertake such assessments in the context of immigration (Home Office, 2009).

The extent of a child-focused process that is essentially political in nature is questionable. The position of disbelief from which the process originates makes a child-centred approach difficult to maintain, particularly when evidence from observers such as Crawley (2007) suggests that assessors are often trying to 'catch the subject out' in order to demonstrate their lack of credibility in their claim to be a child.

There is little theory that underpins the assessment in its current format, concerned as it is with a consistent narrative from the subject, deviation from which is seen as suspicious evidence of adult behaviour. Coherence in narrative form is a subjective process and deviation is a human attribute as stories change in the telling with audience, importance and focus (Cohen, 2001; Kohli, 2007). Internal coherence is essential for the teller but not necessarily the same as perceived coherence for the listener, who may not be party to the internal processes. Additionally, the impact of experiences, including trauma, affect memory and the ability of any narrator to maintain coherence (Herlihy, Scragg and Turner, 2002; Bogner, Herlihy and Brewin, 2007; Herlihy and Turner, 2007). Such factors are not obvious in the Age Assessment Proforma. There are also concerns about the context of the assessment. Within the Assessment Framework, young people, or their parents, are assumed to consent to the process. The age estimation process does not contain any test of consent or indeed any obligation on the assessor to obtain formal consent for the young person. The absence of process and the assumption of consent are potentially harmful. The test of capacity to give informed consent in the medical arena – namely Gillick competence (Gillick, 1985) – can be considered in these circumstances in the absence of other guidance. The key to these guidelines is the understanding that any judgement on capacity requires from the young person both an understanding of the process *and* sufficient maturity to understand what is involved, including any potentially harmful outcomes.

The use of interpreters, while usually helpful, is also very complex. Their training is often limited and they are unlikely to have any mental health training. Few checks can be undertaken to ensure they understand what is being asked of them or what the replies should be. The subtleties of language may be missed. They may come from a different region or the 'opposite side' of the conflict from which the young person is fleeing, which may be completely paralysing and may lead to actual or perceived bias or prejudice by the interpreter. And yet they are also potentially very helpful if these biases can be drawn out and used. They may be able to verify someone's story – if, for example, the person's dialect matches the village they say they come from or they know from their own experiences an event could or could not have happened (Tribe and Ravel, 2003).

Mental health factors add to the complexity of the age estimation process by affecting how a young person presents and how they tell their story (Herlihy and Turner, 2007). Fear, anxiety, depression, shame, guilt and serious mental illness may all contribute to a confusing picture. Asylum seeking young people are at high risk for developing mental health difficulties and a large proportion will do so (Fazel and Stein, 2003; Hodes, 2004). However, it is a complicated picture because they come with multiple motives; they may have been sent away as the last hope for their parents; they may be hopeful for the future, feeling safe and looking forward. They may have been told they need to say certain things, to be consistent and on no account have any variation. This can lead to what Kohli (2007) calls 'thin' stories that may be superficial, the story that is not too hard to tell, that can be consistent, that is 'safe'. The trauma may be pushed to the back – too complex to talk about; too complex to understand; there may even be no words for it as 'war silences children' (Melzak, 1992). As a result of their experiences they may have an uneven psychological development – in some areas, such as fending for themselves, they may be very mature and yet very immature in others, such as their capacity for intimacy.

The effect of listening to unbearable stories of persecution and torture, with no built-in support structures for staff, can lead to 'vicarious traumatization' whereby staff can either show signs of being traumatized themselves, with intrusive dreams or sleeplessness, or switch off and show 'an unexplained general sense of tiredness, boredom and lethargy' (Human Resilience, 2009). The effects can be minimized by ensuring regular discussions with colleagues aware of this possibility and would be protective of the young people as well as the staff.

There appears to be little evidence of consistent application of the Gillick test of competence in relation to the undertaking of age estimations with young people. The concept of understanding the process is difficult enough if one considers the potential language and cultural barriers involved, and adding a test of maturity to understand what is involved and all possible outcomes on which to base a decision to comply, we suggest, lies beyond the ability of most young people who are required to undertake such assessments. The question of context – being assessed in a screening unit as part of a process of immigration determination – means that the ability to give true informed consent is diminished or indeed absent; the option of not complying; that is, being treated as an adult, does not make the test fair and the addition of barriers around comprehension and language would seem to make it meaningless in these circumstances.

5.5 Suggestions for a Framework for Good Practice

It is essential that ethical values and principles of good practice are adhered to by all those involved in assessments; that assessments are needs based, rooted in child development, undertaken by those trained in the area, evidence based, open to scrutiny and feedback and that an estimate of age is given in parallel with a needs assessment.

Table 5.1 Principles of assessment

They:

- are child centred;
- are rooted in child development;
- are ecological in their approach;
- ensure equality of opportunity;
- involve working with children and families;
- build on strengths as well as identify difficulties;
- are inter-agency in their approach to assessment and the provision of services;
- are a continuing process, not a single event;
- are grounded in evidence based knowledge.

(Department of Health, 1999).

Given that in the setting described above, there are rarely the usual context markers available – family, school, reports, certificates and so on – the assessments need to be designed to give us as much information as possible with only the young person present who can give information about his or her life. Therefore, the setting, the timing, the way questions are asked and the tasks set need to be very carefully planned to ensure that as much information as possible can be elicited.

The current guidance available to social workers on the use of assessment with children and young people is clearly articulated through the Framework for the Assessment of Children (Department of Health, 1999). This guidance makes very clear statements about the need for assessments to address a range of issues for children and young people and to account for the unique circumstances that such children and young people find themselves in when subject to interventions by social workers and other welfare professionals (Table 5.1).

5.5.1 Setting

The process of age assessment is stressful in itself (Crawley, 2007). There needs to be careful thought as to how the assessment is set up – where it takes place, who does it and how long it lasts. It is suggested that a setting independent of the Home Office is used and that assessments are conducted by someone trained in health, including mental health, child development and needs assessment (Crawley, 2007). Informed consent needs to be confirmed in writing with signed agreement from the social worker that the information has been explained and understood. Specially trained interpreters need to be used and sufficient time given so that assessment is carried out over more than one meeting and comparisons can be made with how the young person behaves/interacts on different occasions. It is suggested that other informants, such as reception centre staff, teachers or others, are consulted wherever possible to give a description of daily functioning and not only an opinion on age. This practice needs to be standardized across the UK. The principles that are described above are ones that should be considered in all countries and jurisdictions to ensure compliance with the international laws of human rights.

Based on the factors discussed above about location, principles and concerns, the authors of this chapter have devised a framework to be used as guidance in interviewing (see Appendix 5.A).

5.6 Summary and Conclusion

The suggested framework and accompanying tables would allow the interviewers to begin to piece together a picture of a young person and assess appropriately what may be their needs and as a consequence, what might be their likely chronological age. Questions to be asked would include whether the story seems consistent and age appropriate. If the story is not coherent, does it make sense given what the young person describes as having happened? How great are the needs? How would they best be met, given the likely age of the young person? If they seem to be an adult but with a great level of need, how will these needs be addressed?

Clearly, this framework is only a guideline, although broader than the one currently used. As such, or with any other similar framework, it must be emphasized that it needs auditing, validating, standardizing and researching if it is to be used with any degree of reliability. Social work and other practitioners need to have formal assessed training and the work must be performed in a transparent manner to ensure fairness and equity.

Psychological assessment of maturity is a difficult task when the usual context markers are missing and there are added complications of asylum and immigration. This chapter has identified some of the background to the current assessment process, the concerns and challenges, and highlighted the importance of an ethical underpinning of the process. It is important to use as much information as possible in an area where there are few verifiable facts and objective evidence, in order to protect vulnerable children and ensure that wherever possible their needs can be met and a safer system be put in place for their continuing welfare. The framework suggested uses an accepted system of needs assessment, and its application in relation to separated children claiming protection from persecution and torture is identified with the clarification that the primary purpose is to assess needs but in the context of age, making use of specialist skills and inter-agency working, which will lead to safer practice and a more humane system.

Appendix 5.A Proposed Framework, Based on Common Assessment Framework (Department of Schools Families and Children, 2007)

Remember, **benefit of the doubt** is the key underpinning principle.

The following is intended to be a guide to questions and to lead to a conversation, so that it is a way of getting to know someone and what their lives were like and what their concerns and needs might now be. Begin by asking them to 'tell us a bit about yourself' or 'you have been through a lot. Tell us how you are now . . .'.

Needs	Evidence	Met or unmet	Concerns

1. Communication

Can they give informed consent?
  Are they Gillick competent?
  Do they have 'capacity'?

Can an interpreter help with
  assessing language?

Is it what would be expected from a
  child of the claimed age and from
  the claimed village?

2. General health

Do they look generally well,
  sufficiently nourished and
  hydrated?

Do they have any medical condition
  we need to know about?
  Have they had any
  operations/serious illnesses?

Ask about condition of teeth and
  any treatment.

Ask about physical development.
  Are they pubertal/prepubertal, for
  example menstruation, shaving?

Do they look underweight,
  overweight, pale, tired?

3. Emotional and social development

What do they remember of their
  early relationships?
What family did they have?
Who was around?
Who looked after them when they
  were little?

What do they know about their early
  development?

Have they been involved in any risky
  behaviours, like self-harm, now or
  in the past?

Do they have any phobias and how
  do they generally cope with stress?

What kind of person are they:
  happy/sad/irritable/patient?
How would friends describe them?

Needs	Evidence	Met or unmet	Concerns

What are important values and belief systems held within their family?

How are their appetite, mood and sleep? Now and before they came here.

How do they come across in the interview?

4. Behavioural development

What is their behaviour during interview?
Do they make eye contact?
Are they restless?
How do they talk about themselves or tell their story?

What did they do outside school/family?

Did they ever use drugs or alcohol?

Did they witness violence?
Were they involved in it?

Are they sexually active?
Do they have a partner or are they married?
Have they ever been sexually assaulted?

Did they have any problems with concentration?
Do they seem to now in the interview?

How are their peer relationships?
Did they have friends?
What did they do together?
How did it compare to other young people in the area?

Does it seem age appropriate?

5. Identity, self-esteem, self-image and social presentation

Ask what kind of person they are.
How do they feel about being that person?

Needs	Evidence	Met or unmet	Concerns
How do they look: confident, worried, anxious? Is their behaviour appropriate for interview?			

6. Religion and spiritual development

What religion are they?
What does it mean to them?
Can they worship here?
Do they know where to go?
Do they need help with getting there?

7. Family and social relationships

Where is their family now?

Who do they socialize with now?

How isolated are they?

8. Self-care skills and independence

How much cooking did they do before they came here?

Can they look after their money?

Are they good at keeping themselves and their home clean?

How do they think they will manage here?

Do they look clean and well presented?

Who looked after them?
Who did they look after?

What kind of diet do they have?

9. Learning

Did they go to school?

Was this the same as other young people in the area?

How did they do at school?

What was their achievement relative to others?

What kind of school did they attend?
What can they recall about their teachers?

Needs	Evidence	Met or unmet	Concerns

Were they disciplined at school?
What was it like?
Was it any different for them from others?

What books or films do they like?
Do they have the capacity for abstract
  thought and discussion?

Do they tend to think concretely?

10. Aspirations

How realistic are their
  aspirations/expectations of what will
  happen to them or what they can do
  here?

On the basis of the above information we estimate the age of this young person to
be:

13	14	15	16	17	18	19	20	21

And as a consequence of their age and maturity their needs are:

Area of need	Level of need	Urgency	Actions	Area of need	Level of need	Urgency	Actions
General health				Religion and spiritual needs			
Communi-cation				Family and social relations			
Emotional and social development				Self-care and inde-pendence			
Behavioural development				Learning			
Identity and self-esteem				Aspirations			

References

11 Million (2008) Claiming asylum at a screening unit as an unaccompanied child, www.11Million.org (accessed 28 October 2009).

11 Million (2009) The arrest and detention of children subject to immigration control: a report following the Children's Commissioner for England's visit to Yarl's Wood Immigration Removal Centre, www.11Million.org (accessed 28 October 2009).

A vs. *London Borough of Croydon and Secretary of State for the Home Department; WK vs. Secretary of State for the Home Department and Kent County Council* [2009] EWHC 939 (Admin).

Aldgate, J.D. and Jones, D. (2006) The place of attachment in children's development, in *The Developing World of the Child* (eds. J. Aldgate, D. Jones, W. Rose and C. Jeffrey), Jessica Kingsley, London, pp. 67–96.

Aries, P. (1962) *Centuries of Childhood*. Penguin, Harmondsworth.

Ayotte, W. (1998) *Supporting Unaccompanied Children in the Asylum Process*, Save the Children, London.

Bailey, S. (2006) Adolescence and beyond: twelve years onwards, in *The Developing World of the Child* (eds J. Aldgate, D. Jones, W. Rose and C. Jeffery), Jessica Kingsley, London, pp. 208–225.

Barkham, P. (2008) 'You can't come in', *The Guardian* (18 November), www.guardian.co.uk/politics/2008/nov/18/immigration-policy-phil-woolas-racism (accessed 18 November 2009).

BASW (2002) *British Association of Social Work. The Code of Ethics for Social Work*, BASW, Birmingham.

Ben Shahar, T. (2009) Psychological maturity, http://talbenshahar.com/index.php?option=com_content&task=view&id=28&Itemid=51 (accessed 20 October 2009).

Bogner, D., Herlihy, J. and Brewin, C. (2007) Impact of sexual violence on disclosure during Home Office interviews. *British Journal of Psychiatry*, **191**, 75–81.

Burnett, A. and Peel, M. (2001) Asylum seekers and refugees in Britain. What brings asylum seekers to the United Kingdom? *British Medical Journal*, **322**, 485–488.

Children Act 1989, www.opsi.gov.uk/acts/acts1989/ukpga_19890041_en_1 (accessed 28 October 2009).

Cohen, J. (2001) Errors of recall and credibility: can omissions and discrepancies in successive statements reasonably be said to undermine credibility of testimony? *Medico-legal Journal*, **69**, (Pt 1), 25–34.

Crawley, H. (2007) *When Is a Child Not a Child? Asylum, Age Disputes and the Process of Age Assessment*, Immigration Law Practitioners' Association, London.

Davies, G. (2008) An evaluation of the age assessment process in relation to unaccompanied asylum seeking children, Anglia Ruskin University, Faculty of Health and Social Care, Department of Social Studies and Primary Care.

Department for Children, Schools and Families (2007) Common assessment framework, www.dcsf.gov.uk/everychildmatters/strategy/deliveringservices1/caf/cafframework/ (accessed 28 October 2009).

Department of Health (DoH) (1999) Framework for the assessment of children in need and their families, www.archive.official-documents.co.uk/document/doh/facn/facn.htm (accessed 21 November 2009).

Emde, R. (2006) Culture, diagnostic assessment, and identity: defining concepts. *Infant Mental Health Journal*, **27** (6), 606–611.

Erikson, E. (1968) *Identity, Youth and Crisis*, W.W. Norton, New York.

Erikson, E. (1977) *Childhood and Society*, W.W. Norton, New York.

Fazel, M. and Stein, A. (2003) Mental health of refugee children. *British Medical Journal*, **327**, 134–135.

Gillen, S. (2008) Struggle for rights of young asylum seekers ends in triumph, Community Care, www.communitycare.co.uk/Articles/2008/11/12/109928/lifting-uncrc-reservation-offers-hope-for-asylum-seekers.html (accessed 28 October 2009).

Gillick vs. *West Norfolk and Wisbech Area Health Authority and another* [1985] 3 All ER 402 (HL), www.careandhealthlaw.com/Public/Index.aspx?ContentID=-66&IndexType=1& TopicID=245&Category=1 (accessed 20 October 2009).

Gopfert, M. and McClelland, N. (2010) Maternal mental health: an ethical base for good practice, in *Oxford Textbook of Women and Mental Health* (ed. D. Kohen), Oxford University Press, Oxford.

Grady, P. (2004) Social work responses to accompanied asylum seeking children, in *Social Work, Immigration and Asylum* (eds D. Hayes and B. Humphries), Jessica Kingsley, London.

Hayes, D. (2004) History and context: the impact of immigration control on welfare delivery, in *Social Work, Immigration and Asylum* (eds D. Hayes and B. Humphries), Jessica Kingsley, London.

Herlihy, J., Scragg, P. and Turner, S. (2002) Discrepancies in autobiographical memories – implications for the assessment of asylum seekers: repeated interview study. *British Medical Journal*, **324**, 324–327.

Herlihy, J. and Turner, S. (2007) Asylum claims and memory of trauma – sharing our knowledge. *British Journal of Psychiatry*, **191**, 3–4.

Hodes, M. (2004) Refugee children in the UK, in *Mental Health Services for Ethnic Minority Children and Adolescents* (eds M. Malek and C. Joughin), Jessica Kingsley, London.

Home Office (2005) Asylum statistics, 2004, United Kingdom, Home Office, London.

Home Office (2008) Asylum statistics – United Kingdom 2007, Home Office Statistical Bulletin, London, www.homeoffice.gov.uk/rds/pdfs08/hosb1108.pdf (accessed 28 October 2009).

Home Office (2009) Policy and law: asylum process guidance, www.ukba.homeoffice.gov.uk/policyandlaw/guidance/asylumprocess (accessed 18 October 2009).

Human Resilience (2009) Vicarious traumatisation, www.humanresilience.com/home/blog/44-vicarious-traumatisation.html (accessed 13 September 2009).

ICAR Information Centre about Asylum and Refugees (2004) Attitudes towards asylum seekers, refugees and other immigrants, a literature review for the Commission for Racial Equality, www.icar.org.uk/10583/previous-work/public-attitudes-to-asylum.html (accessed 7 May 2010).

James, A., Jenks, C. and Prout, A. (1998) *Theorising Childhood*, Polity Press, Cambridge.

JCHR (2006) Joint Committee on Human Rights 10th report part 5 – Treatment of children – The UK's reservation to the UN convention on the Rights of the Child (CRC), www.publications.parliament.uk/pa/jt200607/jtselect/jtrights/81/8102.htm (accessed 18 November 2009).

Jones, D. and Ramchandani, P. (1999) *Child Sexual Abuse: Informing Practice from Research*, Radcliffe Medical Press, London.

Kohlberg, L. and Turiel, E. (1971) Moral development and moral education, in *Psychology and Educational Practice* (ed. G. Lesser), Scott Foresman, Chicago, IL, pp. 410–465.

Kohli, R. (2007) The meaning of resettlement, in *Social Work with Unaccompanied Asylum Seeking Children*, Palgrave, UK.

Lorek, A., Ehntholt, K. and Wey, E. (2009) Mental and physical health of children in British immigration detention centre. *Child Abuse and Neglect*, **33** (9), 573–585.

Melchiorre, A. (2004) At what age? ... are school-children employed, married and taken to court? www.right-to-education.org/sites/r2e.gn.apc.org/files/age_new.pdf (accessed 19 October 2009).

Melzak, S. (1992) *Secrecy, Privacy, Survival, Repressive Regimes and Growing up*, Anna Freud Centre, London.

Nagel, J. (1994) Constructing ethnicity: creating and recreating ethnic identity and culture. *Social Problems* **41**, 152–176.

Nin, A. (1971) *The Early Diary of Anais Nin*, Vol. 4 (ed. G. Stuhlmann), Quartet, London, pp. 142–143.

Phinney, J.S. and Chavira, V. (1992) Ethnic identity and self-esteem: an exploratory longitudinal study. *Journal of Adolescence*, **15** (3), 271–281.

Phinney, J. (2001) Stages of ethnic identity development in minority group adolescents. *Journal of Early Adolescence*, **9**, 34–59.

Piaget, J. (1952) *The Origins of Intelligence in Children*, W.W. Norton, New York.

Piaget, J. (1972) *To Understand Is To Invent*, Viking, New York.

R (on the application of B) vs. *London Borough of Merton* [2003] EWHC 1689 (Admin).

R (on application of I) vs. *Secretary of State for the Home Department; R (on application of O)* vs. *Secretary of State for the Home Department* [2005] QBD (Admin) EWHC 1025 (Admin).

Rayner, E. (1972) *Human Development*, George Allen & Unwin, London.

Robjant, K. and Robbins, V. (2009) Psychological distress among British immigration detainees. *Journal of Clinical Psychology* **48** (3), 275–286.

Save the Children (2004) Newsletter no. 19, Separated Children in Europe Programme, www.separated-children-europe-programme.org/separated_children/publications/newsletter/Newsletter19.pdf (accessed 28 October 2009).

Schofield, G. (2006) Middle childhood: five to eleven years, in *The Developing World of the Child* (eds J. Aldgate, D. Jones, W. Rose and C. Jeffrey), Jessica Kingsley, London, pp. 196–207.

Topping, A. (2009) Very young children among migrants heading for UK, warns refugee agency, The Guardian (25 September).

Tribe, R. and Ravel, H. (2003) *Working with Interpreters in Mental Health*, Brunner-Routledge, UK.

UKBA (2007) *Planning Better Outcomes and Support for UASC*, UKBA Home Office Consultation Paper, Febrary.

United Nations Children's Fund (Unicef) (2009) Children in war, www.unicef.org/sowc96/childwar.htm (accessed 13 September 2009).

Vygotsky, L. (1978) Interaction between learning and development, in *Mind in Society* (Trans. M. Cole), Harvard University Press, Cambridge, MA.

Vygotsky, L. (1962) *Thought and Language*, MIT Press, Cambridge, MA.

Winefield, H. and Harvey, E. (1996) Psychological maturity in early adulthood: relationships between social development and identity. *Journal of Genetic Psychology* **157**, 93–103.

6

Principles of Physical Age Estimation

Sue Black[1] and George Maat[2]

[1]*Centre for Anatomy and Human Identification, University of Dundee, Dundee, DD1 5EH, UK*
[2]*Barge's Anthropology, Leiden University Medical Centre, Leiden, The Netherlands*

The process of assigning a biological age in an attempt to approximate to the chronological age of an individual (living or deceased) is inextricably linked to the largely predictable and measurable progression of the processes of growth, maturation and, ultimately, senescence. Although the processes are often thought of as a seamless progression, there are significant differences that are relevant to the understanding of the approaches utilized in age estimation. Growth is appropriately defined as 'a quantitative increase in size or mass' whereas maturation is perhaps better defined as 'a progression of changes, either qualitative or quantitative, that leads from an undifferentiated or immature state to a highly organized, specialized and mature state' (Bogin, 1999). While, theoretically, growth and maturation could occur independent of each other, in reality they progress in a relatively harmonious equilibrium to safeguard the normal development of the individual from conception to adulthood. Both growth and maturation are essential and inextricable partners in the complex mammalian journey from a single fertilized cell to the ultimate organized mature adult state, which is comprised of somewhere in the region of 10^{12} cells.

A significant misalignment between growth and maturation quickly results in an alteration to the predicted 'normal' pattern of shape, size, proportions or indeed viability of the individual and will most likely result in a recognizable pathological or restricted function condition. Indeed, such an alteration may not be compatible

Age Estimation in the Living: The Practitioners Guide   Sue Black, Anil Aggrawal and Jason Payne-James
© 2010 John Wiley & Sons, Ltd

with sustained life. However, there are many other factors that may influence both the growth and the maturation of the individual in such a way as to not necessarily disrupt the overall form and survival of the individual but which introduce sufficient variability or imbalance that the idealistic perfect relationship between biological and chronological age is disrupted. These 'interferences' may result in an individual being smaller/taller for age than their genetic potential dictates or perhaps be advanced/retarded in their maturation but they do not necessarily result in a pathological condition, a syndrome, a disease or a congenital abnormality, anomaly or variation. These sometimes relatively minor differences are tolerated by the developing individual but they ensure that when attempting to align the chronological and biological clocks, then the relationship can never be 100% predictive.

These disturbances to optimal achievement of the final mature status occur through a variety of aetiologies that can bring their influences to bear at almost any stage of the growth and maturation process. While some of these will be discussed below, others will be discussed in Chapter 7.

At the other end of the age profile, senescence is defined as the stage of the life process that follows the attainment of full maturity when the body systems surpass their functional optimum and are no longer considered to be operating at their prime. For example, continued mineralization into the joint cartilages will significantly impact on joint mobility and will ultimately result in osteoarthritis. While we may consider this to be a degenerative condition, it is in fact a continuation of growth and remodelling. The onset of senescent change, its rate of progression and its manifestation are all highly variable and therefore the alignment between the biological and chronological clocks is poor in this section of the human life span. Therefore, the relationship between chronological and biological age is strongest during the phase of rapid growth and development in the young, weakens during the phase when growth has slowed substantially but maturation is still active in the young adult, and is at its most weak when senescence commences.

Shakespeare (*As You Like It*, Act II, Scene 7) described the 'Seven Ages of Man' as infancy, boyhood, puberty, youth, manhood, old age and decrepitude, and while there is a certain balance and theatrical alignment to those classifications, they neither follow the biological nor the physicality of the functional pattern of human development. For the purposes of age estimation in this text, there is little merit in examining the earliest stages of growth and development from the divisions of a single cell through the laying down of embryonic tissues to fetal organogenesis, and so this text commences with early fetal development, which is viewed by Sinclair (1969) to be the second phase of human growth. He considered the first phase to be restricted to early embryonic development, which merges into the second, which he proposed to be a balance between growth and differentiated functional activity that would persist until the third phase of 'maturity' was reached. The fourth phase he related to old age when growth is insufficient to keep the body in balance. Given that Sinclair's second phase covers the entire time line when age evaluation is in its most closely aligned position to chronological age and therefore at its most reliable stage (i.e. birth to the end of adolescence), it will be necessary for the purposes of this text to divide this period into further subunits as directed by biological and functional influences.

6.1 Intra-uterine Growth and Development

Prenatal life, the time between fertilization and birth, is both clinically and conveniently separated into three trimesters of pregnancy. The first trimester encompasses the period between fertilization and the end of the twelfth week (third lunar month), and reflects implantation and embryogenesis. The second trimester spans from the fourth through to the sixth lunar months and is the period of most rapid intra-uterine growth; by this stage the differentiation of cells into tissues and organs is largely complete so the individual is now comfortably referred to as a fetus. The third trimester extends between the seventh lunar month and birth, when there is again a period not only of rapid growth in size but also in weight and there is significant organ maturation to prepare the fetus for a semi-independent *extra-uterine* existence.

One of the most obvious influences on normal development will be genetic in origin and as a result many of the most serious abnormalities are not consistent with maintained life and the embryo may be spontaneously aborted. It is suggested that around 10% of embryos fail to implant and of those that do successfully attach to the uterine environment, approximately 50% of these will spontaneously abort. The genetic material not only codes for the developing embryo, but also codes for the development of the protective and nutritive structures that form the embryo–maternal communication. Therefore maintenance and support following implantation is crucial to completion of the intra-uterine growth process and so the normal development and growth of placental structures is of high genetic priority (Ulijaszek, Johnston and Preece, 1998).

The invention of radiography and then ultrasound has allowed clinicians a view into the normal and abnormal development of the individual *in utero*. Extensive studies have permitted any developing fetus to be mapped against a 'norm' and therefore to be assessed in terms of its intra-uterine progression. The most obvious features utilized within this category that are related to age evaluation are the appearance of primary centres of ossification of the skeleton, lengths of bones and indeed lengths of both body parts and the full length of the fetus. More detailed information on ossification can be found in Chapter 11. While the uterus is unquestionably a cocooned environment for the fetus, it still remains susceptible to both intrinsic and extrinsic influences, which may impact on how it grows and develops.

Although prenatal growth is influenced by the child's genetic composition, it is also affected by many factors that are of maternal control or under external environmental influence and these can include:

- Maternal weight

- Maternal age

- Health status and nutrition

- Blood pressure

- Intra-uterine constraints

- Parity

- Smoking

- Alcohol/drugs

- Emotional status

- Environmental pollution

- Altitude and so on.

It is alleged that only 20–40% of the variability in birth weight can be explained through fetal genes, whereas the greatest influences (60–80%) are controlled by epigenetic factors (Ulijaszek, Johnston and Preece, 1998). So while it is true that genetics will likely, in the first instance, take major control over the success of implantation and subsequent maintenance of the developing embryo and fetus, respectively, it is the epigenetic influences that will 'adjust' and fine tune the tempo of fetal growth and maturation, a situation that will continue when the child exits from the intra-uterine environment.

The relationship between the normal development of the fetus and the introduction of a teratogen was particularly evident following the introduction of the drug thalidomide as an anti-emetic to relieve maternal morning sickness. Limb defects are rare in humans, occurring in approximately 6 out of every 10 000 births, that is approx 0.06%, but between 1957 and 1961 a marked rise in the incidence of limb defects was observed. The teratogenic effects of thalidomide were not discovered until this sudden and unexpected increase in limb malformations was retraced to source. However, the drug was not removed from the market before over 7000 infants were affected (Stern, 1981; Brent, 2004; Leroi, 2005).

The introduced teratogen may take many forms, including prescriptive drugs, but more commonly in modern society it is alcohol, recreational drugs and environmental pollutants (including radiation) that result in the most serious and often irrecoverable effects to normal optimal growth and development (Wolraich, 2003). Different tissues present variable temporal windows of heightened sensitivity and so a teratogen introduced at one stage of the pregnancy may have devastating consequences whereas the same substance introduced several weeks later may have limited or indeed no perceivable effect. Once the fertilized ovum has implanted and a safe and adequate nutritional source is established, the developing fetus is not safe, or indeed immune, to teratogenic influences that can still cross the placental barrier.

The enhanced rate of fetal growth and therefore its almost insatiable requirement for a nutrient source, is directly related to the calorific demand placed not only at the organ and tissue levels but also at the cellular level where proliferation is at its peak. Figure 6.1 shows the growth curve for crown rump length (CRL) between 6

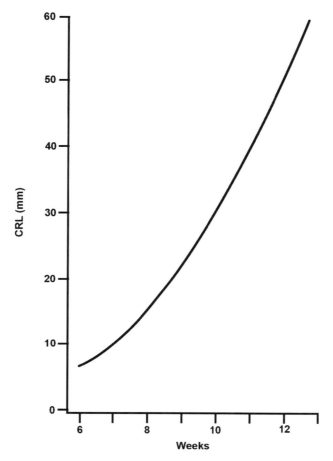

Figure 6.1   Growth in crown rump length in the first 14 weeks of intrauterine development.

Source: Redrawn from Ulijaszek, Johnston and Preece (1998).

and 12 weeks post-conception to show that this phase of development particularly reflects growth in 'size' rather than 'maturation' and therefore any adverse factor introduced or maintained through this stage of pregnancy will most likely affect the final birth size of the individual. Whether that child will be able to experience full 'catch up' when no longer *in utero* is another matter although remarkable catch up is possible (Prader, Tanner and von Harmack, 1963; Kulin *et al.*, 1982; Walker and Golden, 1988; Golden, 1991, 1994). As the uterine environment becomes more cramped for space, the CRL will decelerate in its growth rate and the emphasis on maturation becomes more prevalent in the third trimester of pregnancy to ensure that safe parturition is optimized by limiting the 'size' variable while increasing the 'maturation' capability.

6.2   Birth and Infancy

Birth represents an identifiable and eminently recordable event as the fetus passes from the intra-uterine to the external environment where it must be able to maintain and operate many of its body systems without assistance. Under normal circumstances, the cardiovascular, digestive, respiratory and excretory systems must be independently operational by the time the child is born and therefore these tissues are in advance with regards to maturity compared to other aspects of the body. The child is not required to walk at birth and neither is it expected to be able to feed itself as it is wholly dependent on its parental/caring source. Therefore at birth, several functions are relatively primitive in the human compared to many other mammals, which are largely responsible for self-locomotion and feeding survival either from birth or very shortly thereafter. It is anticipated therefore that mammals with a high social component to their society will generally require a variable period of total dependence following birth. Bogin (1999) refers to the stage of human life that occupies the first three years as 'infancy' and refers to this period as being when a child still retains dependency prior to it adopting a close-to-adult diet and some independence of social interaction.

Infancy is the period in which the child will show the most rapid growth velocity of any of the postnatal stages. Within the first year the child will increase its length by around 50% and double its birth weight. Figure 6.2 shows the velocity in height expressed as centimetres per year over the juvenile life span of the child, and clearly demonstrates that height velocity is at its peak during the first year after birth. During this infancy period, the child will start to develop the mechanism (i.e. the dentition) to prepare for separation from the maternal nutrition source and therefore the early development of the teeth represents a preparative stage for the weaning process.

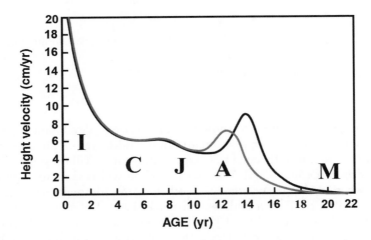

Figure 6.2 Growth height velocity curves for girls (grey) and boys (black) showing the postnatal stages for the pattern of human growth. I = infancy, C = childhood, J = juvenile, A = adolescence and M = mature adult.

Source: Redrawn from Bogin (1999).

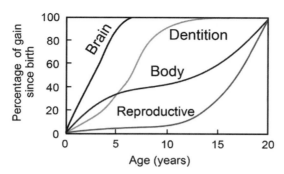

Figure 6.3 Growth curves for different body tissues.
Source: Redrawn from Scammon (1930).

Figure 6.3 shows that during infancy the two body tissues to show the steepest curve for growth and maturation are represented by the dentition and the neurological component of the central nervous system. The brain and spinal cord are precocious in terms of their development and already reach a plateau around 5–6 years of age, when growth will then start to slow down dramatically. For this reason, many of the clinical tests for normal growth and development in the infancy phase are tests of neurological maturation, for example can the child grasp your finger, can the child lift its head or can the child hear sounds or follow lights? All of these tests are designed to assess whether the motor neuronal connections are at the predicted stage of development for the chronological age of the child. When looking at skeletal development in relation to neuronal maturation, the precocious development of the orbits (eyes are direct brain outgrowths), the neurocranium and the vertebral column are all areas of skeletal development that are designed to protect the large neurological structures (Scheuer and Black, 2000) and therefore areas including the fusion of the occipital bone and the neural arch component of the vertebrae reflect this precocious maturation of the nervous system. The human brain grows more rapidly during infancy than almost any other tissue or organ of the body and takes the largest share of basal metabolic rate.

Cartoon artists understand what represents the immature and the adult form and seek to gain sympathy for their 'good' characters by reflecting a non-threatening appearance through representation of the largely infant form. Such characters, for example Elmer Fudd in the Bugs Bunny cartoons, are drawn with a bald large head, large eyes, small ears, small jaws and high voice. In contrast, the villains require to be more threatening and are often drawn to represent the male adult form with a long and large face, small eyes, large ears, head and facial hair, a deep voice and large jaws (e.g. Jafar in the Aladdin cartoons).

6.3 Childhood

The age of emergence of the last deciduous molar largely signals the end of infancy and signals a time when the infant can become virtually maternally independent in terms of breast feeding and enters the phase of childhood, which encompasses approximately ages 3–7 years. There is a rapid deceleration in growth as the child passes from infancy into childhood but the child is still dependent on others for basic survival requirements, including protection, food provision, clothing and so on. Post-weaning dependency is a characteristic of mammals with a highly developed social community, for example wolves, lions, elephants and some primates. No human child would survive if deprived of this care at the childhood stage (Ulijaszek, Johnston and Preece, 1998) and indeed there has been no substantiation of any claims that so-called 'feral' children can survive independently in this age group.

One of the most striking features about growth in this phase of the human life span is its predictability both in relation to the individual and different populations (Johnston, 1986). The epigenetic factors that may have been brought to bear upon the developing fetus *in utero* may now no longer influence the child (although others may have taken their place) and 'catch up' growth may have been established. Therefore there is a striking similarity in the growth profile across groups within this period of development and the growth charts used to form the basis of epidemiological and clinical evaluations are relatively standard throughout most societies (Tanner, Whitehouse and Takaishi, 1966; Cole, Freeman and Preece, 1998; Ulijaszek, 2001; Kuczmarksi *et al.*, 2002; Butte, Garza and de Onis, 2007).

Although perhaps more predictable in this period of the life span, there are still many extraneous factors that can bring about an alteration in the predicted path of growth and development. Possibly the most influential are socio-economic status, nutrition, disease and emotional well-being. Any factor that detracts from normal growth has the potential to leave its mark on the developing skeleton and dentition. A period of growth upset can result in growth being slowed down or even halted for a period of time and this can manifest as lines or bands of increased density in the shafts of the growing long bones, which can be evidenced from radiographs and CT scans. These 'arrest lines' or 'Harris lines' are a clear indication of a period of altered growth rate and are therefore an indicator that perhaps the individual has not reached, or indeed may not reach, their full genetic potential (Maat, 1984; Ogden 1984; Byers, 1991; Kapadia *et al.*, 1992; Aufderheide and Rodriguez-Martin, 1998).

Two of the most important growth-related features within the period defined by childhood are, first, the development of the permanent dentition and its partial eruption as it prepares to replace the deciduous teeth and, second, the completion of the growth of both the brain and the spinal cord. These result in changes being evident in the skull, vertebral column and jaws that can be specifically utilized for age evaluation purposes. Cabana, Jolicoeur and Michaud (1993) showed that human brain growth in terms of weight is largely complete at a mean age of seven years, which supports the timing of the maturation of the occipital bone in the skull and the fusion of the vertebrae at the neuro-central junctions to form a spinal canal that is close to adult size (Scheuer and Black, 2000).

Childhood is therefore also the period where other motor but also cognitive skills are most frequently tested, as this is the final period of neurological maturation. Of course, this also corresponds with the age at which most children commence their formal education and develop full speech-related interaction and independent thought. The mature adult gait is not achieved until around eight years of age and it is no accident that the early phase of childhood is referred to as the 'toddler' stage. By six years of age, the pelvis has grown sufficiently for the previously abdominal organs such as the bladder to fully descend into the pelvic cavity and thus the centre of gravity for mature and efficient bipedal locomotion can be achieved (Meschan, 1975). It is likely that this growth is closely aligned to the skeletal evidence of maturation in the pelvis particularly in relation to fusion at the ischio-pubic ramus, which is reported to occur between five and eight years of age (Scheuer and Black, 2000).

A mid-growth spurt in height was reported by Tanner (1947) to occur towards the end of the childhood period and this short-lived acceleration has been reported in about two thirds of healthy children examined. When it is detected it seems to occur around seven to eight years of age.

6.4   Juvenile

The juvenile stage was defined by Pereira and Altman (1985) as a time when the child is clearly prepubescent but largely dependent on their carer for survival (Blurton-Jones, 1993). It encompasses the period between about 7 and 10 years of age in girls and 12 years in boys. This is the period of the child's life when the acceleration (velocity) of growth is arguably at its lowest level since birth. It applies not only to the individual in general but also to most of the organs and tissues of the individual. There is little difference in growth achieved in this period between boys and girls. Even craniofacial growth is not particularly affected in this period as, for example, the first permanent molars are erupted and the second permanent molars will not erupt until later in the next developmental stage (Wilkinson, 2004). Therefore this is considered to be the time period where there is greatest parity in growth between the sexes, between individuals and allegedly between populations.

There is often a nadir in growth acceleration around 10 to 11 years of age in girls and 12 to 13 years in boys and this marks the end of the juvenile period and is the onset of the next important stage – adolescence.

6.5   Adolescence

The period of adolescence commences with the onset of puberty around 10–11 years in girls and around 12–13 years in boys (Sinclair, 1969). The adolescent period follows the nadir in growth velocity seen at the end of the juvenile period and is characterized by a protracted period of enhanced endocrine activity. The hypothalamic–pituitary–gonadal axis is stimulated and the subsequent hormonal effects influence the majority of tissues throughout the body. This is undeniably the age of sexual maturation but it will also coincide with peak height velocity, changes in fat patterning, hair growth, emotional changes, voice pattern alteration and the culmination of skeletal and dental maturation.

The characteristic secondary sexual changes are considered in some detail in Chapters 9 and 11. While this is an event that has an average age for commencement, duration and cessation, it is one that is greatly influenced by a number of factors, including genetics, nutrition, physical activity levels, medication and so on. The timing of onset and the duration of puberty will each play an important role in the final size and form of the mature adult. A precocious or a delayed puberty that is either curtailed or extended can result in a body size and shape that will largely be set for the remainder of the individual's adult life. Almost every tissue, but especially the skeleton, will be influenced by a rapid growth spurt during adolescence. Different regions will reach peak growth rate at different ages (Satake *et al.*, 1994). For example the study by Greil (1997) showed that while the peak growth velocity for the hand occurred around 10 years of age, it was 12 years for trunk length, leading to the well-known anatomical disharmony between trunk and extremity maturation. Therefore it is important that in the skeletal assessment of age during puberty, different areas of the skeleton should be assessed in relation to their peak growth velocity and maturational schedule.

Puberty is the period of maximum differentiation between the sexes which occurs both through hormonal influences on the skeleton, particularly in relation to alteration of the pelvic shape in preparation for child bearing in females but also in relation to testosterone production, which influences muscle mass in males (Tanner, 1962, 1978; Buckler, 1990). While the female adolescent changes may commence some two years earlier than in males, the duration and dimension of pubertal change is greater in the male and the result within a population is that the average adult male is both taller and heavier than the average female and displays a larger muscle mass (Alexander *et al.*, 1979). While this may be true within a population, the differences that occur between populations and indeed the differences that occur at the individual level will be greatly influenced by both genetic and environmental factors. Therefore it can be difficult to place exactly where an adolescent rests along the time continuum of their sub-adult profile.

Interestingly, Boas (1930) identified a correlation between the timing of onset of puberty and its duration. He found that the earlier the individual commences puberty, the greater will be their peak height velocity. Similarly, Largo *et al.* (1978) identified that children with slow rates of growth prior to the onset of puberty will tend to have an extended growth spurt.

6.6   Adult

Attaining final adult height is considered one of the defining characteristics of moving from adolescence into adulthood and corresponds to between 16 and 18 years in females and 18 to 21 years in males although this will vary significantly between populations. It is accepted that individuals who are exposed to adverse conditions, including under-nutrition, may start their growth spurt later and continue to increase in height up to at least 25 years of age (Maat, 2005). Growth in height will ultimately cease when the long bone epiphyses finally fuse to the diaphyses. The closer an individual progresses towards final cessation of growth, the narrower becomes the space of the growth plate between the epiphysis and the diaphysis until it is finally obliterated (Figure 6.4 and Chapter 11). The final growth

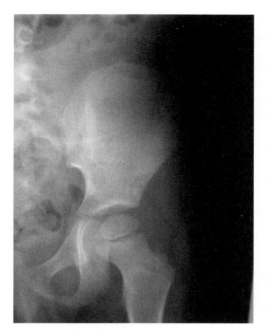

Figure 6.4 Radiograph of the left hip of a four-year-old boy. Note the radiolucent area between the epiphysis of the head of the femur and the diaphysis. This is the growth plate. A second growth area can be seen in the region of the greater trochanter and a third in the region of the ischiopubic ramus.

plate to close is the medial end of the clavicle (collar bone) and this is discussed in Chapter 11.

The transition into adulthood is therefore represented by attaining full reproductive maturation and final adult height. Thereafter the body enters a variable period of homoeostasis where some elements may still continue to exhibit maturation and growth (e.g. the medial end of the clavicle, pubic symphysis, cranial sutures, rib ends etc. – see Chapter 11) but significant changes such as those evidenced throughout childhood are absent.

6.7   Senescence

This period of the human life span is generally represented by a process of inadequate and ever decreasing normal growth processes which will vary significantly not only between individuals but between different populations. Only one event is uniformly experienced by all females and that is the cessation of menstruation at menopause. Although this generally occurs between 45 and 55 years of age, it is a highly variable event (Pavelka and Fedigan 1991; McKinlay, Brambilla and Posner, 1992; Whitehead, Whitcroft and Hillard, 1993). There is no similar recordable event for the human male. While there is a vague pattern of decline witnessed within the body, growth and age-related change is no longer predictable within the narrow limits found for younger individuals. Therefore it becomes extremely difficult to assign an age to an individual with any degree of accuracy when for example the individual is over 40 years of age – see Chapter 12. Under these circumstances, it is advised to use multiple methods of age estimation, each of which produces a range of potential ages and one can search for a likely age within the locale of the overlaps for these ranges.

6.8   Summary

Contrary to Shakespeare's 'seven ages of man' theory, this chapter has seen man's life profile grouped into nine categories dependent upon the changes that can be readily identified to occur within the age boundaries of that cohort:

- Embryo – conception to end of week 8

- Fetus – week 8 to birth

- Birth – a recordable event

- Infant – birth to around 3 years

- Child – approx. 3 years until 7 years

- Juvenile – approx. 7–10 years in girls and 7–12 in boys

- Adolescent – approx. 10–16 in girls and 12–18 in boys

- Adult – approx. 16–18 in girls and 18–20 in boys until around 40 years

- Senescent – around 40+ years.

It is important to realize that these categories are loosely based upon biological and developmental characteristics and are not conveniently arranged to suit the judicial age boundaries set by our legal systems. Therefore a prescribed biological feature used to assign an age to an individual (living or deceased) may not fall within an age cohort that is relevant to the judicial system. The example used in Chapter 13 is particularly pertinent to this realization. The question asked is whether the individual is less than 21 years of age or more than 21 years of age. This age is not characteristic of any particular age marker and therefore accuracy of prediction must be reduced. Within the nine categories listed above it is important to realize that in age estimation of the living, greatest focus will be placed on the boundary between categories 7 and 8 – between adolescence and adulthood.

The clinical investigators interested in child health and normal growth and development recognized that genetic and environmental factors would influence the position of these boundaries between these age groupings and were cognizant of the underlying biochemical, developmental and physical factors that enforced change on the individual within each group.

Child heath studies were prominent throughout Europe, the UK and the USA in the years following both the First and the Second World Wars, where the effects of societal alterations were investigated on the welfare of the child. Obviously longitudinal data was the preferred data set, which involved following the same child on more than one occasion and preferably over a significant number of years. However, this is a costly operation both in monetary terms and in commitment both on behalf of the researchers and the participants. A cross-sectional approach where many individuals from different age cohorts are measured only once is obviously less labour intensive and requires a reduced commitment to the project but its main disadvantage is that growth dynamics including velocity cannot be investigated. Therefore the longitudinal studies were favoured but in time most would fall away through lack of funding and those that spanned a useful period of time have become invaluable sources of data for growth studies of today. To compensate, many studies that commenced with the intention of becoming longitudinal studies were forced to compromise and include cross-sectional data so that many studies are of mixed data type.

It is well recognized though that a child from 1940 is representative only of a child from that era and from those circumstances. Direct comparison to a child of 2010 from a different socio-economic status or populational origin cannot be undertaken without significant cognizance of all potential sources of variation. It has been shown that direct comparisons of groups of individuals from the same genetic background but separated by time will show differences and this is referred to as a 'secular trend'. In a number of successive generations of a similar group it has been shown that average heights and weights are greater in more recent generations while the onset of puberty, adolescent growth spurt and menarche occur at progressively younger ages. For example, age at menarche in Polish girls has decreased by just over 4 months per decade between 1955 and 1978 (Wolanski, 1967; Hulanika and Waliszko, 1991).

Secular trends do not only occur within a static population over time, but are also evident in a migrant population and this has an important impact on child development. It is well known that a move to a higher socio-economic status has a positive impact on secular trend (Bogin, 1988). This phenomenon has been studied extensively in migrant populations in the US and it has been shown that in successive generations, the height of children of migrants continues to increase until it ultimately converges with that of the indigenous population and thus differs markedly from the parent population (Roche, 1979).

6.9 Growth Studies

The University of Iowa Child Welfare Research Station was probably one of the first longitudinal studies to be implemented. It ran from 1917 until 1970 and is generally represented by the work of Baldwin (1921) and Meredith (1935).

The Harvard Growth Study ran from 1922 to 1934 and is represented by the research undertaken by Dearborn, Rothney and Shuttleworth (1938) and Shuttleworth (1937), and the Harvard School of Public Health Study from 1929 to 1954, with research by authors including Stuart *et al.* (1962) and Valadian and Porter (1977).

The University of California Institute of Child Welfare undertook at least three growth studies – Berkley Growth study (1928–1984: Bayley and Pinneau 1952); Child Guidance Study (1930–1950: MacFarland); and Adolescent Growth Study (1932–1939: Stolz and Stolz, 1951; Jones 1949; Shock 1966).

The only study still to be active today is the Fels Research Institute Longitudinal Study at Yellow Springs, which commenced in 1929. Initially there were approximately 600 participants but these were supplemented by a further 350 who were offspring of a Fels participant and then by a further 90 who were grandchildren of the original Fels group. This ongoing data collection is privately funded and boasts a significant publication pedigree from researchers including Sontag (1971), Reynolds and Wines (1948), Garn and Rohmann (1962), Roche (1992) and Falkner (1966). Falkner had been instrumental in setting up the International Children's Centre (ICC) studies in both London and Paris (see below).

The Child Research Council study by the University of Colorado ran between 1930 and 1971 with publications from Washburn, Maresh (1943) and Maresh and Deming (1939).

The Philadelphia Centre for Research in Growth ran a programme from 1948 for which the data was utilized by researchers such as Krogman (1970) and Johnston (1974).

The Brush Foundation at the Western Reserve University in Cleveland, Ohio supported a programme between 1930 and 1971 and this was of course the source for one of the earliest hand/wrist atlases by Todd (1937), which was largely superseded by the work of Greulich and Pyle (1959). Other research on this material was reported by authors including Broadbent, Golden and Brown (1975).

In Europe there were two major studies within the UK that followed the Second World War. In the Oxford Health Survey by John Ryle, which ran between 1944 and 1964, 470 infants and children were recruited and measured between the ages of one month and five years. The data included both anthropometric measurements and radiographs and the results were reported by researchers including Ryle, Stewart and Acheson.

The British Harpenden Growth Study commenced in 1949 and ran until 1971, was directed by Jim Tanner and examined inhabitants of a children's home. A variety of anthropometric measurements were recorded in addition to radiographs of the skeleton and the dentition. The children were measured every 6 months between the age of 3 and 10 years, every 3 months during puberty, yearly until 20 and then every 5 years thereafter. The most prolific research to be produced from this data was by Tanner (1981), Tanner and Whitehouse (1975), Marshall (1975), Hughes and Tanner (1966) and Cameron, Tanner and Whitehouse (1982).

Throughout Europe, the ICC in France set up a series of coordinated studies – 1949–1969 London; 1953–1975 Paris; 1954–1980 Zurich; 1955–1975 Stockholm; 1955–1975 Brussels; 1954–1975 Dakar. All of these studies followed a standardized data recording procedure and resulted in some of the most widely quoted references in the field of auxology.

These twentieth century studies form the core around which age estimation in the child is achieved, certainly by the clinician. It must be recognized, though, that many of these studies are over 30 years old and the effects of secular trends must be taken into consideration if utilizing this data on other populations for the purposes of evaluating age. However, it should be recognized that this growth data was not designed to be used for the purposes of assigning a chronological age to an individual but was collected, analysed and reported for the purposes of studying child growth and development. Therefore caution must be observed when applying the formulae and methodologies from these longitudinal studies to a single individual from a modern era for judicial purposes. While it is unquestionably true that the field of forensic age evaluation stands on the shoulders of auxology giants who had the tenacious temperament to remain with long-term projects, many of these may be of limited applicability to the modern sample. However, longitudinal studies are expensive and it is unlikely that these will ever be repeated and therefore the new discipline of age estimation in the living must be very cautious of interpretation of its results when the mirror it is using reflects life as it was some time ago in the past and perhaps in a different part of the world. Therefore it is beholden upon the forensic community to design its own modern day methodology and establish global data collection strategies if the issue of age evaluation in the living is to become a robust judicial tool.

References

Alexander, R.D., Hoogland, J.L., Howard, R.D. *et al.* (1979) Sexual dimorphisms and breeding systems in pinnipeds, ungulates, primates and humans, in *Evolutionary Biology and Human Social Behavior: An Anthropological Perspective* (eds N.A. Chagnon and W. Irars), Duxbury Press, North Scituate, MA, pp. 402–435.

Aufderheide, A.C. and Rodriguez-Martin, C. (1998) *The Cambridge Encyclopedia of Human Palaeopathology*, Cambridge University Press, Cambridge.

Baldwin, B.T. (1921) *The Physical Growth of Children from Birth to Maturity*. University of Iowa Studies of Child Welfare, Vol. 1, No. 1, State University of Iowa Press, Iowa City, IA.

Bayley, N. and Pinneau, S.R. (1952) Tables for predicting adult height from skeletal age: revised standards for use with the Greulich–Pyle hand standards. *Journal of Pediatrics*, **40**, 423–441.

Blurton-Jones, N.G. (1993) The lives of hunter-gatherer children: effects of parental behaviour and parental reproductive strategy, in *Juvenile Primates* (eds M.E. Pereira and L.A. Fairbanks), Oxford University Press, Oxford, pp. 309–326.

Boas, F. (1930) Observations on the growth of children. *Science*, **72**, 44–48.

Bogin, B. (1988) Rural-to-urban migration, in *Aspects of Human Migration* (eds C.G.N. Mascie-Taylor and G.W. Lasker), Cambridge University Press, Cambridge, pp. 90–129.

Bogin, B. (1999) *Patterns of Human Growth*, 2nd edn, Cambridge University Press, Cambridge.

Brent, R.L. (2004) Utilization of animal studies to determine the effects and human risks of environmental toxicants (drugs, chemicals and physical agents). *Pediatrics*, **113**, 984–995.

Broadbent, B.H., Golden, W.H. and Brown R.G. (1975) *Bolton Standards of Dentofacial Developmental Growth*, C.V. Mosby, St Louis, MO.

Buckler, J. (1990) *A Longitudinal Study of Adolescent Growth*, Springer-Verlag, London.

Butte, N.F., Garza, C. and de Onis, M. (2007) Evaluation of the feasibility of international growth standards for school-aged children and adolescents. *Journal of Nutrition*, **137**, 153–157.

Byers, S. (1991) Technical note: calculation of age at formation of radiopaque transverse lines. *American Journal of Physical Anthropology*, **85**, 339–343.

Cabana, T., Jolicoeur, P. and Michaud, J. (1993) Prenatal and postnatal growth and allometry of stature, head circumference and brain weight in Quebec children. *American Journal of Human Biology*, **5**, 93–99.

Cameron, J., Tanner, J.M. and Whitehouse, R.H. (1982) A longitudinal analysis of the growth of limb segments in adolescence. *Annals of Human Biology*, **9**, 211–220.

Cole, T.J., Freeman, J.V. and Preece, M.A. (1998) British 1990 growth reference centiles for weight, height, body mass index and head circumference fitted by maximum penalized likelihood. *Statistics in Medicine*, **17**, 407–429.

Dearborn, W.F., Rothney, J.W.M. and Shuttleworth, F.K. (1938) *Data on the Growth of Public School Children*, Monographs of the Society for Research in Child Development, Vol. 3, No. 1, Society for Research in Child Development, Washington, DC.

Falkner, F. (1966) *Human Development*, W.B. Saunders, Philadelphia, PA.

Garn, S.M. and Rohmann, C.G. (1962) X-linked inheritance of developmental timing in man. *Nature*, **196**, 695–696.

Golden, M.H. (1991) The nature of nutritional deficiency in relation to growth failure and poverty. *Acta Paediatrica Scandinavica*, **374**, 95–110.

Golden, M.H. (1994) Is complete catch-up possible for stunted malnourished children? *European Journal of Clinical Nutrition*, **48**, S58–S71.

Greil, H. (1997) Sex, body type and timing in bodily development – trend statements based on a cross-sectional anthropometric study, in *Growth and Development in a Changing World* (eds D.F. Roberts, P. Rudan and T. Skaric-Juric), Croatian Anthropological Society, Zagreb, pp. 57–88.

Greulich, W.W. and Pyle, S.I. (1959) *Radiographic Atlas of Skeletal Development of the Hand and Wrist*, 2nd edn, Stanford University Press, Stanford, CA.

Hughes, P.C.R. and Tanner, J.M. (1966) The development of carpal bone fusion as seen in serial radiographs. *British Journal of Radiology*, **39**, 943–949.

Hulanika, B. and Waliszko, A. (1991) Deceleration of age at menarche in Poland. *Annals of Human Biology*, **18**, 507–513.

Johnston, F.E. (1974) Control of age at menarche. *Human Biology*, **46**, 159–171.

Johnston, F.E. (1986) Somatic growth of the infant and preschool child, in *Human Growth*, 2nd edn, Vol. 2 (eds F. Falkner and J.M. Tanner), Plenum Press, New York, pp. 3–24.

Jones, H.E. (1949) *Motor Performance and Growth: A Developmental Study of Static Dynamomometric Strength*, University of California Press, Berkeley, CA.

Kapadia, Y.K., Bowman, J.E., MacLaughlin, S.M. and Scheuer, J.L. (1992) A study of Harris lines in the juvenile skeletons from St Brides. *Annals of Human Biology*, **19**, 328–329.

Krogman, W.M. (1970) *Growth of the Head, Face, Trunk and Limbs of Philadelphia White and Negro Children of Elementary and High School Age*, Monographs of the Society for Research in Child Development, Vol. **35**, No. 3, Society for Research in Child Development, Washington, DC.

Kuczmarksi, R.J., Ogden, C.L., Guo, S.S. *et al.* (2002) 2000 CDC growth charts for the United States: methods and Developments, *Vital and Health Statistics*, Series 11, No. 246.

Kulin, H.E., Bwibo, N., Mutie, D. and Santner, S.J. (1982) The effect of chronic childhood malnutrition on pubertal growth and development. *American Journal of Clinical Nutrition*, **36**, 527–536.

Largo, R.H., Gasser, Th., Prader, A. *et al.* (1978) Analysis of the adolescent growth spurt using smoothing spline functions. *Annals of Human Biology*, **5**, 421–434.

Leroi, A.M. (2005) *Mutants: On the Form, Varieties and Errors of the Human Body*, Harper Perennial, London.

Maat, G.J.R. (1984) Dating and rating of Harris lines. *American Journal of Physical Anthropology*, **63**, 291–299.

Maat, G.J.R. (2005) Two millennia of male stature development and population health and wealth in the Low Countries. *International Journal of Osteoarchaeology*, **15**, 276–290.

Maresh, M.M. (1943) Growth of major long bones in healthy children. *American Journal of Diseases of Children*, **66**, 227–257.

Maresh, M.M. and Deming, J. (1939) The growth of the long bones in 80 infants. Roentgenograms versus anthropometry. *Child Development*, **10**, 91–106.

Marshall, W.A. (1975) The relationship of variations in children's growth rates to season climatic variation. *Annals of Human Biology*, **2**, 243–250.

McKinlay, S.M., Brambilla, D.J. and Posner, J.G. (1992) The normal menopause transition. *American Journal of Human Biology*, **4**, 37–46.

Meredith, H.V. (1935) *The Rhythm of Physical Growth*, University of Iowa Studies of Child Welfare, Vol. **11**, No. 3, State University of Iowa Press, Iowa City, IA.

Meschan, I. (1975) *An Atlas of Anatomy Basic to Radiology*, W.B. Saunders, Philadelphia, PA.

Ogden, J.A. (1984) Growth slowdown and arrest lines. *Journal of Pediatric Orthopedics*, **4**, 409–415.

Pavelka, M.S. and Fedigan, L.M. (1991) Menopause: a comparative life history perspective. *Yearbook of Physical Anthropology*, **34**, 13–38.

Pereira, M.E. and Altman, J. (1985) Development of social behaviour in free-living nonhuman primates, in *Nonhuman Primate Models for Human Growth and Development* (ed. E.S. Watts), Alan R. Liss, New York, pp. 217–309.

Prader, A., Tanner, J.M. and von Harmack, G.A. (1963) Catch-up growth following illness or starvation. An example of developmental canalization in man. *Journal of Pediatrics*, **62**, 646–659.

Reynolds, E.L. and Wines, J.V. (1948) Individual differences in physical changes associated with adolescent girls. *American Journal of Diseases in Children*, **75**, 329–350.

Roche, A.F. (1979) *Secular Trends in Human Growth, Maturation and Development*, Monographs of the Society for Research in Child Development, Vol. **44**, Society for Research in Child Development, Washington, DC.

Roche, A.F. (1992) *Growth, Maturation and Body Composition: The Fels Longitudinal Study 1929–1991*, Cambridge University Press, Cambridge.

Satake, T., Malina, R.M., Tanaka, S. and Kirutka, F. (1994) Individual variation in the sequence of ages at peak velocity in seven body dimensions. *American Journal of Human Biology*, **6**, 359–367.

Scammon R.E. (1930) The measurement of the body in childhood, in *The Measurement of Man* (eds J.A. Harris, C.M. Jackson, D.G. Peterson and R.E. Scammon). University of Minnesota Press, Minneapolis, MN, pp. 173–215.

Scheuer, L. and Black, S. (2000) *Developmental Juvenile Osteology*, Academic Press, London.

Shock, N.W. (1966) Physiological growth, in *Human Development* (ed. F Falkner), W.B. Saunders, Philadelphia, PA, pp. 150–177.

Shuttleworth, F.K. (1937) *Sexual Maturation and the Physical Growth of Girls Age Six to Nineteen*, Monographs of the Society for Research in Child Development, Vol. 4, No. 3, Society for Research in Child Development, Washington, DC.

Sinclair, D. (1969) *Human Growth after Birth*, Oxford University Press, London.

Sontag, L.W. (1971) The history of longitudinal research: implications for the future. *Child Development*, **42**, 987–1002.

Stern, L. (1981) In vivo assessment of the teratogenic potential of drugs in humans. *Obstetrics and Gynecology*, **58** (5 suppl), 3S–8S.

Stolz, H.R. and Stolz, L.M. (1951) *Somatic Development of Adolescent Boys: A Study of the Growth of Boys during the Second Decade of Life*, Macmillan, New York.

Stuart, H.C., Pyle, S.I., Cornoni, J. and Reed, R.B. (1962) Onsets, completions and spans of ossification in the 29 bone growth centres of the hand and wrist. *Pediatrics*, **29**, 237–249.

Tanner, J.M. (1947) The morphological level of personality. *Proceedings of the Royal Society of Medicine*, **40**, 301–303.

Tanner, J.M. (1962) *Growth at Adolescence*, 2nd edn, Blackwell Scientific, Oxford.

Tanner, J.M. (1978) *Foetus into Man: Physical Growth from Conception to Maturity*, Open Books, London.

Tanner, J.M. (1981) *A History of the Study of Human Growth*, Cambridge University Press, Cambridge.

Tanner, J.M., Whitehouse, R.H. and Takaishi, M. (1966) Standards from birth to maturity for height, weight, height velocity and weight velocity: British children, 1965. *Archives of Disease in Childhood*, **41**, 613–635.

Tanner, J.M. and Whitehouse, R.H. (1975) Clinical longitudinal standards for height, weight, height velocity, weight velocity and the stages of puberty. *Archives of Disease in Childhood*, **51**, 170–179.

Todd, T.W. (1937) *Atlas of Skeletal Maturation*, C.V. Mosby, St Louis, MO.

Ulijaszek, S.J. (2001) Secular trends in growth: the narrowing of ethnic differences in stature. *Nutrition Bulletin*, **26**, 43–51.

Ulijaszek, S.J., Johnston, F.E. and Preece, M.A. (1998) *The Cambridge Encyclopedia of Human Growth and Development*, Cambridge University Press, Cambridge.

Valadian, I. and Porter, D. (1977) *Physical Growth and Development from Conception to Maturity*, Little, Brown, and Co., Boston, MA.

Walker, S.P. and Golden, M.H. (1988) Growth in length of children recovering from severe malnutrition. *European Journal of Clinical Nutrition*, **42**, 395–404.

Whitehead, M.I., Whitcroft, S.I.J. and Hillard, T.C. (1993) *An Atlas of Menopause*, Parthenon, New York.

Wilkinson, C. (2004) *Forensic Facial Reconstruction*, Cambridge University Press, Cambridge.

Wolanski, N. (1967) Basic problems in physical development in man in relation to the evaluation of development of children and youth. *Current Anthropology*, **8**, 355–360.

Wolraich, M.L. (2003) *Disorders of Development and Learning*, 3rd edn, B.C. Decker, Ontario.

7

Growth, Maturation and Age

Noël Cameron and Laura L. Jones
Centre for Human Development, Department of Human Sciences,
Loughborough University, Loughborough, Leicestershire LE11 3TU, UK

7.1 Growth, Maturation and Age

Growth, maturation and age are related within the scientific study of human growth (auxology) like the muses of Delphi producing a pleasing harmony only when played with an understanding of their complexity and interdependence. To describe one without regard for the biological status of the others is to ignore this fundamentally important relationship.

The process of maturation is continuous throughout life – it begins at conception and ends at death (Cameron, 1984), thus encompassing the full range of chronological time associated with the life span. Because maturation is intimately linked with physical growth, it is important to differentiate between the two. Bogin (1999) defines growth as 'a quantitative increase in size or mass', such as increases in height and weight. In contrast, maturation is defined as 'a progression of changes, either quantitative or qualitative, that lead from an undifferentiated or immature state to a highly organized, specialized and mature state'.

7.1.1 The Concept of Time

To understand the process of maturation, one must first consider the relationship between maturation and chronological age. Maturation is not linked to time in a chronological sense. In other words, one year of chronological time is not equivalent to one year of maturational 'time'. This is clearly demonstrated in Figure 7.1, which illustrates three boys and three girls of precisely the same chronological age but displaying different degrees of maturity, as evidenced by the appearance of

Age Estimation in the Living: The Practitioners Guide   Sue Black, Anil Aggrawal and Jason Payne-James
© 2010 John Wiley & Sons, Ltd

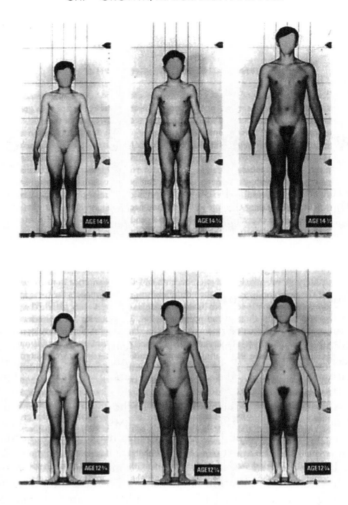

Figure 7.1 Three boys aged 14.75 years and three girls aged 12.75 years at differing stages of maturity. (With kind permission from Tanner, J.M. (1962) *Growth at Adolescence*, 2nd edn, Blackwell Scientific Publications, Oxford. Facing, Page 29).

secondary sexual characteristics (genitalia in boys, breasts in girls and pubic hair in both sexes). In addition, they exhibit differences in the proportion and distribution of subcutaneous fat and the development of the skeleton and musculature that result in sexually dimorphic adult body shapes. There is clearly variation of maturity about any chronological age and while each individual has passed through the same chronological time span, they have done so at differing rates of maturation or at different maturational 'tempos'.

Roy M. Acheson (1966) elegantly described the problem of 'time' within the development of skeletal maturity.

Because maturation is distinct from growth it merits a distinct scale of measurement, indeed the whole basis of the medical and scientific interest it attracts is that it does not proceed at the same rate in the various members of a random group of healthy children. The corollary of this is that the unit of measurement, 'the skeletal year', does not have the same meaning for any two healthy children, nor even … does a skeletal year necessarily have the same meaning for two bones in a single healthy child.

—Acheson, 1966, p. 471.

There is therefore a problem with the use of an age scale to represent maturity. It fails at the extreme because no particular age can be associated with full maturity and prior to full maturity, it fails because of the lack of a constant relationship between maturity and time both between and within the sexes. For instance, when using an 'atlas' technique to assess skeletal maturity (e.g. the Greulich-Pyle atlas of the hand and wrist; Greulich and Pyle, 1959) the final 'standards' for males and females correspond to an 'age' of 18 years but in fact represent full maturity or the maturity to be found in any individual who has achieved total epiphyseal fusion regardless of his or her actual chronological age.

To overcome this problem in the assessment of skeletal maturity Acheson (1954, 1957) and later Tanner and his colleagues (1959; Tanner, Whitehouse and Healy, 1962, 1983) developed the 'bone-specific scoring' techniques in which numerical scores were assigned to the maturity of each bone rather than a bone 'age'. Acheson's earlier attempt (the 'Oxford method') gave scores of 1, 2, 3 and so on to each stage. However, this was a nominal rather than an interval scale and thus the differences between scores were not equivalent; the 'difference' between stage 1 and stage 2 was not necessarily equivalent, in terms of the advancement of maturity, to the difference between stages 2 and 3. Tanner's basic principle was that the development of each single bone, within a selected area, reflected the *single* process of maturation. Ideally, the scores from each bone in a particular area should be the same and the common score would be the individual's maturity. However, such scores would not be the same because of the large gaps between successive events in a single bone. Thus the scoring process would need to minimize the overall disagreement between different bones. The disagreement is measured by the sum of squares of deviations of bone scores about the mean score, and it is this sum that is minimized. In order to avoid what Tanner described as the 'trivial solution' of perfect agreement by giving the same scores to each stage, the scores were constrained on a scale of 0 to 100, that is each bone starts at zero and matures at 100. In essence, each maturity indicator is rated on a maturity scale from 0% maturity to 100% maturity. Without dwelling on the mathematics, which are given in detail by Tanner *et al.* (1983), the principle is an important one and should be applied to any *new* system of assessing maturity. In addition, the bone-specific scoring approach can be applied to an appropriate sample of radiographs from any population to derive maturity norms.

The principle of scoring maturity indicators was later applied to the assessment of dental maturity by Demirjian, Goldstein and Tanner (1973) but, to date, has not been applied to other attempts at maturational assessment such as secondary sexual development. The reason for this apparent neglect may be because we still use the staging system originally developed by Nicholson and Harley (1952) and modified by Tanner and his colleagues (Tanner, 1962). Only five stages are used within any particular area and these are often difficult to assess accurately. Also secondary sexual development takes place over a relatively short period of time, say between 9 and 17 years in girls, compared to the birth to adulthood temporal basis of skeletal maturity. Thus one is faced with fewer maturity indicators within a short period of time and the application of a scoring technique has seemed inappropriate. However, other aspects of skeletal maturity may lend themselves to a scoring system. Cranial suture closure, for instance, has rarely been investigated as an indicator of maturity in children. Yet this latter technique is important in biological anthropology in which the maturity of skeletal remains is of forensic interest to determine chronological age. Meindl and Lovejoy (1985) have described a 'revised method' for determining skeletal age using the lateral-anterior sutures. They use a scoring system which is the equivalent of Acheson's scoring system for the Oxford method and in so doing repeat the erroneous selection of a nominal scale implying that differences between scores are equivalent, that is, that the difference between stages 1 and 2 is the same as that between stages 2 and 3.

7.1.2   Maturity Indicators

In order to quantify maturational variation and create standards of normal variation, various 'maturity indicators' have been identified that have a known distribution at each chronological age. Maturity indicators are defined as 'definable and sequential changes in any part or parts of the body that are characteristic of the progression of the body from immaturity to maturity' (Cameron, 1997). Cameron (1997, 2002) identified six key criteria that maturity indicators must meet for them to be considered useful:

1. they must possess *universality* in that they must be present in all normal children of both sexes,

2. they must appear *sequentially* and in the same sequence in all children,

3. they must easily *discriminate* between those who are immature and those who are mature,

4. maturity indicators must be *reliable* so that they provide consistent results when repeated,

5. they must show a *valid* measure of maturity, and

6. they must show the *complete* path from immaturity to maturity.

The maturity indicators most commonly used āre within the processes of (i) skeletal development, (ii) dental development, and (iii) the development of secondary sexual characteristics. These indicators will be discussed in brief here as they are internationally accepted as being reliable in the estimation of maturity but will be covered in greater detail in Chapters 9–11.

7.1.3   Maturational Variation

We must appreciate that there is variability of maturation *within* the individual. For instance, while skeletal and secondary sexual maturation are associated they are not correlated so significantly that one can categorically associate a particular stage of sexual maturation with a particular skeletal 'age' (Marshall and Tanner, 1969, 1970). In the closest association, of skeletal age to menarcheal age, it is possible to state that a girl with a skeletal age less than 12 years is unlikely to have experienced menarche and that one with a skeletal age of 15 years is likely to be post-menarcheal. We cannot state with any real degree of confidence that the association of these two maturational processes is closer than that.

7.1.4   Uneven Maturation

Maturational variation covers two aspects: (i) the variation of maturation *within* a process, and (ii) the variation of maturation *between* processes. The former aspect may be observed within sexual maturation from the data published by Marshall and Tanner (1969, 1970) on British children. They illustrated variation by investigating the percentage of girls or boys within any particular stage of development of one indicator of maturation when they entered a particular stage of another indicator. For instance, 84% of girls were in at least stage 2 of breast development when they entered stage 2 of pubic hair development. In other words, they did not enter pubertal maturation in both breast and pubic hair development simultaneously. Breast development for the vast majority was the first stage of puberty followed by pubic hair development. Similarly 39% of girls were already adult for breast development when they became adult for pubic hair development.

A similar pattern of variation was observed in males, with 99% of boys starting genitalia development prior to pubic hair development. This variation is critical when combining different maturity indicators to arrive at a single score. Within clinical situations, for instance, the difficulties in rating accurately the various stages of breast, genitalia or pubic hair development within the Tanner five-point classification have led to the combination of the stages into a three- or four-point 'pubertal' staging technique. In the three-point technique, stage P1 represents the pre-pubertal state (B1/G1; PH1) and stage P3 the post-pubertal state (B5/G5; PH5). All indicators of maturational change between these two extremes have been combined into the P2 stage. Using this method, variations within individuals between the different aspects of secondary sexual development are impossible to quantify and, in terms of research to investigate variability in maturation, the pubertal staging technique loses significant sensitivity. The variation of maturation between different aspects of maturity presents difficulties in implying a general maturational level to the individual. Entry into the early stages of puberty is not, for instance, associated with any particular level of skeletal maturity except in the broadest sense. The only real exception to this rule, with regard to skeletal and sexual maturation, is menarcheal age, in which skeletal age and chronological age are correlated at a level of $r = 0.35$ and in which menarche tends to occur at a skeletal age of 12.5–14.0 'years' regardless of chronological age (Marshall and Tanner, 1969).

7.1.5   Sexual Dimorphism

Ideally, any method that assesses maturity should be able to assess the same process of maturation in both males and females. That criterion is true of skeletal and dental maturity assessment methods. It is not, of course, true of all aspects of secondary sexual development although the sex-specific assessment methods have a great deal in common. In the former methods, sexual dimorphism is accounted for by having sex-specific scores for each bone or tooth, and in the latter by identifying equivalent functional processes in the different sexes. However, the interpretation of maturation, or the meaning of the attainment of a particular level of maturity, may be different within the sexes. For instance, it could be argued that spermarche and menarche are equivalent stages of maturation in males and females yet their position within the pattern of growth is quite different and thus their association with other aspects of maturation also differs. Extensive data on menarche demonstrates that it occurs following peak height velocity and towards the latter part of secondary sexual development, that is, in breast stage 3, 4 or 5. Relatively sparse data on spermarche identifies its occurrence at approximately between 13 and 14 years in boys, which would be in the early or middle part of the adolescent growth spurt and thus indicative of an earlier stage of pubertal maturation (Nielsoen *et al.*, 1986; Guízar-Vázquez *et al.*, 1992).

7.1.6   Maturity and Size

Maturation is not related to size except in very general terms; a small human is likely to be a child and thus less mature than a large human, who is more likely to be an adult. This might indicate that size should in some way be included in a consideration of maturation. Indeed, the early methods of skeletal maturity assessment by planimetry used precisely that reasoning. It is now clearly recognized that, except in very general terms, size does not play a part in the assessment of maturation. Size does, however, enter assessment as a maturity indicator, as a ratio measure. For example, the maturity indicator for stage D in the radius of the TWII system is the fact that the epiphysis is 'half or more' the width of the metaphysis, that is the size is relative to another structure within the same area. However, except for such a ratio situation, the only maturity assessment method that uses a quantitative indicator of maturity is testicular volume: 4 ml represents the initiation of pubertal development and 12 ml mid-puberty (Tanner and Whitehouse, 1976). This is not to say that there is no variation in testicular volume. Like all aspects of growth and development, variability is an inherent aspect of testicular growth.

There are six considerations that have governed the development of techniques for the assessment of maturation:

1. the relationship of maturity to time,

2. the quantification of the continuous process of maturation by using discrete events,

3. the relative independence of different processes of maturation within the individual,

4. the appreciation of uneven maturation,

5. sexual dimorphism, and

6. the lack of a relationship between maturity and size.

7.2   Assessment of Maturation

7.2.1   Skeletal Maturity

Skeletal maturity is a measure of how far the bones in an anatomical area have progressed towards maturity. This progression is not usually related to size but to shape, the appearance of articular surfaces and their position relative to other neighbouring bones as visualized from a radiograph. An easily identifiable set of maturity indicators may be applied to the maturation of the skeleton providing that the radiographs of the pertinent areas of the body (typically the hand–wrist) are obtained in the correct way, that is with correct positioning of the limb, the correct X-ray tube–film distance and correct exposure. Two approaches for the assessment of skeletal maturity are regularly used in the literature: (i) the atlas technique (Greulich and Pyle, 1959) and (ii) bone-specific scoring techniques (Tanner *et al.*, 1975, 1983, 2001; Roche, Chumlea and Thissen, 1988; Chumlea, Roche and Thissen, 1989). Atlas and bone-specific scoring techniques rely on the fact that the epiphyses of long bones and ossification centres of round bones pass through a series of visible changes in shape and in the appearance of articular surfaces as they mature. These changes in shape and appearance constitute the maturity indicators. The rating and scoring of these indicators leads to the determination of a 'skeletal age' or 'bone age'.

7.2.2   Dental Maturity

Dental development is best assessed using the method proposed by Demirjian, Goldstein and Tanner (1973) and Demirijian and Goldstein (1976). This method involves taking panoramic radiographs of the mandible and maxilla and scoring the stages of formation and calcification of seven mandibular teeth, much like the method used to assess skeletal maturation of the hand–wrist. Concern over the exposure of children to radiation has led to tooth emergence in the oral cavity being the most commonly used method to assess dental development. The emergence of teeth above the level of the gum is recorded through oral inspection or in a dental impression. There are, however, inherent limitations to this method: (i) while this application may be useful for population groups it must be recognized that there is a high probability of inaccuracies for any individual child, (ii) little information is available during periods when no variation in the number of teeth occurs, and (iii) different definitions of 'eruption' exist in the literature, including the moment the tooth pierces the gum to when the tooth is halfway between the gum and its final position.

7.2.3 Secondary Sexual Development

It is obvious from Figure 7.1 that one of the most visible indicators of maturity is the advancement of the secondary sexual characteristics from their pre-pubertal to their post-pubertal configurations. The majority of studies investigating secondary sexual characteristic development use the Tanner staging technique (Tanner, 1962). The continuous processes of breast development in girls, genital development in boys and pubic hair development in both sexes are split into five discrete stages (B1–B5, G1–G5 and PH1–PH5). Stage 1 is pre-pubertal, stages 2–4 peri-pubertal and stage 5 post-pubertal. The initiation of puberty occurs when an adolescent progresses from stage 1 to stage 2 and adulthood is reached when an adolescent progresses from stage 4 to stage 5. The fact that genitalia/breasts and pubic hair are rated separately is in recognition of their development occurring via two different endocrine pathways, the former via the hypothalamic–pituitary–gonadal (HPG) axis and the latter via the hypothalamic–pituitary–adrenal axis.

7.2.4 Independence of Methods

These three systems of assessing maturity are those currently employed by the vast majority of experts in this field of human sciences. It is evident that the systems have all acquired measurement scales either of discrete or continuous type to facilitate numeration and to assess variation in the appearance of maturity indicators. Because they are under different forms of biological control it would be inappropriate to combine the skeletal, dental and sexual indicators to provide an overall estimate of maturity. They should all be viewed as independent assessments of maturity with general but not specific association. A child may not conform to the same maturational age when assessed by the three different systems. Even within the same process, variations in maturity may be apparent. Thus an understanding of the underlying biology is required for appropriate interpretation.

7.3 Secular Trends

There is a further factor that confounds the interpretation of maturational timing. Maturity indicators are known to be subject to a phenomenon known as the 'secular trend'. A secular trend refers to the process of change in size or maturation over at least one biological generation (approximately 20–25 years); in other words, this is a trend for maturity indicators to occur at progressively younger ages with each succeeding generation. To use secondary sexual development as an example, over the past two decades, there have been numerous papers that have provided evidence for a secular trend in the timing of sexual maturation in different populations worldwide. For example in the USA (Wattigney *et al.*, 1999; Freedman *et al.*, 2002; Sun *et al.*, 2002; Anderson, Dallaland and Must, 2003; Herman-Giddens, 2006), the UK (Kaplowitz and Oberfield, 1999), the Netherlands (Fredriks *et al.*, 2000), Brazil (Silva and Padez, 2006), Italy (Danubio *et al.*, 2004), Egypt (Hosny *et al.*, 2005), South Korea (Hwang *et al.*, 2003), Thailand (Mahachoklertwattana *et al.*, 2002), Cameroon (Pasquet *et al.*, 1999) and South Africa (Jones *et al.*, 2009a). In contrast, other studies have suggested that in recent decades there has been a slowing down or even a halt in the secular trend towards earlier puberty in several populations, including the USA (Viner, 2002; Slyper, 2006), the UK (Whincup *et al.*, 2001), Denmark (Juul *et al.*, 2006), Belgium (Hauspie, Vercauteren and Susanne, 1996), Norway (Hauspie, Vercauteren and Susanne, 1996) and South Africa (Jones *et al.*, 2009b).

So why are the results from these different studies somewhat contradictory? First, making comparisons between studies is difficult due to a number of confounding influences, including socio-economic status (SES), ethnic group, the temporal context of the study, the assessment procedure and the statistical methods employed. Second, the evidence for a secular trend is often based on the assumption that the relationship is linear; however, the relationship may well be curvilinear with a lower 'genetic or physiological ceiling' for age at sexual maturation being attained if there are no environmental constraints such as poor nutrition. From the data that are available it is clear that in developing countries, particularly those undergoing transition, there is a continuing secular trend towards earlier maturation; that is, they have not yet reached a plateau as environmental conditions continue to constrain the genetic predisposition for pubertal timing. In contrast to these data for developing countries, there is robust evidence to suggest that in developed countries, there has been a plateau in the age at sexual maturation over recent decades (Whincup *et al.*, 2001; Viner, 2002; Chumlea *et al.*, 2003). This idea of a lower genetic or physiological limit has been further supported by the fact that a number of European countries are still experiencing secular increases in height in parallel to a plateau in age at menarche (Cole, 2000).

In contrast to the large number of studies examining the evidence for a secular trend in sexual maturation, there are relatively few contemporary studies of secular trends in skeletal and dental development. There is evidence to suggest a secular trend in skeletal maturation in Australia (boys only) (Ranjitkar, 2006), South Africa (Hawley *et al.*, 2009) and Hong Kong (girls only) (So, 1990). It is not proven that a secular trend in dentition exists although there are published reports both proposing and opposing a secular trend (Derijian, 1978). A small number of more recent studies have shown evidence for advanced tooth emergence in Japan (Höffding, 1984) and Finland (Eskeli, 1999). Studies of secular trends in skeletal and dental development are infrequent, due in part to a lack of comparable methodologies across time.

Therefore, it is difficult to examine the influence of secular trends on these maturity indicators; that is, we do not know if they have reached their 'genetic ceiling' in unconstrained populations.

7.4   Worldwide Variation in the Timing of Maturation

Historically there have been a number of studies of dental, skeletal and secondary sexual development, in particular age at menarche, both within and between populations across the world. However, comparisons are difficult because of variation in the study design, the characteristics of the samples of interest and the methods used to determine maturity. While we only present examples of some of the most recent data, comprehensive summaries of the variation in the rate of maturation between different population groups are to be found in Eveleth and Tanner (1976, 1976) and Parent *et al.* (2003).

7.4.1   Secondary Sexual Development

Secondary sexual development is perhaps the easiest of the three maturational processes to compare within and between populations because age at menarche and the initiation of puberty can be identified as specific maturational events. Figures 7.2, 7.3 and 7.4 provide contemporaneous estimates of age at menarche and age at the initiation of breast development in girls, and genital development in boys, from different urban populations split by ethnic group. While studies of urban populations have been included in this chapter, it is well documented that rural populations are generally delayed in comparison to their urban peers (Eveleth and Tanner, 1990).

Contemporary estimates of age at menarche (Figure 7.2) for Black (including African American) girls show that they are, on average, in advance of their Asian and White peers with the exception of Greek and Hong Kong girls. Average age at menarche for Black/African American girls varies between 12.2 years (95% confidence interval [95% CI] = 12.0, 12.4 (Wu, Mendola and Buck, 2002), 12.2 years (95% CI = 12.0, 12.4)) for high SES Nigerian girls (Ofuya, 2007) and 12.4 years (95% CI = 12.2, 12.6) for low-middle SES Black South African girls (Jones *et al.*, 2009a). These data highlight that there is no statistically significant difference in age at menarche between Black girls living in differing socio-economic and nutritional milieu. In Asian and White girls, there is evidence of statistically significant differences in age at menarche between girls living in different environments. Urban Chinese girls (12.8 years, 95% CI = 12.7, 12.9) (Hesketh, Ding and Tomkins, 2002) are significantly delayed compared to Hong Kong girls (12.1 years, 95% CI = 12.0, 12.2) (Lam *et al.*, 2002) and delayed compared to Thai girls (12.5 years, no variance reported) (Pawloski, 2008). For European White girls, Greek girls present with the youngest age at menarche at 12.3 years (95% CI = 12.2, 12.4) (Papadimitriou, 2008) and Danish girls present with the oldest age at menarche at 13.4 years (95% CI = 13.2, 13.6) (Juul *et al.*, 2006). Swedish, Dutch and English girls all present with similar ages of 12.8 years (no variance reported) (Edgardh, 2000), 12.9 (95% CI =

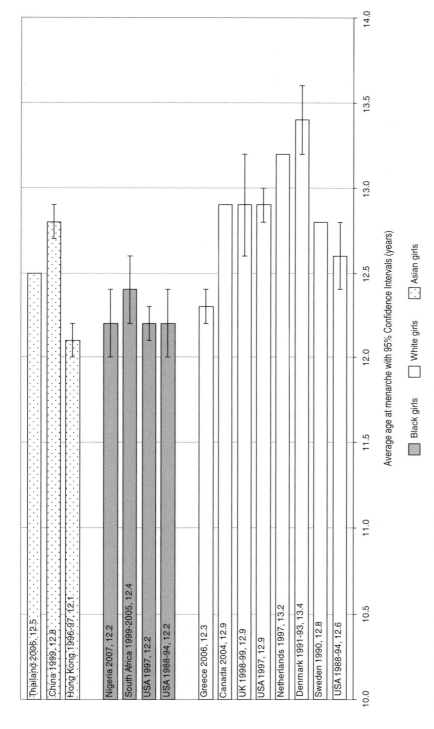

Figure 7.2 Contemporary estimates of average age (95% confidence interval) at menarche (first menstrual period) for urban Black, White and Asian girls.

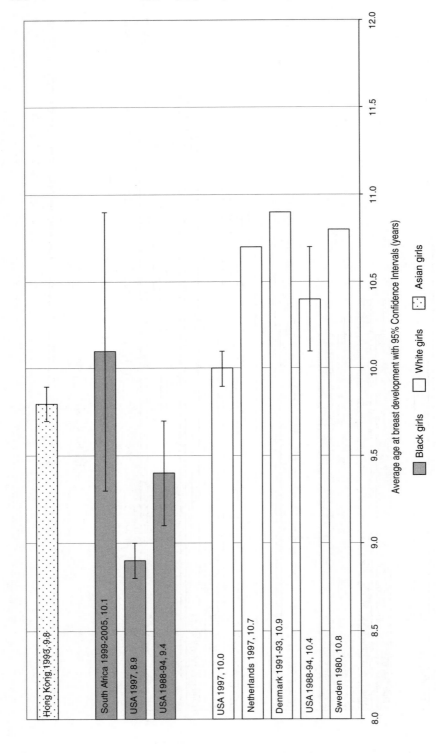

Figure 7.3 Contemporary estimates of average age (95% confidence interval) at the initiation of breast development (B2) for urban Black, White and Asian girls.

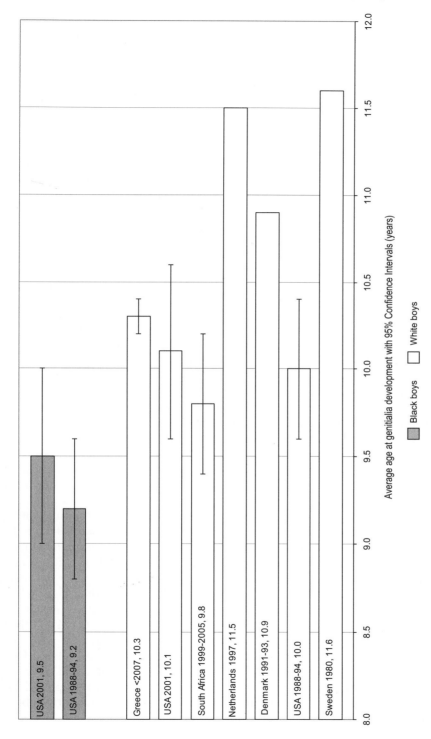

Figure 7.4 Contemporary estimates of average age (95% confidence interval) at the initiation of genitalia development (G2) for urban Black and White boys.

12.6, 13.2) (Mul *et al.*, 2001) and 13.2 years (no variance reported) (Whincup *et al.*, 2001) years, respectively. Figure 7.2 highlights that the estimates for White American (12.9 years, 95% CI = 12.8, 13.0; Herman-Giddens *et al.*, 1997; 12.6 years, 95% CI = 12.4, 12.8; Wu, Mendola and Buck, 2002) and Canadian girls (12.9 years, no variance reported) (Harris, Prior and Koehoorn, 2008) overlap those of the majority of White girls from European countries (with the exception of Greece and Denmark), indicating that there is no statistically significant difference in age at menarche between urban White European, American and Canadian girls.

Compared to age at menarche, there are relatively less data available within the literature for the onset of puberty, particularly for males. This probably reflects the relative ease of assessment of menarche. Figure 7.3 shows the average age of commencement of breast development for urban Black, White and Asian girls. African American girls are, on average, achieving breast development significantly earlier than their White and Asian peers. However, it is important to review critically the American studies, particularly the Pediatric Research in Office Settings (PROS) study published by Herman-Giddens *et al.* (1997) as this study has been criticized within the literature (see for example, Parent *et al.* 2003). This study examined 17 000 girls and reported a mean age for onset of breast development of 8.9 years (95% CI = 8.8, 9.0) for African American girls and 10.0 years (95% CI = 9.9, 10.1) for White girls. These ages were significantly younger than any previous study of American adolescents (Slyper, 2006). As the girls within the Herman-Giddens *et al.* (1997) sample were seen in paediatric clinics, it has been suggested that the early onset of breasts and/or pubic hair may have been the reason for visiting the clinic and thus the sample would not have been random (Sun *et al.*, 2002). In addition, breast palpation techniques were not employed for 63% of the sample, which raises further questions about the accuracy of the results (Herman-Giddens *et al.*, 1997; Sun *et al.*, 2002; Slyper, 2006). Following the publication of the PROS study, a number of more nationally representative studies have been published (Herman-Giddens, Wang and Koch, 2001; Wu, Mendola and Buck, 2002; Chumlea *et al.*, 2003) that have some of the limitations of the PROS study, for example a lack of breast palpation, but used a wider age range of participants to include later maturers and so are, in general, more methodologically robust.

A recent paper by Jones *et al.* (2009b) has reported an average age for initiation of breast development for low-middle SES urban Black girls living in South Africa to be 10.1 years (95% CI = 9.3, 10.9). This estimate is slightly delayed compared to girls from Hong Kong and America, but similar to that of White girls from Europe and America. Asian girls from Hong Kong are achieving breast development at 9.8 years (95% CI = 9.7, 9.9) (Huen *et al.*, 1997), which is slightly earlier than their White European and American peers. If one considers the more representative estimate of Sun *et al.* (2002) for White American girls (10.4 years, 95% CI = 10.1, 10.7) then Figure 7.3 would suggest that White European and American girls are achieving initiation of breast development at similar times, on average, between 10.4 and 10.9 years of age (Lindgren, 1996; Fredriks *et al.*, 2000; Juul *et al.*, 2006).

Figure 7.4 shows the average age at the initiation of genital development for urban Black and White boys. Urban White American, Greek and South African boys are initiating genitalia development at similar times between 9.8 and 10.3 years of age (Herman-Giddens, Wang and Koch, 2001; Sun *et al.*, 2002; Pantsiotou, 2007; Jones *et al.*, 2009b). Other White European boys from the Netherlands (Fredriks *et al.*, 2000), Denmark (Lindgren, 1996) and Sweden (Juul *et al.*, 2006) are delayed in comparison to their White peers; however, it is not possible to determine if these differences are statistically significant as a number of authors did not report measures of variance. Of the two studies of African American boys, mean age at the initiation of genitalia development varied between 9.2 (95% CI = 8.8, 9.6) (Sun *et al.*, 2002) and 9.5 years (95% CI = 9.0, 10.0) (Herman-Giddens, Wang and Koch, 2001), which is generally in advance of their White American, South African and European peers.

7.4.2   Dental Development

As discussed previously, the most commonly used method to assess dental development is to record the emergence of teeth above the gum line, by oral examination or by dental impression (Eveleth and Tanner, 1990). Eveleth and Tanner (1990) describe three different standards for assessing variation in tooth emergence between populations: (i) average number of teeth emerged at a specified age, (ii) average age when 1, 2, 3 and so on teeth have emerged and (iii) median age in a population for the emergence of a specific tooth or pair of teeth. In addition, one must also take into account that children experience both deciduous and permanent tooth eruption and that these two phases occur at different times between and within different populations.

In a study of Japanese, Javanese, Bangladeshi and Guatemalan children, Holman and Jones (2003) showed that deciduous tooth emergence was significantly advanced in urban, well-nourished Japanese children compared to the rural, chronically malnourished Bangladeshi children. This pattern of urban precocity is similar to that seen for sexual and skeletal maturation. Eveleth and Tanner (1990) provide a number of useful summary tables for both deciduous and permanent tooth eruption. For any given age in infancy (i.e. at 12 months), European children, in general, have a greater number of emerged teeth compared to African American, African and Indian children (Eveleth and Tanner, 1990). With regards to the emergence of permanent teeth, there is considerable overlap in age estimation between populations.

7.4.3   Skeletal Development

Worldwide, populations differ in mean skeletal maturity at any given chronological age and in their rate of maturation (Tanner *et al.*, 2001). Contemporary studies of skeletal maturity are scarce and this may be attributable to evolving assessment methods. The majority of studies use either the Greulich–Pyle (GP) technique or Tanner–Whitehouse methods. Table 7.1 shows a summary of the most recent (post-1990) studies of skeletal maturation from a number of developed and developing country samples. It is difficult to provide an overall summary of these studies given that they are based upon relatively small, homogenous samples and the results vary

Table 7.1 Summary of the most recent (post-1990) studies of skeletal maturation from a number of developed and developing country samples.

Authors	Year	Method	Sample	Age (yrs)	n	Summary
Dhar and Dangerfield	1992	TW2	English	2–17	273 170 males 103 females	Both males and females were not significantly different from TW2 references at any age
Vignolo et al.	1992	TW2	Italian	1–17	327 171 males 156 females	Both sexes were in advance of TW2 references at all ages by approximately 7–9 months. The largest advancement was seen in boys, particularly around puberty
Ashizawa et al.	1996	TW2	Japanese	3–18	1457 753 males 704 females	Males mirror TW2 standards closely until 12 years of age after which they are consistently in advance Females are in advance of TW2 standards at all ages
Jimenez-Castellanos et al.	1996	GP	Spanish	0–14	239	Males show, on average, a three-month delay in comparison with the GP references Females show consistently similar skeletal ages to the GP references
Aicardi et al.	2000	TW2	Italian	2–15	589 339 males 250 females	Males were delayed in comparison to TW2 references by around 0.5 years, increasing to over a year after age 13 Females were consistently in advance of TW2 references by approximately 0.2 years
Freitas et al.	2004	TW2	Portuguese	8-16	507 256 males 251 females	Males were consistently in advance of TW2 references at each age studied Females showed a delay in comparison to TW2 references until approximately 11 years of age. Thereafter, they remained advanced

Study	Year	Reference	Population	Age range	Sample size	Findings
Lin et al.	2006	GP	Australian	9–18	2497 1255 males 1242 females	Males aged 9 were skeletally advanced compared to GP references but became delayed by 0.3 years at age 17 Females were concordant with GP references at all ages
Pathmanathan and Raghavan	2006	TW2	Indian	4–18	787 445 males 342 females	Males were delayed in comparison to TW2 references at all ages. The degree of delay was between 0.39 and 0.72 years Females were delayed in comparison to TW2 references at all ages. The of delay varied between 0.33 and 0.64 years
Büken et al.	2007	GP	Turkish	11–19	492 251 males 241 females	Males were delayed in comparison to GP references between 11 and 14 years (0.01 to 0.58 years). Between 15 and 17 years males were advanced by around 0.95 years Females were advanced until 18 years by between 0.2 and 1.1 years. Females were delayed by 0.4 years at age 19
Zhang et al.	2008	TW3	Chinese	1–20	17 401 8685 males 8716 females	Males before 6 years of age showed similar rates of maturation to the TW3 references. After 6 they were increasingly advanced to a maximum of 1.0–1.3 years between 13 and 16 years Females showed skeletal ages that mirrored TW3 references until 6 years of age before becoming delayed from 6–8 years; 9- and 10-year-olds mirrored TW3 references before becoming advanced by between 0.2 and 1.0 year until 16 years

Source: Adapted from Hawley (2009).

even within a specified population. There is no consistent pattern of advancement or delay according to population (i.e. developed vs. developing country) or ethnic group.

7.5   Factors Associated with the Timing of Maturation

A range of factors, including genetics, demographic, biological and environmental influences, have been associated with the timing of maturation (Figure 7.5). Given the much larger literature on the factors affecting sexual maturation as opposed to skeletal and dental maturation, this review will focus on determinants of pubertal development with data for the other maturity indicators highlighted where appropriate.

7.5.1   Genetic Variability

The genetic component or heritability of age at menarche is said to account for a large proportion of the variation in the individual timing of menarche (van den Berg and Boomsma, 2007). As the timing of menarche and breast development is regulated by similar genetic effects, the heritability of menarche can be used as a proxy for the heritability of pubertal development (Pickles *et al.*, 1998; van den Berg

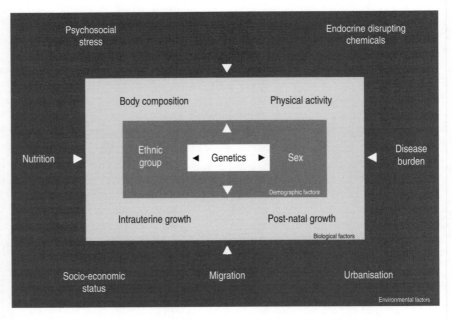

Figure 7.5   The genetic, demographic, biological and environmental factors influencing the timing of maturation. (Source: adapted from Jones, 2008, p. 60).

et al., 2006). Depending on the definition of heritability and the research design, heritability coefficients range from 50% to 80% (Meyer *et al.*, 1991; Palmert and Hirschhorn, 2003; Towne *et al.*, 2005; van den Berg and Boomsma, 2007). There are a limited number of papers that report heritability statistics for skeletal maturation. Garn, Rohmann and Davis (1963) have reported heritability coefficients for ossification rate and timing of 0.40–0.60 for siblings and 0.90 for monozygotic twins. It is well established that dental development is less susceptible to environmental insults in comparison to sexual and skeletal development (Eveleth and Tanner, 1990) and this is clearly demonstrated if one examines heritability coefficients for dental development. In a recent study of Australian twins, Hughes *et al.* (2007) reported narrow-sense heritability rates of between 0.82 and 0.94 for boys and between 0.71 and 0.96 for girls for emergence of primary incisors. The findings from the above studies indicate that as much as 60% of the variation in the timing of sexual and skeletal development is due to the interaction between genetics and the environment.

7.5.2 Demographic Factors

Demographic factors that influence maturation include sex and ethnic group. Girls are consistently in advance of boys in terms of their maturation and this is evident as early as 20 weeks of gestation. At this point, the female skeleton is advanced by some three weeks compared to males (Tanner, 1989). At birth, this difference is four to six weeks, by six to eight years it is two to three months and by adolescence it can be as great as two years (Tanner, 1962). This consistent evidence of sexual dimorphism in skeletal maturation has led to the development of separate standards of skeletal maturation for males and females from birth to adulthood. There is some evidence of girls being advanced in relation to boys for the initiation of secondary sexual development; however, these differences are not statistically significant, indicating that in reality males and females from the same ethnic group are entering puberty at a similar time (see, for example, Sun *et al.*, 2002; Jones *et al.*, 2009b). For dental maturation, most studies find that males are advanced relative to females for emergence of anterior deciduous teeth, but that the pattern is reversed for the emergence of posterior deciduous teeth (Holman and Jones, 2003).

Differences in the timing of pubertal development have been reported between ethnic groups. Reports from developed countries have shown that Black girls are advanced compared to White girls for age at the initiation of puberty and at menarche (Herman-Giddens *et al.*, 1997; Kaplowitz *et al.*, 2001; Freedman *et al.*, 2002; Sun *et al.*, 2002; Wu, Mendola and Buck, 2002; Anderson, Dallal and Must, 2003; Chumlea *et al.*, 2003). The advancement of Black girls has been shown consistently between different countries, time periods and between different study designs. It has been reported that this difference between ethnic groups is independent of relative weight, with several studies showing that ethnic group is an independent predictor of the timing of menarche, having controlled for socio-economic status, body composition and age (Wattigney *et al.*, 1999; Kimm *et al.*, 2001; Anderson and Must, 2005).

This pattern of Black precocity is also found in skeletal maturation, with ossification centres appearing earlier in infancy and early childhood in Black children compared to White children (Malina, Bouchard and Bar-Or, 2004). The skeletal maturity of Black girls is consistently in advance of White girls in late childhood and into adolescence. However, this advancement is not consistent in later childhood and adolescence for boys, where there is no statistically significant difference in skeletal maturation for a given chronological age between Black and White boys (Malina, Bouchard and Bar-Or, 2004).

Eveleth and Tanner (1990) presented data on tooth emergence that was consistent with that of sexual and skeletal development, with Black children being in advance of White children. In a study of Black and White Brazilian children, De Melo, Freitas and Salzano (1975) found that Black children, in particular girls, were precocious in the emergence of permanent teeth compared to White children, although these differences were not statistically significant. Holman and Jones (2003) have also shown ethnic differences in mean age at emergence of deciduous teeth, but have suggested that these may be mediated by nutritional socio-economic factors.

7.5.3   Biological Factors

Several biological factors have also been associated with the timing of maturation. It has been shown that the intra-uterine milieu may influence physiological and pathological events in later life. For example, low birth weight (LBW) has been associated with an increased risk of cardiovascular disease and type II diabetes in adulthood (Barker, 1990, 1994a, 1994b; Barker et al., 1993). Given that the development of teeth occurs during the prenatal period, it is appropriate to hypothesize that a shorter prenatal growth period, growth restriction in utero and poor perinatal and early postnatal development may influence the development of deciduous dentition. It has been shown that dental development, dental eruption and tooth size may be delayed or reduced in premature LBW infants (Fearne and Brook, 1993; Harris et al., 1993; Seow, 1996; Seow and Wan, 2000).

There have been relatively few studies that have examined the early life predictors of skeletal maturation and only one paper has reported statistically significant associations (Demerath et al. 2009). Demerath and colleagues have shown that rapid infant weight gain is associated with advanced skeletal maturation and taller stature at nine years of age independent of birth weight and body mass index (BMI). These relationships held true for both American ($n = 467$, boys $= 245$) and South African ($n = 196$, boys $= 109$) infants despite their exposure to demonstrably different growth and nutritional environments. In contrast, to the findings from the Demerath et al. study, Malina, Katzmarzyk and Beunen (1999) and Cameron et al. (2003) found no statistically significant associations between early life factors and later skeletal maturation. Malina, Katzmarzyk and Beunen (1999) investigated the association between birth weight, skeletal age and the rate of skeletal maturation in European children aged 6 to 11 years ($n = 235$, 127 boys). Birth weight was found to be associated with mass and stature in boys, stature in girls, but was not significantly associated with skeletal maturation in either sex.

Cameron et al. (2003) examined the association between infant weight gain and skeletal maturity at nine years of age in urban Black South African children ($n = 193$, boys $= 108$). There was no significant difference in skeletal maturity between infants who experienced rapid infant weight gain and those who experienced normal/catch down growth at nine years of age. However, the analysis did not control for a number of potential confounding factors such as sex, chronological age and pubertal status, which may have influenced the results.

With respect to pubertal development, girls who were born with LBW exhibited earlier initiation of breast development and menarche, in contrast to LBW boys, who have been shown to mature later than their average birth weight peers (Delemarre-van de Waal, van Coeverden and Engelbregt, 2002). Persson et al. (1999) investigated the influence of perinatal factors such as size and weight at birth on the timing of pubertal development in Swedish children ($n = 1238$). The authors found that girls born small for gestational age (SGA) entered puberty, on average, 0.4 years earlier ($P < 0.05$) than their non-SGA counterparts. Although the result for SGA vs. non-SGA girls was statistically significant, this may not be a true difference in the onset of puberty as the individuals were seen at two yearly intervals and so the potential for error in the estimate of pubertal timing may be greater than the difference reported. This was further confirmed when childhood growth factors such as height and weight were added into the model as the difference in pubertal timing became insignificant. This suggests that differences in pubertal timing in this cohort were explained by differences in childhood growth patterns rather than by perinatal factors such as SGA. There was no association between perinatal factors and the timing of pubertal development in boys from this Swedish sample.

A number of other studies, with more robust measures of pubertal development (such as Tanner scaling) have reported that being born LBW or SGA was associated with an earlier age at the initiation of puberty and menarche for girls (Bhargava et al., 1995; Ibáñez et al., 2000a; Ghirri et al., 2001). One important consideration is whether SGA girls experience the same sequence and tempo of pubertal events given the altered timing of puberty. Bhargava and colleagues (1995) examined the growth of 428 (252 LBW, 45 SGA) urban Indian children from birth to 14 years of age. The results from this study showed that while LBW and SGA babies entered puberty earlier, they experienced the same sequence and tempo of pubertal development compared to their non-LBW/SGA peers.

Therefore, it appears that those children who are born small but grow rapidly during infancy and childhood are more likely to enter puberty early and have a shorter final adult stature (Ibáñez et al., 2000a, Ibáñez and de Zegher, 2006). This reduction in final adult stature has been attributed to sub-optimal growth during infancy and childhood, as opposed to during puberty (Bhargava et al., 1995; Persson et al., 1999; Ghirri et al., 2001). The mechanism that links SGA and rapid growth in infancy with altered pubertal timing is currently unknown. It has been reported that SGA babies present lower levels of neonatal and childhood serum leptin, IGF-1 and insulin-like growth factor 3 binding protein (Boguszewski et al., 1996, 1997a, 1997b; Harigaya et al., 1997; Cance-Rouzaud et al., 1998; Luo et al., 2003), suggesting that this altered infantile hormone profile may programme the HPG axis to mature earlier (Luo et al., 2003). A number of other reports have suggested that in addition to programming of the HPG axis, intra-uterine growth restriction may lead to altered target organ responsiveness to hormonal stimulation by, for example, follicle stimulating hormone

(FSH), inhibin and growth hormone (GH) (Achermann *et al.*, 1998; Ibáñez *et al.*, 1999, 2000b; Cacciari *et al.*, 1999; Ibáñez, Potau and de Zegher, 2000).

7.5.4   Environmental Factors

Bones show greater variability in their development compared to teeth and therefore it has been suggested that teeth are less sensitive to environmental insults and are hence under greater/tighter genetic control (Swindler and Emel, 1990). Having said this, a small percentage of the variation in tooth emergence has been attributed to environmental influences, including dietary intake, nutritional status and socio-economic status (Ulijaszek *et al.*, 1998). In a study of 114 Japanese children, Holman and Yamaguchi (2005) found a strong and statistically significant effect of nutritional status on the timing of deciduous tooth eruption, with children of the poorest nutritional status experiencing the greatest delays.

The environmental factors that have been shown to be associated with the timing of pubertal development and age at menarche are far greater in number compared to those associated with dental and skeletal maturation, and include nutrition, socio-economic status, urbanization, disease burden, psychosocial stress and endocrine disrupting chemicals (EDCs). Nutrition is perhaps the most complex of these factors, due to its interaction with socio-economic status and disease burden (Parent *et al.*, 2003). Nutrition is an important regulator of the tempo of growth and pubertal development (Dunger, Ahmed and Ong, 2005, 2006). Chronic illness and malnutrition in childhood has been shown to reduce growth tempo and cause a delay in the onset of puberty (see, for example, Pozo and Argente, 2002). Disease and malnutrition are closely linked as the interaction is typically cyclic, particularly in lower SES households; that is, an episode of diarrhoea may lead to malnutrition, which depresses the immune system leading to an increased likelihood of further diarrhoeal episodes (Nandy *et al.*, 2005).

In contrast to under-nutrition, over-nutrition or obesity has been linked with rapid growth in infancy and earlier pubertal development (Dunger, Ahmed and Ong, 2005). A number of studies have examined the association between weight status and the timing of pubertal development and age at menarche, because adiposity has been suggested as a causal factor for earlier puberty in girls (Frisch and McArthur, 1974). There is evidence that suggests that girls who are overweight and/or obese experience pubertal development at a younger age compared to their leaner peers (Garn, LaVelle and Pilkington, 1983; Adair and Gordon-Larsen, 2001; Kaplowitz *et al.*, 2001; Anderson, Dallal and Must, 2003). In a longitudinal study of 180 White girls, Davison, Susman and Birch (2003) showed that a higher BMI at five years of age and a greater increase in BMI between five and nine years were associated with earlier puberty. He and Karlberg (2001) have also shown that children who have the greatest gain in BMI during childhood (two to eight years) entered puberty at an earlier age compared to their leaner peers. In a more recent study of 354 American girls, Lee *et al.* (2007) reported that higher BMI z scores at three years of age and a greater increase in BMI z score between three and five years of age was significantly associated with earlier puberty, independent of ethnic group, maternal education and maternal age at menarche. While there is clear evidence from both cross-sectional and longitudinal studies showing that greater adiposity is linked with earlier puberty, it is somewhat difficult to explain the mechanism through which increased adiposity is associated with the timing of pubertal development as a significant correlation may indicate a direct link that can be causal or consequential; that is, does increased adiposity lead to earlier puberty or does earlier puberty lead to increased adiposity? This association is further confounded, as the pubertal period is associated with significant changes in body composition, including increases in total body and fat mass (Rogol *et al.*, 2002). It appears that there are conflicting views within the literature about the causal or consequential nature of adiposity and the timing of pubertal development. Therefore there is a need for further longitudinal research that examines the association between body composition and the timing of pubertal development.

The roles of SES, body composition and the timing of pubertal development are intricately linked. This is also true for skeletal maturity. It is difficult to isolate the specific factors that are responsible for the observed differences in pubertal timing between those from higher and lower socio-economic groups as studies use different measures of SES to represent different factors such as maternal education, access to health care, consumer durable ownership, family size, parental marital status, calorie intake and energy expenditure, among others (Ellis, 2004). In societies that experience inequalities in health and nutritional status (e.g. Sudan, Mozambique, Iran, Morocco, Philippines and China) adolescents from higher socio-economic groups experience earlier pubertal development in relation to their lower socio-economic peers (Abioye-Kuteyi *et al.*, 1997; Montero *et al.*, 1999; Adair, 2001; Ayatollahi, Dowlatabadi and Ayatollahi, 2002; Wang and Murphy, 2002; Padez, 2003; Ku *et al.*, 2006).

What a number of these studies fail to recognize is that there appears to be an interaction between body composition and SES. A small number of more recent studies have shown that while SES was an independent predictor of the timing of pubertal development, once body composition was controlled for in the analysis, SES was no longer an independent predictor (Onat and Ertem, 2005; Kirchengast and Bauer, 2007; Hernández *et al.*, 2007). For example, in a study of 1302 Chilean females aged 7 to 19 years, Hernandez *et al.* (2007) found that type of school (public vs. private), a proxy for SES in Chile, influenced age at menarche due to differences in body composition. These results suggest that socio-economic status differences are mediated through body composition. In a recent paper, Griffiths *et al.* (2008) have shown the need to control for pubertal development when examining the SES predictors of body composition in a sample of South African adolescents. Given the results from the Griffiths *et al.* (2008) study, it may be appropriate to suggest that if one needs to control for pubertal development when examining the influence of SES on body composition, then one needs to consider the role of body composition when looking at the association between SES and pubertal development.

The association between SES and skeletal maturity is less consistent, with some studies reporting an association between skeletal maturity and SES and others reporting no association. Indian children from high SES backgrounds presented with bone ages in advance of their less affluent peers (Pathmanathan and Raghavan, 2006). In a study of 711 Arab children from two contrasting socio-economic groups, Shakir and Zaini (1974) reported that the higher SES children were in advance of both their lower SES peers and British standards from birth to six years of age. In contrast to these studies, Waldmann *et al.* (1977) reported no statistically significant differences in skeletal maturity between children from low, middle and high SES backgrounds born in Hong Kong. However, the lowest and highest SES groups were not representative and therefore potential differences in skeletal maturity may not have been observed. In the Madeira Growth Study, Freitas *et al.* (2004) reported no significant association between SES and skeletal maturity for 507 Portuguese adolescents from three social class groups. It appears that when extremes of SES are studied then differences in skeletal maturation are present; however, when more homogenous groups are studied then no SES differences are present. These findings highlight the importance of selecting appropriate measures of SES for the group under investigation and that further studies using robust measures of SES are required to disentangle the relationship between SES and skeletal maturation.

A number of studies have examined the relationship between physical activity prior to adolescence and the timing of pubertal development; the results from these studies are, however, somewhat contradictory. It has been shown that intensive physical training in childhood is associated with delayed age at menarche compared to non-elite age-matched controls, particularly in elite female athletes such as gymnasts, track and field athletes, swimmers and ballet dancers (Constantini and Warren, 1995; Pigeon *et al.*, 1997; Dusek, 2001; Klentrou and Plyley, 2003; Torstveit and Sundgot-Borgen, 2005). This finding has not been replicated in male gymnasts (Gurd and Klentrou, 2003). Several studies have argued that a delay in pubertal development is not associated with training *per se*, but rather with genetic factors that predispose an individual to be successful in a particular sport and/or dietary factors such as calorie intake that is inadequate to meet the energetic demands of training and growth and development (Ledoux, Brisson and Peronnet, 1983; Ersoy, 1991; Klentrou, 2006).

A further environmental factor that interacts with nutrition, SES and physical activity to influence the timing of pubertal development is urbanization. Urbanization is an economic change that facilitates the nutrition transition in developing countries. The nutrition transition refers to a shift from a diet low in fat and refined carbohydrates to a diet high in fat and low in fibre, with consequential increases in obesity and non-communicable diseases (Popkin and Gordon-Larsen, 2004). In addition, the economic changes such as urbanization that drive the nutrition transition result in the globalization of food production, increased media and marketing, increased sedentary behaviours and changes to working patterns and hours (Lang, 2002). Living in urban areas and improving socio-economic conditions have been shown to be associated with greater food availability, less seasonal fluctuations and increased access to and consumption of fast foods (Popkin and Bisgrove, 1988; Popkin *et al.*, 1995). Each of these factors – increased overweight/obesity, improving SES and reduced physical activity, driven by urbanization – has been associated with a decreasing age at pubertal development, age at menarche and advancing skeletal maturation.

It has been reported that internationally adopted children achieve puberty earlier than their non-adopted peers and are at a significantly greater risk of developing precocious puberty (PP) (generally accepted age limits for PP are the onset of puberty prior to eight years of age for girls and nine years of age for boys; Adolfsson and Westphal, 1981; Proos, Hofvander and Tuvemo, 1991; Baron et al., 2000; Krstevska-Konstantinova et al., 2001; Teilmann et al., 2002; Ritzén, 2003; Mason and Narad, 2005; Parent et al., 2005; Cataldo, Accomando and Porcari, 2006; Teilmann et al., 2006; Olmo, Anuncibay and Prado, 2008). In a population-based study of native ($n = 1\,062\,333$), immigrant ($n = 72\,181$) and internationally adopted ($n = 128\,152$) Danish children, Teilmann et al. (2006) have shown that adopted children were 10 to 20 times more likely to develop PP compared with the Danish reference group. The immigrant children (mother and baby born outside of Denmark, but residing in Denmark at the time of the study) were; however, at no greater risk of PP compared to the native children. Teilmann et al. (2006) also showed that the older the age at adoption, the greater the risk of PP, independent of country of birth, with children adopted after two years of age being at the greatest risk. However, it is important to consider this finding within the context of age estimation bias in adopted children. Age estimation is often problematic for adopted children due to incomplete or unavailable birth records. Given that infants are more likely to be adopted than older children (George, 1990), it could be hypothesized that children's ages are underestimated (to improve their adoption chances) and so this may lead to over-inflated estimates of adopted children with PP.

Several mechanisms have been proposed to explain why adopted children are more likely to enter puberty early compared to their non-adopted counterparts. At the time of adoption, adopted children are typically under-nourished, with low height and weight for age (Virdis et al., 1998) due to their constrained growth in early life. If the new environment is unconstrained, significant catch-up growth may occur, which may in turn promote earlier pubertal development. Virdis et al. (1998) have proposed that rapid weight gain in adopted children, due to dietary changes, may lead to increased circulating levels of free active sex steroids, which could promote the maturation of the HPG axis, leading to earlier pubertal development. In addition, it has been proposed that exposure to EDCs in food (e.g. phytoestrogens) and in the environment (e.g. organochlorine pesticides) may stimulate oestrogen-sensitive tissues or inhibit gonadotrophins via negative feedback, leading to earlier puberty (Virdis et al., 1998).

Other environmental factors associated with the timing of pubertal development include organic pollutants such as phthalates that are regularly found in cosmetics, toys and plastic food containers (Colón et al., 2000) and psychosocial stress such as parental divorce and conflict (Wierson, Long and Forehand, 1993). A number of studies have highlighted that exposure to pollutants and other EDCs may contribute to earlier achievement of female pubertal development and menarche by influencing physiological pathways (Colburn, Dumanoski and Myers, 1996; Blanck et al., 2000; Schell et al., 2006). There are few, if any, studies of which the authors are aware that look at EDCs and skeletal maturation. Humans that have been exposed to the effect of polychlorinated biphenyls (PCBs), persistent organic pollutants that are stored in fat tissue, have been shown to present with a smaller size at birth, advanced sexual maturation and altered hormone profiles for thyroid regulation (Denham et al., 2005; Schell et al., 2006). However, while there is some evidence in the literature to suggest that exposure to environmental pollutants influences the underlying mechanisms that control growth and development, human populations are simultaneously exposed to a number of pollutants at any one time, making it very difficult to isolate the individual effect of one specific pollutant (Parent *et al.*, 2003; Schell *et al.*, 2006).

7.6   Summary

Size, maturity, and the passage of time are seen to have complex and changing relationships. The methods used to assess maturity must be sensitive to the temporal context of maturity indicators; some changing rapidly and others slowly within the same passage of time. The selection and evaluation of such indicators also pays heed to the degree of variation in expression to be found both within and between any particular process of maturation, and within and between individuals of the same and opposite sexes. While sexual, skeletal and dental maturity are the most common methods of evaluation, they are seen to be largely independent of each other except across broad spans of chronological time and should not be combined into a single indicator. Secular trends and worldwide variations in different populations in the time of appearance and progression of maturity indicators and the age at which full maturity is reached confound any attempt to link a particular maturational level with a chronological age. Demographic, biological and environmental factors influence the expression of the genetically determined processes of maturation and thus add to this complex picture.

References

Abioye-Kuteyi, E., Ojofeitimi, E., Aina, O. *et al.* (1997) The influence of socioeconomic and nutritional status on menarche in Nigerian school girls. *Nutrition and Health*, **11**, 185–195.

Achermann, J., Hamdani, K., Hindmarsh, P. and Brook, C. (1998) Birth weight influences the initial response to growth hormone treatment in growth hormone-insufficient children. *Pediatrics*, **102**, 342–345.

Acheson, R. (1966) Maturation of the skeleton, in *Human Development* (ed. F. Falkner), W.B. Saunders, Philadelphia, PA, pp. 465–502.

Acheson, R. (1957) The Oxford method of assessing skeletal maturity. *Clinical Orthopaedics*, **10**, 19–39.

Acheson, R. (1954) A method of assessing skeletal maturity from radiographs; a report from the Oxford child health survey. *Journal of Anatomy*, **88**, 498–508.

Adair, L. (2001) Size at birth predicts age at menarche. *Pediatrics*, **107** (4), E59.

Adair, L. and Gordon-Larsen, P. (2001) Maturational timing and overweight prevalence in US adolescent girls. *American Journal of Public Health*, **91**, 642–644.

Adolfsson, S. and Westphal, O. (1981) Early pubertal development of girls adopted from Far-Eastern countries. *Pediatric Research*, **15** (1), 82.

Aicardi, G., Vignolo, M., Milani, S. *et al.* (2000) Assessment of skeletal maturity of the hand–wrist and knee: a comparison among methods. *American Journal of Human Biology*, **12**, 610–615.

Anderson, S., Dallal, G. and Must, A. (2003) Relative weight and race influence average age at menarche: results from two nationally representative surveys of US girls studied 25 years apart. *Pediatrics*, **111**, 844–850.

Anderson, S. and Must, A. (2005) Interpreting the continued decline in the average age at menarche: results from two nationally representative surveys of US girls studied 10 years apart. *Journal of Pediatrics*, **147**, 753–760.

Ashizawa, K., Asami, T., Anzo, M. *et al.* (1996) Standard RUS skeletal maturation of Tokyo children. *Annals of Human Biology*, **23**, 457–469.

Ayatollahi, S., Dowlatabadi, E. and Ayatollahi, S. (2002) Age at menarche in Iran. *Annals of Human Biology*, **29**, 355–362.

Barker, D. (1994a) *Mothers, Babies, and Disease in Later Life*, BMJ Publishing, London.

Barker, D. (1994b) Outcome of low birth weight. *Hormone Research*, **42**, 223–230.

Barker, D. (1990) The fetal and infant origins of adult disease. *British Medical Journal*, **301**, 1111.

Barker, D., Hales, C., Fall, C. *et al.* (1993) Type 2 (non-insulin-dependent) diabetes mellitus, hypertension and hyperlipidaemia (syndrome X): relation to reduced fetal growth. *Diabetologia*, **36**, 62–67.

Baron, S., Battin, J., David, A. and Limal, J. (2000), Puberté précoce chez des enfants adoptés de pays étrangers. *Archives of Pediatrics and Adolescent Medicine*, **7**, 809–816.

Bhargava, S., Ramji, S., Srivastava, U. *et al.* (1995) Growth and sexual maturation of low birth weight children: a 14 year follow up. *Indian Pediatrics*, **32**, 963–970.

Blanck, H., Marcus, M., Tolbert, P. *et al.* (2000) Age at menarche and Tanner stage in girls exposed in utero and postnatally to polybrominated biphenyl. *Epidemiology*, **11**, 641–647.

Bogin, B. (1999) *Patterns of Human Growth*, 2nd edn, Cambridge University Press, Cambridge.

Boguszewski, M., Bjarnason, R., Jansson, C. *et al.* (1997a) Hormonal status of short children born small for gestational age. *Acta Paediatrica Supplement*, **423**, 189–192.

Boguszewski, M., Dahlgren, J., Bjarnason, R. *et al.* (1997b) Serum leptin in short children born small for gestational age: relationship with the growth response to growth hormone treatment. The Swedish Study Group for Growth Hormone Treatment. *European Journal of Endocrinology*, **137**, 387–395.

Boguszewski, M., Jansson, C., Rosberg, S. and Albertsson-Wikland, K. (1996) Changes in serum insulin-like growth factor I (IGF-I) and IGF-binding protein-3 levels during growth hormone treatment in prepubertal short children born small for gestational age. *Journal of Clinical Endocrinology and Metabolism*, **81**, 3902–3908.

Büken, B., Safak, A., Yazici, B. *et al.* (2007) Is the assessment of bone age by the Greulich–Pyle method reliable at forensic age estimation for Turkish children? *Forensic Science International*, **173**, 146–153.

Cacciari, E., Zucchini, S., Cicognani, A. *et al.* (1999) Birth weight affects final height in patients treated for growth hormone deficiency. *Clinical Endocrinology*, **51**, 733–739.

Cameron, N. (2002) Assessment of maturation, in *Human Growth and Development* (ed. N. Cameron), Academic Press, London, pp. 363–382.

Cameron, N. (1997) The assessment of maturation. *South African Journal of Science*, **93**, 18–23.

Cameron, N. (1984) *The Measurement of Human Growth*, Croom Helm, London.

Cameron, N., Pettifor, J., De Wet, T. and Norris, S. (2003) The relationship of rapid weight gain in infancy to obesity and skeletal maturity in childhood. *Obesity Research*, **11**, 457–460.

Cance-Rouzaud, A., Laborie, S., Bieth, E. *et al.* (1998) Growth hormone, insulin-like growth factor-I and insulin-like growth factor binding protein-3 are regulated differently in small-for-gestational-age and appropriate-for-gestational-age neonates. *Biology of the Neonate*, 73, 347–355.

Cataldo, F., Accomando, S. and Porcari, V. (2006) Internationally adopted children: a new challenge for pediatricians. *Minerva Pediatrics*, 58, 55–62.

Chumlea, W., Roche, A. and Thissen, A. (1989) The FELS method for assessing the skeletal maturity of the hand–wrist. *American Journal of Human Biology*, 1, 175–183.

Chumlea, W., Schubert, C., Roche, A. *et al.* (2003) Age at menarche and racial comparisons in US girls. *Pediatrics*, 111, 110–113.

Colburn, T., Dumanoski, D. and Myers, J. (1996) *Our Stolen Future*, Plume, New York.

Cole, T. (2000) Secular trends in growth. *Proceedings of the Nutrition Society*, 59, 317–324.

Colón, I., Caro, D., Bourdony, C. and Rosario, O. (2000) Identification of phthalate esters in the serum of young Puerto Rican girls with premature breast development. *Environmental Health Perspectives*, 108, 895–900.

Constantini, N. and Warren, M. (1995) Menstrual dysfunction in swimmers: a distinct entity. *Journal of Clinical Endocrinology and Metabolism*, 80, 2740–2744.

Danubio, M., De, S.M., Vecchi, F. *et al.* (2004) Age at menarche and age of onset of pubertal characteristics in 6–14-year-old girls from the Province of L'Aquila (Abruzzo, Italy). *American Journal of Human Biology*, 16, 470–478.

Davison, K., Susman, E. and Birch, L. (2003) Percent body fat at age 5 predicts earlier pubertal development among girls at age 9. *Pediatrics*, 111, 815–821.

De Melo, M., Freitas, E. and Salzano, F. (1975) Eruption of permanent teeth in Brazilian Whites and Blacks. *American Journal of Physical Anthropology*, 42, 145–150.

Delemarre-van de Waal, H., van Coeverden, S. and Engelbregt, M. (2002) Factors affecting onset of puberty. *Hormone Research*, 57, 15–18.

Demerath, E.W., Jones, L.L., Hawley, N., *et al.* (2009) Rapid infant weight gain and advanced skeletal maturation in childhood. *Journal of Pediatrics*, 155, 355–361.

Demirjian, A. and Goldstein, H. (1976) New systems for dental maturity based on seven and four teeth. *Annals of Human Biology*, 3, 411–421.

Demirjian, A., Goldstein, H. and Tanner, J. (1973), A new system of dental age assessment. *Human Biology*, 45, 211–227.

Denham, M., Schell, L., Deane, G. *et al.* (2005) Relationship of lead, mercury, mirex, dichlorodiphenyldichloroethylene, hexachlorobenzene, and polychlorinated biphenyls to timing of menarche among Akwesasne Mohawk girls. *Pediatrics*, 115, e127.

Derijian, A. (1978) Dentition, in *Human Growth*, Vol. 2 (eds F. Falkner and J. Tanner), Plenum Press, New York.

Dhar, S. and Dangerfield, P. (1992) Skeletal maturity in normal children from Liverpool, United Kingdom. *Clinical Anatomy*, 5, 458–465.

Dunger, D., Ahmed, M. and Ong, K. (2005) Effects of obesity on growth and puberty. *Best Practice and Research Clinical Endocrinology and Metabolism*, 19, 375–390.

Dunger, D., Ahmed, M. and Ong, K. (2006) Early and late weight gain and the timing of puberty. *Molecular and Cellular Endocrinology*, 254–255, 140–145.

Dusek, T. (2001) Influence of high intensity training on menstrual cycle disorders in athletes. *Croatian Medical Journal*, 42, 79–82.

Edgardh, K. (2000) Sexual behaviour and early coitarche in a national sample of 17 year old Swedish girls. *Sexually Transmitted Infections*, 76, 98–102.

Ellis, B. (2004) Timing of pubertal maturation in girls: an integrated life history approach. *Psychological Bulletin*, 130, 920–958.

Ersoy, G. (1991) Dietary status and anthropometric assessment of child gymnasts. *Journal of Sports Medicine and Physical Fitness*, 31, 577–580.

Eskeli, R. (1999) Standards for permanent tooth emergence in Finnish children. *Angle Orthodontist*, **69**, 529–533.

Eveleth, P. and Tanner, J. (1976) *Worldwide Variation in Human Growth*, 1st edn, Cambridge University Press, Cambridge.

Eveleth, P. and Tanner, J. (1990) *Worldwide Variation in Human Growth*, 2nd edn, Cambridge University Press, Cambridge.

Fearne, J. and Brook, A. (1993) Small primary tooth-crown size in low birth weight children. *Early Human Development*, **33**, 81–90.

Fredriks, A., van Buuren, S., Burgmeijer, R. *et al.* (2000) Continuing positive secular growth change in The Netherlands 1955–1997. *Pediatric Research*, **47**, 316–323.

Freedman, D., Khan, L., Serdula, M. *et al.* (2002) Relation of age at menarche to race, time period, and anthropometric dimensions: the Bogalusa Heart Study. *Pediatrics*, **110**, e43.

Freitas, D., Maia, J., Beunen, G. *et al.* (2004) Skeletal maturity and socio-economic status in Portuguese children and youths: the Madeira growth study. *Annals of Human Biology*, **31**, 408–420.

Frisch, R. and McArthur, J. (1974) Menstrual cycles: fatness as a determinant of minimum weight for height necessary for their maintenance or onset. *Science*, **185**, 949–951.

Garn, S., Rohmann, C. and Davis, A. (1963) Genetics of hand–wrist ossification. *American Journal of Physical Anthropology*, **21**, 33–40.

Garn, S., LaVelle, M. and Pilkington, J. (1983) Comparisons of fatness in premenarcheal and postmenarcheal girls of the same age. *Journal of Pediatrics*, **103**, 328–331.

George, R. (1990) The reunification process in substitute care. *Social Service Review*, **64**, 422–457.

Ghirri, P., Bernardini, M., Vuerich, M. *et al.* (2001) Adrenarche, pubertal development, age at menarche and final height of full-term, born small for gestational age (SGA) girls. *Gynecological Endocrinology*, **15**, 91–97.

Greulich, W. and Pyle, S. (1959) *Radiographic Atlas of the Skeletal Development of the Hand and Wrist*, Stanford University Press, Palo Alto, CA.

Griffiths, P., Rousham, E., Norris, S. *et al.* (2008) Socio-economic status and body composition outcomes in urban South African children. *Archives of Disease in Childhood*, **93**, 862–867.

Guízar-Vázquez, J.J., Rosales-López, A., Ortiz-Jalomo, R. *et al.* (1992) Age at onset of spermaturia (spermarche) in 669 Mexican children and its relation to secondary sexual characteristics and height. *Boletín médico del Hospital Infantil de México*, **49**, 12–17.

Gurd, B. and Klentrou, P. (2003) Physical and pubertal development in young male gymnasts. *Journal of Applied Physiology*, **95**, 1011–1015.

Harigaya, A., Nagashima, K., Nako, Y. and Morikawa, A. (1997) Relationship between concentration of serum leptin and fetal growth. *Journal of Clinical Endocrinology and Metabolism*, **82**, 3281–3284.

Harris, E., Barcroft, B., Haydar, S. and Haydar, B. (1993) Delayed tooth formation in low birth weight African-American children. *Pediatric Dental Journal*, **15**, 30–35.

Harris, M., Prior, J. and Koehoorn, M. (2008) Age at menarche in the Canadian population: secular trends and relationship to adulthood BMI. *Journal of Adolescent Health*, **43**, 548–554.

Hauspie, R., Vercauteren, M. and Susanne, C. (1996) Secular changes in growth. *Hormone Research*, **45**, 8–17.

Hawley, N. (2009) Skeletal maturation and its variation in South African children, PhD Thesis, Loughborough University.

Hawley, N., Rousham, E., Norris, S., *et al.* (2009) Secular trends in skeletal maturity in South Africa: 1962–2001. *Annals of Human Biology*, **36**, 584–594.

He, Q. and Karlberg, J. (2001) BMI in childhood and its association with height gain, timing of puberty, and final height. *Pediatric Research*, **49**, 244–251.

Herman-Giddens, M. (2006) Recent data on pubertal milestones in United States children: the secular trend toward earlier development. *International Journal of Andrology*, **29**, 241–246.

Herman-Giddens, M., Wang, L. and Koch, G. (2001) Secondary sexual characteristics in boys: estimates from the National Health and Nutrition Examination Survey III, 1988–1994. *Archives of Pediatrics and Adolescent Medicine*, **155**, 1022–1028.

Herman-Giddens, M., Slora, E.J., Wasserman, R. *et al.* (1997) Secondary sexual characteristics and menses in young girls seen in office practice: a study from the Pediatric Research in Office Settings network. *Pediatrics*, **99**, 505–512.

Hernández, M., Unanue, N., Gaete, X. *et al.* (2007) Age of menarche and its relationship with body mass index and socio-economic status. *Revista Medica de Chile*, **135**, 1429–1436.

Hesketh, T., Ding, Q. and Tomkins, A. (2002) Growth status and menarche in urban and rural China. *Annals of Human Biology*, **29**, 348–352.

Höffding, J. (1984) Emergence of permanent teeth and onset of dental stages in Japanese children. *Community Dentistry and Oral Epidemiology*, **12**, 55–58.

Holman, D. and Jones, R. (2003) Longitudinal analysis of deciduous tooth emergence: III. Sexual dimorphism in Bangladeshi, Guatemalan, Japanese, and Javanese children. *American Journal of Physical Anthropology*, **122**, 269–278.

Holman, D. and Yamaguchi, K. (2005) Longitudinal analysis of deciduous tooth emergence: IV. Covariate effects in Japanese children. *American Journal of Physical Anthropology*, **126**, 352–358.

Hosny, L., El-Ruby, M., Zaki, M. *et al.* (2005) Assessment of pubertal development in Egyptian girls. *Journal of Pediatric Endocrinology and Metabolism*, **18**, 577–584.

Huen, K., Leung, S., Lau, J. *et al.* (1997) Secular trend in the sexual maturation of southern Chinese girls. *Acta Paediatrica*, **86**, 1121–1124.

Hughes, T., Bockmann, M., Seow, K. *et al.* (2007) Strong genetic control of emergence of human primary incisors. *Journal of Dental Research*, **86**, 1160–1165.

Hwang, J., Shin, C., Frongillo, E. *et al.* (2003) Secular trend in age at menarche for South Korean women born between 1920 and 1986: the Ansan Study. *Annals of Human Biology*, **30**, 434–442.

Ibáñez, L. and de Zegher, F. (2006) Puberty after prenatal growth restraint. *Hormone Research*, **65**, 112–115.

Ibáñez, L., Potau, N. and de Zegher, F. (2000) Ovarian hyporesponsiveness to follicle stimulating hormone in adolescent girls born small for gestational age. *Journal of Clinical Endocrinology Metabolism*, **85**, 2624–2626.

Ibáñez, L., Potau, N., Marcos, M. and de Zegher, F. (1999) Exaggerated adrenarche and hyperinsulinism in adolescent girls born small for gestational age. *Journal of Clinical Endocrinology Metabolism*, **84**, 4739–4741.

Ibáñez, L., Ferrer, A., Marcos, M. *et al.* (2000a) Early puberty: rapid progression and reduced final height in girls with low birth weight. *Pediatrics*, **106**, E72.

Ibáñez, L., Potau, N., Enriquez, G. and de Zegher, F. (2000b) Reduced uterine and ovarian size in adolescent girls born small for gestational age. *Pediatric Research*, **47**, 575–577.

Jiménez-Castellanos, J., Carmona, A., Catalina-Herrera, C. and Viñuales, M. (1996) Skeletal maturation of wrist and hand ossification centers in normal Spanish boys and girls: a study using the Greulich–Pyle method. *Acta Anatomica (Basel)*, **155**, 206–211.

Jones, L. (2008) Determinants of pubertal development in an urban South African cohort, PhD Thesis, Loughborough University.

Jones, L., Griffiths, P., Norris, S. *et al.* (2009a) Age at menarche and the evidence for a positive secular trend in urban South Africa. *American Journal of Human Biology*, **21**, 130–132.

Jones, L., Griffiths, P., Norris, S. *et al.* (2009b) Is puberty starting earlier in urban South Africa? *American Journal of Human Biology,* **21** (3), 395–397.

Juul, A., Teilmann, G., Scheike, T. *et al.* (2006) Pubertal development in Danish children: comparison of recent European and US data. *International Journal of Andrology,* **29,** 247–255.

Kaplowitz, P. and Oberfield, S. (1999) Reexamination of the age limit for defining when puberty is precocious in girls in the United States: implications for evaluation and treatment. Drug and Therapeutics and Executive Committees of the Lawson Wilkins Pediatric Endocrine Society. *Pediatrics,* **104,** 936–941.

Kaplowitz, P., Slora, E., Wasserman, R. *et al.* (2001) Earlier onset of puberty in girls: relation to increased body mass index and race. *Pediatrics,* **108,** 347–353.

Kimm, S., Barton, B., Obarzanek, E. *et al.* (2001) Racial divergence in adiposity during adolescence: The NHLBI Growth and Health Study. *Pediatrics,* **107,** E34.

Kirchengast, S. and Bauer, M. (2007) Menarcheal onset is associated with body composition parameters but not with socioeconomic status. *Collegium Antropologicum,* **31,** 419–425.

Klentrou, P. (2006) Puberty and athletic sports in female adolescents. *Annales Nestlé (English ed.),* **64,** 85–94.

Klentrou, P. and Plyley, M. (2003) Onset of puberty, menstrual frequency, and body fat in elite rhythmic gymnasts compared with normal controls. *British Journal of Sports Medicine,* **37,** 490–494.

Krstevska-Konstantinova, M., Charlier, C., Craen, M. *et al.* (2001) Sexual precocity after immigration from developing countries to Belgium: evidence of previous exposure to organochlorine pesticides. *Human Reproduction,* **16,** 1020–1026.

Ku, S., Kang, J., Kim, H. *et al.* (2006) Age at menarche and its influencing factors in North Korean female refugees. *Human Reproduction,* **21,** 833–836.

Lam, T., Shi, H., Ho, L. *et al.* (2002) Timing of pubertal maturation and heterosexual behaviour among Hong Kong Chinese adolescents. *Archives of Sexual Behaviour,* **31,** 359–366.

Lang, T. (2002) Can the challenges of poverty, sustainable consumption and good health governance be addressed in an era of globalisation? in *The Nutrition Transition: Diet and Disease in the Developing World* (eds B. Caballero and B. Popkin), Academic Press, London.

Ledoux, M., Brisson, G. and Peronnet, F. (1983) Nutritional habits of young female gymnasts. *Medicine and Science in Sports and Exercise,* **14,** 145.

Lee, J., Appugliese, D., Kacirot, N. *et al.* (2007) Weight status in young girls and the onset of puberty. *Pediatrics,* **119,** e624–e630.

Lin, N., Ranjitkar, S., Macdonald, R. *et al.* (2006) New growth references for assessment of stature and skeletal maturation in Australians. *Australian Orthodontic Journal,* **22,** 1–10.

Lindgren, G. (1996) Pubertal stages 1980 of Stockholm schoolchildren. *Acta Paediatrica,* **85,** 1365–1367.

Luo, Z., Cheung, Y., He, Q. *et al.* (2003) Growth in early life and its relation to pubertal growth. *Epidemiology,* **14,** 65–73.

Mahachoklertwattana, P., Suthutvoravut, U., Charoenkiatkul, S. *et al.* (2002) Earlier onset of pubertal maturation in Thai girls. *Journal of the Medical Association of Thailand,* **85,** S1127.

Malina, R., Bouchard, C. and Bar-Or, O. (2004) *Growth, Maturation, and Physical Activity,* 2nd edn, Human Kinetics, Champaign, IL.

Malina, R., Katzmarzyk, P. and Beunen, G. (1999) Relation between birth weight at term and growth rate, skeletal age, and cortical bone at 6–11 years. *American Journal of Human Biology,* **11,** 505–511.

Marshall, W. and Tanner, J. (1969) Variations in pattern of pubertal changes in girls. *Archives of Disease in Childhood*, **44**, 291–303.

Marshall, W. and Tanner, J. (1970) Variations in the pattern of pubertal changes in boys. *Archives of Disease in Childhood*, **45**, 13–23.

Mason, P. and Narad, C. (2005) Long-term growth and puberty concerns in international adoptees. *Pediatric Clinics of North America*, **52**, 1351–1368.

Meindl, R. and Lovejoy, C. (1985) Ectocranial suture closure: a revised method for the determination of skeletal age at death based on the lateral-anterior sutures. *American Journal of Physical Anthropology*, **68**, 57–66.

Meyer, J., Eaves, L., Heath, A. and Martin, N. (1991) Estimating genetic influences on the age-at-menarche: a survival analysis approach. *American Journal of Medical Genetics*, **39**, 148–154.

Montero, P., Bernis, C., Loukid, M. *et al.* (1999) Characteristics of menstrual cycles in Moroccan girls: prevalence of dysfunctions and associated behaviours. *Annals of Human Biology*, **26**, 243–249.

Mul, D., Fredriks, A., van Buuren, S. *et al.* (2001) Pubertal development in The Netherlands 1965–1997. *Pediatric Research*, **50**, 479–486.

Nandy, S., Irving, M., Gordon, D. *et al.* (2005) Poverty, child under-nutrition and morbidity: new evidence from India. *Bulletin of the World Health Organization*, **83**, 210–216.

Nicholson, A. and Harley, C. (1952) Indices of physiological maturity. *Child Development*, **24**, 3–38.

Nielsoen, C.T., Skakkebaek, N.E., Richardson, D.W. *et al.* (1986) Onset of the release of spermatozoa (spermarche) in boys in relation to age, testicular growth, pubic hair, and height. *Journal of Clinical Endocrinology and Metabolism*, **62**, 532–535.

Ofuya, Z. (2007) The age at menarche in Nigerian adolescents from two different socioeconomic classes. *Online Journal of Health and Allied Sciences*, **6**, 3.

Olmo, R., Anuncibay, J. and Prado, C. (2008) Maturational profiles and migration in the female adolescent population of Madrid: is there a need for a new perspective? *Collegium Antropologicum*, **32**, 15–19.

Onat, T. and Ertem, B. (2005) Age at menarche: relationships to socioeconomic status, growth rate in stature and weight, and skeletal and sexual maturation. *American Journal of Human Biology*, **7**, 741–750.

Padez, C. (2003) Social background and age at menarche in Portuguese university students: a note on the secular changes in Portugal. *American Journal of Human Biology*, **15**, 415–427.

Palmert, M. and Hirschhorn, J. (2003) Genetic approaches to stature, pubertal timing, and other complex traits. *Molecular Genetics and Metabolism*, **80**, 1–10.

Pantsiotou, K. (2007) Data on pubertal development in Greek boys. A longitudinal study. *Hormones (Athens)*, **6**, 148–151.

Papadimitriou, A. (2008) Age at menarche in contemporary Greek girls: evidence for levelling-off of the secular trend. *Acta Paediatrica*, **97**, 812–815.

Parent, A., Teilmann, G., Juul, A. *et al.* (2003) The timing of normal puberty and the age limits of sexual precocity: variations around the world, secular trends, and changes after migration. *Endocrine Reviews*, **24**, 668–693.

Parent, A., Rasier, G., Gerard, A. *et al.* (2005) Early onset of puberty: tracking genetic and environmental factors. *Hormone Research*, **64**, 41–47.

Pasquet, P., Biyong, A., Rikong-Adie, H. *et al.* (1999) Age at menarche and urbanization in Cameroon: current status and secular trends. *Annals of Human Biology*, **26**, 89–97.

Pathmanathan, G. and Raghavan, P. (2006) Bone age based linear growth and weight of under privileged north west Indian children compared with their well-off north west Indian peers. *Journal of the Anatomical Society of India*, **55**, 34–42.

Pawloski, L. (2008) A cross-sectional examination of growth indicators from Thai adolescent girls: evidence of obesity among Thai youth? *Annals of Human Biology*, 35, 378–385.

Persson, I., Ahlsson, F., Ewald, U. *et al.* (1999) Influence of perinatal factors on the onset of puberty in boys and girls: implications for interpretation of link with risk of long term diseases. *American Journal of Epidemiology*, 150, 747–755.

Pickles, A., Pickering, K., Simonoff, E. *et al.* (1998) Genetic 'clocks' and 'soft' events: a twin model for pubertal development and other recalled sequences of developmental milestones, transitions, or ages at onset. *Behaviour Genetics*, 28, 243–253.

Pigeon, P., Oliver, I., Charlet, J. and Rochiccioli, P. (1997) Intensive dance practice. Repercussions on growth and puberty. *American Journal of Sports Medicine*, 25, 243–247.

Popkin, B. and Bisgrove, E. (1988) Urbanization and nutrition in low-income countries. *Food and Nutrition Bulletin*, 10, 3–23.

Popkin, B. and Gordon-Larsen, P. (2004) The nutrition transition: worldwide obesity dynamics and their determinants. *International Journal of Obesity*, 28, S2.

Popkin, B., Paeratakul, S., Zhai, F. and Ge, K. (1995) A review of dietary and environmental correlates of obesity with emphasis on developing countries. *Obesity Research*, 3, 145s.

Pozo, J. and Argente, J. (2002) Delayed puberty in chronic illness. *Best Practice and Research: Clinical Endocrinology and Metabolism*, 16, 73–90.

Proos, L., Hofvander, Y. and Tuvemo, T. (1991) Menarcheal age and growth pattern of Indian girls adopted in Sweden. I. Menarcheal age. *Acta Paediatrica*, 80, 852–858.

Ranjitkar, S. (2006) Stature and skeletal maturation of two cohorts of Australian children and young adults over the past two decades. *Australian Orthodontics Journal*, 22, 47–58.

Ritzén, E. (2003) Early puberty: what is normal and when is treatment indicated? *Hormone Research*, 60, 31–34.

Roche, A., Chumlea, W. and Thissen, D. (1988) *Assessing the Skeletal Maturity of the Hand–Wrist*, Charles C. Thomas, Springfield, IL.

Rogol, A., Roemmich, J. and Clark, P. (2002) Growth at puberty. *Journal of Adolescent Health*, 31, 192–200.

Schell, L., Gallo, M., Denham, M. and Ravenscroft, J. (2006) Effects of pollution on human growth and development: an introduction. *Journal of Physiological Anthropology and Applied Human Science*, 25, 103–112.

Seow, W. (1996) A study of the development of the permanent dentition in very low birthweight children. *Pediatric Dental Journal*, 18, 379–384.

Seow, W. and Wan, A. (2000) A controlled study of the morphometric changes in the primary dentition of pre-term, very-low-birth weight children. *Journal of Dental Research*, 79, 63–69.

Shakir, A. and Zaini, S. (1974) Skeletal maturation of the hand and wrist of young children in Baghdad. *Annals of Human Biology*, 1, 189–199.

Silva, H. and Padez, C. (2006) Secular trends in age at menarche among Caboclo populations from Pará, Amazonia, Brazil: 1930–1980. *American Journal of Human Biology*, 18, 83–92.

Slyper, A. (2006) The pubertal timing controversy in the USA, and a review of possible causative factors for the advance in timing of onset of puberty. *Clinical Endocrinology*, 65, 1–8.

So, L. (1990) Secular trend in skeletal maturation in southern Chinese girls in Hong Kong. *Zeitschrift für Morphologie und Anthropologie*, 78, 145–153.

Sun, S., Schubert, C., Chumlea, W. *et al.* (2002) National estimates of the timing of sexual maturation and racial differences among US children. *Pediatrics*, 110, 911–919.

Swindler, D. and Emel, L. (1990) Dental development, skeletal maturation and body weight at birth in pig-tail macaques (*Macaca nemestrina*). *Archives of Oral Biology*, 35, 289–294.

Tanner, J. (1962) *Growth at Adolescence*, 2nd edn, Blackwell, Oxford.

Tanner, J. (1989) *Fetus into Man: Physical Growth from Conception to Maturity*, 2nd edn, Castlemead, Ware.

Tanner, J. and Whitehouse, R. (1959) *Standards for Skeletal Maturity. Part I*, International Children's Centre, Paris.

Tanner, J.M. and Whitehouse, R.H. (1976) Clinical longitudinal standards for height, weight, height velocity, weight velocity, and the stages of puberty. *Archives of Disease in Childhood*, 51, 170–179.

Tanner, J., Whitehouse, R. and Healy, M. (1962) *A New System for Estimating the Maturity of the Hand and Wrist, with Standards Derived from 2600 Healthy British Children. Part II*, International Children's Centre, Paris.

Tanner, J.M., Whitehouse, R.H., Marshall, W.A. *et al.* (1975) *Assessment of Skeletal Maturity and Prediction of Adult Height*, Academic Press, Oxford.

Tanner, J.M., Healy, M.J.R., Goldstein, H. and Cameron, N. (2001) *Assessment of Skeletal Maturity and Prediction of Adult Height: TW3 Method*, 3rd edn, W.B. Saunders, London.

Tanner, J., Whitehouse, R., Cameron, N. *et al.* (1983) *Assessment of Skeletal Maturity and Prediction of Adult Height (TW2 Method)*, 2nd edn, Academic Press, Oxford.

Teilmann, G., Main, K., Skakkebaek, N. and Juul, A. (2002) High frequency of central precocious puberty in adopted and immigrant children in Denmark. *Hormone Research*, 58 (Suppl 2), 135.

Teilmann, G., Pedersen, C., Skakkebaek, N. and Jensen, T. (2006) Increased risk of precocious puberty in internationally adopted children in Denmark. *Pediatrics*, 118, e391.

Torstveit, M. and Sundgot-Borgen, J. (2005) Participation in leanness sports but not training volume is associated with menstrual dysfunction: a national survey of 1276 elite athletes and controls. *British Journal of Sports Medicine*, 39, 141–147.

Towne, B., Czerwinski, S., Demerath, E. *et al.* (2005) Heritability of age at menarche in girls from the Fels Longitudinal Study. *American Journal of Physical Anthropology*, **128**, 210–219.

Ulijaszek, S., Johnston, F. and Preece, M. (eds) (1998) *The Cambridge Encyclopedia of Human Growth and Development*, Cambridge University Press, Cambridge.

Van Den Berg, S. and Boomsma, D. (2007) The familial clustering of age at menarche in extended twin families. *Behaviour Genetics*, 37, 661–667.

Van Den Berg, S., Setiawan, A., Bartels, M. *et al.* (2006) Individual differences in puberty onset in girls: Bayesian estimation of heritabilities and genetic correlations. *Behaviour Genetics*, 36, 261–270.

Vignolo, M., Milani, S., Cerbello, G. *et al.* (1992) FELS, Greulich–Pyle, and Tanner–Whitehouse bone age assessments in a group of Italian children and adolescents. *American Journal of Human Biology*, 4, 493–500.

Viner, R. (2002) Splitting hairs. *Archives of Disease in Childhood*, 86, 8–10.

Virdis, R., Street, M., Zampolli, M. *et al.* (1998) Precocious puberty in girls adopted from developing countries. *Archives of Disease in Childhood*, 78, 152–154.

Waldmann, E., Baber, F., Field, C. *et al.* (1977) Skeletal maturation of Hong Kong Chinese children in the first five years of life. *Annals of Human Biology*, 4, 343–352.

Wang, D. and Murphy, M. (2002) Trends and differentials in menarcheal age in China. *Journal of Biosocial Science*, 34, 349–361.

Wattigney, W., Srinivasan, S., Chen, W. *et al.* (1999) Secular trend of earlier onset of menarche with increasing obesity in black and white girls: the Bogalusa Heart Study. *Ethnicity and Disease*, 9, 181–189.

Whincup, P., Gilg, J., Odoki, K. *et al.* (2001) Age of menarche in contemporary British teenagers: survey of girls born between 1982 and 1986. *British Medical Journal*, **322**, 1095–1096.

Wierson, M., Long, P. and Forehand, R. (1993) Toward a new understanding of early menarche: the role of environmental stress in pubertal timing. *Adolescence*, **28**, 913–924.

Wu, T., Mendola, P. and Buck, G. (2002) Ethnic differences in the presence of secondary sex characteristics and menarche among US girls: the Third National Health and Nutrition Examination Survey, 1988–1994. *Pediatrics*, **110**, 752–757.

Zhang, S., Liu, L., Wu, Z. *et al.* (2008) Standards of TW3 skeletal maturity for Chinese children. *Annals of Human Biology*, **35**, 349–354.

8

Practical Imaging Techniques for Age Evaluation

Andreas Schmeling[1], Sven Schmidt[1], Ronald Schulz[1], Andreas Olze[2],
Walter Reisinger[3] and Volker Vieth[4]

[1] Institut für Rechtsmedizin, Universitätsklinikum Münster, Röntgenstraße 23,
48149 Münster, Germany
[2] Institut für Rechtsmedizin, Charité – Universitätsmedizin Berlin, Turmstraße
21, 10559 Berlin, Germany
[3] Institut für Radiologie (CCM), Charité – Universitätsmedizin Berlin,
Schumannstraße 20/21, 10117 Berlin, Germany
[4] Institut für Klinische Radiologie, Universitätsklinikum Münster,
Albert-Schweitzer-Straße 33, 48149 Münster, Germany

8.1 Introduction

In 2001 the international and interdisciplinary Study Group on Forensic Age Diagnostics (http://rechtsmedizin.klinikum.uni-muenster.de/agfad/index) published recommendations for forensic age estimations in living individuals between the ages of 14 and 21 in criminal proceedings (Schmeling et al., 2001). These were updated in 2008 (Schmeling et al., 2008). The updated recommendations advised that the following be performed:

- a physical examination with determination of anthropometric measures (body height and weight, constitutional type),

- inspection of signs of sexual maturation,

- identification of age-relevant developmental disorders,

- an X-ray examination of the left hand,

- dental examination including the determination of the dental status and evaluation of an orthopantomogram.

If the skeletal development of the hand is completed, an additional X-ray examination, computerized tomography (CT) or magnetic resonance imaging (MRI) scan of the medial clavicle should be carried out.

Guidelines for the use of ionizing radiation vary from country to country and with different professional groups (see Chapter 4). When utilizing X-rays the local regulations, statutes or professional guidelines should be observed.

The recommended methods should be combined to increase the diagnostic accuracy and to improve the identification of age-relevant developmental disorders. The individual examinations should be performed by experienced clinicians and forensic specialists. In addition to the established age-relevant findings, the individual expert reports must quote the methods and/or staging as well as the reference studies on which the age estimation is based. The criteria for reference studies on forensic age diagnostics are listed in the recommendations. For each examined feature, the report must indicate the most probable age and the range of scatter of the reference population. The coordinating expert has to provide a final age diagnosis on the basis of the findings of the individual expert reports.

This chapter describes imaging techniques of forensic age diagnostics in juveniles and adolescents and instructions on how to interpret the radiological findings.

8.2   Radiation Exposure in X-ray Examinations for the Purpose of Age Estimation

Since the X-ray examinations are arguably carried out for forensic age estimations without a medical therapeutic reason the question arises whether there are any risks to the individual due to the radiation exposure.

The effective dose from an X-ray examination of the hand is 0.1 microsievert (µSv) (Okkalides and Fotakis, 1994), from an orthopantomogram (OPG) 26 µSv (Frederiksen, Benson and Sokolowski, 1994), from a conventional X-ray examination of the clavicles 220 µSv (Okkalides and Fotakis, 1994) and from a CT scan of the clavicles 600 µSv (Jurik, Jensen and Hansen, 1996). According to the relatively high effective dose of the X-ray and CT examinations of the clavicles, their use should be restricted to individuals with completed hand ossification.

The levels of naturally occurring and other ambient civilian radiation exposure can be compared to amounts of radiation exposure from radiological procedures to assess the potential risk to the individual. The dose from naturally occurring radiation exposure in Germany is 2.1 millisievert (mSv) on average per year. Apart from the direct cosmic radiation of 0.3 mSv and the direct terrestrial radiation of 0.4 mSv, the ingestion of naturally occurring radioactive substances in food contributes 0.3 mSv to the radiation exposure. For the inhalation of radon and its disintegration products 1.1 mSv must be added (Bundesministerium für Umwelt, Naturschutz und Reaktorsicherheit, 2007). Compared to naturally occurring radiation exposure one hand X-ray equals the naturally occurring radiation exposure of 25 minutes, one OPG is equivalent to 4.5 days, one X-ray of the clavicles equates to 38 days and one CT scan of the clavicles equates to 104 days.

The highest contribution to civilian radiation exposure comes from medical procedures with about 2.0 mSv per inhabitant per year (Bundesministerium für Umwelt, Naturschutz und Reaktorsicherheit, 2007). The radiation exposure from an intercontinental flight at an altitude of 12 000 metres is 0.008 mSv per hour. It follows that the dose for a flight from Frankfurt to New York is 0.05 mSv (Bundesministerium für Umwelt, Naturschutz und Reaktorsicherheit, 2007). That means that the radiation exposure from two OPGs is equivalent to the radiation exposure from an intercontinental flight. On the basis of this comparison a true health risk as a result of X-ray examinations for forensic age estimations can largely be excluded (Schmeling et al., 2000b).

Concerning a possible health risk, the biological effect of X-rays needs to be discussed as well. In this case a distinction between stochastic and non-stochastic radiation effects has to be made. Non-stochastic effects appear above 100 mSv and are therefore irrelevant to radiological diagnostics. DNA damage leading to mutations of the genotype and malignant diseases is one of the stochastic effects. To assess the risk of these stochastic effects in the low-dose region, the observed risk of high doses, for example of survivors of the nuclear bombs in Hiroshima and Nagasaki, is extrapolated to low doses on the assumption of a linear dose–effect curve without a threshold dose. This procedure is a controversial issue. A group of radiation scientists even postulated biopositive effects – so-called 'radiation hormesis' (also called radiation homoeostasis) – in the low-dose region resulting in a stimulation of the cellular detoxification of chemically aggressive metabolic products, stimulation of DNA repair and an improved immune defence response. So far these biopositive effects have only been detected at the cellular level (Feinendegen, 1994). By contrast, Rothkamm and Löbrich (2003) identified that DNA double-strand breaks after radiation exposure in the low-dose region remained unrepaired, while DNA damages that were caused by high doses were repaired within a few days. These studies were undertaken on isolated cell cultures and the extent to which the results can be transferred to the complete organism remains unclear.

Cancer mortality risks can be calculated for adults and children on the assumption that there is a linear dose–effect relationship and thus even X-rays in the low-dose region can cause a malignant disease although there is no identifiable threshold between the risk of radiation exposure and the delivered radiation dose. The risk for children is considered to be twice the risk for adults and these cancer mortality risks can be compared to other life risks (see Table 8.1). The mortality risks of the X-rays are much lower than other life risks.

The German radiation biologist Jung (2000) compared the mortality risk of X-ray examinations for age estimations with the mortality risk resulting from the participation in traffic with the risk to have a fatal accident. He came to the conclusion that the mortality risk of an OPG is comparable to the participation in traffic for 2.5 hours. Thus, the radiation risk of the X-ray examination is comparable to the

Table 8.1 Comparison of different life risks and the likelihood of fatal event.

Life risk	Likelihood of fatal event
X-ray hand (child)	1 : 10 000 000
X-ray hand (adult)	1 : 20 000 000
OPG (child)	1 : 380 000
OPG (adult)	1 : 770 000
X-ray clavicle (adult)	1 : 90 000
CT clavicle (adult)	1 : 30 000
Drowning	1 : 2 900
Homicide	1 : 530
Accident	1 : 220
Fall	1 : 140
Myocardial infarction	1 : 20
Malignant tumour	1 : 7

(*Source*: Statistisches Bundesamt, 2004; Aebi *et al.*, 2006; Ramsthaler *et al.*, 2009)

risk of the examined individual's exposure to traffic *en route* to the examination or perhaps the trial. If the risk of an appointment for an age estimation is deemed to be acceptable, then perhaps this should also apply to the radiation risk of the X-ray examination itself (Jung, 2000).

However, as long as the discussion about the biological radiation effect in the low-dose region is undecided, the so-called minimizing order remains valid without restrictions. It demands that any necessary examination is carried out with the minimum amount of radiation and without unnecessary exposure. Thus, no X-rays should be made beyond the examination range specified in scientific recommendations (Schmeling *et al.*, 2008; Cunha *et al.*, 2009).

8.3 Radiological Examination of the Hand

Within the area of forensic age estimations in adolescents, skeletal maturation is a vital diagnostic pillar. In this regard, the hand skeleton is particularly suitable until the developmental processes are completed at around the age of about 18 years. The maturity status of the hand may, in some regards, be considered representative of the entire skeletal system (Greulich and Pyle, 1959; Schmid and Moll, 1960; Hansman and Maresh, 1961; Gefferth, 1970; Hägg and Taranger, 1980; Thiemann and Nitz, 1991).

A basic prerequisite for radiological age estimation is a physical examination in order to establish whether the proband exhibits a clinical condition that may affect skeletal development. Most diseases delay development and are thus conducive to underestimation of age. Such underestimation of age would not disadvantage the person concerned in terms of criminal prosecution. By contrast, overestimating age due to a disease that accelerates development should be avoided at all costs. Such diseases occur very rarely and include, above all, endocrinal disorders, which may affect not only the attainment of height and sexual development, but also skeletal development. Endocrine disorders that may accelerate skeletal development include precocious puberty, adrenogenital syndrome and hyperthyroidism (Stöver, 1983), among others.

An X-ray of the left hand is taken as, in all populations, the number of right-hand dominants is higher and, as a result, the right hand is more often exposed to traumata that can impair skeletal development (Greulich and Pyle, 1959; Graham, 1972). However, there are no reported significant differences in the ossification rates of right and left hands (Roche, 1963; Liliequist and Lundberg, 1971).

Criteria for evaluating hand radiographs include the form and size of bone elements and the degree of epiphyseal ossification. To this effect, either a given X-ray image is compared with standard images of the relevant age and sex (radiographic atlas) (Greulich and Pyle, 1959; Thiemann, Nitz and Schmeling, 2006), or the degree of maturity or bone age is determined for selected bones (single bone method) (Greulich and Pyle, 1959; Roche, Chumlea and Thissen, 1988; Tanner *et al.*, 1975, 2001).

Various studies have demonstrated that although the single bone method requires more time, it does not necessarily yield more accurate results (Andersen, 1971; Weber, 1978; Cole, Webb and Cole, 1988; King *et al.*, 1994). Therefore, the two atlas methods developed by Greulich and Pyle (1959) and by Thiemann, Nitz and Schmeling (2006) seem to be a valid approach for forensic age estimation.

Probably the best known and the most widely used is the Greulich–Pyle (GP) atlas method (Greulich and Pyle, 1959). Their *Radiographic Atlas of Skeletal Development of the Hand and Wrist* was published in 1950 and again in 1959, with the most recent reprint in 2001. The work is based on a collection of radiological films produced between 1931 and 1942 as part of the Brush Foundation longitudinal study. The reference population consisted of 1000 Americans born in the United States, most of Northern European origins, living in Cleveland, Ohio, and aged 0–18 years. The subjects came from financially comfortable backgrounds (Greulich and Pyle, 1959). The method is illustrated by means of Figure 8.1.

The skeletal age to be determined on the basis of a hand radiograph is consistent with the respective Greulich–Pyle standard image with the highest radiomorphological conformity. Between the hand radiograph to be evaluated (Figure 8.1B) and the Greulich–Pyle standard image 25 for male individuals (Figure 8.1A), the following similarities indicating a skeletal age of 14 years have been detected:

- The epiphysis of the radius and the epiphysis of all phalanges of the second, third, fourth and fifth fingers have begun to cap their shafts.

- The sides of the epiphysis of the second to the fifth metacarpals are now aligned closely with the sides of their shafts. The growth cartilage plates are uniformly narrow and some portions of the epiphyseal shaft spaces are fuzzy.

In contrast to the Greulich–Pyle standard image 26 for male individuals (Figure 8.1C), the following features indicating a skeletal age of 15 cannot be found in the hand radiograph to be evaluated (Figure 8.1B):

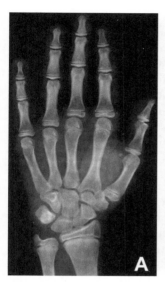 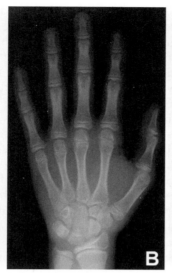 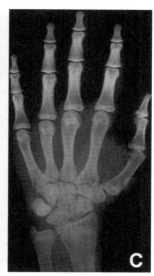

Figure 8.1 Greulich–Pyle method. (A) Male standard 25 of the Greulich–Pyle atlas (skeletal age: 14 years). (B) Hand radiograph of the individual to be evaluated. (C) Male standard 26 of the Greulich–Pyle atlas (skeletal age: 15 years).

– The epiphysis of the ulna is not as wide as its shaft and does not follow its contour closely.

– Fusion is not under way in the epiphysis of all distal phalanges.

In the synopsis, this results in a skeletal age of 14.0 years for the hand radiograph to be evaluated.

  In a recent study, Schmidt *et al.* (2008) studied the applicability of the GP method in forensic age diagnostics. They presented statistical measurement data separately for each sex and for age increments from 5.0 to 16.0 years and the standard deviations ranged from 0.4 to 1.7 years for the girls and 0.3 to 1.3 years for the boys. If a more or less normal statistical distribution of chronological age within the sample groups is assumed, the standard deviation can be used as a parameter for the margin of error of an estimate. In 68% of the probands of a certain skeletal age, the chronological age equals the mean value ± the standard deviation, and in 95% of the probands it equals the mean value ± twice the standard deviation. According to their results, the authors concluded that if the GP method is used exclusively, it can be claimed with a probability of 95% that a young man has reached the age of 14 years and thus the age of criminal liability in many countries if his skeletal age is at least 15.5 years. In the case of female subjects, even if they are estimated as being 16.0 years old, it cannot be asserted with a probability of 95% that they have reached the age of 14.

  Compared to the GP method, the Thiemann–Nitz radiographic atlas method is based on a more recent sample. In the former German Democratic Republic in 1977,

20 medical institutions collated and analysed 5200 hand X-rays taken from healthy subjects aged between 0 and 18 years. The children were selected in accordance with a standardized study design. Height and body weight had to be within the double standard deviation of the standard value tables of height and body weight by Sälzler (1967) for 0- to 3-year-olds and by Marcusson (1961) for 4- to 18-year-olds. The first edition of the atlas was published in 1986 and the second edition in 1991. Due to the missing ranges of scatter for skeletal age, the forensic applicability of the Thiemann–Nitz atlas was limited. This shortcoming was resolved in the third revised and amended edition published in 2006. For the forensically relevant age interval the simple standard deviation of skeletal ages is between 0.2 and 1.2 years (Thiemann, Nitz and Schmeling, 2006).

An innovative method to determine the skeletal age of the hand was presented by Cameriere *et al.* (2006). In this method, the ratio of the carpal area and the total area of carpal bones and epiphyses of the radius and ulna are determined. A simple linear regression model was used to describe the relationship between age and this ratio. In this regression analysis, the standard error of estimate was 1.2 years.

Since the subjects of forensic examination mostly belong to populations for which no detailed reference studies are available that could be used for forensic purposes, the question arises as to whether there are significant developmental differences between various ethnic groups that would prohibit the application of relevant age standards to members of ethnic groups other than the reference population. In this respect the term 'ethnicity' shall be used only to identify the affinity of various populations in terms of origin.

Numerous studies are available on skeletal maturation of all major ethnic groups (Africans, Australians, Caucasoids and Mongoloids) (Schmeling *et al.*, 2000a). Because there are several potential factors of influence, their simultaneous action makes assessment of population differences a difficult exercise, all the more so as the validity of some of those investigations seems to be limited to small sample sizes, the exclusive consideration of non-relevant age groups, lack of information on health, ethnic identity and socio-economic status and absence of confirmed data on proband age. Hence, for the problem at hand, greatest relevance may be claimed for studies on various ethnic groups of similar socio-economic status and living in one and the same region or populations of one and the same socio-economic status living in different regions. Such studies are available from the USA, where research has been conducted on descendants of Caucasoids, Mongoloids and Africans, as well as from numerous ethnic groups of the former Soviet Union.

In a comparison with the GP standards, Sutow (1953) discussed racial differences as one of the causes of retarded skeletal maturation of Japanese children living in Japan. His findings were checked by Greulich (1957), who referred to Japanese individuals living in the USA. He studied hand bone development in 898 children of Japanese descent aged between 5 and 18 years living in the San Francisco Bay area of California. While retarded skeletal maturation, in comparison with the GP standards, was recorded by Sutow for all age groups of Japanese living in their own country, such retardation was detected by Greulich only in boys aged between 5 and 7 years. Boys aged between 13 and 17 and girls between 10 and 17 years even exhibited comparative acceleration. Greulich concluded that the significant retardation, in comparison with the GP standards, recorded for children living in Japan was attributable to less favourable nutritional and environmental conditions rather than to racial differences. Improved living standards in recent decades resulted in accelerated skeletal maturation even in Japanese living in Japan (Kimura, 1977a,b) which, in the meantime has come to lie within the range of socio-economically advanced European populations (Wenzel, Droschl and Melsen, 1984; Beunen et al., 1990).

Whereas some authors (Massé and Hunt, 1963; Garn et al., 1972) reported comparatively accelerated skeletal development in Africans in early childhood, ethnic origin obviously has no significant impact on the bone growth rate in later childhood and adolescence. Platt (1956) studied skeletal maturation in 100 Black inhabitants of Florida, 143 Blacks in Philadelphia and 100 Whites in Philadelphia aged between 5 and 14 years. In none of these three groups was skeletal age, as determined by identical X-ray standards, significantly different from chronological age. Platt compared his results with studies on Black residents of Africa. Mackay (1952) recorded retardation by 1.5 to 2 years for East Africans, while Weiner and Thambipillai (1952) recorded an average retardation of 16 months for West Africans. The assumption of an ethnic impact on skeletal maturation would justify expectation of a continuous series of phenomena ranging from severe retardation in Blacks in Africa to moderate retardation in Black Americans who had mixed with Whites through to absence of retardation in Whites. Such continuous series do not exist, and consequently Platt postulated that health and nutrition are likely to be the major factors influencing skeletal maturation, not ethnic origin.

Skeletal maturation in 461 Black and 380 White Americans in the Lake Erie region was studied by Loder et al. (1993) between 1986 and 1990. Using the atlas method of Greulich and Pyle on the age group of 13–18 years, they recorded comparative acceleration of 0.45 years for White boys, 0.16 years for White girls, 0.38 years for Black boys and 0.52 years for Black girls. Johnston (1963) studied the same age group of White Americans in Philadelphia by the same method and found acceleration values of 0.39 years for boys and 0.58 years for girls. Johnston's data for White Americans were almost identical to Loder's findings for Black Americans, which seems to clearly underline that in the populations of the age group studied, there were no ethnic differences with regard to skeletal maturation. Roche, Roberts and Hamill (1975, 1978) investigated skeletal maturation in the context of race, geographic region, family income and educational standards of parents in a representative cross-section of the US population aged between 6 and 17 years. They found no consistent Black–White differences, with no significant differences between regions nor any urban–rural differences.

Comprehensive studies were conducted on skeletal maturation in different ethnic groups of the former Soviet Union, and 16 studies of 17 ethnic groups in different climatic and geographic zones of the former Soviet Union were evaluated by Pashkova and Burov (1980). Included were Russians, Ukrainians, Georgians, Armenians, Azerbaijanis, Balkarians, Cabardines, Kazakhs, Tadchiks, Uzbeks, Ingushi, Chechenians, Udmurtians, Chukchen, Koryaks, Intelmenians and Evenkians. The range of variation at all stages of skeletal maturation was less than one year in all populations studied. However, the causes of those variations were attributed by the authors to relatively small samples, different methods and techniques used in the studies or undiagnosed clinical conditions of probands but were not attributed to ethnic, regional or climatic differences.

Studies evaluated so far seem to suggest that there is a genetically determined element to skeletal maturation that does not appear to depend on ethnicity and may be exploited under optimum environmental conditions (i.e. high socio-economic status), whereas a less favourable environment may lead to retardation of skeletal maturation. Applying X-ray standards to individuals of a socio-economic status lower than that of the reference population usually leads to underestimating a person's age. In terms of criminal responsibility, this has no adverse effect on the person concerned as it may remove them from the age where they can be charged with criminal acts. It may, however, have adverse effects on a victim's ability to pursue redress.

8.4   Radiological Examination of the Teeth

The main criteria for dental age estimation in adolescents and young adults are eruption and mineralization of the third molars.

Tooth eruption is a parameter of developmental morphology that, unlike tooth mineralization, can be determined in two ways: by clinical examination and/or by evaluation of dental X-rays. While 'eruption' incorporates the entire journey of the tooth from its formation in the alveolar crypts to full occlusion, 'emergence' is restricted to the time when any part of the tooth finally clears the gingival margin and becomes visible in the mouth until the stage when the tooth finally comes into occlusion with its partner tooth from the opposing jaw (Scheuer and Black, 2000). Olze et al. (2007) defined a stage classification of third molar eruption based on evidence from conventional OPGs (Figure 8.2):

Stage A: Occlusal plane covered with alveolar bone.

Stage B: Alveolar emergence; complete resorption of alveolar bone over occlusal plane.

Stage C: Gingival emergence; penetration of gingiva by at least one dental cusp.

Stage D: Complete emergence in occlusal plane.

Olze et al. (2007) analysed and compared the chronological course of third molar eruption in German, Japanese and South African populations. They found that their German sample had an intermediate rate of dental development as determined by comparing the different ages of third molar eruption. The defined eruption stages occurred at earlier ages in the investigated South African sample, and at later ages in the Japanese sample. Statistically significant population differences were observed in males at stages A and B. The South African males were on average 3.0 to 3.2 years younger than the German males at these stages of development, and the Japanese males were on average 3.1 to 4.2 years older than their South African counterparts for the same developmental stage. The females exhibited statistically

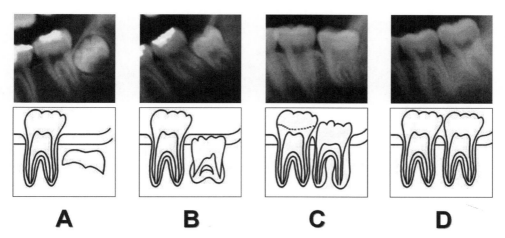

Figure 8.2 Stages of third molar eruption.

significant population differences at stages A, B and C. The South African females reached the target stages on average 1.6 to 1.8 years earlier than the German females, whereas the Japanese females were on average 0.9 to 3.3 years older than their German counterparts. It was concluded that population-specific reference data should be used when evaluating third molar eruption for the purpose of forensic age estimation.

Various classifications have been devised for evaluating tooth mineralization (Gleiser and Hunt, 1955; Nolla, 1960; Haavikko, 1970; Liliequist and Lundberg, 1971; Demirjian, Goldstein and Tanner, 1973; Gustafson and Koch, 1974; Nortje, 1983; Harris and Nortje, 1984; Kullman, Johanson and Akesson, 1992; Köhler et al., 1994). They differ with regard to the number of stages, the definition of each stage and the presentation. Since the validity of an age estimate depends crucially on the classification method used, practitioners should select the most appropriate one. Olze et al. (2005) assessed the validity of five basic types of classification. They selected the methods by Gleiser and Hunt (1955), Demirjian, Goldstein and Tanner (1973), Gustafson and Koch (1974), Harris and Nortje (1984) and Kullman, Johanson and Akesson (1992). Of these methods the most accurate results were obtained following Demirjian's classification system (Figure 8.3):

Stage A: Cusp tips are mineralized but have not yet coalesced.

Stage B: Mineralized cusps are united so the mature coronal morphology is well defined.

Stage C: The crown is about half formed; the pulp chamber is evident and dentinal deposition is occurring.

Stage D: Crown formation is complete to the dentoenamel junction. The pulp chamber has a trapezoidal form.

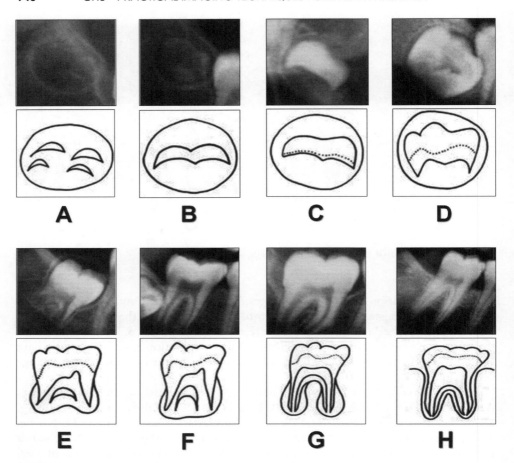

Figure 8.3 Demirjian's stages of third molar mineralization.

Stage E: Formation of the inter-radicular bifurcation has begun. Root length is less than the crown length.

Stage F: Root length is at least as great as crown length. Roots have funnel-shaped endings.

Stage G: Root walls are parallel, but apices remain open.

Stage H: Apical ends of the roots are completely closed, and the periodontal membrane has a uniform width around the root.

Demirjian's classification performed best not only for observer agreement but also for the correlation between estimated and true age. It is argued that this is due to the fact that Demirjian's classification is based on a sufficient number of stages, which are defined independently of speculative estimations of length. This leads to the conclusion that the method devised by Demirjian should be used for evaluating the mineralization of third molars for purposes of forensic age determination.

One question of major practical relevance to estimating age from a dental view is whether the reference data customarily used for forensic diagnosis, derived from White North Americans on the one hand and Central and Northern Europeans on the other, can also be applied to members of other ethnic groups.

Few comparative studies are available on the subject of third molar mineralization. Gorgani, Sullivan and DuBois (1990) examined 229 Black and 221 White US citizens aged 6–14 years. Among the Black subjects, crown mineralization of the third molars was completed one year earlier. Harris and McKee (1990) studied 655 White and 335 Black US citizens aged 3.5–13 years. Whereas the Black subjects reached the earlier stages of third molar mineralization about one year earlier, the gap appeared to narrow for later stages. This trend is confirmed by the work of Mincer, Harris and Berryman (1993). They examined 823 US citizens (80% White, 19% Black) aged 14–25 years but did not establish any significant differences in the time frame for third molar mineralization. Daito, Tanaka and Hieda (1992) addressed third molar mineralization in 9111 Japanese children aged 7–16 years and compared their data with the values provided by Gravely (1965), Rantanen (1967) and Haavikko (1970) for Caucasoid populations. No significant differences were discovered. These studies only lend themselves to limited comparison due to small sample sizes, varying methods and assessment by different observers. A further problem lies in the fact that the age data for subjects of Black African origin often was not verified. Moreover, most available studies focus on the earlier stages of mineralization.

A comparative study of third molar mineralization (Olze et al., 2004) was carried out on three population samples: German, Japanese and South African. To this end, 3652 conventional OPGs were evaluated on the basis of Demirjian's stages. Statistically significant differences between the samples investigated were established for the age at which stages D–G of third molar mineralization were achieved. Significant differences between German and Japanese males were noted for stages D–G of mineralization. Significant differences between Japanese and German females were observed for stages D–F. According to these findings, Japanese males and females were approximately 1–2 years older than their German counterparts when they reached stages D–F. Significant age differences between South African and German males applied to stages D–E. Significant age differences between South African and German females were observed for stages E and G. The South African subjects were approximately 1–2 years younger than the German subjects upon achieving these stages of mineralization. Significant age differences between the South African and Japanese samples were ascertained for both sexes at stages D–G. The South African subjects were approx. 1–4 years younger than the Japanese subjects upon reaching these stages.

The population differences observed here may be due to differences in palatal dimensions between the ethnic groups surveyed. The largest palatal dimensions are observed in Africans and the smallest in Mongoloids, with Caucasoids assuming the middle rank (Byers, Churchill and Curran, 1997). Inadequate space in the maxillary crest causes delay in third molar eruption, if not retention (Fanning, 1962). In turn, retained third molars mineralize later than teeth whose eruption has not been impeded (Köhler *et al.*, 1994). This would explain why Caucasoid populations occupy the middle position in relative terms when it comes to third molar mineralization, while Mongoloid populations display a comparative delay and African populations a relative acceleration.

8.5   Radiological Examination of the Clavicles

To answer the question of whether a person has reached the age of 18 it is particularly helpful to evaluate the ossification status of the medial epiphysis of the clavicle, because all other examined developmental systems may already have completed their growth by that age.

While traditional classification systems differentiate between four stages of clavicle ossification (stage 1: ossification centre not ossified; stage 2: ossification centre ossified, epiphyseal plate not ossified; stage 3: epiphyseal plate partly ossified; stage 4: epiphyseal plate fully ossified), Schmeling *et al.* (2004) divided the stage of total epiphyseal fusion into two additional stages (stage 4: epiphyseal plate fully ossified, epiphyseal scar visible; stage 5: epiphyseal plate fully ossified, epiphyseal scar no longer visible) (Figure 8.4).

The possible approaches to examine the medial clavicular epiphysis in living individuals are conventional radiography, CT, as well as new approaches using MRI and ultrasound, as presented in previous pilot studies (Schmidt *et al.*, 2007; Schulz *et al.*, 2008b; Quirmbach, Ramsthaler and Verhoff, 2009).

There is only one study referring to conventional radiography that meets the requirements of a reference study as stated by the Study Group on Forensic Age

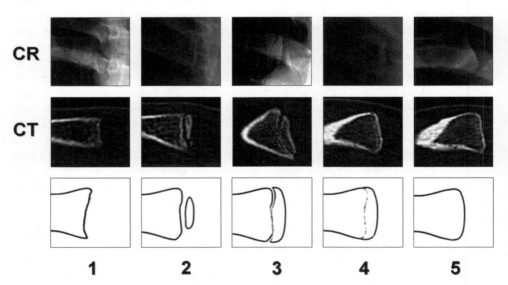

Figure 8.4 Stages of clavicular ossification (CR = conventional radiography; CT = computed tomography).

Diagnostics. In this study the earliest age at which stage 3 was detected in either sex was 16 years. Stage 4 was first observed in women at 20 years and in men at 21 years. Stage 5 was first achieved by both sexes at age 26 (Schmeling *et al.*, 2004). It was concluded that plain chest postero-anterior (PA) radiographs can essentially provide a basis for assessing clavicular ossification. If overlap in PA views impedes evaluation, additional oblique images should be taken to facilitate age estimation (Bontrager and Lampignano, 2009).

In 1997 and 1998, Kreitner *et al.* published the first CT-based studies in which the medial epiphyseal ossification of the clavicle was evaluated applying a four-stage scheme. Since these studies did not discriminate results by sex, their forensic value is limited. In a CT study conducted by Schulz *et al.* in 2005, presenting more cases and results discriminated by sex, the five-stage classification by Schmeling *et al.* (2004) was used. The earliest occurrence of stage 3 in females was noted at age 16 and in males at age 17. Stage 4 was first achieved by both sexes at age 21. Stage 5 was first noted in females at age 21 and in males at age 22, which is 4 or 5 years earlier than is reported in the conventional radiographic studies. Schulz *et al.* (2005) raised the question whether CT scans with a slice thickness of >1 mm could cause misinterpretation of clavicle ossification status and recommended examining the influence of slice thickness on the age intervals of ossification stages in additional studies.

In a study on the influence of the slice thickness on the ability to assess the stages of clavicular ossification, Mühler *et al.* (2006) retrospectively analysed the CTs of 40 individuals that had been examined within the scope of age diagnostics. Scans with slice thicknesses of 1, 3, 5 and 7 mm were reconstructed from the obtained data. Seven out of eighty clavicular epiphyseal plates showed differences depending on the layer thickness in the particular stages of ossification. In one case a slice thickness of 1 mm led to a different diagnosis of the ossification stage than a slice thickness of 3 mm, in three cases the diagnoses differed between slice thicknesses of 3 mm and of 5 mm, and in another three cases between 5 and 7 mm. The authors therefore concluded that for age estimation purposes the slice thickness should be 1 mm in order to ensure maximum accuracy and diagnostic reliability.

Recently, Kellinghaus *et al.* (2009) published data from a thin-slice CT study. In this study stage 3 was first achieved by male individuals at age 17 and in females at age 16. The occurrence of stage 4 was first found in both sexes at the age of 21. In either sex, the earliest observation of stage 5 was at age 26. These findings are consistent with the data from the conventional study of the clavicle (Schmeling *et al.* 2004).

Schulz *et al.* (2008a) comparatively assessed conventional chest PA radiographs and CT scans of sternoclavicular joints used to perform forensic age assessments in 57 individuals undergoing criminal proceedings. Because of superimposition of other structures, it was not possible to determine reliably the ossification stage of the clavicle by conventional radiography in 15 out of 114 clavicles assessed. Regarding agreement between the methods, both radiography and CT produced identical staging results in 97 out of 99 clavicular epiphyses. In two cases, however, ossification was classified as stage 2 by CT and as stage 3 by conventional radiography. They therefore concluded that in forensic age estimation practice, it is necessary that conventional radiographic reference studies be used for ossification stage classification by conventional radiography and that CT reference studies be used for ossification stage classification by computed tomography.

For forensic age estimations in living individuals, non-ionizing procedures for the presentation of the medial clavicular epiphyseal cartilage would be desirable, as the radiation exposure from the necessary imaging examination could be decreased considerably. Against this background an MRI study (Schmidt *et al.*, 2007) and ultrasound studies (Schulz *et al.*, 2008b; Quirmbach, Ramsthaler and Verhoff, 2009) were performed to determine whether the degree of ossification of the medial clavicular epiphyseal cartilage could be assessed using these techniques. It was shown that the age intervals observed for the ossification stages were consistent with the known data from radiological and CT assessments. Due to the small sample sizes it was proposed to confirm the results in a larger number of cases. This is clearly a route for further investigation (Mentzel *et al.*, 2005; Dvorak *et al.*, 2007; Khan *et al.*, 2009).

8.6   Summary and Conclusions

The results of any and all of the factors incorporated in the analysis of age, whether via physical examination, radiographic examination of the hand, dental examination and/or the radiographic (CT) examination of the clavicles, should be compiled by a coordinating clinical/forensic expert prior to making a final age estimation. The overall age estimate should include a discussion of the age-relevant variations resulting from application of the reference studies in an individual case, including factors of ethnicity and socio-economic status and their potential effect on the developmental status, or clinical conditions that may affect the development of the individual examined, including their effect on the estimated age. If possible, a quantitative assessment of any such effect should be given.

However, for age diagnoses obtained with a combination of methods there is still no satisfactory way to scientifically determine the margin of error. While a number of reference studies collected data on individual features and some studies both on skeletal maturation and tooth mineralization (Lamons and Gray, 1958; Grön, 1962; Lacey, 1973; Pfau and Sciulli, 1994), there is still no reference study available analysing all required features for a single reference population. If independent features are examined as part of an age diagnosis that combines several methods it may be assumed that the margin of error for the combined age diagnosis is smaller than that for each individual feature. However, it has not yet been possible to quantify this reduction. Combining methods makes it possible to identify statistical outliers, which should also reduce the scale of variation of the overall diagnosis to a certain non-quantifiable extent.

Indirect conclusions about the range of combined overall age diagnoses were possible after verifying age estimates carried out at the Institute of Legal Medicine in Berlin. To this effect, the court's case files of the persons originally examined for age estimation purposes at the institute were consulted to see whether the actual age of these persons was indeed established during the court proceedings. In the

43 cases where the age of the person concerned could be verified beyond doubt, the deviation between estimated and actual age ranged between plus and minus 12 months (Schmeling *et al.*, 2003).

References

Aebi, M.F., Aromaa, K., de Cavarlay, B.A. *et al.* (2006) *European Sourcebook of Crime and Criminal Justical Statistics*, 3rd edn, WODC, Den Haag.

Andersen, E. (1971) Comparison of Tanner–Whitehouse and Greulich–Pyle methods in a large scale Danish survey. *American Journal of Physical Anthropology*, **35**, 373–376.

Beunen, G., Lefevre, J. and Ostyn, M. *et al.* (1990) Skeletal maturity in Belgian youths assessed by the Tanner–Whitehouse method (TW2). *Annals of Human Biology*, **17**, 355–376.

Bontrager, K.L. and Lampignano, J.P. (2009) *Textbook of Radiographic Positioning and Related Anatomy*, C.V. Mosby/Elsevier, St Louis, MO.

Bundesministerium für Umwelt, Naturschutz und Reaktorsicherheit (2007) Umweltradioak-tivität und Strahlenbelastung im Jahr 2007, www.bmu.de/files/pdfs/allgemein/ application/pdf/parlamentsbericht07.pdf (accessed 28 December 2009).

Byers, S.N., Churchill, S.E. and Curran, B. (1997) Identification of Euro-Americans, Afro-Americans, and Ameridians from palatal dimensions. *Journal of Forensic Sciences*, **42**, 3–9.

Cameriere, R., Ferrante, L., Mirtella, D. and Cingolani, M. (2006) Carpals and epiphyses of radius and ulna as age indicators. *International Journal of Legal Medicine*, **120**, 143–146.

Cole, A.J.L., Webb, L. and Cole, T.J. (1988) Bone age estimation: a comparison of methods. *British Journal of Radiology*, **61**, 683–686.

Cunha, E., Baccino, E., Martrille, L. *et al.* (2009) The problem of aging human remains and living individuals: a review. *Forensic Science International*, **193**, 1–13.

Daito, M., Tanaka, M. and Hieda, T. (1992) Clinical observations on the development of third molars. *Journal of Osaka Dental University*, **26**, 91–104.

Demirjian, A., Goldstein, H. and Tanner, J.M. (1973) A new system of dental age assessment. *Human Biology*, **45**, 221–227.

Dvorak, J., George, J., Junge, A. and Hodler, J. (2007) Age determination by magnetic resonance imaging of the wrist in adolescent male football players. *British Journal of Sports Medicine*, **41**, 45–52.

Fanning, E.A. (1962) Third molar emergence in Bostonians. *American Journal of Physical Anthropology*, **20**, 339–346.

Feinendegen, L.E. (1994) Die mögliche Bedeutung günstiger Strahleneffekte in Zellen für den Gesamtorganismus. *Röntgenpraxis*, **47**, 289–292.

Frederiksen, N.L., Benson, B.W. and Sokolowski, T.W. (1994) Effective dose and risk assessment from film tomography used for dental implant diagnostics. *Dentomaxillofacial Radiology*, **23**, 123–127.

Garn, S.M., Sandusky, S.T., Nagy, J.M. and McCann, M.B. (1972) Advanced skeletal development in low income Negro children. *Journal of Pediatrics*, **80**, 965–969.

Gefferth, K. (1970) Ein Verfahren zur Bestimmung des biologischen Knochenalters. *Acta Paediatrica Academiae Scientiarum Hungaricae*, **1**, 59–66.

Gleiser, I. and Hunt, E.E. (1955) The permanent mandibular first molar; its calcification, eruption and decay. *American Journal of Physical Anthropology*, **13**, 253–284.

Gorgani, N., Sullivan, R.E. and DuBois, L. (1990) A radiographic investigation of third-molar development. *Journal of Dentistry for Children*, **57**, 106–110.

Graham, C.B. (1972) Assessment of bone maturation – methods and pitfalls. *Radiologic Clinics of North America*, **10**, 185–202.

Gravely, J.F. (1965) A radiographic survey of third molar development. *British Dental Journal*, **119**, 397–401.

Gustafson, G. and Koch, G. (1974) Age estimation up to 16 years of age based on dental development. *Odontologisk Revy*, **25**, 297–306.

Greulich, W.W. (1957) A comparison of the physical growth and development of American-born and native Japanese children. *American Journal of Physical Anthropology*, **15**, 489–515.

Greulich, W.W. and Pyle, S.I. (1959) *Radiographic Atlas of Skeletal Development of the Hand and Wrist*, Stanford University Press, Stanford, CA.

Grön, A.-M. (1962) Prediction of tooth emergence. *Journal of Dental Research*, **41**, 573–585.

Haavikko, K. (1970) The formation and the alveolar and clinical eruption of the permanent teeth. *Suomen Hammaslaakariseuran Toimituksia*, **66**, 103–170.

Hägg, U. and Taranger, J. (1980) Skeletal stages of the hand and wrist as indicators of the pubertal growth spurt. *Acta Odontologica Scandinavica*, **38**, 187–200.

Hansman, C.F. and Maresh, M.M. (1961) A longitudinal study of skeletal maturation. *American Journal of Diseases of Children*, **101**, 305–321.

Harris, E.F. and McKee, J.H. (1990) Tooth mineralization standards for blacks and whites from the Middle Southern United States. *Journal of Forensic Sciences*, **35**, 859–872.

Harris, M.J.P. and Nortje, C.J. (1984) The mesial root of the third mandibular molar. A possible indicator of age. *Journal of Forensic Odonto-Stomatology*, **2**, 39–43.

Johnston, F.E. (1963) Skeletal age and its prediction in Philadelphia children. *Human Biology*, **35**, 192–202.

Jung, H. (2000) Strahlenrisiken durch Röntgenuntersuchungen zur Altersschätzung im Strafverfahren. *RöFo: Fortschritte auf dem Gebiete der Röntgenstrahlen und der Nuklearmedizin*, **172**, 553–556.

Jurik, A.G., Jensen, L.C. and Hansen, J. (1996) Radiation dose by spiral CT and conventional tomography of the sternoclavicular joints and the manubrium sterni. *Skeletal Radiology*, **25**, 467–470.

Kellinghaus, M., Schulz, R., Vieth, V. *et al.* (2009) Forensic age estimation in living subjects based on the ossification status of the medial clavicular epiphysis as revealed by thin-slice multidetector computed tomography. *International Journal of Legal Medicine*, **124**(2), 149–154.

Khan, K.M., Miller, B.S., Hoggard, E. *et al.* (2009). Application of ultrasound for bone age estimation in clinical practice. *Journal of Pediatrics*, **154**, 243–247.

Kimura, K. (1977a) Skeletal maturity of the hand and wrist in Japanese children by the TW2 method. *Annals of Human Biology*, **4**, 353–356.

Kimura, K. (1977b) Skeletal maturity of the hand and wrist in Japanese children in Sapporo by the TW2 method. *Annals of Human Biology*, **4**, 449–454.

King, D.G., Steventon, D.M., O'Sullivan, M.P. *et al.* (1994) Reproducibility of bone ages when performed by radiology registrars: an audit of Tanner and Whitehouse II versus Greulich and Pyle methods. *British Journal of Radiology*, **67**, 848–851.

Köhler, S., Schmelzle, R., Loitz, C. and Püschel, K. (1994) Die Entwicklung des Weisheitszahnes als Kriterium der Lebensalterbestimmung. *Annals of Anatomy*, **176**, 339–345.

Kreitner, K.-F., Schweden, F., Schild, H.H. *et al.* (1997) Die computertomographisch bestimmte Ausreifung der medialen Klavikulaepiphyse – Eine additive Methode zur Altersbestimmung im Adoleszentenalter und in der dritten Lebensdekade? *Fortschritte auf dem Gebiete der Röntgenstrahlen und der Nuklearmedizin*, **166**, 481–486.

Kreitner, K.-F., Schweden, F.J., Riepert, T. *et al.* (1998) Bone age determination based on the study of the medial extremity of the clavicle. *European Radiology*, **8**, 1116–1122.

Kullman, L., Johanson, G. and Akesson, L. (1992) Root development of the lower third molar and its relation to chronological age. *Swedish Dental Journal*, **16**, 161–167.

Lacey, K.A. (1973) Relationship between bone age and dental development. *Lancet*, **302**, 736–737.

Lamons, F.F. and Gray, S.W. (1958) A study of the relationship between tooth eruption age, skeletal development age, and chronological age in sixty-one Atlanta children. *American Journal of Orthodontics*, **44**, 687–691.

Liliequist, B. and Lundberg, M. (1971) Skeletal and tooth development: a methodologic investigation. *Acta Radiologica: Diagnosis*, **11**, 97–112.

Loder, R.T., Estle, D.T., Morrison, K. *et al.* (1993) Applicability of the Greulich and Pyle skeletal age standards to black and white children of today. *American Journal of Diseases of Children*, **147**, 1329–1333.

Mackay, D.H. (1952) Skeletal maturation in the hand: a study of development in East African children. *Transactions of the Royal Society of Tropical Medicine and Hygiene*, **46**, 135–150.

Marcusson, H. (1961) *Das Wachstum von Kindern und Jugendlichen in der Deutschen Demokratischen Republik*, Akademie-Verlag, Berlin.

Massé, G. and Hunt, E.E. (1963) Skeletal maturation of the hand and wrist in West African children. *Human Biology*, **35**, 3–25.

Mentzel, H.-J., Vilser, C., Eulenstein, M. *et al.* (2005). Assessment of skeletal age at the wrist in children with a new ultrasound device. *Pediatric Radiology*, **35**, 429–433.

Mincer, H.H., Harris, E.F. and Berryman, H.E. (1993) The ABFO study of third molar development and its use as an estimator of chronological age. *Journal of Forensic Sciences*, **38**, 379–390.

Mühler, M., Schulz, R., Schmidt, S. *et al.* (2006) The influence of slice thickness on assessment of clavicle ossification in forensic age diagnostics. *International Journal of Legal Medicine*, **120**, 15–17.

Nolla, C.M. (1960) The development of the permanent teeth. *Journal of Dentistry for Children*, **27**, 254–266.

Nortje, C.J. (1983) The permanent mandibular third molar. Its value in age determination. *Journal of Forensic Odonto-Stomatology*, **1**, 27–31.

Okkalides, D. and Fotakis, M. (1994) Patient effective dose resulting from radiographic examinations. *British Journal of Radiology*, **67**, 564–572.

Olze, A., Schmeling, A., Taniguchi, M. *et al.* (2004) Forensic age estimation in living subjects: the ethnic factor in wisdom tooth mineralization. *International Journal of Legal Medicine*, **118**, 170–173.

Olze, A., Bilang, D., Schmidt, S. *et al.* (2005) Validation of common classification systems for assessing the mineralization of third molars. *International Journal of Legal Medicine*, **119**, 22–26.

Olze, A., van Niekerk, P., Ishikawa, T. *et al.* (2007) Comparative study on the effect of ethnicity on wisdom tooth eruption. *International Journal of Legal Medicine*, **121**, 445–448.

Pashkova, V.I. and Burov, S.A. (1980) Possibility of using standard indices of skeletal ossification for the forensic medical expertise of determining the age of children and adolescents living throughout the whole territory of the USSR. *Sudebno-Meditsinskaia Ekspertiza*, **23**, 22–25 [in Russian].

Pfau, R.O. and Sciulli, P.W. (1994) A method for establishing the age of subadults. *Journal of Forensic Sciences*, **39**, 165–176.

Platt, R.A. (1956) The skeletal maturation of negro school children, MA thesis, University of Pennsylvania.

Quirmbach, F., Ramsthaler, F. and Verhoff, M.A. (2009) Evaluation of the ossification of the medial clavicular epiphysis with a digital ultrasonic system to determine the age threshold of 21 years. *International Journal of Legal Medicine*, **123**, 241–245.

Ramsthaler, F., Proschek, P., Betz, W. and Verhoff, M.A. (2009) How reliable are the risk estimates for X-ray examinations in forensic age estimations? A safety update. *International Journal of Legal Medicine*, **123**, 199–204.

Rantanen, A.V. (1967) The age of eruption of the third molar teeth. *Acta Odontologica Scandinavica. Supplementum*, **25**, 1–86.

Roche, A.F. (1963) Lateral comparisons of the skeletal maturity of the human hand and wrist. *American Journal of Roentgenology, Radium Therapy, and Nuclear Medicine*, **89**, 1272–1280.

Roche, A.F., Roberts, J. and Hamill, P.V.V. (1975) Skeletal maturity of children 6–11 years: racial, geographic area and socioeconomic differentials, United States, Vital and Health Statistics, Series 11, No. 149, Government Printing Office, Washington, DC.

Roche, A.F., Roberts, J. and Hamill, P.V.V. (1978) Skeletal maturity of youth 12–17 years: racial, geographic area and socioeconomic differentials, United States, Vital and Health Statistics, Series 11, No. 167, Government Printing Office, Washington, DC.

Roche, A.F., Chumlea, W.C. and Thissen, D. (1988) *Assessing the Skeletal Maturity of the Hand–Wrist: Fels Method*, C.C. Thomas, Springfield, IL.

Rothkamm, K. and Löbrich, M. (2003) Evidence for a lack of DNA double-strand break repair in human cells exposed to very low X-ray doses. *Proceedings of the National Academy of Sciences of the United States of America*, **100**, 5057–5062.

Sälzler, A. (1967) *Ursachen und Erscheinungsformen der Akzeleration*, Verlag Volk und Gesundheit, Berlin.

Schmeling, A., Reisinger, W., Loreck, D. *et al.* (2000a) Effects of ethnicity on skeletal maturation – consequences for forensic age estimations. *International Journal of Legal Medicine*, **113**, 253–258.

Schmeling, A., Reisinger, W., Wormanns, D. and Geserick, G. (2000b) Strahlenexposition bei Röntgenuntersuchungen zur forensischen Altersschätzung Lebender. *Rechtsmedizin*, **10**, 135–137.

Schmeling, A., Kaatsch, H.-J., Marré, B. *et al.* (2001) Empfehlungen für die Altersdiagnostik bei Lebenden im Strafverfahren. *Rechtsmedizin*, **11**, 1–3.

Schmeling, A., Olze, A., Reisinger, W. *et al.* (2003) Statistical analysis and verification of forensic age estimation of living persons in the Institute of Legal Medicine of the University Hospital Charité. *Legal Medicine*, **5**, 367–371.

Schmeling, A., Schulz, R., Reisinger, W. *et al.* (2004) Studies on the time frame for ossification of medial clavicular epiphyseal cartilage in conventional radiography. *International Journal of Legal Medicine*, **118**, 5–8.

Schmeling, A., Grundmann, C., Fuhrmann, A. *et al.* (2008) Criteria for age estimation in living individuals. *International Journal of Legal Medicine*, **122**, 457–460.

Schmid, F. and Moll, H. (1960) *Atlas der Normalen und Pathologischen Handskelettentwicklung*, Springer-Verlag, Berlin.

Schmidt, S., Mühler, M., Schmeling, A. *et al.* (2007) Magnetic resonance imaging of the clavicular ossification. *International Journal of Legal Medicine*, **121**, 321–324.

Schmidt, S., Koch, B., Schulz, R. *et al.* (2008) Studies in use of the Greulich–Pyle skeletal age method to assess criminal liability. *Legal Medicine*, **10**, 190–195.

Scheuer, L. and Black, S. (2000) *Developmental Juvenile Osteology*, Academic Press, London.

Schulz, R., Mühler, M., Mutze, S. *et al.* (2005) Studies on the time frame for ossification of the medial epiphysis of the clavicle as revealed by CT scans. *International Journal of Legal Medicine*, **119**, 142–145.

Schulz, R., Mühler, M., Reisinger, W. *et al.* (2008a) Radiographic staging of ossification of the medial clavicular epiphysis. *International Journal of Legal Medicine*, **122**, 55–58.

Schulz, R., Zwiesigk, P., Schiborr, M. *et al.* (2008b) Ultrasound studies on the time course of clavicular ossification. *International Journal of Legal Medicine*, **122**, 163–167.

Statistisches Bundesamt (2004) Todesursachen in Deutschland 2003. Sterbefälle nach ausgewählten Todesursachen, Altersgruppen und Geschlecht, Fachserie 12, Reihe 4, Wiesbaden.

Stöver, B. (1983) Röntgenologische Aussagekraft des Handradiogrammes. *Röntgenpraxis*, **36**, 119–129.

Sutow, W.W. (1953) Skeletal maturation in healthy Japanese children, 6 to 19 years of age. Comparison with skeletal maturation in American children. *Hiroshima Journal of Medical Sciences*, **2**, 181–193.

Tanner, J.M., Whitehouse, R.H., Marshall, W.A. *et al.* (1975) *Assessment of Skeletal Maturity and Prediction of Adult Height (TW2 Method)*, Academic Press, London.

Tanner, J.M., Healy, M.J. R., Goldstein, H. and Cameron, N. (2001) *Assessment of Skeletal Maturity and Prediction of Adult Height (TW3 Method)*, W.B. Saunders, London.

Thiemann, H.-H. and Nitz, I. (1991) *Röntgenatlas der normalen Hand im Kindesalter*, Thieme, Leipzig.

Thiemann, H.-H., Nitz, I. and Schmeling, A. (2006) *Röntgenatlas der normalen Hand im Kindesalter*, Thieme, Stuttgart.

Weber, R. (1978) Genauigkeit der Skelettalterbestimmungen und Größenprognosen nach den Methoden von Greulich & Pyle sowie Tanner & Whitehouse, Medical Thesis, Berlin.

Weiner, J.S. and Thambipillai, V. (1952) Skeletal maturation of West-African negroes. *American Journal of Physical Anthropology*, **10**, 407–418.

Wenzel, A., Droschl, H. and Melsen, B. (1984) Skeletal maturity in Austrian children assessed by the GP and the TW-2 methods. *Annals of Human Biology*, **11**, 173–177.

9

External Soft Tissue Indicators of Age from Birth to Adulthood

Anil Aggrawal[1], Puneet Setia[2], Avneesh Gupta[3] and Anthony Busuttil[4]
[1]*Maulana Azad Medical College, New Delhi, 110002, India*
[2]*Department of Forensic Medicine, Vir Chandra Singh Garhwali Government Medical Sciences and Research Institute, Srinagar, Garhwal, Uttrakhand, India*
[3]*Cochise County Medical Examiner, 75 Colonia de Sauld, Suite 200D, Sierra Vista, AZ 85635, USA*
[4]*Forensic Medicine Unit, Medical School, University of Edinburgh, Edinburgh EH 8 9 A G*

Age is one of the most important criteria in knowing a person's true identity. If one can determine the age of an individual, one gets very close to knowing their true identity. In the Western world, the need for age estimation most often arises in cases of refugees and asylum seekers, whose records may not be available or for whom there may be questions about document validity (see Chapter 3). For indigenous populations, there is generally excellent record keeping which obviates the need for age determination. However, in the developing world, or after natural disasters, record keeping may be less efficient, non-existent or destroyed. Many births take place at home (NFHS, 2006), the deliveries being conducted by local elders, for which there is no written record of time or place of birth. In this setting the requirement for the determination of age is heightened and more so in the younger age groups, where disputes are more frequent in both civil and criminal settings (Aggrawal and Busuttil, 1991; Aggrawal, 2000, 2003, 2009). Whenever there is a formal requirement for age evaluation, the expertise of the forensic practitioner is essential.

Traditionally, it has always been thought that age can only be determined using the teeth and skeleton of the individual – and this is somewhat of an oversimplification. Dental and skeletal charting are important, but they are not the only parameters that can be used for the estimation of age, especially in the younger age group.

Age Estimation in the Living: The Practitioners Guide   Sue Black, Anil Aggrawal and Jason Payne-James
© 2010 John Wiley & Sons, Ltd

Figure 1 Net migration rate based on data from https://www.cia.gov/library/ publications/the-world-factbook/fields/2112.html (accessed 1 June 2009).

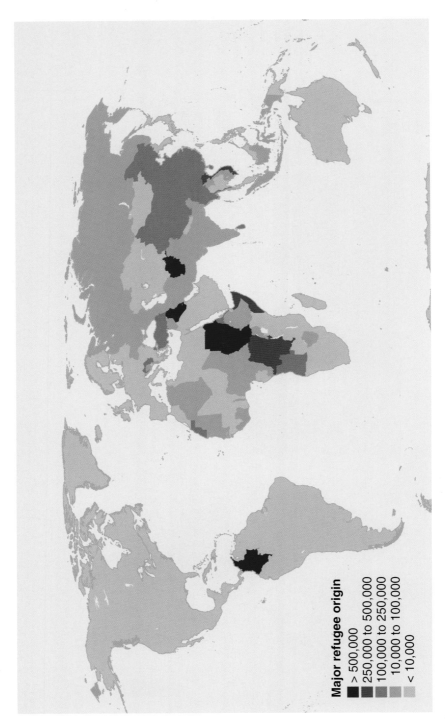

Major refugee origin

> 500,000
250,000 to 500,000
100,000 to 250,000
10,000 to 100,000
< 10,000

Figure 2 Major source countries of refugees, end 2007. UNHCR, 2009a.

Various anthropometric values, including height, weight, head circumference, chest circumference and so on may be more important in age evaluation of the child, especially in the first two to three years of life. Then again during the pubertal growth spurt, the pubertal changes can be used as an effective adjunct to dental and skeletal charting for the exact determination of age. This chapter considers soft tissue markers of age. However, it must always be remembered that these parameters are not infallible and they should not replace the more accurate and reliable dental and skeletal examinations but be used to augment and support other means of age evaluation – they should be considered to be corroborative of other methods and may identify or raise the possibility of inaccuracies.

9.1   Growth Patterns

Human growth is not uniform. It occurs in spurts that occur at different ages, and at each age the factors that affect the spurt can be different. In intra-uterine life, the growth of the fetus is dependent entirely on the intra-uterine environment whereas during the neonatal period, growth is dependent on the perinatal factors (see Chapter 6). After the early neonatal period environmental factors play a more prominent role in the regulation of the growth of the child. The first growth spurt occurs during the first few years of life, culminating at about seven years of age. The second spurt occurs at the time of puberty. In between these two periods, there is a steady state of growth which is much more predictable for age estimation (Molinari, Largo and Prader, 1980; Tanner, 1986). During the periods of these two spurts, changes occur at multiple levels in the body, which can be mapped and used for the purpose of age estimation.

The growth spurt at the time of puberty is due to the growth of all the skeletal and muscular dimensions of the body. However, among them, the head, hands and feet reach their adult status earlier than the other parts of the body (Tanner, 1986). Along with the growth of height and weight, there are also physiological changes in the body at the time of puberty. These are discussed in detail in Chapter 6.

9.2   Anthropometric Parameters in Children

Growth charts are simple tools that are used all over the world by health service providers to monitor the growth of children. But knowing the growth status of the child is not the only use for these charts as they can also be used for determining the age of the individual despite this not being their primary function. Although used most commonly, weight of the child is one of the least useful of the parameters in this regard. The weight of a child varies almost on a daily basis and even within a single day, and the result will be dependent upon the time when the data was collected. For example, weight will be heavier following consumption of a meal. Therefore, other parameters including height (or recumbent length, if the child is less than two years of age), head circumference, abdominal circumference, motor development and so on may be more useful in determining the age of the child. These parameters do not show such large fluctuations as the weight of the child and will only change substantially in cases of chronic malnutrition or if the child is suffering from some serious ailment, for example hydrocephalus for head circumference. In either of these situations (malnutrition or illness) other more accurate parameters including dental and/or skeletal development will also likely be affected. Large deviations from 'normal' growth charts in the absence of any pathology or nutritional influence may identify inaccurate ages.

One of the earliest instances of large-scale anthropometric evaluation of children by recording the relationship between height and weight was undertaken by Wood-bury in 1921 (Robert, 1921). Although the rationale for this project was to evaluate anthropometric parameters for children (up to six years of age), these findings can be utilized to assess the age of the child. Since then, many authors have conducted similar studies and presented their findings for different age and ethnic groups for both height and weight (Hrdlicka, 1921; Woodbury, 1921; Meredith, 1939; Chan, Chang and Hsu, 1961; Garn, Rohmann and Robinow, 1961; Chang et al., 1963; Ashcroft and Lovell, 1964; Ashcroft, Heneage and Lovell, 1966; Tanner, White-house and Takaishi, 1966a,b; Tanner and Whitehouse, 1976; Hamill et al., 1979; Billewicz, Thomson and Fellowes, 1983; Hayes et al., 1983; Buckler, 1985; Tanner and Davies, 1985; Hoey, Tanner and Cox, 1987; Cameron, 1991; Hosseini, Carpenter and Mohammad, 1999; Bordom et al., 2008; Kim et al., 2008; Olivieri et al., 2008), head circumference (Nellhaus, 1968; Hayes et al., 1983; Ounsted, Moar and Scott, 1985; Paul, Ahmed and Whitehead, 1986; Hoey and Cox, 1990; Karabiber et al., 2001), height-weight index and sitting height (Greulich, 1951).

9.2.1 Growth Charts

Growth charts permit evaluation of the 'normal' development of the child. They are predominantly used in paediatric practice to chart development and identify any issue of abnormality/delay in development (Healy, 1962; Tanner and Davies, 1985). For a normally developing child, measurement of parameters including the child's weight, height, head circumference and so on can be plotted against the known or alleged age of the child. Charts 9.1–9.6 are examples that are used for this purpose. It must be noted that there are separate charts for boys and girls for each parameter, indicating that the rate of growth is different for boys and girls.

The growth charts depicted here have been taken from CDC (2009). These charts are based on American children but most countries prepare their own charts based on local demographic profiles. It is not possible to include the values for each and every country in the present text and so it is strongly recommended that each centre should prepare their own growth charts, taking data from the local population wherever possible. The present CDC charts show the 3rd, 5th, 10th, 25th, 50th, 75th, 90th, 95th and 97th percentiles of the various parameters. Many people find these charts too exhaustive and prefer to use smaller, simpler ones, displaying a reduced number of percentiles. Most frequently only three lines are utilized – 3rd, 50th and 97th percentiles – as they are easier to interpret. Which chart and percentile is going to be used in a particular country or state is determined by local authorities and legislation.

CDC Growth Charts: United States

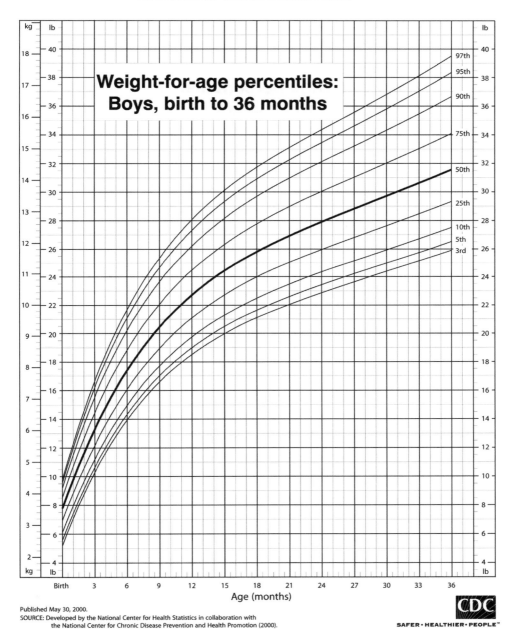

Chart 9.1 CDC growth chart for boys showing weight for age percentile from birth to 36 months

CDC Growth Charts: United States

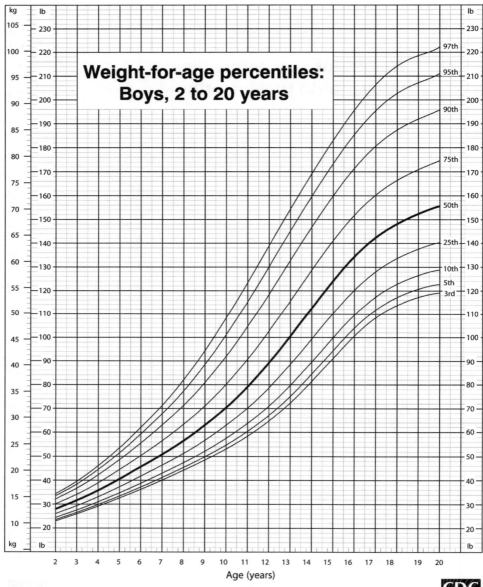

Weight-for-age percentiles: Boys, 2 to 20 years

Age (years)

Published May 30, 2000.
SOURCE: Developed by the National Center for Health Statistics in collaboration with
   the National Center for Chronic Disease Prevention and Health Promotion (2000).

Chart 9.2   CDC growth chart for boys showing weight for age percentile from 2 to 20 years

CDC Growth Charts: United States

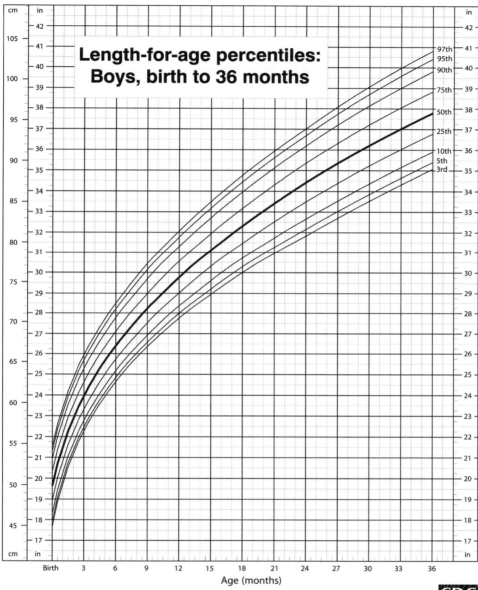

**Length-for-age percentiles:
Boys, birth to 36 months**

Age (months)

Published May 30, 2000.
SOURCE: Developed by the National Center for Health Statistics in collaboration with
the National Center for Chronic Disease Prevention and Health Promotion (2000).

SAFER·HEALTHIER·PEOPLE™

Chart 9.3   CDC growth chart for boys showing length for age percentile from birth
to 36 months

CDC Growth Charts: United States

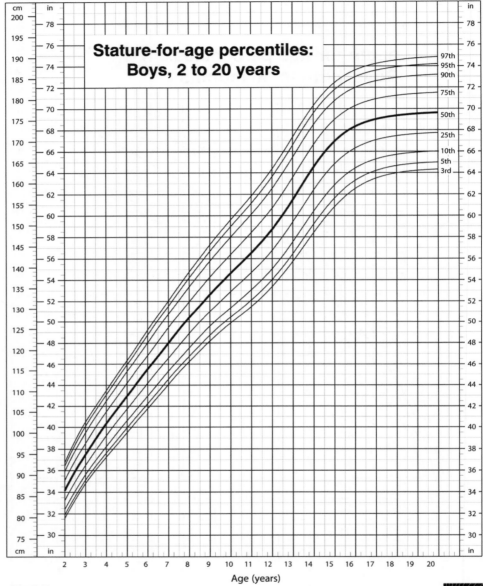

Published May 30, 2000.
SOURCE: Developed by the National Center for Health Statistics in collaboration with
the National Center for Chronic Disease Prevention and Health Promotion (2000).

Chart 9.4 CDC growth chart for boys showing stature for age percentile from 2 to 20 years

CDC Growth Charts: United States

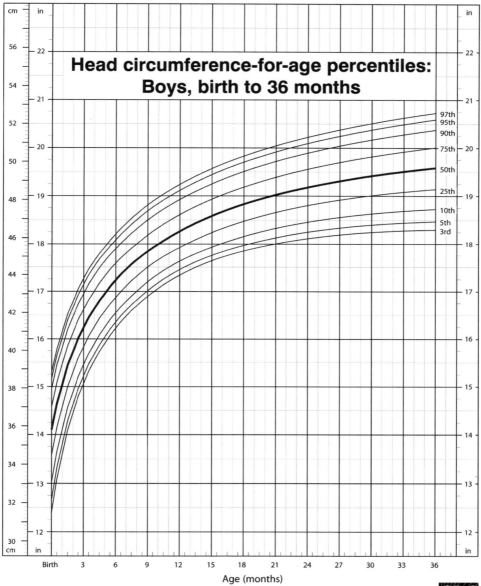

Chart 9.5 CDC growth chart for boys showing head circumference for age percentile from birth to 36 months

CDC Growth Charts: United States

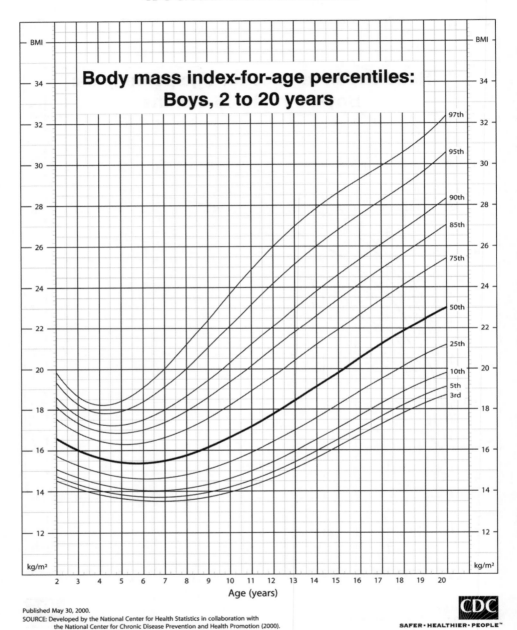

Body mass index-for-age percentiles: Boys, 2 to 20 years

Published May 30, 2000.
SOURCE: Developed by the National Center for Health Statistics in collaboration with the National Center for Chronic Disease Prevention and Health Promotion (2000).

SAFER·HEALTHIER·PEOPLE™

Chart 9.6 CDC growth chart for boys showing body mass index for age percentile from 2 to 20 years

9.2.2   Developmental Milestones

Developmental milestones are recognized stages that are expected to have been achieved by a child of a particular age if growth and maturation are progressing in a normal manner. By recording which milestones have been secured and which have not, one can make a reasonably reliable estimate of the child's age. Individually, there can be wide variations in the appearance of these milestones, but taken together and in combination with growth charts, these are relatively reliable at indicating an age range for the child. The milestones detailed below are abstracted and summarized from Rudolph *et al.* (2003).

9.2.2.1   Head Control   Head control is examined in various positions. These include prone, ventral suspension and pull to sit.

9.2.2.1.1   Prone Position   When the child is placed on a mattress in prone position the following activities are expected at the ages indicated:

1	Head turns to one side:	one month
2	Lifts head momentarily:	one month
3	Lifts head by 45°:	two months
4	Lifts head by 90°:	three to four months
5	Bears weight on forearms:	three to five months
6	Bears weight on hands with arms extended:	five to six months

9.2.2.1.2   Ventral Suspension   When the child is suspended ventrally by lifting from the back, the following activities are noted at different ages:

1	Head hangs completely down:	newborn
2	Momentarily holds head in plane of body:	one and half month
3	Head sustained in plane of body:	two months
4	Head sustained in plane above body:	three months

9.2.2.1.3   Pull to Sit   When the child is gently pulled to a sitting position from supine, the following activities are noted at the respective ages:

1	Complete head lag, back uniformly rounded:	newborn
2	Slight head lag:	three months
3	No head lag, back straightening:	five months
4	Lifts head off the table when about to be pulled up:	six months
5	Raises head spontaneously from supine position:	seven months

9.2.2.2   Rolling   Rolling indicates the independent ability of the child to move from a prone to a supine position and vice versa, without any external help. Rolling occurs first from the supine to the prone position at the age of about four to five months while independent turning from the prone to the supine position occurs about a month later.

9.2.2.3 Sitting A child starts sitting in various stages. These depend on the stage of development of the secondary curvatures of the vertebral column. As we know, the column of the newborn is generally maintained in a flexed and rounded manner. As the child grows, the cervical and lumbar curves develop. It is the development of these secondary curves that permits the upright posture of the child. The stages of sitting are as follows:

1	Back uniformly rounded, cannot sit unsupported:	newborn
2	Back straightening, sits with propping:	five to six months
3	Back straight, sits with arms forward for support:	six to seven months
4	Sits without support:	seven months

9.2.2.4 Gross Motor The gross motor movements involve activities like standing, walking and running. These movements, like the ones described earlier, appear at a specific age and are an important indicator for assessing the child's stage of development and thus by proxy, its age. Since these are gross developments, they do not require any specialized knowledge to be appreciated and so can be used even by laypeople to determine a likely age for the child but of course the range of ages can be very individualistic.

1	Some weight bearing:	three months
2	Supports most weight:	six months
3	Pulls to stand:	nine months
4	Walks holding onto furniture:	eleven months
5	Walks with one hand held:	twelve months
6	Walks without help:	thirteen months
7	Walks well:	fifteen months
8	Runs well:	two years
9	Climbs up and down the stairs, with both feet at each step:	two years
10	Climbs up and down the stairs, one foot on each step while coming down and both feet on each step while going up:	three years
11	Climbs up and down the stairs, with one foot at each step:	four years
12	Jumps off the ground with both feet:	two and a half years
13	Hops on one foot:	four years
14	Skips:	five to six years
15	Balance on one foot for two to three seconds:	three years
16	Balance on one foot for six to ten seconds:	four years

9.2.2.5 Fine Motor These involve the fine movements of fingers of hands.

1 Hands predominantly closed:	one month
2 Hands predominantly open:	three months
3 Hands come together:	four months
4 Voluntary grasp:	five months
5 Transfer object from hand to hand:	six months
6 Ulnar grasp of cube:	five to six months
7 Grasp cube against thenar eminence:	six to eight months
8 Grasp cube against lower limb:	eight to ten months
9 Mature cube grasp – fingertips and distal thumb:	ten to twelve months
10 Index finger approach to small objects and finger – thumb apposition:	ten months
11 Voluntary release of objects:	ten months
12 Plays pat-a-cake:	nine to ten months
13 Enjoys putting objects in and out of box:	ten to eleven months
14 Casting objects:	ten to thirteen months
15 Makes tower of two cubes:	thirteen to fifteen months
16 Makes tower of four cubes:	eighteen months
17 Makes tower of six to seven cubes:	two years
18 Makes tower of ten cubes:	three years
19 Good use of cup and spoon:	fifteen to eighteen months

9.2.2.6 Social and cognitive The developmental milestones that come under this category are the ones that signify the social behaviour of the child.

1 Social smile:	one to two months
2 Smiles at image in mirror:	five months
3 Looks for dropped toy:	six months
4 Separation anxiety/stranger awareness:	six to twelve months
5 Interactive games – peek-a-boo:	nine to twelve months
6 Waves bye-bye:	ten months
7 Rolls ball to examiner:	one year
8 Feeds self with cup and spoon:	fifteen to eighteen months
9 Autonomy and independent issues begin:	one and a half to two years
10 Magical thinking and symbolic (pretend) play:	one and a half to five years
11 Parallel play:	one to two years
12 Dresses self, except for buttons in back:	three years
13 Cooperative play:	three to four years
14 Able to distinguish fantasy from reality:	five years
15 Ties shoe laces:	five years

9.2.2.7 Speech and language Speech and language is an important aspect of the development of the child.

1 Cooing:	two to four months
2 Babbles with labial consonants (ba, ma, ga):	five to eight months
3 Imitates sounds made by others:	nine to twelve months
4 First words (mama, dada):	nine to twelve months
5 Understanding one-step command:	fifteen months
6 Jargon (expressive, unintelligible language):	fifteen months to two years
7 Vocabulary of ten to fifty words:	thirteen to eighteen months
8 Vocabulary of fifty to seventy-five words:	eighteen to twenty-four months
9 Two-word sentences:	one and a half to two years
10 Three-word sentences:	two to three years
11 Vocabulary of 250 words:	three years
12 Four-word sentences:	three to four years
13 Five-word sentences:	four to five years

9.3 Pubertal Changes

The stages of development of pubertal changes have been described in great detail by Tanner (1962). These stages have stood the test of time and have not been disputed or changed significantly since their first publication. The development of these characteristics is dependent on genetic and environmental factors, with genetics playing a predominant role (van den Berg *et al.*, 2006). Among the various secondary sexual characteristics, breast development has been found to be one of the most important (Hoffman *et al.*, 2005), although Tanner states pubic hair development to be the most important criterion (Tanner, 1986). The Tanner stages have global acceptance as a realistic means for examining and describing the soft tissue changes that occur during puberty. This text follows Tanner's staging system for the development of all the changes during puberty. For most of the characteristics, stage 2 is the stage when that particular characteristic first starts to display alterations in relation to puberty. Therefore, when using pubertal changes as a proxy for age estimation, stage 2 is recognized as the stage of initial appearance of that character.

Before moving to the specific change in detail, the pattern of changes that occur at the time of puberty requires to be examined. Not all changes occur at the same time and there is a relatively common sequence in which the changes occur, which is different in males and females. In males, the first change (or the first sign of puberty) is the growth of testes and scrotum, followed by the growth of pubic and axillary hair in that order. The breaking of the voice occurs over a period of time and thus is not considered a good marker for age determination (Tanner, 1986). In females, the appearance of the breast bud is the first sign of pubertal development. This is followed by the development of pubic and axillary hair, in that order, although sometimes pubic hair may develop along with or before the appearance of the breast bud. Menarche is the last stage of sexual development in the female and is a recordable single event (Tanner, 1986).

Peak height velocity is another significant event that occurs during puberty. However, its appreciation requires the examination of the person over a period of time, with serial measurements and thus is of restricted importance for age estimation procedures, which are generally recorded at a single point in time.

9.3.1 Stages of Pubic Hair Development Derived from Tanner (1962)

See Figure 9.1:

Stage 1 (PH1): Pre-adolescent; the vellus over the pubes is not further developed than that over the anterior abdominal wall; that is, no pubic hair.

Stage 2 (PH2): Sparse growth of long, slightly pigmented, downy hair, straight or only slightly curled and in females, appearing chiefly along the labia.

Stage 3 (PH3): Considerably darker, coarser and more curled. The hair spreads sparsely over the junction of the pubes.

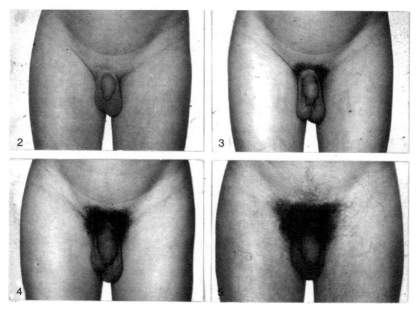

Figure 9.1 Tanner stages 2–5 for penile and scrotal development.

Stage 4 (PH4): Hair is now adult in type, but the area covered by it is still considerably smaller than in most adults. There is no spread to the medial surface of the thighs.

Stage 5 (PH5): Adult in quantity and type, distributed like adult pattern in both males and females. Spread to the medial surface of the thighs.

9.3.1.1 Pubic Hair Development in Males In Egypt (Ghaly, Hussein and Abdelghaffar, 2008), the mean age of attainment of pubic hair stage 2 was 11.86 years. In the US (RosenfHussein and Abdelghaffarield *et al.*, 2009), the mean age of attainment of stage 3 of pubic hair was 12.61 years, with the range being from 12.34 to 12.86 years. In another study (Sun *et al.*, 2002), the median age for development of stage 2 of pubic hair in non-Hispanic White boys was 11.98 years; for non-Hispanic Black boys, it was 11.16 years; and for Mexican American boys, the median age was 12.30 years. In their study on adolescent boys, De Simone *et al.* (2004) found that the median age for the development of pubic hair was 11.47 years, with the range being 11.26 to 11.67 years. In Kazakhstan (Facchini *et al.*, 2008), the median age for development of stage 2 pubic hair in urban Kazakh and Russian boys was 12.48 and 11.87 years, respectively, and for the rural population it was 13.27 and 13.47 years respectively. In Britain (Marshall and Tanner, 1970), the mean age for development of stage 2 pubic hair was 13.44 years. See Table 9.1 for a summary of these findings.

9.3.1.2 Pubic Hair Development in Females In Egypt (Ghaly, Hussein and Abdelghaffar, 2008), the mean age of attainment of pubic hair stage 2 was 10.46 years. In the US (Rosenfield, Lipton and Drum, 2009), stage 3 of pubic hair development was attained at the mean age of 11.57 years with the range being 11.30 to 11.92. The range was extended in groups of different ethnic origin. Sun *et al.* (2002) reported that the median age for development of stage 2 pubic hair in non-Hispanic White girls was 10.57 years; for non-Hispanic Black girls it was 9.43 years; and for Mexican American girls it was 10.39 years. In Kazakhstan, Facchini *et al.* (2008) reported that the median age for development of stage 2 pubic hair in urban Kazakh and Russian girls was 11.60 and 11.45 years, respectively, whereas for the rural population it was 12.41 and 11.90 years, respectively. In Iran (Razzaghy-Azar *et al.*, 2006), the median age of stage 2 development of pubic hair was 10.49 years, with the range being 8.86 to 12.17 years. In Lithuanian girls (Zukauskaite *et al.*, 2005), the mean age for development of pubic hair was 11.2 years. In the UK, Marshall and Tanner (1969) reported that the mean age for development of stage 2 pubic hair in girls was 11.69 years. See Table 9.1 for a summary of these findings.

9.3.2 Stages of Axillary Hair Development Derived from Tanner (1962)

Stage 1 (A1): No axillary hair present.

Stage 2 (A2): Axillary hair is scanty and slightly pigmented.

Stage 3 (A3): Axillary hair is darker and curly, with adult pattern.

Table 9.1 Various ages of pubertal development in different regions of the world (all ages in years).

Country	Source	Males			Females			
		Pubic hair	Axillary hair	Genital development	Pubic hair	Axillary hair	Breast development	Menarche
Poland	Wronka and Pawlinska-Chmara (2005)							12.78–13.26
Bologna (north Italy)	Veronesi and Gueresi (1994)							12.53 ± 0.05
Portugal	Gama (2008)							13.59–14.81[a]
South Africa	Cameron and Nagdee (1996)							12.52 ± 1.25
Argentina	Lejarraga, Cusminsky and Castro (1976)			11.8 ± 0.15	11 ± 0.03		10.8 ± 0.09	
Italy (Abruzzo)	De Simone (2004)	11.17 ± 0.88		11.47 ± 0.41				
Kazakhstan[b]	Facchini et al. (2008)	10.21–15.75		11.26–12.41	9.83–14.18		11.69–12.50	12.79–13.40
Iran[c]	Razzaghy-Azar et al. (2006)				8.86–12.17		8.23–11.94	11.27–15.96
Lithuania	Zukauskaite et al. (2005)				11.2 ± 0.3	12.7 ± 0.7	11.3 ± 0.2	
Britain	Marshall and Tanner (1969)				11.69 ± 1.21		11.15 ± 1.10	13.47 ± 1.02
Britain	Marshall and Tanner (1970)	13.44 ± 1.09		11.64 ± 1.07				
US	Sun, Schubert et al. (2002)	11.48–12.20		10.79–11.09	10.25–11.17		10.25–11.05	
Egypt	Ghaly, Hussein and Abdelghaffar (2008)	11.86 ± 1.45	13.55 ± 1.52		10.46 ± 1.36	11.65 ± 1.62	10.71 ± 1.30	12.44
Taiwan	Chang and Chen (2008)							13 ± 1.26
Egypt	Attallah (1978)							13.23 ± 0.08

[a] shows the range of mean ages.
[b] This study gives a range of four different ethnic groups, of which two are urban and two rural. The values for pubic hair (both boys and girls) are medians while the rest are means.
[c] The values given here are the range of median from 10th to 90th percentile.

In Egypt (Ghaly, Hussein and Abdelghaffar, 2008), the mean age of appearance for stage 2 axillary hair in males was 13.55 years and that for development of adult type hair (stage 3) was 15.25 years. In females the same ages were 11.65 years and 14.19 years, respectively. In Lithuanian girls (Zukauskaite et al., 2005), the mean age for the development of axillary hair was 12.7 years.

In is generally accepted that in the male, hair is first evident in the pubic region followed by the axilla and then finally hair growth commences on the face. In the male, fine downy pubic hair begins to appear around 14 years of age and is evident in the axilla by 15 years, and on the chin and upper lip between 16 and 18 years. The colour of the hair may darken and become more coarse within a couple of years. Hair on the inner sides of the thigh and on the scrotum may appear after 18 years (Aggrawal, 2003). See Table 9.1 for a summary of age in relation to stage of axillary hair development.

9.3.3 Stages of Development of Male Genitalia Derived from Tanner (1962)

See Figure 9.1:

Stage 1 (G1): The genitalia are pre-adolescent. Penis, scrotum and testis are of the same size as in early childhood.

Stage 2 (G2): There is enlargement of scrotum and testis. There is some reddening to scrotal skin.

Stage 3 (G3): The scrotum enlarges further and the penis elongates.

Stage 4 (G4): The scrotum becomes larger and darker; the penis becomes longer. There is development of the glans and the breadth also increases.

Stage 5 (G5): The penis and scrotum are of adult size.

In Egypt (Ghaly, Hussein and Abdelghaffar, 2008), the mean age of stage 2 for male genital pubertal development was 10.56 years. In Italian boys (De Simone et al., 2004), the median age for development of stage 2 was reported as 11.17 years, with the range being 10.69 to 11.57 years. In Kazakhstan (Facchini et al., 2008), the median age for the presence of stage 2 in urban Kazakh and Russian boys was 9.67 and 9.52 years, respectively, while the same age for a rural population was 10.51 and 11.44 years, respectively. In the US, Sun et al. (2002) reported that the median age for development of stage 2 of external genitalia in non-Hispanic White boys was 10.03 years; for non-Hispanic Black boys it was 9.20 years; and for Mexican American boys, the median age was 10.29 years. In the UK, Marshall and Tanner (1970) reported the mean age for development of stage 2 of male genitalia to be 11.64 years. See Table 9.1 for a summary of these results.

9.3.3.1 Testicular Volume Testicular volume is another of the parameters used for determining the sexual maturity of an individual. It can be measured either by the use of an orchidometer or directly by using a ruler and simply recording length and width of the testis. Currently, ultrasound may be utilized for measuring testicular volume. It has been shown (Rivkees *et al.*, 1987) that the results obtained using either an orchidometer or by direct measurement are neither accurate nor reproducible. Alternatively, ultrasound measurement could provide both accurate and reproducible results. So it is recommended that for qualitative estimates, orchidometer and direct measurement should be used and for quantitative estimates ultrasound should be used. Other studies (Diamond *et al.*, 2000; Sakamoto *et al.*, 2007) have also reported similar results. In a study undertaken to compare the three methods (Taskinen, Taavitsainen and Wikström, 1996), it was found that none of the three methods gave any superior advantage to another and thus it was recommended that a simple ruler, due to its ease, availability and low cost, should be the method used for the determination of testicular volume. In a study using a graphical approach (Chipkevitch *et al.*, 1996), six ellipses of volume 2 ml to 25 ml were drawn on a sheet of paper and the testes were compared visually with the drawn outlines. In this study it was mentioned that there was no significant difference in their results with any of the previous methods utilized.

Kuijper *et al.* measured the testicular volume in boys up to the age of six years and found that the testicular volume increased during the first five months of age, from $0.27 \, cm^3$ to $0.44 \, cm^3$, then decreased to $0.31 \, cm^3$ at nine months of age, and then remained the same until six years of age (Kuijper *et al.*, 2008).

Daniel *et al.* investigated the difference between testicular volume in Black and White populations in America, but failed to find any significant difference. They concluded that there was no significant difference in testicular volume between the two ethnic groups. They also concluded that testicular volume correlated more closely with genital maturity and pubic hair development than with age, height, weight or any other parameter examined. The testicular volume increased from about $4.76 \, cm^3$ to $30.25 \, cm^3$, almost in a linear fashion (Daniel *et al.*, 1982). However the authors could not identify any literature that described a regression equation for the normal testicular volume in adolescents. This can form one of the many research projects for the future. It is reported by Tanner and Whitehouse (1976) that testicular volume is approximately 4 ml prior to any indication of puberty and this will increase to approximately 12 ml by the point of mid-pubertal development.

9.3.3.2 Age of First Erection and Ejaculation   The age of first erection and ejaculation (oigarche) are two physiological changes that herald sexual maturation in boys. Although related, these two are functionally different processes involving a separate set of neuro-muscular connections. The general belief is that both occur together and commence around the time of puberty. However, with puberty being a process and not an event, which spans several years, this belief cannot hold the test of scientific reasoning. The first awareness of penile tumescence is often during the night and has been reported in 3.7% of boys at the age of 11 and 16% by the age of 16 years (Ramsey, 1943; Karacan *et al.*, 1975). Reports have suggested that the age at first conscious ejaculation is around 13 years of age with a range between 12.5 and 15.5 considered to be normal (Richardson and Short, 1978; Laron *et al.*, 1980; Carlier and Steeno, 1985). Penile tumescence and nocturnal emission are a common indication of male maturation throughout puberty.

Spermarche is the stage at which viable sperm are produced within the testes. There is little information on the timing of this stage of maturation but it is believed to be around 13–14 years (Nielsoen *et al.*, 1986; Guízar-Vázquez, Rosales-López and Ortiz-Jalomo, 1992). One could equate spermarche in the male to menarche in the female – see below.

9.3.4 Stages of breast development as derived from Tanner (1962)

See Figure 9.2:

Stage 1 (B1): Pre-adolescent; elevation of papilla only.

Stage 2 (B2): Breast bud stage; elevation of breast and papilla as a small mound, enlargement of areola diameter.

Stage 3 (B3): Further enlargement of breast and areola, with no separation of their contours.

Stage 4 (B4): Projection of areola and papilla to form a secondary mound above the level of the breast.

Stage 5 (B5): Mature stage; projection of papilla only, due to recession of the areola to the general contour of the breast.

In Egypt, Ghaly, Hussein and Abdelghaffar (2008) reported the mean age for the attainment of stage 2 of breast development was 10.71 years. In one US study (Rosenfield, Lipton and Drum, 2009), the mean age for commencement of breast development was 10.18 years, with the range being from 9.93 to 10.41 years. In another study, Sun *et al.* (2002) reported that the median age for development of stage 2 of breast in non-Hispanic White girls was 10.38 years, for non-Hispanic Black girls was 9.48 years and for Mexican American girls was 9.80 years. In Kazakhstan (Facchini *et al.*, 2008), the median age for stage 2 breast development in urban Kazakh and Russian girls was 10.54 and 10.48 years, respectively, and for a rural population was 11.50 and 11.53 years, respectively. In Iran (Razzaghy-Azar *et al.*, 2006), the median age for stage 2 breast development was 9.74 years, with the range being 8.23 to 11.94 years. In Lithuanian girls, Zukauskaite *et al.* (2005) reported that the mean age of commencement of breast development was 10.2 years. In the UK, Marshall and Tanner (1969) reported that the mean age of appearance for stage 2 of breast development was 11.15 years. See Table 9.1 for a summary of these results.

9.3.5 Age of Menarche

Menarche is the last of the reproductive changes that occur in the female at the time of puberty. Its occurrence is generally taken to signify that the development of the girl has progressed to a stage where she is now sufficiently biologically mature to bear children – and is a clear indication of her sexual reproductive maturity. There are many factors that determine the age of onset of menarche. The immediate cause is the increase in the frequency of the gonadotropin releasing hormone (GnRH). However,

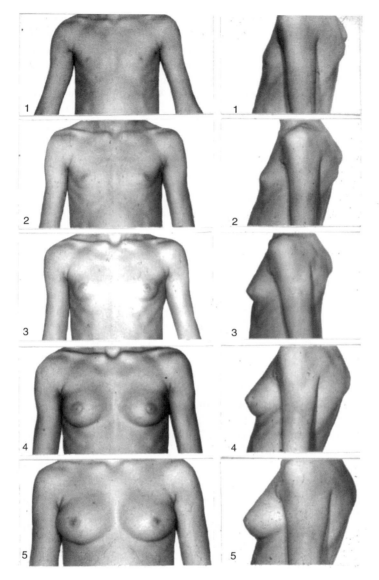

Figure 9.2   Tanner stages 1–5 for breast development.

this increase is dependent on various factors, which include fat distribution (Frisch, 1976, 1990, 1994, 1996; Lassek and Gaulin, 2007), nutritional status (Thomas *et al.*, 2001; Gluckman and Hanson, 2006), peak height and bi-iliac breadth (van't Hof and Roede, 1977; Ellison, 1982; Stark, Peckham and Moynihan, 1989; Elizondo, 1992). The age of menarche has been a particularly important developmental characteristic to allow demographers and auxologists to examine features including populational health status and secular trend. This is a single and memorable event and its accurate recall can be extremely important in the estimation of the age of an individual.

In Egypt (Ghaly, Hussein and Abdelghaffar, 2008), the average age of menarche was reported to be 12.44 years while in the US (Rosenfield, Lipton and Drum, 2009), the mean age of attainment of menarche was 12.57 years, with the range being from 12.39 to 12.77 years. In Kazakhstan (Facchini *et al.*, 2008), the median age for menarche in urban Kazakh and Russian girls was 12.89 and 13.16 years, respectively, and for a rural population was 13.28 and 13.43 years, respectively. In Iran (Razzaghy-Azar *et al.*, 2006), the median age of menarche was 12.68 years, with the range being 11.27 to 15.96 years. In the UK, Marshall and Tanner (1969) reported the mean age of menarche to be 13.47 years. With a well-documented secular trend in this biological event (see Chapter 7) it is essential that this be taken into account if age at menarche is to form a component of an age estimation process.

9.4 Areas of New Research

Apart from some of the topics that have been mentioned earlier, there are others that need to be addressed in the present section. The first is the use of variation in colour of teeth to determine age (Martin-de las Heras *et al.*, 2003). This work was undertaken on deceased individuals and required removal of the teeth and their processing before they could be used for colour estimation. They used teeth from individuals varying in age from 10 to 89 years and found encouraging results. Although their method cannot be directly applied to the living, it can form the basis for further research. Earlier, an attempt was made to find the colour of the teeth *in vivo* using a fibre-optic colorimeter (Goodkind and Schwabacher, 1987). The combination of these two methods can be utilized as an area of potential research for estimating the age of an individual using colour changes in the teeth.

Colour change in the soft tissues is another area that has the potential of being used for age estimation in forensic practice. The preliminary study on this topic has been undertaken by Pilin, Pudil and Bencko (2007a,b,c). In their study on age estimation using colour change in intervertebral disc, tendocalcaneus and costal cartilage, they have reported some encouraging results. However, their study was undertaken on post-mortem tissues, which is not applicable to living individuals, but it has opened new avenues of research by showing that there are colour changes in the tissues with age that are measurable and quantifiable. It is now perhaps just a matter of time before the same can be utilized in living individuals.

9.5 Conclusion

A physical estimation of age in children is undertaken predominantly by using dental and skeletal parameters. The soft tissue indicators are not particularly accurate indicators and can never replace the more definite skeletal and dental markers, although they have great value as corroborators of an opinion. These parameters are restricted in the time period of value as they are most applicable at the time of growth spurts, that is in the very young or at the time of puberty, as at other ages, soft tissue changes are not sufficiently discriminative. However, it must be remembered that the soft tissue parameters also offer advantages. They can provide a valuable corroboration to more reliable methods and they do not carry the same health and safety concerns as for example does a radiographic analysis. They may also highlight disparities in the results of other assessment techniques and raise awareness of either precocious or delayed maturation events that could indicate an underlying clinical issue. Examination and documentation of soft tissue indicators for age estimation are essential elements although they do require access to the most intimate and private anatomy of the person being assessed.

References

Aggrawal, A. (2009) Estimation of age in the living: in matters civil and criminal. *Journal of Anatomy* [Epub ahead of print] PMID: 19470083.

Aggrawal, A. and Busuttil, A. (1991) Age estimation in the living. *The Police Surgeon (Journal of the Association of Police Surgeons)*, **38** (Jan), 33–36.

Aggrawal, A. (2000) Age estimation in the living – some medicolegal considerations. *Anil Aggrawal's Internet Journal of Forensic Medicine and Toxicology* [serial online], **1** (1), www.geradts.com/anil/ij/vol_001_no_002/ug001.html (accessed 15 August 2009).

Aggrawal, A. (2003) Age estimation in the living, in *Forensic Medicine: Clinical and Pathological Aspects* (eds J.J. Payne-James, A. Busuttil and W. Smock), Greenwich Medical Media, San Francisco, CA, pp. 391–408.

Ashcroft, M.T. and Lovell, H.G. (1964) Heights and weights of Jamaican children of various racial origins. *Tropical and Geographical Medicine*, **16**, 346–353.

Ashcroft, M.T., Heneage, P. and Lovell, H.G. (1966) Heights and weights of Jamaican schoolchildren of various ethnic groups. *American Journal of Physical Anthropology*, **24** (1), 35–44.

Attallah, N.L. (1978) Age at menarche of schoolgirls in Egypt. *Annals of Human Biology*, **5** (2), 185–189.

Billewicz, W.Z., Thomson, A.M. and Fellowes, H.M. (1983) Weight-for-height in adolescence. *Annals of Human Biology*, **10** (2), 119–124.

Bordom, J.H., Billot, L., Gueguen, R. and Deschamps, J.R. (2008) New growth charts for Libyan preschool children. *Eastern Mediterranean Health Journal*, **14** (6), 1400–1412.

Buckler, J.M. (1985) Are Tanner growth charts applicable to children at school entry in Leeds? *Archives of Disease in Childhood*, **60** (12), 1188–1191.

Cameron, N. (1991) Human growth, nutrition, and health status in Sub-Saharan Africa. *Yearbook of Physical Anthropology*, **34**, 211–250.

Cameron, N. and Nagdee, I. (1996) Menarcheal age in two generations of South African Indians. *Annals of Human Biology*, **23** (2), 113–119.

Carlier, J.G. and Steeno, O.P. (1985) Oigarche: the age at first ejaculation. *Andrologia*, **17** (1), 104–106.

Centers for Disease Control and Prevention, National Center for Health Statistics (2009) Growth charts, www.cdc.gov/growthcharts (accessed 1 March 2009).

Chan, S.T., Chang, K.S.F. and Hsu, F.K. (1961). Growth and skeletal maturation of Chinese children in Hong Kong. *American Journal of Physical Anthropology*, **19**, 289–300.

Chang, K.S., Lee, M.M., Low, W.D. and Kvan, E. (1963) Height and weight of southern Chinese children. *American Journal of Physical Anthropology*, **21**, 497–509.

Chang, S.R. and Chen, K.H. (2008) Age at menarche of three-generation families in Taiwan. *Annals of Human Biology*, **35** (4), 394–405.

Chipkevitch, E., Nishimura, R.T., Tu, D.G. and Galea-Rojas, M. (1996) Clinical measurement of testicular volume in adolescents: comparison of the reliability of 5 methods. *Journal of Urology*, **156** (6), 2050–2053.

Daniel, W.A. Jr., Feinstein, R.A., Howard-Peebles, P. and Baxley, W.D. (1982) Testicular volumes of adolescents. *Journal of Pediatrics*, **101** (6), 1010–1012.

De Simone, M., Danubio, M.E., Amicone, E. *et al.* (2004) Age of onset of pubertal characteristics in boys aged 6–14 years of the Province of L'Aquila (Abruzzo, Italy). *Annals of Human Biology*, **31** (4), 488–493.

Diamond, D.A., Paltiel, H.J., DiCanzio, J. *et al.* (2000) Comparative assessment of pediatric testicular volume: orchidometer versus ultrasound. *Journal of Urology*, **164** (3 Pt 2), 1111–1114.

Elizondo, S. (1992) Age at menarche: its relation to linear and ponderal growth. *Annals of Human Biology*, **19** (2), 197–199.

Ellison, P.T. (1982) Skeletal growth, fatness and menarcheal age: a comparison of two hypotheses. *Human Biology*, **54** (2), 269–281.

Facchini, F., Fiori, G., Bedogni, G. *et al.* (2008) Puberty in modernizing Kazakhstan: a comparison of rural and urban children. *Annals of Human Biology*, **35** (1), 50–64.

Frisch, R.E. (1976) Fatness of girls from menarche to age 18 years, with a nomogram. *Human Biology*, **48** (2), 353–359.

Frisch, R.E. (1990) The right weight: body fat, menarche and ovulation. *Baillières Clinical Obstetrics and Gynaecology*, **4** (3), 419–439.

Frisch, R.E. (1994) The right weight: body fat, menarche and fertility. *Proceedings of the Nutrition Society*, **53** (1), 113–129.

Frisch, R.E. (1996) The right weight: body fat, menarche, and fertility. *Nutrition*, **12** (6), 452–453.

Gama, A. (2008) Age at menarche in Portuguese rural women from Oleiros. *Annals of Human Biology*, **35** (6), 639–655.

Garn, S.M., Rohmann, C.G. and Robinow, M. (1961) Increments in handwrist ossification. *American Journal of Physical Anthropology*, **19**, 45–53.

Ghaly, I., Hussein, F.H. and Abdelghaffar, S. (2008) Optimal age of sexual maturation in Egyptian children. *Eastern Mediterranean Health Journal*, **14** (6), 1391–1399.

Gluckman, P.D. and Hanson, M.A. (2006) Evolution, development and timing of puberty. *Trends in Endocrinology and Metabolism*, **17** (1), 7–12.

Goodkind, R.J. and Schwabacher, W.B. (1987) Use of a fiber-optic colorimeter for in vivo color measurements of 2830 anterior teeth. *Journal of Prosthetic Dentistry*, **58** (5), 535–542.

Greulich, W.W. (1951) The growth and developmental status of Guamanian school children in 1947. *American Journal of Physical Anthropology*, **9** (1), 55–70.

Guízar-Vázquez, J.J., Rosales-López, A., Ortiz-Jalomo, R. *et al.* (1992) Age at onset of spermaturia (spermarche) in 669 Mexican children and its relation to secondary sexual characteristics and height. *Boletín médico del Hospital Infantil de México*, **49**, 12–17.

Hamill, P.V., Drizd, T.A., Johnson, C.L. *et al.* (1979) Physical growth: National Center for Health Statistics percentiles. *American Journal of Clinical Nutrition*, **32** (3), 607–629.

Hayes, A., Daly, L., O'Brien, N.G. and MacDonald, D. (1983) Anthropometric standards for Irish newborn. *Irish Medical Journal*, **76** (2), 60, 62, 64–66 passim.

Healy, M.J. (1962) The effect of age-grouping on the distribution of a measurement affected by growth. *American Journal of Physical Anthropology*, **20**, 49–50.

Hoey, H.M. and Cox, L.A. (1990) Head circumference standards for Irish children. *Acta Paediatrica Scandinavica*, **79** (2), 162–167.

Hoey, H.M., Tanner, J.M. and Cox, L.A. (1987) Clinical growth standards for Irish children. *Acta Paediatrica Scandinavica. Supplement*, **338**, 1–31.

Hoffman, W.H., Barbeau, P., Litaker, M.S. *et al.* (2005) Tanner staging of secondary sexual characteristics and body composition, blood pressure, and insulin in black girls. *Obesity Research*, **13** (12), 2195–2201.

Hosseini, M., Carpenter, R.G. and Mohammad, K. (1999) Weight-for-height of children in Iran. *Annals of Human Biology*, **26** (6), 537–547.

Hrdlicka, A. (1921) Heights and weights of American children. *American Journal of Physical Anthropology*, **4** (3), 269–275.

Karabiber, H., Durmaz, Y., Yakinci, C. *et al.* (2001) Head circumference measurement of urban children aged between 6 and 12 in Malatya, Turkey. *Brain Development*, **23** (8), 801–804.

Karacan, I., Williams, R.L., Thornby, J.I. and Salis, P.J. (1975) Sleep related penile tumescence as a function of age. *American Journal of Psychiatry*, **132**, 932–937.

Kim, J.Y., Oh, I.H., Lee, E.Y. *et al.* (2008) Anthropometric changes in children and adolescents from 1965 to 2005 in Korea. *American Journal of Physical Anthropology*, **136** (2), 230–236.

Kuijper, E.A., van Kooten, J., Verbeke, J.I. *et al.* (2008) Ultrasonographically measured testicular volumes in 0- to 6-year-old boys. *Human Reproduction*, **23** (4), 792–796.

Laron, Z., Arad, J., Gurewitz, R. and Grunebaum, M. (1980) Age at first conscious ejaculation – a milestone in male puberty. *Helvetica Paediatrica Acta*, **35** (1), 13–20.

Lassek, W.D. and Gaulin, S.J. (2007) Brief communication: menarche is related to fat distribution. *American Journal of Physical Anthropology*, **133** (4), 1147–1151.

Lejarraga, H., Cusminsky, M. and Castro, E.P. (1976) Age of onset of puberty in urban Argentinian children. *Annals of Human Biology*, **3** (4), 379–381.

Marshall, W.A. and Tanner, J.M. (1969) Variations in pattern of pubertal changes in girls. *Archives of Disease in Childhood*, **44** (235), 291–303.

Marshall, W.A. and Tanner, J.M. (1970) Variations in the pattern of pubertal changes in boys. *Archives of Disease in Childhood*, **45** (239), 13–23.

Martin-de las Heras, S., Valenzuela, A., Bellini R. *et al.* (2003) Objective measurement of dental color for age estimation by spectroradiometry. *Forensic Science International*, **132** (1), 57–62.

Meredith, H.V. (1939) Stature of Massachusetts children of north European and Italian ancestry. *American Journal of Physical Anthropology*, **24** (3), 301–346.

Molinari, L., Largo, R.H. and Prader, A. (1980) Analysis of the growth spurt at age seven (mid-growth spurt). *Helvetica Paediatrica Acta*, **35** (4), 325–334.

Nellhaus, G. (1968) Head circumference from birth to eighteen years. Practical composite international and interracial graphs. *Pediatrics*, **41** (1), 106–114.

NFHS (2006) National Family Health Survey (NFHS), India, www.nfhsindia.org/pdf/India.pdf (accessed 22 September 2009).

Nielsoen C.T., Skakkebaek, N.E., Richardson, D.W. *et al.* (1986) Onset of the release of spermatozoa (spermarche) in boys in relation to age, testicular growth, pubic hair, and height. *Journal of Clinical Endocrinology and Metabolism*, **62**, 532–535.

Olivieri, F., Semproli, S., Pettener, D. and Toselli, S. (2008) Growth and malnutrition of rural Zimbabwean children (6–17 years of age). *American Journal of Physical Anthropology*, **136** (2), 214–222.

Ounsted, M., Moar, V.A. and Scott, A. (1985) Head circumference charts updated. *Archives of Disease in Childhood*, **60** (10), 936–939.

Paul, A.A., Ahmed, E.A. and Whitehead, R.G. (1986) Head circumference charts updated. *Archives of Disease in Childhood*, **61** (9), 927–928.

Pilin, A., Pudil, F. and Bencko, V. (2007a) Changes in colour of different human tissues as a marker of age. *International Journal of Legal Medicine*, **121** (2), 158–162.

Pilin, A., Pudil, F. and Bencko, V. (2007b) The image analysis of colour changes of different human tissues in the relation to the age. Part 1. Methodological approach. *Soudní lékarství*, **52** (2), 26–30.

Pilin, A., Pudil, F. and Bencko, V. (2007c) The image analysis of colour changes of different human tissues in the relation to the age. Part 2: practical applicability. *Soudní lékarství*, **52** (3), 36–42.

Ramsey, G.V. (1943) The sexual development of boys. *American Journal of Psychology*, **56** (2), 217–233.

Razzaghy-Azar, M., Moghimi, A., Sadigh, N. *et al.* (2006) Age of puberty in Iranian girls living in Tehran. *Annals of Human Biology*, **33** (5–6), 628–633.

Richardson, D.W. and Short, R.V. (1978) Time of onset of sperm production in boys. *Journal of Biosocial Science. Supplement*, **5**, 15–25.

Rivkees, S.A., Hall, D.A., Beopple, P.A. and Crawford, J.D. (1987) Accuracy and re-producibility of clinical measures of testicular volume. *Journal of Pediatrics*, **110** (6), 914–917.

Robert, W.M. (1921) Statures and weights of children under six years of age. *American Journal of Physical Anthropology*, **5** (1), 5–16.

Rosenfield, R.L., Lipton, R.B. and Drum, M.L. (2009) Thelarche, pubarche, and menarche attainment in children with normal and elevated body mass index. *Pediatrics*, **123** (1), 84–58.

Rudolph, C.D., Rudolph, A. M, Hosetter, M.K. *et al.* (2003) *Rudolph's Pediatrics*, 21st edn, McGraw Hill, New York.

Sakamoto, H., Saito, K., Oohta, M. *et al.* (2007) Testicular volume measurement: comparison of ultrasonography, orchidometry, and water displacement. *Urology*, **69** (1), 152–157.

Stark, O., Peckham, C.S. and Moynihan, C. (1989) Weight and age at menarche. *Archives of Disease in Childhood*, **64** (3), 383–387.

Sun, S.S., Schubert, C.M., Chumlea, W.C. *et al.* (2002) National estimates of the timing of sexual maturation and racial differences among US children. *Pediatrics*, **110** (5), 911–919.

Tanner, J.M. (1962) *Growth at Adolescence*, Blackwell, Oxford.

Tanner, J.M. (1986) Normal growth and techniques of growth assessment. *Clinical Endocrinology and Metabolism*, **15** (3), 411–451.

Tanner, J.M. and Davies, P.S. (1985) Clinical longitudinal standards for height and height velocity for North American children. *Journal of Pediatrics*, **107** (3), 317–329.

Tanner, J.M. and Whitehouse, R.H. (1976) Clinical longitudinal standards for height, weight, height velocity, weight velocity, and stages of puberty. *Archives of Disease in Childhood*, **51** (3), 170–179.

Tanner, J.M., Whitehouse, R.H. and Takaishi, M. (1966a) Standards from birth to maturity for height, weight, height velocity, and weight velocity: British children, 1965. I. *Archives of Disease in Childhood*, **41** (219), 454–471.

Tanner, J.M., Whitehouse, R.H. and Takaishi, M. (1966b) Standards from birth to maturity for height, weight, height velocity, and weight velocity: British children, 1965. II. *Archives of Disease in Childhood*, **41** (220), 613–635.

Taskinen, S., Taavitsainen, M. and Wikström, S. (1996) Measurement of testicular volume: comparison of 3 different methods. *Journal of Urology*, **155** (3), 930–933.

Thomas, F., Renaud, F., Benefice, E. *et al.* (2001) International variability of ages at menarche and menopause: patterns and main determinants. *Human Biology*, **73** (2), 271–290.

van't Hof, M.A. and Roede, M.J. (1977) A Monte Carlo test of weight as a critical factor in menarche, compared with bone age and measures of height, width, and sexual development. *Annals of Human Biology*, **4** (6), 581–585.

Van Den Berg, S.M., Setiawan, A., Bartels, M. *et al.* (2006) Individual differences in puberty onset in girls: Bayesian estimation of heritabilities and genetic correlations. *Behavior Genetics*, **36** (2), 261–270.

Veronesi, F.M. and Gueresi, P. (1994) Trend in menarcheal age and socioeconomic influence in Bologna (northern Italy). *Annals of Human Biology*, **21** (2), 187–196.

Woodbury, R.M. (1921) Statures and weights of children under six years of age. *American Journal of Physical Anthropology*, **5** (3), 279–282.

Wronka, I. and Pawlinska-Chmara, R. (2005) Menarcheal age and socio-economic factors in Poland. *Annals of Human Biology*, **32** (5), 630–638.

Zukauskaite, S., Lasiene, D., Lasas, L. *et al.* (2005) Onset of breast and pubic hair development in 1231 preadolescent Lithuanian schoolgirls. *Archives of Disease in Childhood*, **90** (9), 932–936.

10

Age Evaluation and Odontology in the Living ·

Jane Taylor and Matthew Blenkin
School of Health Sciences, University of Newcastle, Australia, Health Precinct, Ourimbah, NSW 2258, Australia

10.1 Introduction

Examination of the dental tissues as a method for estimating the age of an individual has strong historical precedence dating back to the early nineteenth century (Miles, 1963a) or even possibly to Roman times (Müller, 1990). Today the developmental stages of the dentition are widely and regularly used in dentistry and medicine to time interventionist treatment, and in archaeology and forensic contexts, including odontology and anthropology, to estimate the age of the living and the deceased.

Dental development is thought to be the most accurate and reliable way of correlating growth and development, as it is a system little affected by environmental factors (Gustafson and Koch, 1974; Smith, 1991; Liversidge, Herdeg and Rösing, 1998; Heuzé and Cardoso, 2008) and tooth formation stages exhibit lower levels of variation than is evidenced in the skeletal system (Lewis and Garn, 1960). Dental maturation is also believed to be independent of somatic, skeletal and sexual maturation as teeth are derived from different embryonic origins and thus are under alternative mechanisms of control, the former being mesodermal in origin whereas dental structures are derived from the ectomesenchyme (Demirjian *et al.*, 1985; Holtgrave, Kretschmer and Muller, 1997).

Dental age estimation techniques are considered to be highly reliable in children and less accurate in adults (Hägg and Matsson, 1985; Mincer, Harris and Berryman, 1993; Solheim and Vonen, 2006). The more teeth there are in various stages of development, the more data is available for analysis and the more reliable and accurate are the predictions (Hägg and Taranger, 1985; Smith, 1991).

Age Estimation in the Living: The Practitioners Guide Sue Black, Anil Aggrawal and Jason Payne-James
© 2010 John Wiley & Sons, Ltd

Smith (1991) divided dental ageing techniques into three categories:

1. age attainment of developmental stages, which gives an indication of the age at which a given event usually occurs;

2. age prediction, which ascribes a dental age according to the level of development and how closely it approximated to chronological age;

3. maturity assessment, which indicates if the given individual is advanced or retarded in development compared to a given reference population.

All can have application in age estimation of a living individual but it is important that practitioners appreciate the differences between each of the techniques and the information produced.

This chapter will provide an overview of dental development and discuss dental age estimation techniques for both sub-adult and adult groups, with a particular emphasis on those that have applicability for living individuals. Recommendations will be made for the use of appropriate techniques in different situations.

10.2 Overview of the Development of the Dentition

Human teeth, both primary (deciduous) and secondary (permanent), develop through a succession of stages that are predictable and observable, and it is the observation of these stages that many methods of age estimation are based upon.

The developmental process of teeth is the most complex, and one of the longest, of any structure or organ in the body as it involves both a formative and an eruptive phase (Schour and Massler, 1940; Smith, 1991). The primary teeth (deciduous dentition) commence odontogenesis around week 6 *in utero* and mineralization of the incisal edge of the upper incisors begins around 13–16 weeks of gestational age (Lunt and Law, 1974). The development of the primary dentition then continues in a well-documented sequence through to the point where mineralization is completed with closure of the root apices of the second molars at about three years of age. During this period the primary teeth emerge into the oral cavity in a more or less predictable pattern by about the age of two years.

The secondary (permanent) dentition commences formation around the time of birth with the mineralization of the cusp tips of the first permanent molars. Development continues until the closure of the root apices of the third permanent molars between 18 and 25 years of age. The process of eruption of secondary teeth, and associated exfoliation of primary teeth, commences around 6 years of age and is completed by about 18 years of age (Logan and Kronfeld, 1933). The tooth begins its eruptive journey into the oral cavity when enamel apposition on the crown is complete and the root is beginning to develop. The formation and eruption of the secondary dentition also occurs in a predictable sequence.

Liversidge, Herdeg and Rösing (1998) have summarized, in order of influence, the factors that affect growth, and presumably dental growth, in general:

1. chance;

2. genetic differences;

3. sex;

4. regional variation;

5. secular trends;

6. human ecology;

7. climate;

8. age.

It is reasonable that dental development would also be under similar influences. If the degree of dental development is to be used as an indication of chronological age, it is essential that any factors that affect the timing and rate of development are thoroughly understood and taken into account.

It has been estimated that the contribution of genetic control is as much as 90% (Garn, Lewis and Polacheck, 1960; Pelsmaekers *et al.*, 1997; Merwin and Harris, 1998). The timing of the emergence of deciduous incisors has also been shown to be under strong genetic control (Hughes *et al.*, 2007). Even within a population of similar genetic heritage there will be a range of rates of development due to natural biological variation, which can be considered to be variation due to chance.

Studies of the pattern of dental mineralization show that the early stages of tooth development are almost the same for both males and females and the sexual dimorphism in developmental rates occurs at around the crown completion stage and continues to increase during the root development stage, when girls reach the majority of developmental stages ahead of boys (Gleiser and Hunt, 1955; Moorrees, Fanning and Hunt 1963; Demirjian and Levesque, 1980; Chaillet *et al.*, 2004).

Regional variation is thought to be exhibited in dental development. Numerous studies have shown dental maturation rates that are consistent for a given racial group, but vary significantly between groups (Fanning and Moorees, 1969; Loevy, 1983; Owsley and Jantz, 1983; Hägg and Matsson, 1985; Nyström, 1986, 1988; Harris and McKee, 1990; Staaf, Mörnstad and Welander, 1991; Davis and Hägg, 1994; Mörnstad, 1995; Tompkins, 1996), although some have posited that these differences may reflect differences in methodology or be due to secular trends and therefore geographic-specific standards may not be necessary (Liversidge and Speechly, 2001; Braga *et al.*, 2005; Liversidge *et al.*, 2006, Maber, Liversidge and Hector, 2006).

Nutrition (Fess, 1963; Billewicz and MacGregor, 1975; Demirjian, 1986), hygiene, health, education and income (Mukherjee, 1973), low birth weight (Backström *et al.*, 2000), genetic syndromes, and endocrine and metabolic disorders (Lukacs, 1989) are all known to impact on dental development to some degree. Interestingly, neither climate (Townsend and Hammel, 1990), nor a fluoridated water supply (El Badrawy, 1984) has been shown to affect the rate of dental development.

Consistent with other body systems, variation in dental development increases with increasing age. The early developmental stages of early forming teeth are notably less variable than the later developmental stages of the later forming teeth (Garn, Lewis and Polacheck, 1959; Demirjian and Levesque, 1980), and thus with increasing age, the range of variation for age prediction must also rise.

10.3 Techniques of Dental Age Estimation

Age estimation techniques are frequently divided into those applicable to children or sub-adults and those relevant to adults. The following discussion will make an (arbitrary) division between the two groups at 18 years of age. For dental age estimation techniques the cut-off point is usually allied to a stage of development of the third molars. It is important to remember that there will be some cross-over in applicability of techniques, a good example being the use of third molars.

Techniques of dental age assessment can be divided into physical, radiographic and destructive. Destructive techniques are, obviously, less likely to be applied in living individuals as they require sacrifice of a vital or functioning tooth, but in some situations, with informed consent, an individual may be willing to lose a tooth, and as such these techniques will be discussed briefly.

Certain technical criteria should be met for any method that is to be used in a forensic context. The reference sample should have been generated from a large sample of people of known age, with a wide and even age distribution (Schmeling *et al.*, 2008), and should be appropriate for the sex, regional and ancestral background of the person being evaluated (Liversidge, Herdeg and Rösing, 1998; Chaillet, Nyström and Demirjian, 2005; Schmeling *et al.*, 2006b).

Ritz-Timme *et al.* (2000) recommended that the reference data must have been presented to the scientific community (usually via peer reviewed publication) and should contain clear information concerning accuracy of the technique and the representation of the sample source.

The accuracy, precision and appropriateness of the various techniques should be considered by practitioners when deciding on a technique of choice, but ease of use is also an important consideration.

The accuracy of a method is defined by the proximity of the estimated age to the chronological (i.e. known) age. Mörnstad, Staaf and Welander (1994) commented that the natural range of variation in the dental maturity of 95% of the population is about ±1.5–2 years, so accuracy greater than that would theoretically be impossible to achieve and results showing a greater degree of accuracy than this would be potentially irrelevant and misleading. Average error rates of ±1–2 years for children (Willems, Moulin-Romsee and Solheim, 2002) and ±5 years (Smith, 1991), ±10 years (Willems, Moulin-Romsee and Solheim, 2002; Solheim and Vonen, 2006) and ±14 years (Rösing and Kvaal,1997) for adults have been stated.

The level of accuracy required is case specific. Rösing and Kvaal (1997) opined that an error rate of greater than ±14 years could be of no forensic benefit, but practitioners need to consider the circumstances of each case. It may be that a larger error rate is still useful if no other information is available or when it is able to corroborate the findings of other methods.

Precision is defined by the repeatability measurements and is an indicator of the reproducibility of a technique. Inter- and intra-observer rates of error are one indicator of precision, and the ease by which a technique can be applied can also impact on precision and confidence.

Practitioners need to be confident that a technique is simple, yet robust, reliable and sufficiently accurate to be of value and admissible in a legal setting.

10.4   The Sub-adult Dentition

For children or sub-adults, clinical examinations predominantly use physical tooth counts in the mouth, radiographic techniques to assess the developing tooth and destructive methods, which may include histological examinations and amino acid racemization.

10.4.1   Sub-adult: Physical/Anatomical

10.4.1.1   Tooth Counts   Observation of the number and type of teeth present in the oral cavity is widely used, but it is a difficult technique that requires appropriate dental experience primarily for tooth identification purposes. This technique is based on the assumption that different teeth erupt at different ages, in a relatively constant chronological order, and by observing which teeth are present one can estimate the dental age of the individual.

Limitations include that emergence times are affected by a diverse range of factors, including infection, pathology, trauma, crowding, extraction, agenesis and the presence of supernumerary teeth (Fanning, 1961; Moorrees, Fanning and Hunt, 1963; Hägg and Taranger, 1985; Suri, Gagari and Vasterdis, 2004). A number of resources do not address sexual dimorphism in emergence times and the data may be sourced from small sample sizes for which the reliability and accuracy of information is unknown. This approach to ageing is limited to those periods when teeth are emerging, that is 0–3 years for the deciduous and 5–14 years for the permanent dentition.

Studies have provided diverse levels of confidence in this approach. Hägg and Taranger (1985) found emergence of the tooth into the oral cavity to be a reliable indicator of age, giving errors of ±4 months for deciduous teeth and ±3 years for permanent teeth, both at the 95% confidence interval. Townsend and Hammel (1990), in a review of 42 separate studies, found it an accurate method for use during the 6–30 month period of deciduous emergence and that it seemed unaffected by sex or race. Foti *et al.* (2003) reported prediction errors of ±3.5 years at the 95% confidence interval for a regression model based on a sample of 6- to 20-year-olds.

The technique is only easy to use and reliable if the practitioner is familiar with the anatomy of all human teeth and the potential for variation in shape, agenesis and retention possibilities.

Application of this technique on living individuals involves a full clinical examination. The use of smiling photographs to determine teeth present would be limited by the quality of the photograph and the ability of the examiner to identify teeth accurately in less than optimal conditions. It is not easy to account for abnormalities in position under these circumstances.

With either a full clinical examination or the use of social photographs, the limiting factor in the use of tooth counts is that once a tooth has erupted there is no reliable means to tell how long it has been in the mouth, meaning that the most reliable age estimation would only be able to indicate that the individual in question is over a certain age, using age attainment statistics.

References frequently used in these comparisons include those of Schour and Massler (1940, 1941), Haaviko (1974), Moorrees and Kent (1978), Smith (1991) and Foti *et al.* (2003). Smith and Garn (1987) provide a practical reference for this technique, reproduced in Figure 10.1.

Most national dental associations also publish data relevant to their specific population groups. Geographically specific reference data has been published: see (but not limited to) Brown (1978) (Australian Aborigines); Hägg and Taranger (1985) (Swedish); Kochhar and Richardson (1998) (Northern Irish); Choi and Yang (2001) (Korean); Nyström *et al.* (2001) (Finnish); Mugonzibwa *et al.* (2002) (Tanzanian); Diamanti and Townsend (2003) (Australian); Holman and Jones

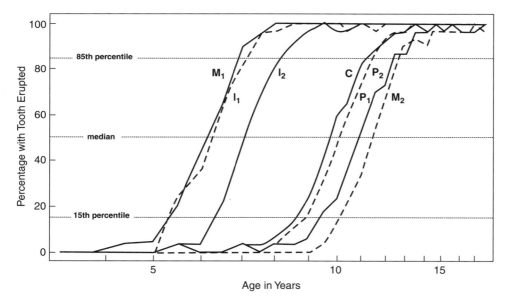

Figure 10.1 Example of determining age of attainment of a growth stage. Data is based upon a sample of 2990 females. Such curves can be used as an indication of age based upon erupted teeth; however, the limitations of such estimates need to be taken into account. Smith, B.H. and Garn, S.M. (1987) Polymorphisms in eruption sequence of permanent teeth in American children. *American Journal of Physical Anthropology*, **74**, 289–303. Copyright © (1987 Wiley & Sons). Reprinted with permission of John Wiley & Sons, Inc.

(2003) (Bangladeshi, Guatemalan, Japanese, Javanese); Nizam, Naing and Mokhtar (2003) (Malaysian); Psoter *et al.* (2003) (American, White and Hispanic); Rousset *et al.* (2003) (French); Liversidge and Molleson (2004) (British); Holman and Yamaguchi (2005) (Japanese); Friedrich *et al.* (2006) (German); Bastos *et al.* (2007) (Brazilian); Folayan *et al.* (2007) (Nigerian); Leroy *et al.* (2008) (Flemish); and Blenkin and Evans (2010) (Australian).

10.4.2   Sub-adult: Radiographic

Although dental development studies have been reported as far back as the late nineteenth century (see Smith, 1991) the first work to be regularly referred to in the dental and forensic literature is that of Logan and Kronfeld (1933).

Subsequent to this, numerous techniques for the radiographic evaluation of mineralization stages of the developing dentition have been described, including, but not limited to: Schour and Massler (1941); Gleiser and Hunt (1955); Nolla (1960); Fanning (1961); Morrees, Fanning and Hunt (1963); Wolanski (1966); Calonius, Lunin and Stout (1970); Demirjian, Goldstein and Tanner (1973); Gustafson and Koch (1974); Haavikko (1974); Anderson, Thompson and Popovich (1976); Demirjian and Goldstein (1976); Ciapparelli (1985, 1992); Carels *et al.* (1991); Mörnstad, Staaf and Welander (1994); Liversidge and Molleson (1999); Teivens and Mörnstad (2001); Willems *et al.* (2001); Blenkin (2009); and Cameriere, Ferrante and Cingolani (2006).

It is frequently acknowledged that direct comparison between such a vast array of methods is impractical as some lack rigorous descriptive scientific criteria; both cross-sectional and longitudinal approaches have been employed and sample sizes and statistical analyses vary (see Liversidge, Herdeg and Rösing, 1998). One approach to enable some form of comparison is to divide the methods into those that rely on a diagrammatic or atlas style presentation of the developmental stages for comparison and those requiring some form of measurement of the developing tooth. This latter group can then be further subdivided into those presenting the results as population- and sex-specific standards against those using a regression formula to calculate estimated age.

Irrespective of the technique used, it is essential to have high quality radiographic images of the teeth being assessed. Either panoramic tomographs, single tooth intra-oral periapical films or CT scans provide the greatest detail; however, extra-oral oblique views using plain film can also be used.

10.4.2.1   Atlas Style Techniques   Of the atlas style presentations the most regularly cited is that of Schour and Massler (1941), reproduced in Figure 10.2. This chart summarized the development of the human dentition from birth to 35 years and is still widely used today. Application involves comparison of a radiograph of, preferably, the entire maxilla and mandible to diagrams depicting the stage of the development of the dentition that can be expected at each year in the life of a child. By matching the radiographic image to a specific diagram, the estimated age of the child is assigned in accordance with the associated diagram.

DEVELOPMENT OF THE HUMAN DENITION

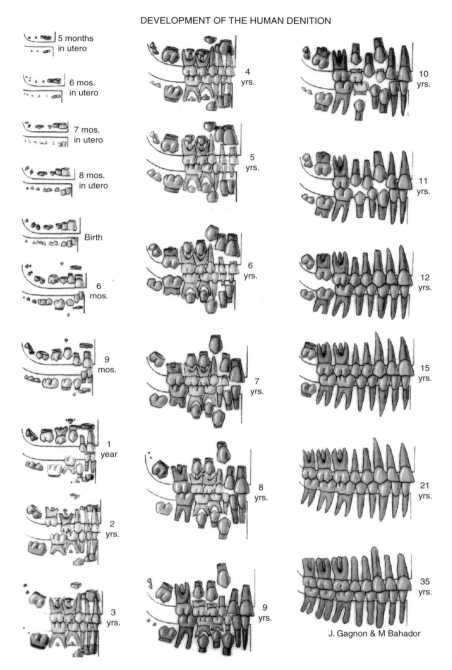

Figure 10.2 Atlas style age estimation charts developed by Schour and Massler. Schour, I., Massler, M. The development of the human dentition. *Journal of the American Dental Association* 1941; **28**, 1154. Copyright © 1941 American Dental Association. All rights reserved. Reprinted by permission.

Valid criticisms of this method include the fact that it is based on the work of Logan and Kronfeld and as such is a very small, biased sample, being one sample per age group up to 15 years of chronically ill, institutionalized and potentially malnourished children. In assigning a different diagram to each year, the range about a mean age can only be six months, and this is likely to be too narrow a range to support credible age estimation.

Updated versions of these charts are still used today (Ciapparelli, 1992), and adaptations include those of Ubelaker (1989) for Native Americans of archaeological origin.

The charts of Gustafson and Koch (1974) can also be considered in this category. These authors sought to develop a schematic representation of tooth development based upon data from published papers. Data was reclassified according to four developmental stages and converted into a graphic that depicted development in two monthly intervals up to one year of age and thereafter in yearly intervals. The reported accuracy for a single age estimation was ±4.97 months at the 95% confidence interval. Hägg and Matsson (1985) and Mörnstad (1995) found the technique to be more reliable for boys than for girls.

Although simple to use, atlas type systems do have limitations. Some stages, for example clinical emergence, can be almost impossible to determine from a radiograph, making application unreliable and any comparisons subject to a higher degree of inter-observer disagreement.

10.4.2.2 Techniques Employing Measurement   Most radiographic age estimation techniques require measurement of the stage of development of the forming tooth. The vast majority utilize indirect or relative measurements, usually via reference to a diagrammatic schema (e.g. Gleiser and Hunt, 1955; Wolanski, 1966; Haavikko, 1974; Anderson, Thompson and Popovich, 1976; Demirjian, Goldstein and Tanner, 1973; Ciapparelli, 1985, 1992; Willems *et al.*, 2001; Blenkin, 2009) while others require estimation of a percentage of final root development (e.g. Nolla, 1960; Fanning, 1961; Moorrees, Fanning and Hunt, 1963). A small number utilize direct linear measurement of the developing tooth (e.g. Carels *et al.*, 1991; Mörnstad, Staaf and Welander, 1994; Liversidge and Molleson, 1999; Cameriere, Ferrante and Cingolani, 2006).

The majority of techniques use these measurements to generate some form of sum of stages or maturity score, which is then referenced against a table or graph to indicate age. Some, including the techniques using direct measurements, have preferred to use regression equations to calculate estimated age.

Many of the published techniques are developments or modifications of two original techniques. The first group, Anderson, Thompson and Popovich (1976) and Ciapparelli (1985, 1992), described modifications of the Moorrees, Fanning and Hunt (1963) model. Morress, Fanning and Hunt designated a number of stages of development for each tooth based upon the stages described by Gleiser and Hunt (1955). They undertook a qualitative study to provide norms for the ages of attainment of 14 specific stages of tooth development for each of the 8 mandibular and maxillary teeth. It was the intention that these norms, including percentile bands, be used in conjunction with the known chronological age in clinical diagnosis and treatment planning by dentists and orthodontists. As a sexual dimorphism was noted, tables were divided into results for male and female.

The second group of researchers, including Teivens and Mörnstad (2001), Willems *et al.* (2001) and Blenkin (2009), presented adaptations of the Demirjian, Goldstein and Tanner (1973) technique. Demirjian, Goldstein and Tanner modified the defined system of stages previously published by Moorrees, Fanning and Hunt. They simplified this system by defining only eight stages of development, depicted in Figure 10.3. Further, the assessment of these stages relied on relative, not absolute, measurements. The written descriptions of these stages were modified in a later paper by Demirjian in order to provide further clarification of the defining features of each stage (Demirjian and Goldstein, 1976). By examining radiographs the teeth 47 to 41

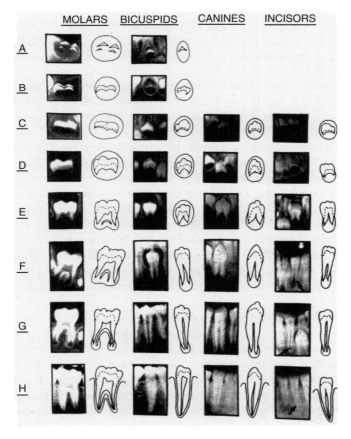

Figure 10.3 The Demirjian system for rating eight developmental stages for permanent molars and premolars and six stages for canines and incisors. Reprinted from figure 1 from Demirjian, A., Goldstein, H. and Tanner, JM. A new system of dental age assessment. *Human Biology*, 1973; **45**, 211–227. Copyright © Wayne State University Press, with the permission of Wayne State University Press.

inclusive are assessed in terms of their developmental stage and assigned a rating of A to H. The attributed stage for each is then converted to a self-weighted numerical score. This conversion gives a set of tooth scores for each case, the sum of which results in a summative 'Maturity Score' for that case. Centile charts for both males and females were then derived that allowed for conversion of this total maturity score to dental age.

A modification of the Demirjian technique, suggested by Blenkin (2009), allows for standardization against a sample from a given population. Population-specific regression formulae and predictive curves can be produced using a standardization study.

For the Moorrees, Fanning and Hunt (1963) system, the range of age variation from the norm for 2 standard deviations (SD) was reported at about 3–5 years for teeth in the root formation stages and up to 8 years in the apical closure of third molars, although Smith (1991) reported an accuracy of ±0.2 years. Using his own system, Demirjian reported a range of up to 3 years between the 3rd and 97th percentiles (Demirjian, Goldstein and Tanner, 1973), while Haag and Matsson (1985) found the predicted ages were associated with a 95% confidence interval of ±2 years.

Those techniques using estimates of percentage of root formation (e.g. Nolla, 1960; Fanning, 1961; Moorrees, Fanning and Hunt, 1963) have been criticized as being imprecise as it is difficult, if not impossible, to predict a measure of an unknown final dimension with any degree of accuracy.

Moorrees, Fanning and Hunt quoted the intra-observer agreement figure of 75% for incisors and 90% for posterior teeth but made no allowance for the situation where two separate assessments match but only because of random chance. Demirjian, Goldstein and Tanner (1973) reported an inter-observer agreement level of 90%. Other studies applying the Demirjian technique have reported lower, but acceptable levels at 75% or better (Demirjian and Leveresque, 1980; Nyström, 1986, 1988; Staff, Mörnstad and Welander, 1991; Nykanen et al., 1998; Liversidge, Speechly and Hector, 1999; Nyström et al., 2000; Blenkin, 2009). The inter-observer agreement levels are reported to be higher when participants avail themselves of the training and pre-calibration course available for the Demirjian technique (Demirjian, 1994).

Higgins (2006) identified the ease of use of a number of radiographic techniques and described the Demirjian technique as simple to moderate, the Gleiser and Hunt and the Moorrees, Fanning and Hunt techniques as moderately difficult, and the Nolla technique as difficult. Many authors have indicated that the Demirjian technique is the technique of choice as it provides radiographs, drawings and clear written instructions to aid in determining developmental stages (Hägg and Matsson, 1985; Nyström, 1988; Staaf, Mörnstad and Welander, 1991; Kullman et al., 1996; Liversidge, Herdeg and Rösing, 1998; Frucht et al., 2000; Chaillet et al., 2004).

Increased accuracy is reported when self-weighted maturity scores and regression models are modified to reflect local samples (see, but not limited to, Davis and Hägg, 1994; Willems et al., 2001; Liversidge, Lyons and Hector, 2003; Olze et al., 2004; Blenkin, 2009; Chaillet, Nyström and Demirjian, 2005; Leurs et al., 2005; Maber,

Liversidge and Hector, 2006; Liversidge *et al.*, 2006; Cameriere *et al.*, 2007; Lee *et al.*, 2008).

10.4.3 Sub-adult: Destructive

As previously indicated, destructive techniques will be touched on only briefly for those very rare situations where an individual, with informed consent, may be willing to sacrifice a tooth as part of the age assessment process (see also Chapter 4). The necessity of this approach is one that may require the advice of medical or dental defence organizations or professional bodies. The majority of these techniques require specialist trained laboratory assistance, and practitioners are referred to the cited references for more detail prior to use.

10.4.3.1 Histological Techniques While enamel and dentine are still forming, the amount of dentine laid down after the formation of the neonatal line in the deciduous dentition (Schour, 1936), and the counting of cross-striations and striae of Retzius in primary and secondary enamel are all reported to correlate positively with chronological age (Dean and Beynon, 1991, Huda and Bowman, 1995).

Once enamel deposition is complete the use of cemental annulation rings has been found to offer reasonable correlations with chronological age (Lovejoy *et al.*, 1985; Charles *et al.*, 1986; Lipsinic, 1986; Solheim, 1990; Wittwer-Backofen, Gampe and Vaupel, 2004).

10.4.3.2 Aspartic Acid Racemization Aspartic acid racemization uses the ratio of the L- and D-enantiomers of aspartic acid to give an indication of the time that has lapsed since the dentine was laid down and when the ratio was zero. The correlation between the ratio of D- and L-forms and the age of the tooth has been shown to be high, with an error of just ± 3 years in younger age groups (Ohtani and Yamamoto, 1991; Ohtani *et al.*, 1995; Ritz *et al.*, 1995; Pilin *et al.*, 2001) and ± 12–20 years in older age groups (Helfman and Bada, 1976; Mörnstad, Staaf and Welander, 1994; Ohtani, Ito and Yamamoto, 2003).

10.5 The Adult Dentition

Once development of most of the dentition ceases, it is the observation of time-related degradational changes of the dental tissues that allows for estimates of age to be made in adults. Physical examinations can look at teeth present and tooth wear; radiographic examinations are largely limited to third molars and secondary dentine; while destructive techniques can use changes in the histological structure of the various dental tissues and amino acid racemization.

10.5.1   Adult: Physical

10.5.1.1   Tooth Wear   Dental attrition, or occlusal wear, has been used by many authors to estimate chronological age, with varying degrees of success (Murphy, 1959; Miles, 1963a; Brothwell 1965; Molnar, 1970; Nowell, 1978; Lovejoy, 1985; Solheim, 1988; Kim, Kho and Lee, 2000).

Murphy's (1959) initial positive results based on an Australian aboriginal population did not correlate well when applied to other groups and highlight the inherent variability of this trait. There are many factors that may influence the amount and rate of dental attrition within a population, let alone between populations that are geographically and culturally diverse, including tooth number, angulation, size and position, bruxism, size and shape of the mandibular condyles, the presence of dental restorations, occupational/habitual factors such as pipe smoking or tooth-pick chewing, and diet (Yun *et al.*, 2007, Prince, Kimmerle and Konigsberg, 2008).

In an attempt to address the inherent population variability in dental wear, Miles developed a method from archaeological samples that could be used within any given population as it established a baseline from within that sample (Miles, 1963a). Miles hypothesized that dental wear is continuous throughout the functional life of the tooth; wear on all three permanent molars occurs at comparable rates through similar states and patterns; and that both wear and diet are effectively uniform throughout a given population. The amount of wear can then be assessed and an age estimation made on the basis of comparison to the baseline. In 1965, Brothwell simplified the Miles method by basing the assessment of the extent of the wear on patterns of dentine islands remaining on the occlusal surface in archaeological material (Brothwell, 1965).

Smith (1984) modified the method first proposed by Murphy, producing diagrams and descriptions of eight stages of wear for comparison. The stages (Figure 10.4) commence at 1 with little or no wear and proceed to the most extreme stage (8), where the crown is entirely worn away. A comparable but more detailed scale was developed by Lovejoy (1985). Any such grading system may be used to establish a serialized baseline for population-specific comparison.

Much of the work in this field has been focused on historical skeletal populations and was not originally intended to age the living. Secular changes in diet have resulted in significantly less occlusal wear in modern Western populations (Miles, 1962) and applicability of these older techniques to a modern case may be limited. In such circumstances the availability of other individuals from the same population for standardization is advisable. As an example, a new scoring system developed by Kim, Kho and Lee (2000) and modified by Yun *et al.* (2007) produced results of age estimates with an error of ±5.0 years in about 60% of cases in a Korean population.

10.5.2   Adult: Radiographic

Once the dentition has completed mineralization, by about 25 years of age, the use of the radiographic techniques of age estimation mentioned in the sub-adult section have little application. Only one tooth group, the third molar or wisdom teeth, may still be developing, although two dental tissues, cementum and secondary dentine, do

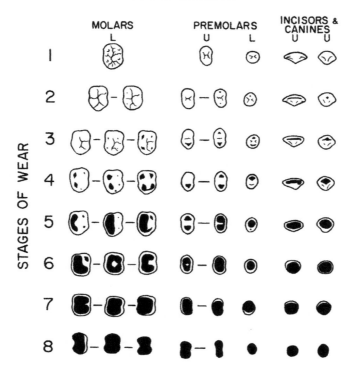

Figure 10.4 Diagrams of crown surfaces used to score stages of tooth wear. Smith, B.H. (1984) Patterns of molar wear in hunter-gatherers and agriculturalists. *American Journal of Physical Anthropology*, **63**, 39–56. Copyright © (1984 Wiley & Sons). Reprinted with permission of John Wiley & Sons, Inc.

continue to be laid down. The observation of post-developmental changes, such as the apposition of secondary dentine on the walls of the pulp chamber, via radiography can be of use and is covered separately in a following section (Kvaal *et al.*, 1995; Drusini, Toso and Ranzato, 1997; Cameriere *et al.*, 2006; Cameriere *et al.*, 2007).

10.5.2.1 Third Molars Third molars, or wisdom teeth, have traditionally been eschewed as too biologically variable in development to be a reliable measure for age estimation (Thorson and Häag, 1991; Mörnstad, 1995; Kullman, Johanson and Akesson, 1992; Bolaños *et al.*, 2000). These teeth exhibit higher levels of congenital absence, malformation and left–right asymmetry in size than any other teeth, and are frequently impacted and subsequently extracted.

At the time of the development of the third molars, from the mid-teens to the early 20s, there are few other reliable dental methods of age estimation, and a considerable amount of recent research has concentrated on the use of third molar development in age assessment. These studies have found analysis of third molar development to be accurate and sufficiently highly correlated with chronological age to be of forensic value (Nortjé, 1983; Engström, Engström and Sagne, 1983; Mincer,

Harris and Berryman, 1993, Mesotten *et al.*, 2002; Gunst *et al.*, 2003; Bhat and Kamath, 2007; Sisman *et al.*, 2007; Martin-de las Heras *et al.*, 2008). One study in particular obtained an accuracy of ±2.4 years at the 95% confidence level (Nortjé, 1983).

Third molar statistics are often presented as evidence of the likelihood that the individual has attained an age of 18 years (complete closure of the apex of the root), or as a percentage of the population who would be aged 18 years when the third molar has completed development. These statistics are presented as being forensically relevant as 18 is the age of legal maturity in many jurisdictions. As examples, Mincer, Harris and Berryman (1993) found that the mean age for third molars to achieve apex closure was 20.5 years in both Negroid and Caucasoid American children. In an Austrian sample, Meinl *et al.* (2007a) indicated that 99.5% of males and 99.3% of females would be over 18 years of age when the roots of the third molars were seen to have completed development. Other authors presenting similar statistics include Gunst *et al.* (2003), De Salvia *et al.* (2004), Olze *et al.* (2004) and Blakenship *et al.* (2007).

Most third molar studies use modifications of the Demirjian or Moorrees, Fanning and Hunt techniques, and precision and ease of use are similar as for the rest of the dentition.

Regional or geographic variation in the development of third molars, as with all other teeth in the dentition, is thought to be present (Gorgani, Sullivan and DuBois, 1990; Mincer, Harris and Berryman, 1993; Nyström *et al.*, 1988; Olze *et al.*, 2003; Olze *et al.*, 2004; Prieto *et al.*, 2005; Orhan *et al.*, 2007). Practitioners are encouraged to use reference tables and formulae that are directly applicable to the population group under investigation in all cases; for example, see Engström, Engström and Sagne (1983), Nortjé (1983), Mincer, Harris and Berryman (1993), Solari and Abramovitch (2002), Garamendi *et al.* (2005), Olze *et al.* (2007, 2008a,b), Sisman *et al.* (2007) and Bai *et al.* (2008).

10.5.2.2 Secondary Dentine Apposition   Measures of the amount of secondary dentine present can give an indication of the time that has elapsed since the tooth was formed and hence provide an estimation of chronological age (Ikeda *et al.* 1985; Drusini, 1993; Drusini, Toso and Ranzato, 1997; Soomer *et al.*, 2003). Kvaal *et al.* (1995) used up to six different ratios of varying pulp chamber and tooth size measurements, which gave a significant correlation, with an r^2 of 0.76 and an error rate of ±17.2 years. Willems, Moulin-Romsee and Solheim (2002) found the Kvaal method reliable but precision and ease of use were not high, while a recent study by Meinl *et al.* (2007b) reported some inaccuracy when applied to a younger population.

Cameriere, Ferrante and Cingolani (2004) investigated the ratio of pulp area to entire tooth area to age and found a significant correlation of $r^2 = 0.85$ and an error of about ±10.0 years at the 95% confidence level. More recent work has refined this technique whereby the pulp/tooth area ratios for an upper and lower canine are inserted into a regression formula to give an estimate of age (Cameriere *et al.*, 2006, 2007). The r^2 value was reported as 0.925 with a 95% confidence interval of about ±8.1 years.

10.5.3   Adult: Destructive

10.5.3.1   The Gustafson Method   The Gustafson method is based on the observation of six different dental criteria (attrition, secondary dentine apposition, periodontal recession, cementum build-up, root resorption and dentinal sclerosis) which
undergo age-related changes throughout life (Gustafson, 1950). The original study
claimed a standard error of about ±4.5 years; however, later studies have been unable
to reproduce this level of accuracy (Miles, 1963b; Burns and Maples, 1976; Maples,
1979; Lucy and Pollard, 1995). Today it is generally accepted that the average error
of the Gustafson method is ±10–15 years.

Many variations on the Gustafson method have been published, most focusing
on the use of one or more of the modified criteria (Dalitz, 1963; Johanson, 1971;
Maples, 1978; Metzger, 1980; Lamendin *et al.*, 1992; Solheim, 1993).

10.5.3.2   Root Transparency   Studies of transparent or sclerotic dentine have reported errors of about ±9.2–10.5 years at the 65% confidence interval (Miles,
1963b; Bang and Ramm, 1970; Whittaker and Bakri, 1996). More recently the
use of biomedical computer imaging equipment to estimate the amount of transparent dentine in three dimensions has provided promising results (Vasiliadis, Darling
and Levers, 1983; Sognnaes, Gratt and Papin, 1985; Lopez-Nicolas, Morales and
Luna, 1996).

10.5.3.3   Amino Acid Racemization and Histological Techniques   Amino acid
racemization and histological techniques are also applicable in adult cases. Examination of cemental annulation rings is one of the few histological techniques applicable
to an adult case.

10.6   Summary

The choice of dental age estimation techniques depends on the circumstances of
each individual case, including the level of accuracy deemed necessary and the
availability and accessibility of information and data (Ritz-Timme *et al.*, 2000;
Heuzé and Cardoso, 2008). Practitioners are encouraged to be familiar with a
number of different techniques that will be appropriate in different situations.

Of the non-destructive techniques, those assessing stages of development of the
mineralization of the teeth, via radiographs, are considered more reliable than those
that use tooth counts (Moorrees, Fanning and Hunt, 1963; Nolla, 1960; Solheim
and Vonen, 2006). Amino acid racemization is considered to be the most reliable
destructive method of dental age estimation (Liversidge, Herdeg and Rösing, 1998).

Although there are currently no generally accepted guidelines concerning quality
assurance in age estimation (except for amino acid racemization) (Ritz-Timme *et al.*,
2000; Solheim and Vonen, 2006; Schmeling *et al.*, 2007), a number of published
suggestions do exist to ensure viable techniques are used and reliable conclusions
presented. The Study Group of Forensic Age Diagnostics (an interdisciplinary group
of German-speaking forensic specialists – see Chapter 1) recommend a physical

examination, a radiographic examination of the left wrist, and a dental examination, including recording of the dental status and a radiograph of the dentition for age assessment in living persons (Schmeling *et al.*, 2006a,b). Benson and Williams (2008) have made similar recommendations in their discussion of age estimation for refugee children in Australia.

It is recommended that for the dental component, a full clinical examination, with informed consent, is undertaken, including information on teeth status (eruption, attrition, colour, staining, periodontal health, restorations, agenesis, retention etc.); a detailed medical and dental history is recorded; and an orthopantomogram (panoramic radiograph) is undertaken (Solheim and Vonen, 2006; IOFOS, 2008).

Many authors recommend using more than one technique (Liversidge, Herdeg and Rösing, 1998; Solheim and Vonen, 2006) and warn that it is inadvisable to assess total maturation from one tissue system alone (Tanner, 1962; Moorrees, Fanning and Hunt, 1963; Demirjian *et al.*, 1985).

Ritz-Timme *et al.* (2000) and Schmeling *et al.* (2006a) recommend that dental age estimations be performed by people with specialist training and forensic experience and that there is adequate validation of the competency of the practitioner through continued professional development.

Table 10.1 presents the authors' recommended techniques for various situations. Practitioners are reminded to select techniques according to the individual case and the associated reporting requirements, and to undertake appropriate training and familiarization prior to use in a forensic situation.

Table 10.1   Recommended age estimation techniques for the living.

Sub-adult	No radiographs	Physical (tooth counts, emergence times)
		1. Smith and Garn (1987)
		2. Schour and Massler (1941)
		3. Gustafson and Koch (1974)
	Radiographs	Radiographic
		1. Demirjian, Goldstein and Tanner (1973) modified to local standards, e.g. Blenkin (2009)
		2. Moorrees, Fanning and Hunt (1963)
Adult	No radiographs	Physical (tooth wear)
		1. Smith (1984)
		2. Miles (1963a)
	Radiographs	For 18–25 years
		1. Modified Demirjian with reference to third molars
		Over 25 years
		1. Cameriere *et al.* (2006, 2007)
		2. Kvaal *et al.* (1995)

References

Anderson, D.L., Thompson, G.W. and Popovich, F. (1976) Age of attainment of mineralization stages of the permanent dentition. *Journal of Forensic Sciences,* **21**, 191–200.

Backström, M.C., Aine, L., Mäki, R. *et al.* (2000) Maturation of primary and permanent teeth in preterm infants. *Archives of Disease in Childhood. Fetal and Neonatal Edition*, **83**, 104–108.

Bai, Y., Mao, J., Zhu, S. and Wei, W. (2008) Third-molar development in relation to chronological age in young adults of central China. *Journal of Huazhong University of Science and Technology. Medical Sciences*, **28**, 487–490.

Bang, G. and Ramm, E. (1970) Determination of age in humans from root dentin transparency. *Acta Odontologica Scandinavica*, **28**, 3–35.

Bastos, J.L., Peres, M.A., Peres, K.G. and Barros, A.J.D. (2007) Infant growth, development and tooth emergence patterns: a longitudinal study from birth to 6 years of age. *Archives of Oral Biology*, **52**, 598–606.

Benson, J. and Williams J. (2008) Age determination in refugee children. *Australian Family Physician*, **37**, 821–824.

Bhat, V.J. and Kamath, G.P. (2007) Age estimation from root development of mandibular third molars in comparison with skeletal age of wrist joint. *American Journal of Forensic Medicine and Pathology*, **28**, 238–241.

Billewicz, W.Z. and MacGregor, I.A. (1975) Eruption of permanent teeth in West African (Gambian) children in relation to age, sex and physique. *Annals of Human Biology*, **2**, 117–128.

Blakenship, J.A., Mincer, H.H., Anderson, K.M. *et al.* (2007) Third molar development in the estimation of chronological age in American blacks as compared with whites. *Journal of Forensic Sciences,* **52**, 428–433.

Blenkin, M. (2009) *Forensic Odontology and Age Estimation: An Introduction to Concepts and Methods*, VDM Verlag, Saarbrücken.

Blenkin, M. and Evans, W. (2010) Age estimation from the teeth using a modified Demirjian system. *Journal of Forensic Sciences,* in press.

Bolaños, M.V., Manrique, M.C., Bolaños, M.J. and Briones, M.T. (2000) Approaches to chronological age assessment based on dental calcification. *Forensic Science International*, **110**, 97–106.

Braga, J., Heuze, Y., Chabedel, O. *et al.* (2005) Non-adult dental age assessment: correspondence analysis and linear regression versus Bayesian predictions. *International Journal of Legal Medicine*, **119**, 260–274.

Brothwell, D.R. (1965) *Digging up Bone*, British Museum, London.

Brown, T. (1978) Tooth emergence in Australian Aboriginals. *Annals of Human Biology*, **5**, 41–54.

Burns, K.R. and Maples, W.R. (1976) Estimation of age from individual adult teeth. *Journal of Forensic Sciences*, **21**, 343–356.

Calonius, P.E., Lunin, M. and Stout, F. (1970) Histologic criteria for age estimation of the developing human dentition. *Oral Surgery, Oral Medicine, and Oral Pathology*, **29**, 869–876.

Cameriere, R., Ferrante, L. and Cingolani, M. (2004) Variations in pulp/tooth area ratio as an indicator of age: a preliminary study. *Journal of Forensic Sciences*, **49**, 1319–1323. Erratum in *Journal of Forensic Sciences*, 2005, **50**, 486.

Cameriere, R., Ferrante, L. and Cingolani, M. (2006) Age estimation in children by measurement of open apices in teeth. *International Journal of Legal Medicine*, **120**, 49–52.

Cameriere, R., Brogi, G., Ferrante, L. *et al.* (2006) Reliability in age determination in pulp/tooth ratio in upper canines in skeletal remains. *Journal of Forensic Sciences,* 51, 861–864.

Cameriere, R., Ferrante, L., Belcastro, M.G. *et al.* (2007) Age estimation by pulp/tooth ratio in canines by peri-apical X-rays. *Journal of Forensic Sciences,* 52, 166–170.

Carels, C.E., Kuijpers-Jagtman, A.M., Van Der Linden, F.P. and Van't Hof, M.A. (1991) Age reference charts of tooth length in Dutch children. *Journal de biologie buccale,* 19, 297–303.

Chaillet, N., Nyström, M. and Demirjian, A. (2005) Comparison of dental maturity in children of different ethnic origins. International maturity curves for clinicians. *Journal of Forensic Sciences,* 50, 1164–1174.

Chaillet, N., Nyström, M., Kataja, M. and Demirjian, A. (2004) Dental maturity curves in Finnish children. Demirjian's method revisited and polynomial functions for age estimation. *Journal of Forensic Sciences,* 49 (6), 1324–1331.

Charles, D., Condon, K., Cheverud, J. and Buikstra, J. (1986) Cementum annulations and age determination in *Homo sapiens.* I: Tooth variability and observer error. *American Journal of Physical Anthropology,* 71, 311–320.

Choi, N.K. and Yang, K.H. (2001) A study on the eruption timing of primary teeth in Korean children. *ASDC Journal of Dentistry for Children,* 68, 244–249, 228.

Ciapparelli, L. (1985) An assessment of dental age in Essex schoolchildren using panoral radiographs with forensic application, Dissertation, Diploma in Forensic Odontology, London Hospital Medical College, London.

Ciapparelli, L. (1992) The chronology of dental development and age assessment, in *Practical Forensic Odontology* (ed. D.H. Clark), Wright, Oxford, pp. 22–42.

Dalitz, G.D. (1963) Age determination of adult human remains by teeth examination. *Journal of the Forensic Science Society,* 21, 11–21.

Davis, P.J. and Hägg, U. (1994) The accuracy and precision of the Demirjian system when used for age determination in Chinese children. *Swedish Dental Journal,* 18, 113–116.

Dean, M.C. and Beynon, A.D. (1991) Histological reconstruction of crown formation times and initial root formation times in a modern human child. *American Journal of Physical Anthropology,* 86, 215–228.

Demirjian, A. (1986) Dentition, in *Human Growth* (eds F. Falkner and J.M. Tanner), Plenum, New York.

Demirjian, A. (1994) Dental development on CD-ROM. Available from SilverPlatter Education Inc., 100 River Ridge Drive, Norwood, MA 02062–5043, USA.

Demirjian, A. and Goldstein, H. (1976) New systems for dental maturity based on seven and four teeth. *Annals of Human Biology,* 3, 411–421.

Demirjian, A. and Levesque, G.-Y. (1980) Sexual differences in dental development and prediction of emergence. *Journal of Dental Research,* 59, 1110–1122.

Demirjian, A., Goldstein, H. and Tanner, J.M. (1973) A new system of dental age assessment. *Human Biology,* 45, 211–227.

Demirjian, A., Buschang, P.H., Tanguay, R. and Kingnorth-Patterson, D. (1985) Interrelationships among measures of somatic, skeletal, dental, and sexual maturity. *American Journal of Orthodontics,* 88, 433–438.

De Salvia, A., Calzettac, C., Orrico, M. and De Leo, D. (2004) Third mandibular molar radiological development as an indicator of chronological age in a European population. *Forensic Science International,* 146S, S9–S12.

Diamanti, J. and Townsend, G.C. (2003) New standards for permanent tooth emergence in Australian children. *Australian Dental Journal,* 48, 39–42.

Drusini, A.G. (1993) Age estimation from teeth using soft X-ray findings. *Anthropologischer Anzeiger*, **51**, 41–46.

Drusini, A.G., Toso, O. and Ranzato, C. (1997) The coronal pulp cavity index: a biomarker for age determination in human adults. *American Journal of Physical Anthropology*, **103**, 353–363.

El Badrawy, H.E. (1984) Dental development in optimal and suboptimal fluoride communities. *Journal de l Association Dentaire Canadienne*, **50**, 761–764.

Engström, C., Engström, H. and Sagne, S. (1983) Lower third molar development in relation to skeletal maturity and chronological age. *The Angle Orthodontist*, **53**, 97–106.

Fanning, E. (1961) A longitudinal study of tooth formation and root resorption. *New Zealand Dental Journal*, **57**, 202–217.

Fanning, E. and Moorees, C. (1969) A comparison of mandibular molar formation in Australian Aborigines and Caucasoids. *Archives of Oral Biology*, **14**, 999–1006.

Fess, L.R. (1963) Tooth eruption and malnutrition: Cali, Columbia, December 1962–March 1963, DPH Thesis, Tulane University, New Orleans.

Folayan, M., Owotade, F., Adejuyigbe, E. *et al.* (2007) The timing of eruption of the primary dentition in Nigerian children. *American Journal of Physical Anthropology*, **134**, 443–448.

Foti, B., Lalys, L., Adalian, P. *et al.* (2003) New forensic approach to age determination in children based on tooth eruption. *Forensic Science International*, **132**, 49–56.

Friedrich, R.E., Katerjim, H., Wedl, J.S. and Scheuer, H.A. (2006) [Eruption times of permanent teeth in children and adolescents of Paderborn, Westphalia, Germany]. *Archiv für Kriminologie*, **217**, 20–35 (in German).

Frucht, S., Schnegelsberg, C., Schulte-Mönting, J. *et al.* (2000) Dental age in southwest Germany. A radiographic study. *Journal of Orofacial Orthopedics*, **61**, 318–329.

Garamendi, P.M., Landa, M.I., Ballesteros, J. and Solano, M.A. (2005) Reliability of the methods applied to assess age minority in living subjects around 18 years old. A survey on a Moroccan origin population. *Forensic Science International*, **154**, 3–12.

Garn, S.M., Lewis, A.B. and Polacheck, D.L. (1960) Sibling similarities in dental development. *Journal of Dental Research*, **39**, 170–175.

Gleiser, I. and Hunt, E. (1955) The permanent first molar: its calcification, eruption and decay. *American Journal of Physical Anthropology*, **13**, 253–281.

Gorgani, N., Sullivan, R.E. and DuBois, L. (1990) A radiographic investigation of third-molar development. *ASDC Journal of Dentistry for Children*, **57**, 106–110.

Gunst, K., Mesotten, K., Carbonez, A. and Willems, G. (2003) Third molar development in relation to chronological age: a large sample sized retrospective study. *Forensic Science International*, **136**, 52–57.

Gustafson, G. (1950) Age determination on teeth. *Journal of the American Dental Association*, **41**, 45–54.

Gustafson, G. and Koch, G. (1974) Age estimation up to 16 years of age based on dental development. *Odontologisk revy*, **25**, 297–306.

Haavikko, K. (1974) Tooth formation age estimated on a few selected teeth. A simple method for clinical use. *Proceedings of the Finnish Dental Society*, **70**, 15–19.

Hägg, U. and Matsson, L. (1985) Dental maturity as an indicator of chronological age: the accuracy and precision of three methods. *European Journal of Orthodontics*, **7**, 25–34.

Hägg, U. and Taranger, J. (1985) Dental development, dental age and tooth counts. *The Angle Orthodontist*, **55**, 93–107.

Harris, E. and McKee, J. (1990) Tooth mineralization standards for blacks and whites from the middle southern United States. *Journal of Forensic Sciences*, **35**, 859–872.

Haavikko, K. (1974) Tooth formation age estimated on a few selected teeth. A simple method for clinical use. *Proceedings of the Finnish Dental Society*, **70**, 15–19.

Helfman, P.M. and Bada, J.L. (1976) Aspartic acid racemization in dentine as a measure of ageing. *Nature*, **262**, 279–281.

Heuzé, Y. and Cardoso, F.V. (2008) Testing the quality of nonadult Bayesian dental age assessment methods to juvenile skeletal remains: the Lisbon collection children and secular trend effects. *American Journal of Physical Anthropology*, **135**, 275–283.

Higgins, D. (2006) Recommendations for age estimation protocols in South Australia, Dissertation, Graduate Diploma in Forensic Odontology, University of Adelaide, Adelaide.

Holman, D.J. and Jones, R.E. (2003) Longitudinal analysis of deciduous tooth emergence III. Sexual dimorphism in Bangladeshi, Guatemalan, Japanese, and Javanese children. *American Journal of Physical Anthropology*, **122**, 269–278.

Holman, D.J. and Yamaguchi, K. (2005) Longitudinal analysis of deciduous tooth emergence IV. Covariate effects in Japanese children. *American Journal of Physical Anthropology*, **126**, 352–358.

Holtgrave, E.A., Kretschmer, R. and Muller, R. (1997) Acceleration in dental development: fact or fiction. *European Journal of Orthodontics*, **19**, 703–710.

Huda, T.F. and Bowman, J.E. (1995) Age determination from dental microstructure in juveniles. *American Journal of Physical Anthropology*, **97**, 135–150.

Hughes, T.E., Bockmann, M.R., Seow, K. *et al.* (2007) Strong genetic control of emergence of human primary incisors. *Journal of Dental Research*, **86** (12), 1160–1165.

Ikeda, N., Umetsu, K., Kashimura, S. *et al.* (1985) Estimation of age from teeth with their soft X-ray findings. *Japanese Journal of Forensic Medicine*, **39**, 56–68.

IOFOS (2008) Dental age estimation. Quality assurance, www.odont.uio.no/foreninger/iofos/quality/Age-IOFOS.htm (accessed 6 January 2009).

Johanson, G. (1971) Age determination from human teeth: a critical evaluation with special consideration of changes after fourteen years-of-age. *Odontologisk revy*, **22**, 1–26.

Kim, Y.K., Kho, H.S. and Lee, K.H. (2000) Age estimation by occlusal tooth wear. *Journal of Forensic Sciences*, **45**, 303–309.

Kochhar, R. and Richardson, A. (1998) The chronology and sequence of eruption of human permanent teeth in Northern Ireland. *International Journal of Paediatric Dentistry*, **8**, 243–252.

Kullman, L., Johanson, G. and Akesson, L. (1992) Root development of the lower third molar and its relation to chronological age. *Swedish Dental Journal*, **16**, 161–167.

Kullman, L., Tronje, G., Teivens, A. and Lundholm, A. (1996) Methods of reducing observer variation in age estimation from panoramic radiographs. *Dento-Maxillo-Facial Radiology*, **25**, 173–178.

Kvaal, S.I., Kolltveit, K.M., Thomsen, I.O. and Solheim, T. (1995) Age estimation of adults from dental radiographs. *Forensic Science International*, **74**, 175–185.

Lamendin, H., Baccino, E., Humbert, J.F. *et al.* (1992) A simple technique for age estimation in adult corpses: the two criteria dental method. *Journal of Forensic Sciences*, **37**, 1373–1379.

Lee, S.E., Lee, S.-H., Lee, J.-Y. *et al.* (2008) Age estimation of Korean children based on dental maturity. *Forensic Science International*, **178**, 125–131.

Leroy, R., Cecere, S., Lesaffre, E. and Declerck, D. (2008) Variability in permanent tooth emergence sequences in Flemish children. *European Journal of Oral Sciences*, **116**, 11–17.

Leurs, I.H., Wattel, E., Aartman, I.H.A. *et al.* (2005) Dental age in Dutch children. *European Journal of Orthodontics*, **27**, 309–314.

Lewis, A.B. and Garn, S.M. (1960) The relationship between tooth development and other maturational factors. *The Angle Orthodontist*, **30**, 70–77.

Lipsinic, F.E. (1986) Correlation of age and incremental lines in the cementum of human teeth. *Journal of Forensic Sciences*, **31**, 982–989. Erratum in *Journal of Forensic Sciences*, 1987, **32**, 843.

Liversidge, H.M. and Molleson, T. (1999) Developing permanent tooth length as an estimate of age. *Journal of Forensic Sciences*, **44**, 917–920.

Liversidge, H.M. and Molleson, T. (2004) Variation in crown and root formation and eruption of human deciduous teeth. *American Journal of Physical Anthropology*, **123**, 172–180.

Liversidge, H.M. and Speechly, T. (2001) Growth of permanent mandibular teeth of British children aged 4 to 9 years. *Annals of Human Biology*, **28**, 256–262.

Liversidge, H.M., Herdeg, B. and Rösing, F.W. (1998) Dental age estimation of non-adults. A review of methods and principles, in *Dental Anthropology: Fundamentals, Limits and Prospects* (eds W.K. Alt, F.W. Rösing and M. Teschler-Nicola), Springer, New York, pp. 419–442.

Liversidge, H.M., Lyons, F. and Hector, M.P. (2003) The accuracy of three methods of age estimation using radiographic measurements of developing teeth. *Forensic Science International*, **131**, 22–29.

Liversidge, H.M., Speechly, T. and Hector, M.P. (1999) Dental maturation in British children: are Demirjian's standards applicable? *International Journal of Paediatric Dentistry*, **9**, 263–269.

Liversidge, H.M., Chaillet, N., Mörnstad, H. *et al.* (2006) Timing of Demirjian's tooth formation stages. *Annals of Human Biology*, **33**, 454–470.

Loevy, H.T. (1983) Maturation of permanent teeth in black and Latino children. *Acta de odontología pediátrica*, **4**, 59–62.

Logan, W.H.G. and Kronfeld, R. (1933) Development of the human jaws and surrounding structures from birth to the age of fifteen years. *Journal of the American Dental Association*, **20**, 379–427.

Lopez-Nicolas, M., Morales, A. and Luna, A. (1996) Application of dimorphism in teeth to age calculation. *Journal of Forensic Odonto-Stomatology*, **14**, 9–12.

Lovejoy, C.O. (1985) Dental wear in the Libben population: its functional pattern and role in the determination of skeletal age at death. *American Journal of Physical Anthropology*, **68**, 47–56.

Lovejoy, C.O., Meindl, R.S., Mensforth, R.P. and Barton, T.J. (1985) Multifactorial determination of skeletal age at death: a method and blind tests of its accuracy. *American Journal of Physical Anthropology*, **68**, 1–14.

Lucy, D. and Pollard, A.M. (1995) Further comments on the estimation of error associated with the Gustafson dental age estimation method. *Journal of Forensic Sciences*, **40**, 222–227.

Lukacs, J.R. (1989) Dental paleopathology: methods for reconstructing dietary patterns, in *Reconstruction of Life from the Skeleton* (eds M.Y. Iscan and K.A.R. Kennedy), Wiley-Liss, New York.

Lunt, R.C. and Law, D.B. (1974) A review of the chronology of calcification of human teeth. *Journal of the American Dental Association*, **89**, 599–606.

Maber, M., Liversidge, H.M. and Hector, M.P. (2006) Accuracy of age estimation of radiographic methods using developing teeth. *Forensic Science International*, **159S**, S68–S73.

Maples, W.R. (1978) An improved technique using dental histology for estimation of adult age. *Journal of Forensic Sciences*, **23**, 764–770.

Maples, W.R. (1979) Some difficulties in the Gustafson dental age estimations. *Journal of Forensic Sciences*, **24**, 168–172.

Martin-de las Heras, S., Garcia-Fortea, P., Ortega, A. *et al.* (2008) Third molar development according to chronological age in populations from Spanish and Magrebian origin. *Forensic Science International*, **174**, 47–53.

Meinl, A., Tangl, S., Huber, C. *et al.* (2007a) The chronology of third molar mineralization in the Austrian population – a contribution to forensic age estimation. *Forensic Science International*, **169**, 161–167.

Meinl, A., Tangl, S., Pernicka, E. *et al.* (2007b) On the applicability of secondary dentine formation to radiological age estimation in young adults. *Journal of Forensic Sciences,* **52,** 438–441.

Merwin, D.R. and Harris, E.F. (1998) Sibling similarities in the tempo of human tooth mineralization. *Archives of Oral Biology,* **43,** 205–210.

Mesotten, K., Gunst, K., Carbonez, A. and Willems, G. (2002) Dental age estimation and third molars: a preliminary study. *Forensic Science International,* **26,** 110–115.

Metzger, Z. (1980) Gustafson's method for age determination from teeth – a modification for the use of dentists in identification teams. *Journal of Forensic Sciences,* **25,** 742–749.

Miles, A.E.W. (1962) Assessment of the ages of Anglo-Saxons from their dentitions. *Proceedings of the Royal Society of Medicine,* **55,** 881–886.

Miles, A.E.W. (1963a) Dentition in the estimation of age. *Journal of Dental Research,* **42,** 255–263.

Miles, A.E.W. (1963b) The dentition in assessment of individual age in skeletal material, in *Dental Anthropology* (ed. D.R. Brothwell), Pergamon, New York, pp. 191–210.

Mincer, H.H., Harris, E.F. and Berryman, H.E. (1993) The ABFO study of third molar development and its use as an estimator of chronological age. *Journal of Forensic Sciences,* **38,** 379–390.

Molnar, S. (1970) Human tooth wear, tooth function and cultural variability. *American Journal of Physical Anthropology,* **34,** 175–190.

Moorrees, C.F.A. and Kent, R.L. (1978) A step function model using tooth counts to assess the developmental timing of the dentition. *Annals of Human Biology,* **5,** 55–68.

Moorrees, C.F.A., Fanning, E.A, and Hunt, E.E. (1963) Age variation of formation stages for ten permanent teeth. *Journal of Dental Research,* **42,** 1490–1502.

Mörnstad, H. (1995) The validity of four methods for age determination by teeth in Swedish children: a multicentre study. *Swedish Dental Journal,* **19,** 121–130.

Mörnstad, H., Staaf, V. and Welander, U. (1994) Age estimation with the aid of tooth development: a new method based on objective measurements. *Scandinavian Journal of Dental Research,* **102,** 137–143.

Mugonzibwa, E.A., Kuijpers-Jagtman, A.M., Laine-Alava, M.T. and van't Hof, M.A. (2002) Emergence of permanent teeth in Tanzanian children. *Community Dentistry and Oral Epidemiology,* **30,** 455–462.

Mukherjee, D.K. (1973) Deciduous dental eruption in low income group Bengali Hindu children. *Journal of Tropical Pediatrics and Environmental Child Health,* **19,** 207–211.

Müller, N. (1990). Zur Altersbestimmung beim Menschen unter besonderer Berücksichtigung der Weisheitszähne, MD Thesis, University of Erlangen-Nürnberg.

Murphy, T.R. (1959) The changing pattern of dentine exposure in human tooth attrition. *American Journal of Physical Anthropology,* **17,** 167–178.

Nizam, A., Naing, L. and Mokhtar, N. (2003) Age and sequence of eruption of permanent teeth in Kelantan, north-eastern Malaysia. *Clinical Oral Investigations,* **7,** 222–225.

Nolla, C.M. (1960) The development of the permanent teeth. *Journal of Dentistry for Children,* **27,** 254–266.

Nortjé, C.J. (1983) The permanent mandibular third molar. *Journal of Forensic Odonto-Stomatology,* **1,** 27–31.

Nowell, G.W. (1978) An evaluation of the Miles method of ageing using the Tepe Hissar dental sample. *American Journal of Physical Anthropology,* **49,** 271–276.

Nykanen, R., Espeland, L., Kvaal, S.I. and Krogstad, O. (1998) Validity of the Demirjian method for dental age estimation when applied to Norwegian children. *Acta Odontologica Scandinavica,* **56,** 238–244.

Nyström, M. (1986) Dental maturity in Finnish children, estimated from the development of seven permanent mandibular teeth. *Acta Odontologica Scandinavica*, **44**, 193–198.

Nyström, M. (1988) Comparisons of dental maturity between the rural community of Kuhmo in northeastern Finland and the city of Helsinki. *Community Dentistry and Oral Epidemiology*, **16**, 215–217.

Nyström, M., Ranta, R., Kataja, M. and Silvola, H. (1988) Comparison of dental maturity between the rural community of Kuhmo in northeastern Finland and the city of Helsinki. *Community Dentistry and Oral Epidemiology*, **16**, 215–217.

Nyström, M., Aine, L., Peck, L. *et al.* (2000) Dental maturity in Finns and the problem of missing teeth. *Acta Odontologica Scandinavica*, **58**, 49–56.

Nyström, M., Kleemola-Kujala, E., Evlahti, M. *et al.* (2001) Emergence of permanent teeth and dental age in a series of Finns. *Acta Odontologica Scandinavica*, **59**, 49–56.

Ohtani, S. and Yamamoto, K. (1991) Age estimation using the racemization of amino acid in human dentine. *Journal of Forensic Sciences,* **36**, 792–800.

Ohtani, S., Ito, R. and Yamamoto, T. (2003) Differences in D/L aspartic acid ratios in dentin among different types of teeth from the same individual and estimated age. *International Journal of Legal Medicine*, **117**, 149–152.

Ohtani, S., Sugimoto, H., Sugeno, H. *et al.* (1995) Racemization of aspartic acid in human cementum with age. *Archives of Oral Biology*, **40**, 91–95.

Olze, A., Taniguchi, M., Schmeling, A. *et al.* (2003) Comparative study on the chronology of third molar mineralization in a Japanese and a German population. *Legal Medicine (Tokyo)*, **5** (Sup 1), S367–S371.

Olze, A., Schmeling, A., Taniguchgi, M. *et al.* (2004) Forensic age estimation in living subjects: the ethnic factor in wisdom tooth mineralisation. *International Journal of Legal Medicine*, **118**, 170–173.

Olze, A., van Niekerk, P., Schulz, R. and Schmeling, A. (2007) Studies of the chronological course of wisdom tooth eruption in a Black African population. *Journal of Forensic Sciences,* **52**, 1161–1163.

Olze, A., Peschke, C., Schulz, R. and Schmeling, A. (2008a) Studies of the chronological course of wisdom tooth eruption in a German population. *Journal of Forensic and Legal Medicine*, **15**, 426–429.

Olze, A., Ishikawa, T., Zhu, B.L. *et al.* (2008b) Studies of the chronological course of wisdom tooth eruption in a Japanese population. *Forensic Science International*, **174**, 203–206.

Orhan, K., Ozer, L., Orhan, A.I. *et al.* (2007) Radiographic evaluation of third molar development in relation to chronologic age among Turkish children and youth. *Forensic Science International*, **165**, 46–51.

Owsley, D. and Jantz, R. (1983) Formation of the permanent dentition in the Arikira Indians: timing differences that affect dental age assessments. *American Journal of Physical Anthropology*, **61**, 467–471.

Pelsmaekers, B., Loos, R., Carels, C. *et al.* (1997) The genetic contribution to dental maturation. *Journal of Dental Research*, **76**, 1337–1340.

Pilin, A., Cabala, R., Pudil, F. and Bencko, V. (2001) The use of D-, L-aspartic ratio in decalcified collagen from human dentin as an estimator of human age. *Journal of Forensic Sciences,* **46**, 1228–1231.

Prieto, J.L., Barberia, E., Ortega, R. and Magaña, C. (2005) Evaluation of chronological age based on third molar development in the Spanish population. *International Journal of Legal Medicine*, **119**, 349–354.

Prince, D.H., Kimmerle, E.H. and Konigsberg, L.W. (2008) A Bayesian approach to estimate skeletal age-at-death utilizing dental wear. *Journal of Forensic Sciences*, **53**, 588–593.

Psoter, W.J., Morse, D.E., Pendrys, D.G. *et al.* (2003) Median ages of eruption of the primary teeth in white and Hispanic children from Arizona. *Pediatric Dentistry*, **25**, 257–261.

Ritz, S., Stock, R., Schutz, H.-W. and Kaatsch, H.-J. (1995) Age estimation in biopsy specimens of dentin. *International Journal of Legal Medicine*, **108**, 135–139.

Ritz-Timme, S., Cattaneo, C., Collins, M.J. *et al.* (2000) Age estimation: the state of the art in relation to the specific demands of forensic practice. *International Journal of Legal Medicine*, **113**, 129–136.

Rösing, F.W. and Kvaal, S.I. (1997) Dental age in adults. A review of estimation methods, in *Dental Anthropology. Fundamentals, Limits and Prospects* (eds W.K. Alt, F.W. Rösing and M. Teschler-Nicola), Springer, New York, pp. 443–468.

Rousset, M.-M., Boualam, N., Delfosse, C. and Roberts, W.E. (2003) Emergence of permanent teeth: secular trends and variance in a modern sample. *Journal of Dentistry for Children*, **70**, 208–214.

Schmeling, A., Reisinger, W., Geserick, G. and Olze A. (2006a) Age estimation of unaccompanied minors, Part I. General considerations. *Forensic Science International*, **159S**, S61–S64.

Schmeling, A., Reisinger, W., Geserick, G. and Olze, A. (2006b) Age estimation of unaccompanied minors, Part II. Dental aspects. *Forensic Science International*, **159S**, S65–S67.

Schmeling, A., Geserick, G., Reisinger, W. and Olze, A. (2007) Age estimation. *Forensic Science International*, **165**, 178–181.

Schmeling, A., Grundmann, C., Fuhrmann, A. *et al.* (2008) Criteria for age estimation in living individuals. *International Journal of Legal Medicine*, **122**, 457–460.

Schour, I. (1936) The neonatal line in the enamel and dentine of the human deciduous teeth and first permanent molar. *Journal of the American Dental Association*, **23**, 1946–1955.

Schour, I. and Massler, M. (1940) Studies in tooth development: the growth pattern of human teeth, Part II. *Journal of the American Dental Association*, **27**, 1918–1931.

Schour, I. and Massler, M. (1941) The development of the human dentition. *Journal of the American Dental Association*, **28**, 1153–1160.

Sisman, Y., Uysal, T., Yagmur, F. and Ramoglu, S.I. (2007) Third-molar development in relation to chronologic age in Turkish children and young adults. *The Angle Orthodontist*, **77**, 1040–1045.

Smith, B.H. (1984) Patterns of molar wear in hunter-gatherers and agriculturalists. *American Journal of Physical Anthropology*, **63**, 39–56.

Smith, B.H. (1991) Standards of human tooth formation and dental age assessment, in *Advances in Dental Anthropology* (eds M.A. Kelly and C.S. Larsen), Wiley-Liss, New York, pp. 143–168.

Smith, B.H. and Garn, S.M. (1987) Polymorphisms in eruption sequence of permanent teeth in American children. *American Journal of Physical Anthropology*, **74**, 289–303.

Sognnaes, R.F., Gratt, B.M. and Papin, P.J. (1985) Biomedical image processing for age measurement of intact teeth. *Journal of Forensic Sciences*, **30**, 1082–1089.

Solari, A.C. and Abramovitch, K. (2002) The accuracy and precision of third molar development as an indicator of chronological age in Hispanics. *Journal of Forensic Sciences*, **47**, 531–535.

Solheim, T. (1988) Dental attrition as an indicator of age. *Gerodontics*, **4**, 299–304.

Solheim, T. (1990) Dental cementum apposition as an indicator of age. *Scandinavian Journal of Dental Research*, **98**, 510–519.

Solheim, T. (1993) A new method for dental age estimation in adults. *Forensic Science International*, **59**, 137–147.

Solheim, T. and Vonen A. (2006) Dental age estimation, quality assurance and age estimation of asylum seekers in Norway. *Forensic Science International*, **159S**, S56–S60.

Soomer, H., Ranta, H., Lincoln, M.J. *et al.* (2003) Reliability and validity of eight dental age estimation methods for adults. *Journal of Forensic Sciences,* **48**, 149–152.

Staaf, V., Mörnstad, H. and Welander, U. (1991) Age estimation based on tooth development: a test of reliability and validity. *Scandinavian Journal of Dental Research*, **99**, 281–286.

Suri, L., Gagari, E. and Vastardis, H. (2004) Delayed tooth eruption: pathogenesis, diagnosis and treatment. A literature review. *American Journal of Orthodontics and Dentofacial Orthopedics*, **126**, 432–445.

Tanner, J.M. (1962) *Growth at Adolescence*, Blackwell Scientific, London.

Teivens, A. and Mörnstad, H.A. (2001) Comparison between dental maturity rates in Swedish and Korean populations using a modified Demirjian method. *Journal of Forensic Odonto-Stomatology*, **19**, 31–15.

Thorson, J. and Häag, U. (1991) The accuracy and precision of the third molar as an indicator of chronological age. *Swedish Dental Journal*, **15**, 15–22.

Tompkins, R.L. (1996) Human population variability in relative dental development. *American Journal of Physical Anthropology*, **99**, 79–102.

Townsend, N. and Hammel, E.A. (1990) Age estimation from the number of teeth erupted in young children. An aid to demographic surveys. *Demography*, **27**, 165–174.

Ubelaker, D.H. (1989) *Human Skeletal Remains*, Taraxacum, Washington, DC.

Vasiliadis, L., Darling, A.J. and Levers, B.G. H. (1983) The amount and distribution of sclerotic human root dentine. *Archives of Oral Biology*, **28**, 645–649.

Whittaker, D.K. and Bakri, M. (1996) Racial variations in the extent of tooth root translucency in ageing individuals. *Archives of Oral Biology*, **41**, 15–19.

Willems, G., Moulin-Romsee, C. and Solheim, T. (2002) Non-destructive dental-age calculation methods in adults: intra- and inter-observer effects. *Forensic Science International*, **126**, 221–226.

Willems, G., Van Olmen, A., Spiessens, B. and Carels, C. (2001) Dental age estimation in Belgian children: Demirjian's technique revisited. *Journal of Forensic Sciences,* **46**, 893–895.

Wittwer-Backofen, U., Gampe, J. and Vaupel, J.W. (2004) Tooth cementum annulation for age estimation: results from a large known age validation study. *American Journal of Physical Anthropology*, **123**, 119–129.

Wolanski, N. (1966) A new method for the evaluation of tooth formation. *Acta Genetica et Statistica Medica*, **16**, 186–197.

Yun, J.I., Chung, J.W., Kho, H.S. and Kim, Y.K. (2007) Age estimation of Korean adults by occlusal tooth wear. *Journal of Forensic Sciences,* **52**, 678–683.

11

Age Evaluation from the Skeleton

S. Lucina Hackman[1], Alanah Buck[2] and Sue Black[1]
[1]Centre for Anatomy and Human Identification, University of Dundee, Dundee
DD1 5EH, UK
[2]Forensic Pathology, PathWest, Locked Bag, WA 6909, Australia

11.1   Background

The chronological age of an individual is generally recognized as a measure of the period of time that has passed since they were born. However, if the date of birth is not known, is concealed or is falsely attested, assessing the true chronological age of an individual, whether living or dead, presents a number of difficulties for the clinician and the forensic practitioner. The strength of the relationship between chronological age and a proxy indicator then becomes extremely important and an assessment of biological age is usually selected as the most relevant factor for further investigation. Biological age is generally measured through recognition of growth and/or maturational milestones achieved either in the skeleton (skeletal age), the dentition (dental age) or soft tissue developments usually associated with secondary sexual development (indicators of puberty) or indicators of growth. Clearly the greater the number of dependent variables that can be incorporated into an assessment of biological age, the stronger will be the correlation with chronological age.

While the external anthropometric features of height, weight, head circumference, breast development and so on that are so favoured by paediatricians can be readily recorded for the living and do have a significant correlation with chronological age, there is no doubt that the ability to visualize the hard tissues of the body (bones and teeth) through radiography, computed tomography (CT), ultrasound and other clinical imaging techniques plays an enormously important part, particularly in the investigative and diagnostic approaches to the evaluation of age.

This chapter concerns the evaluation of skeletal age and this can generally be achieved with a similar degree of reliability whether the individual is living or

Age Estimation in the Living: The Practitioners Guide   Sue Black, Anil Aggrawal and Jason Payne-James
© 2010 John Wiley & Sons, Ltd

deceased. Indeed, the majority of the methods utilized in the evaluation of skeletal age were developed either to assign an age to the deceased or to evaluate clinical
maturational status and so have subsequently been transferred, with some degree
of success, to the requirements of age estimation in the living for judicial and investigative purposes. However, it should be appreciated that often the methodology
available to the forensic practitioner for age evaluation in the living has not been
specifically designed for the purpose for which it is being utilized and as such, is to
be applied with some considerable degree of caution and should only be considered
by those with sufficient experience in this field.

All methods of age assessment that utilize the skeleton are essentially 'measuring' or 'recognizing' changes in skeletal maturation (Cameron, 1982) as an indication of how far the individual has progressed along the age continuum towards
full maturity (Cameron, 1982; Scheuer and Black, 2000). Fortunately, skeletal
maturation is a relatively reliable indicator of growth and development and has
been used for this purpose in clinical diagnosis for many years (Filly *et al.*, 1981;
Fishman, 1982; Cole, Webb and Cole, 1988; Even, Bronstein and Hochberg, 1998;
Flores-Mir, Nebbe and Major, 2004; Charles *et al.*, 2007; Kant *et al.*, 2007; Alkhal
et al., 2008; Soegiharto, Moles and Cunningham, 2008b; Lee *et al.*, 2009). Studies
that assess the accuracy with which the age assessment methods correctly predict
chronological age show that, even with limited training, clinicians are able to perform this function with acceptable levels of inter- and intra-observer error, indicating that the approach has an attractive element of easy operability (Roche and
French, 1970; Lynnerup *et al.*, 2008; van Rijn and Lequin, 2009). However, this
apparent ease of application brings a warning for the judicial authorities as ease
does not necessarily equate to expertise, especially when an element of professional
judgement and opinion is necessary, particularly in relation to issues that must
take into account racial variation, nutritional impacts and concepts such as secular
trend.

With the advent of radiological imaging, research was undertaken to investigate the
strength of the relationship between skeletal maturation and chronological age, and
it was apparent from the outset that it was neither linear nor consistent (Cameron,
1982). The extent to which natural variation affected evaluation was highlighted
and although it is recognized, there is little that the practitioner can do to take this
into account other than to give a wide range for their age evaluation (Scheuer and
Black, 2000). Therefore the practical requirement of this approach rarely, if ever,
lives up to the desired accuracy.

The assessment of age from bones relies on a number of changes that occur
within the skeleton as the individual matures. It utilizes both the growth in size
of the skeletal elements (Maresh and Deming, 1939; Anderson, Green and Messner, 1963; Kimura, 1976; Fazekas and Kosa, 1978; Rissech and Black, 2007)
and the changes in shape and form that occur with advancing skeletal maturity
(Scheuer and Black, 2000). In an appropriate temporal window of opportunity,
the assessment of the appearance of both primary and secondary ossification centres can be taken into account and this can be married to their individual change
in shape over time, bone size and eventual fusion to other bone centres (Davies
and Parsons, 1927; Joseph, 1951; Moss and Noback, 1958; Garn, Rohmann and

Apfelbaum, 1961; Garn, Rohmann and Blumenthal, 1966). The assessment of chronological age is therefore directly associated with the process by which the cartilaginous anlage (the precursors of the skeletal elements) are replaced by ossified tissue (Pludowski, Lebiedowski and Lorenc, 2004). These changes in shape and size and eventual fusion of ossification centres in a human skeleton have been shown to have a relatively stable and predictable pattern of progression, and it is this that the clinician relies upon when performing their assessment of skeletal age in relation to maturity and which the forensic practitioner will use to predict chronological age.

The modern methods of assessment of skeletal age in the living have a history that is soundly rooted at the beginning of the twentieth century. This was the time when longitudinal radiographic studies on growing children made the study of the appearance, growth and fusion of ossification centres possible (Poland, 1898; Todd, 1937; Greulich and Pyle, 1959; Bleich, 1960; Tanner, Whitehouse and Healy, 1962; Pyle and Hoerr, 1969; Brodeur, Silberstein and Gravis, 1981; Roche, Chumlea and Thissen, 1988). Prior to this, analysis depended on the removal of soft tissue from cadavers to allow histological or gross study of stages of development (Fazekas and Kosa, 1978). Using bone from deceased individuals had some evident drawbacks. First, it only gave an immediate snapshot of the stage of ossification or fusion reached by the bone in that one individual, and, second, there was often no accounting for influential factors, including racial background, pathological status or poor nutrition. The use of radiographs allowed researchers not only a window into the process of development that had not previously been afforded, but also a method of recording the development that occurred to each skeletal element over the time that it took for each and every part of that individual to reach maturity. Of course this type of research can never be repeated, but its value was immense and since that time, access to comparable material to continue the research has become increasingly scarce.

The remainder of this chapter will consider the different stages of development of the human and offer a summary on what may be achieved within that age range when considering evaluation of age of the living from the skeleton.

11.2   Fetal Age

For the purposes of this chapter the term fetus will be used to describe the individual from the eighth week of intra-uterine life until birth.

If chronological age is defined by the passage of time since birth, an equivalent earlier marker is required for age evaluation in the fetus. The date of conception is generally considered to be inaccurate both in terms of maternal recall and in recognition of the variable period from fertilization to implantation. Therefore the date of the maternal last menstrual period (LMP) is usually selected as the preferred indicator to predict the date of birth and therefore the potential *in utero* age of the fetus (Taipale and Hiilesmaa, 2001).

The precursor for bone development is in evidence from the third week of intra-uterine life with the development and positioning of the mesodermal germ layer in the embryo. This embryonic mesoderm differentiates into most of the connective tissue structures of the body, and many aspects subsequently migrate to adopt the positions within the body where the bones of the skeleton will ultimately form. Bones form either as a result of direct ossification of a rich vascular membrane (periosteal or intra-membranous ossification) or by ossification of a hyaline cartilage precursor (endochondral ossification) (Sadler, 1985; Scheuer and Black, 2000). Each bone will commence ossification at a primary locus within the template and this is referred to as the primary centre of ossification (Ogden, 2000). The timing of the appearance of these centres is well documented for every bone in the body and can be readily viewed from a radiographic perspective (Scheuer and Black, 2000, 2004; Schaefer, Black and Scheuer, 2009). So for example, the first bone in the skeleton to evidence ossification is found in the midshaft region of the clavicle between weeks 5 and 6 of intra-uterine life. However, not all primary centres of ossification appear in the body prior to birth and indeed the last primary centre to appear is in the fourth coccygeal vertebra around the time of puberty. Tables 11.1–11.3 give a brief summary of the approximate timings of appearance of the initial primary centres of ossification associated with each bone in the human skeleton.

Once ossification commences, it spreads out from the primary centre, replacing growth-related proliferation of the soft tissue template until eventually it replaces

Table 11.1 Approximate times of appearance of the initial primary centres of ossification for the cranial bones.

Skull bone	Approx. age of appearance of primary centre of ossification
Maxilla	Week 6 IU[a]
Mandible	Week 6 IU
Frontal	Weeks 6–7 IU
Temporal	Weeks 7–8 IU
Parietal	Weeks 7–8 IU
Palatine	Weeks 7–8 IU
Zygomatic	Weeks 8–9 IU
Occipital	Weeks 8–10 IU
Sphenoid	Weeks 9–10 IU
Nasal	Weeks 9–10 IU
Vomer	Weeks 9–10 IU
Lacrimal	Weeks 10–12 IU
Ethmoid	Weeks 17–21 IU
Inferior concha	Weeks 16–18 IU

[a]IU = intra-uterine.

Table 11.2 Approximate times of appearance of the initial primary centres of ossification for the bones of the axial and girdle postcranial skeleton.

Bone	Approx. age of appearance of initial primary centre of ossification
Clavicle	Weeks 5–6 IU
Scapula	Weeks 7–8 IU
Ribs	Weeks 6–10 IU
Vertebral column	Weeks 7–10 IU
Ilium	Weeks 8–10 IU
Ischium	Weeks 14–18 IU
Sternum	Weeks 17–21 IU
Pubis	Weeks 18–22 IU

Table 11.3 Approximate times of appearance of the initial primary centres of ossification for the bones of the appendicular (non-girdle) skeleton.

Bone	Approx. age of appearance of initial primary centre of ossification
Humerus	Week 7 IU
Radius	Week 7 IU
Ulna	Week 8 IU
Femur	Weeks 7–8 IU
Tibia	Weeks 7–8 IU
Distal phalanges hand	Weeks 7–9 IU
Fibula	Weeks 8–10 IU
Metacarpals	Weeks 8–10 IU
Metatarsals 2–5	Weeks 8–10 IU
Proximal phalanges hand	Weeks 9–11 IU
Distal phalanges foot	Weeks 9–12 IU
Middle phalanges hand	Weeks 10–12 IU
Metatarsal 1	Weeks 12–13 IU
Proximal phalanges foot	Weeks 14–16 IU
Middle phalanges foot	Weeks 16–20 IU
Calcaneus	Months 5–6 IU
Talus	Months 6–7 IU
Other tarsals	Months 1–3 PP[a]
Carpals	Months 2–4 PP

[a]PP= post-partum

that original structure in its entirety. At birth each bone of the skeleton is represented by some form of primary ossification except the following:

- hyoid bone

- coccygeal vertebrae 2–4

- sternebra 4

- xiphoid process

- capitate and hamate (can sometimes be present at birth)

- triquetral, lunate, trapezium, trapezoid and pisiform

- cuboid, all cuneiforms and navicular.

Age evaluation of the fetus will take account of weight, crown–heel length, crown–rump length and head circumference but it will also place heavy emphasis on the number of primary ossification centres present and their location (Fazekas and Kosa, 1978; Chinn *et al.*, 1983; Hadlock *et al.*, 1984, 1992; De Vasconcellos and Ferreira, 1998; Degani, 2001). Knowledge of the sequence of appearance of these centres permits the investigator to assign a 'most likely' age based on those centres that are present compared to those that have not yet developed (Scheuer and Black, 2000, 2004; Schaefer, Black and Scheuer, 2009). Although the identification of 'term' in a fetus is important, it is the evaluation of the legal age at which life is sustainable without medical support that is important to evaluate and this differs from country to country.

Equally, as ossification progresses, particularly in the long bones, these become amenable to recording lengths and these values are extensively used by the paediatrician to assess the age and maturity of the developing fetus, especially to ensure that it is exhibiting growth that falls within normal parameters (Fazekas and Kosa, 1978; Filly *et al.*, 1981; De Vasconcellos and Ferreira, 1998; Ott, 2006). Ultrasound is now the preferred mode of imaging to capture this data as it does not risk exposing the fetus to harmful radiation (Pretorius, Nelson and Manco-Johnson, 1984; De Vasconcellos and Ferreira, 1998; Taipale and Hiilesmaa, 2001; Salpou *et al.*, 2008). While the most reliable data is derived from recent clinical studies, there is some work that has been undertaken on aborted (natural and induced) fetuses which has allowed a more detailed study of the relationship between growth and age in these early years. However, fetuses that have been aborted spontaneously may not be representative of normal development and therefore information derived from such a source must be treated with caution (Maresh and Deming, 1939; Fazekas and Kosa, 1978).

While radiographs of fetal bones proved to be a relatively accurate way of assessing age, there were difficulties including variation in the object to film distances, aligning the target bones perpendicular to the plate and movement of the fetus while the film was being taken (Filly *et al.*, 1981; Mahony, Callen and Filly, 1985). The development of ultrasound has largely overcome a great number of these issues as it permits images to be recorded in real time, adjusts for fetal movement, is sufficiently sensitive to allow for visualization of both primary and secondary ossification centres and overcomes the health and safety issue associated with radiation (Mahony, Callen and Filly, 1985). This does not mean that ultrasound imaging is not without its own limitations; for example, foreshortening of the bone can occur if the angle of orientation is not correct (Krook, Wawrukiewicz and Hackethorn, 1985) and it is a technique that requires considerable experience for accurate reporting.

With the introduction of imaging techniques there is an associated need to ensure that results are viable. A number of studies have compared the accuracy of ultrasound and radiographic images to assess which is a more true measure of the actual bone. In all cases, both approaches have been shown to have an appropriate and acceptable level of concordance (Maresh and Deming, 1939; Pretorius, Nelson and Manco-Johnson, 1984; Piercecchi-Marti *et al.*, 2002).

In ultrasound the length of the femur is generally used in addition to crown–rump length or biparietal diameter to assess the age of the fetus. Many authors argue that the use of multiple parameters gives a more accurate assessment of age than the use of one in isolation (Hadlock *et al.*, 1984). If only the femoral length is used, the length of the ossified portion of the long bone is the only section that is measured, resulting in a reported accuracy of between ±2.8 weeks. Other long bones can be utilized, including the humerus and the clavicle (Jeanty *et al.*, 1981), although these are argued to be less accurate than relying on the femur alone or utilizing a combination of measurements as described above.

Other methods have been investigated with varying degrees of success. While ultrasound can image the distal femoral epiphyses and the proximal tibial epiphysis, the initial appearances of these are too varied to have much veracity as an age indicator (Chinn *et al.*, 1983; Mahony, Callen and Filly, 1985). Foot bones and their development have also been studied and a positive correlation between the increase in length of the metatarsals and age has been confirmed (De Vasconcellos and Ferreira, 1998).

11.3   Birth

To establish via the skeleton whether a fetus is full term relies on evaluation of not only primary centres of ossification but also selected secondary centres of ossification. A secondary centre is best defined as an additional region within a bone where ossification is located. In the long bones, this may occur at either end in relation to the growth plate or it may occur in areas where strong muscles attach to bone and set up an additional area of bone deposition. These secondary centres are often referred to as epiphyses and they represent the area where the bone is still actively growing and encompasses the growth plate (Ogden, 2000).

There are no secondary centres of ossification associated with the bones of the skull and so all are located in the postcranial skeleton. Tables 11.4 and 11.5 summarize

Table 11.4 Approximate times of appearance of the secondary centres of ossification of the axial and girdle skeleton (f = female, m = male).

Bone	Approx. age of appearance of secondary centres of ossification
Coracoid process	Year 1
Subcoracoid	Years 8–10
Acetabulum	Years 9–11
Anterior inferior iliac spine	Years 10–13
Clavicle (medial)	Years 12–14
Iliac crest	Years 12–14 (f) Years 14–17 (m)
Vertebral column	Puberty (12–18)
Sternum	Puberty (12–18)
Ribs	Puberty (12–18)
Glenoidal rim, acromion and coracoid epiphyses	Years 13–16
Medial scapula and inferior angle	Years 15–17

the approximate times of appearance of the secondary centres of ossification for the postcranial skeleton, and it is clear that these span the period from late fetal life until puberty – the absence of epiphyses signifies either the fetal period or adulthood and of course these could never be confused. Therefore the period just prior to full term and the cessation of growth following puberty is characterized by the appearance, growth and final fusion of a combination of both the primary and secondary centres of ossification for each and every bone of the skeleton.

However, not all bones in the postcranial skeleton have secondary centres of ossification, and these include:

- The first cervical vertebra

- The coccygeal vertebrae

- All carpal bones

- Patella

- Talus and navicular (can have inconstant epiphyses)

- Cuboid and cuneiforms.

It should also be noted that the two large epiphyses associated with the knee are commonly present at full term (the distal femur and the proximal tibia) and in the past, their presence has been taken as an indication of a fetal maturity (Sadler, 1985; Scheuer and Black, 2000).

Table 11.5 Approximate times of appearance of the secondary centres of ossification of the appendicular (non-girdle) skeleton (f = female, m = male).

Bone	Approx. age of appearance of secondary centres of ossification
Femur distal	Months 36–40 IU
Tibia proximal	Weeks 36–40 IU
Humerus head	Months 2–6
Tibia distal	Months 3–10
Distal phalanx 1 foot	Month 9 (f) Month 14 (m)
Fibula distal	Months 9–11
Proximal phalanges hand	Months 10–17 (f) Months 14–24 (m)
Femur head	Year 1
Humerus greater tuberosity and capitulum	Years 1–2
Radius distal	Years 1–2
Middle phalanges foot	Months 11–14 (f) Months 14–24 (m)
Proximal phalanges foot	Months 11–20 (f) Months 18–28 (m)
Metacarpals	Months 16–19 (f) Months 22–29 (m)
Middle phalanges hand	Months 19–24 (f) Months 25–34 (m)
Base metatarsal 1	Months 18–20 (f) Months 26–31 (m)
Metatarsal heads	Months 19–30 (f) Months 27–48 (m)
Distal phalanges hand	Year 2 (f) Years 2–3 (m)
Distal phalanges 2–5 foot	Years 2–3 (f) Years 4–5 (m)
Femur greater trochanter	Years 2–5
Humerus lesser tuberosity and medial epicondyle	Years 4–5
Fibula proximal	Years 4–5
Radius proximal	Year 5
Calcaneus	Years 5–6 (f) Years 7–8 (m)
Ulna distal	Years 5–7
Femur lesser trochanter	Years 7–12
Humerus trochlea	By year 8
Ulna proximal	Years 8–10
Humerus lateral epicondyle	By year 10

11.4   Juvenile/Child

After birth, being able to assess skeletal age in juveniles and adolescents is of interest to clinicians for a number of reasons. Commonly, skeletal age is evaluated in order to identify which stage of skeletal maturation, or biological maturity, has been reached by the juvenile (Maresh, 1971). This enables the clinician to identify any growth impediments that might be present, assess the validity of treatments that might be being considered/undertaken or accurately identify the commencement or progression of the growth spurt for the purposes of either surgical or pharmaceutical intervention (Cole, Webb and Cole, 1988; Even, Bronstein and Hochberg, 1998;

Flores-Mir, Nebbe and Major, 2004; Charles *et al.*, 2007; Kant *et al.*, 2007; Alkhal *et al.*, 2008; Soegiharto, Moles and Cunningham, 2008b; Lee *et al.*, 2009).

Studies into the timings of the appearance and fusion of ossification centres have been undertaken on both the living and the dead (Joseph, 1951; Malina, 1971; Ulijaszek, Johnston and Preece, 1998; Scheuer and Black, 2000). It should be noted that imaging techniques such as radiography of living individuals give a different timing for both appearance and fusion of centres than those reported on dry bone, and as a result there may be discrepancies between these times and the two modalities (Moss and Noback, 1958; Webb and Suchey, 1985; Coqueugniot and Weaver, 2007).

Linking long bone length to chronological age in juveniles via imaging techniques can be dated back to the work of Maresh and Deming (1939). Their research showed that the link between growth and maturity was strong but not linear, displaying periods of both acceleration and stasis, and this has been echoed by many other studies on different parts of the skeleton (Tupman, 1962; Gindhart, 1973; Rissech and Black, 2007). However, this is certainly a popular approach to age evaluation in the fetus, neonate and younger child as it does not require an expert evaluation, simply a matching of a metric value to a reference table. Table 11.6 is an example of one of these tables as it summarizes femoral diaphyseal lengths in males and females between the ages of 2 months *post partum* and 12 years of age. Recourse to these types of tables permits an age evaluation from long bone lengths between birth and puberty, but without detailed knowledge of the origins of the sample investigated, this can lead to overconfidence.

While growth is a defining feature of the juvenile, it is not a linear process through-out childhood as every child undergoes a number of growth spurts and any attempt to evaluate the relationship between skeletal age and chronological age must take these timings into consideration (Tanner, 1962; Hunter, 1966; Bock, 2004). Individ-ual children of the same chronological age can have significantly different biological ages and therefore it is important to have a solid understanding of impact factors that may influence any form of evaluation (Cameron, 1982; Scheuer and Black, 2000). For example, individual variation can mean that the onset of the adolescent growth period may vary by as much as four years for boys and by as much as five years for girls (Hunter, 1966). Despite many studies on both living populations and archaeo-logical remains, separating the influence of these different factors from the core rate of maturation continues to elude the scientist. It is almost impossible to study any of the factors in isolation and because of this, assessment of age remains something that, while more accurate in juveniles than adults, still has a significant error range and this must be reflected in any attempt to assess age in the living individual.

Among these factors, however, it has been established that all ageing techniques must take into account the sex of the child. Females have an accelerated skeletal maturation, being ahead of males by around a week at the time of birth and by approximately 2 years by the time puberty is reached (Molinari, Gasser and Largo, 2004). Girls consistently embark on their growth spurts at an earlier age than boys, reach maximum growth velocity and subsequently complete skeletal maturity well ahead of their male counterparts (Tanner, 1962). For this reason it is absolutely essential to ensure that the sex of the child is known and not simply guessed or

Table 11.6 Diaphyseal length of the femur in males and females between the ages of 2 months *post partum* and 12 years of age.

Age (years)	Male			Female		
	n	Mean	SD	n	Mean	SD
0.125	59	86.0	5.4	68	87.2	4.3
0.25	59	100.7	4.8	65	100.8	3.6
0.50	67	112.2	5.0	78	111.1	4.6
1.00	72	136.6	5.8	81	134.6	4.9
1.5	68	155.4	6.8	84	153.9	6.4
2.0	68	172.4	7.3	84	170.8	7.1
2.5	72	187.2	7.8	82	185.2	7.7
3.0	71	200.3	8.5	79	198.4	8.7
3.5	73	212.1	11.4	78	211.1	10.0
4.0	72	224.1	9.9	80	223.2	10.1
4.5	71	235.7	10.5	78	235.5	11.4
5.0	77	247.5	11.1	80	247.0	11.5
5.5	73	258.2	11.7	74	257.0	12.2
6.0	71	269.7	12.0	75	268.9	13.5
6.5	72	280.3	12.6	81	279.0	13.8
7.0	71	291.1	13.3	86	288.8	13.6
7.5	76	301.2	13.5	83	299.8	15.2
8.0	70	312.1	14.6	85	309.8	15.6
8.5	72	321.0	14.6	82	318.9	15.8
9.0	76	330.4	14.6	83	328.7	16.8
9.5	78	340.0	15.8	83	338.8	18.6
10.0	77	349.3	15.7	84	347.9	19.1
10.5	76	357.4	16.2	75	356.5	21.4
11.0	75	367.0	16.5	76	367.0	22.4
11.5	76	375.8	18.1	75	378.0	23.4
12.0	74	386.1	19.0	71	387.6	22.9

Adapted from Maresh (1970).

assumed. Prior to changes at puberty it can be difficult to assign sex correctly in a fully clothed child just via visual external inspection, especially if they are dressed in items that are not consistent with their true biological sex or are not obviously gender specific.

The longitudinal studies conducted in the first half of the twentieth century have resulted in two different types of assessment being developed. The first is known as the 'atlas technique' and the second, often known as the 'single-bone method', involves assigning bone ages to single bones and combining the results. These are described in more detail below.

The first atlas was created in 1898 (Poland, 1898) and it comprised radiographs of the hand and wrist. It did not take into account sex differences and not every age was represented by a radiographic plate – but it still remains the first of its kind. This was followed in the 1930s by a series of longitudinal studies that encouraged development of a number of atlases. These studies were designed and initiated by Todd (1937) and resulted in the first useable atlas of the hand–wrist. These studies continued after his death and from them came the production of further atlases covering different parts of the body. These atlases relate to the hand–wrist (Todd, 1937; Greulich and Pyle, 1959; Pyle, Waterhouse and Greulich, 1971), foot–ankle (Pyle and Hoerr, 1969) and knee (Hoerr, Pyle and Francis, 1962); an atlas of the elbow also exists which was created at a much later date and on a different population (Brodeur, Silberstein and Gravis, 1981). Each atlas that was devised from the study initiated by Todd was created by taking a series of 100 'best' radiographs for each age. These were chosen to best represent the level of skeletal maturation achieved by a child of that age. From these, one radiograph was chosen which the authors felt represented the gold standard for that given age. Sex differences were taken into account so there were two standards for each sex, although in later atlases these were combined, with a different age range being assigned to each radiograph to accommodate the sex differences. The radiographic standards were taken from white American children of relatively high socio-economic status who took part in the longitudinal study which ran between 1917 and 1942 (Todd, 1937; Hoerr, Pyle and Francis, 1962; Pyle and Hoerr, 1969; Pyle, Waterhouse and Greulich, 1971).

In practical terms, the atlases are used by finding the 'standard' image that most closely resembles the image taken of the child under investigation and then assigning a given age to the child. They are widely applied today in the assessment of skeletal maturation, especially the hand–wrist atlas of Greulich and Pyle, and authors argue that they are reasonably accurate and easy to use. Further atlases have been designed using this method and using an alternative population for the standard radiographs such as the Thiemann–Nitz atlas, which was based on a population from the German Democratic Republic in the 1970s (Schmeling *et al.*, 2006a; Schmidt *et al.*, 2007) or the Gök atlas from Turkey (Büken *et al.*, 2008, 2009).

Figure 11.1 shows the right hand of a young boy aged 2 years and 10 months. All primary centres of ossification for the digits and the radius and the ulna are of course present as these are all represented at birth. However, primary centres are also present for four of the carpal bones. Secondary centres of ossification can be seen at the distal end of the radius but the distal end of the ulna is obscured by the hand of the radiographer. Epiphyses are evident for the base of the first metacarpal and the heads of all other metacarpals and for the bases of all phalanges. Reference to standard texts of age evaluation from the skeleton would place this child quite correctly between 2 and 4 years of age but the inherent variation means that a more accurate evaluation to bring the estimated age closer to the known age is simply not possible.

Figure 11.2 shows an older boy of 8 years and 5 months. In this radiograph, all the same primary centres are visible but now there are seven carpals visible. In addition, the bones are longer and the secondary centres are at a more advanced stage of maturation compared to those in Figure 11.1. Reference to standard texts of age evaluation from the skeleton would place this child quite correctly between 7 and 9 years of age but he is closer to the upper limit than he is to the lower limit.

It is important to ensure that the radiograph is taken in the appropriate plane of view for comparison with the standard images (Brodeur, Silberstein and Gravis, 1981). Figure 11.3a and b show the radiographic appearance of the left elbow of a young girl aged 12 years and 9 months. Figure 11.3a shows a standard lateral view, which allows visualization of fusion at the head of the radius and in the olecranon

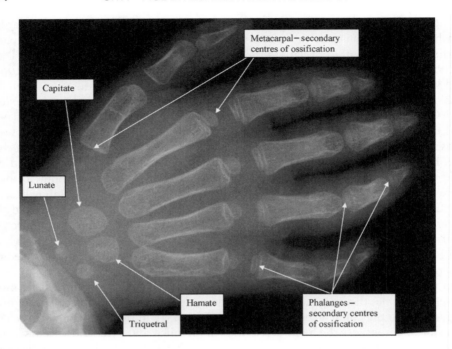

Figure 11.1 Radiograph of the right hand of a juvenile male aged 2 years and 10 months.

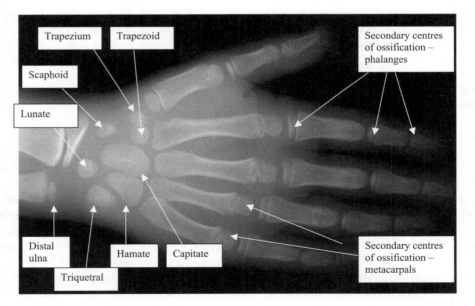

Figure 11.2 Radiograph of the right hand of a juvenile male aged 8 years and 5 months.

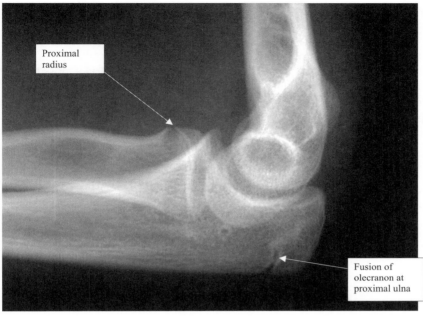

(a)

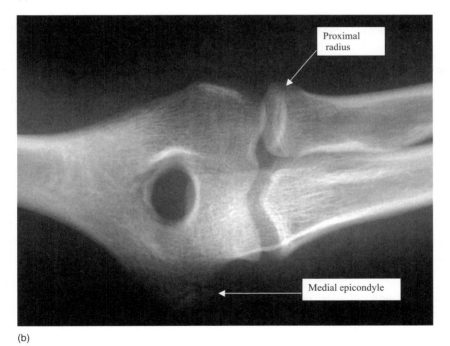

(b)

Figure 11.3 (a) Lateral view and (b) anterior-posterior view of the left elbow of a juvenile female aged 12 years and 9 months.

process of the ulna. However, in the different view shown in Figure 11.3b, the full extent of epiphyseal development in the head of the radius can be seen and fusion in the medial epicondyle but the view of the olecranon process is obscured by the distal humerus. Following standard texts, this girl would be correctly aged at between 11 and 14 years but note now that the range for a possible age has increased markedly as the influences of puberty cause considerable variation. Therefore to view the elbow joint reliably requires two radiographic images and this raises the question of unnecessary and excessive exposure and explains why this joint is not utilized extensively in age evaluation in the living. Table 11.7 shows some

Table 11.7   Approximate dates of completion of epiphyseal fusion in the regions most likely to be investigated for age-related information in the living.

Bone	Approx. age of complete fusion of secondary centres of ossification
Medial clavicle	Starts years 16–21 Completed by 28 years
Iliac crest	Starts years 17–20 Completed by 24 years
Humerus	
Distal fusion	Years 11–15 (f) Years 12–17 (m)
Medial epicondyle	Years 13–15 (f) Years 14–16 (m)
Proximal fusion	Years 13–17 (f) Years 16–20 (m)
Radius	
Proximal fusion	Years 11–13 (f) Years 14–17 (m)
Distal fusion	Years 14–17 (f) Years 16–20 (m)
Ulna	
Proximal fusion	Years 12–14 (f) Years 13–16 (m)
Distal fusion	Years 16–18 (f) Years 17–20 (m)
Hand	
All epiphyses	Years 13–15 (f) Years 15–17 (m)
Femur	
Head fusion	Years 12–16 (f) Years 14–19 (m)
Greater trochanter	Years 14–16 (f) Years 16–18 (m)
Lesser trochanter	Years 16–17
Distal fusion	Years 14–18 (f) Years 16–20 (m)
Tibia	
Distal fusion	Years 14–16 (f) Years 15–18 (m)
Proximal fusion	Years 13–17 (f) Years 15–19 (m)
Fibula	
Distal fusion	Years 12–15 (f) Years 15–18 (m)
Proximal fusion	Years 12–17 (f) Years 15–20 (m)
Foot	
Calcaneus	Years 15–16 (f) Years 18–20 (m)
Distal and mid phalanges and metatarsal heads	Years 11–13 (f) Years 14–16 (m)
Proximal phalanges and base of metatarsal 1	Years 13–15 (f) Years 16–18 (m)

summary statistics for approximate timings of closure of secondary centres of ossification.

The 'single-bone method' involves the assignment of a score to each ossification centre represented in the radiograph. The development of each bone within the hand/wrist complex is divided into a series of stages from (A), not yet visible on the radiograph, to (H), where the bone has achieved full adult morphology. Each of these stages is assigned a numeric score. Each bone is assessed individually and a cumulative score is achieved for the anatomical region under examination. Each cumulative numerical score is then related to a chronological age. The most widely known of these systems is the Tanner–Whitehouse methods – TWI (Tanner, Whitehouse and Healy, 1962), TW2 (Tanner *et al.*, 1975) and TW3 (Tanner *et al.*, 2001) – but there are a number of other methods in existence such as the Fels method (Roche, Chumlea and Thissen, 1988), Fishman's method (Fishman, 1982) and the most recent by Cameriere and colleagues (Cameriere *et al.*, 2006). Each of the above methods uses the ossification centres of the hand and the distal ends of the radius and ulna. In addition to scoring the carpals and long bones of the hand and wrist, the Tanner–Whitehouse methods have also maintained the link between length of long bones and maturity and can also be used to predict final adult height. The original TWI technique was based on the Oxford technique suggested by Acheson (1954), one of the first to suggest this approach as an alternative to the atlas method. The Tanner–Whitehouse method has undergone two revisions since the first one was produced and each revision has based the assignment of maturity scores on the maturational records of a different set of children. The first Tanner–Whitehouse (TWI) method was published in 1962 and utilized information from British children of lower socio-economic status (Tanner, Whitehouse and Healy, 1962); TW2 was the first revision, using information collected from Scottish children of low socio-economic status (Tanner *et al.*, 1975). The third version used more recent information from European children, therefore allowing secular changes that occurred in the time that had passed since the first edition, to be addressed (Tanner *et al.*, 2001). It is of interest to note that Bertaina *et al.* (2007) found that the TW3 system does not represent any significant benefit over the TW2 system, yet argue that for use in forensic age assessment, the TW3 method is more appropriate because it is based on a more contemporary population. Unfortunately, the text for the TW3 method is no longer in production and therefore it is extremely difficult to gain access to the details of this methodology.

The TW method relies on assessment of 20 bones within the hand–wrist to which it applies 9 maturity indices, whereas the Fels method, which was derived from 13 823 radiographs acquired in a longitudinal study of British children, relies on 98 maturity indicators (Roche, Chumlea and Thissen, 1988). The drawback of the Fels method is that it requires training and a computer program to apply it with any degree of competence. These restrictions ensure that it is not the preferred method and is little used despite the arguments proffered by some that it is an appropriate, and reasonably accurate, assessment method (Chumlea, Roche and Thissen, 1989; Van Lenthe, Kemper and Van Mechelen, 1998).

Finally, there are a number of techniques that are not widely used or have perhaps been developed for certain specific situations, for example that devised by Fishman (1982) for the use of dating the time of optimum dental intervention. Work continues to try to develop a more accurate and easy to use system, which also reflects the growth and maturation parameters as evidenced on a modern population (Schmidt *et al.*, 2008; Zhang *et al.*, 2009). Mineralization of the carpals was investigated by Cameriere *et al.* (2006), a methodology which they tested on Slovenian children. They concluded that the method was comparable to the TW3 method and Fels method but was easier to use (Cameriere *et al.*, 2006, 2008). A similar scoring system to that designed by the TW team but using the bones of the foot has been suggested by Whitaker *et al.* (2002). O'Connor *et al.* (2008) returned to the knee atlas in an attempt to develop a system of assessment that reflected the maturity processes in a modern Irish population.

Atlases also exist that are not known outside certain countries and whose use therefore is limited to these areas, such as the Gök atlas which is used in Turkey (Büken *et al.*, 2007, 2008) and the Thiemann–Nitz atlas, whose use is limited to Germany despite studies that indicate that it is a relevant method of assessing chronological age for other populations (Schmeling *et al.*, 2006a; Schmidt *et al.*, 2007).

The rationale in relation to uptake of methodologies is complex and can include simple language barriers, complexity of the process, need for specialist equipment, access to the data or limitations within perhaps the original sample size or in relation to the status of the population under investigation (Schmeling *et al.*, 2006a). Despite the passage of time and many attempts to improve it, the Greulich and Pyle (GP) atlas remains the most commonly used and internationally recognized method today, followed closely by that of Tanner-Whitehouse, with the most popular of these in turn being TW1 and 2. It is of interest and perhaps some concern that these use information based on the oldest studied populations and so there is unquestionably a need to develop a truly international database of images for age evaluation purposes.

The use of the hand-wrist has gained prevalence within forensic arenas for age assessment due to the fact that as a body area it can be isolated safely thereby limiting potential radiological exposure to the trunk (Cobb, 1971; Mazrani, McHugh and Marsden, 2007; Ramsthaler *et al.*, 2009). The 1970s saw an increase in the recognition of the potential harmful effects of exposure to X-rays (Hall, 1991; Brenner *et al.*, 2003). While the use of X-rays for clinical reasons is accepted to diagnose, treat and monitor clinical conditions and interventions (Filly *et al.*, 1981), the use of additional radiographs for non-clinical reasons has become ethically contentious and this includes the use of imaging for age evaluation purposes, and indeed the decision to follow this route has resulted in opposition (RCPCH, 2007). Chapter 8 explores the relative risks of such exposure.

Age estimations link into legal systems that use concrete dates to move individuals from one grouping to another. For example, in the UK, 18 years of age is when an individual is officially recognized as an adult and moves away from the support and protection afforded by the Children Act (2004). Taking the GP atlas as an example, one standard deviation covers 1.1 years and 2 covers 2.2 years (Greulich and Pyle, 1959). If, as Greulich and Pyle found, 90% of all cases fall within 2 standard deviations of the assessed age, every practitioner has to ask if this is an acceptable error, when there is so much riding on the outcome of the assessment. When verifying the accuracy of age assessments undertaken for immigration purposes in Europe, Schmeling *et al.* (2006a) found that of 41 cases where the age of the individual had been established beyond doubt, the error between assessments, using the multiple-method approach outlined above, was ±12 months. When the legality of a system balances between the definition of a juvenile at 17 or an adult at 18, this level of conservative error displays precisely why age evaluation in the living must be undertaken only with due care and attention.

In immigration and forensic age determination, the countries of origin of those undergoing assessment are diverse (Schmeling et al., 2000). Often they originate from a distinct population group, which will most likely differ significantly from the index population studied during the development of the atlas or single-bone method. Therefore any age assessment must take into account the differences that exist between populations. Secular changes in populations have been studied to try to assess their implications on skeletal maturation (Maresh, 1972; Garn, 1987; Richter and Kern, 1987; Henneberg and van den Berg, 1990; Roberts, 1994; Matsuoka et al., 1999; Zhen-Wang and Cheng-Ye, 2005; Kalichman et al., 2008; Özer, 2008). Secular changes as seen in these studies support the argument by Schmeling et al. (2006c) that it is socio-economic and nutritional factors (Tyvalsky, 2004; Fernandez et al., 2007; Rizzoli, 2008) which have the greatest influence on the differences in maturational progress found between populations both geographically and temporally (Matsuoka et al., 1999; Schmeling et al., 2006c). It should be noted that secular trends can operate in both directions, resulting either in an increase in the rate of skeletal maturity and growth or as a decrease in times of less than optimal conditions (Richter and Kern, 1987). The differences that exist between groups both in time and geography are understood to exist; however, performing longitudinal studies is neither ethically nor practically possible. Additionally any study can be argued to be almost immediately redundant as changes in nutrition and medical care create changes in health with resultant effects on maturation rates (Schmeling et al., 2000; Schmeling et al., 2006c).

Due to the need to avoid longitudinal studies that result in regular exposure to ionizing radiation, research into the differences that exist between population groups has taken the form of applying the GP atlas, TW system or one of the ageing methodologies to the population in question. By statistical analysis of the results the difference between skeletal age and chronological age can be analysed and potential error margins highlighted. Studies that have undertaken this have found a varying degree of fit between the original atlas or assessment method and their index population (Sidhom and Derry, 1931; Greulich, 1957; Beunen et al., 1982; Kimura, 1983; Bogin et al., 1989; Ontell et al., 1996; Groell et al., 1999; Rikhasor et al., 1999; Vignolo et al., 1999; Koc et al., 2001; Mora et al., 2001; Ashizawa et al., 2005; Garamendi et al., 2005; Büken et al., 2007; Little and Malina, 2007; Savaridas et al., 2007; Lynnerup et al., 2008; O'Connor et al., 2008; Soegiharto, Cunningham and Moles, 2008a; van Rijn and Lequin, 2009). Studies in Japan, for example, when comparing children from different areas using the TW2 methodology, found that both advanced and retarded skeletal maturity was identified depending upon where in Japan the juvenile originated (Greulich, 1957; Takai and Akiyoshi, 1983; Kimura, 1984). Zhang et al. (2009) developed a hand–wrist atlas that addressed ethnicity and sex. They found that in the USA, while radiologists found bone age was closely linked to chronological age in African American and White children, there were significant differences between the assigned bone age and chronological age in Asian and Hispanic children. It should be noted that they chose to represent only children of proven 'normal' development and avoided the issue of mixed ethnicity. This bias is reflected in all these studies as children are chosen on the basis of health, their link to a normal maturation pattern and their ethnicity. As a result of their findings after assessing the fit between a Danish cohort of children and the GP atlas, Lynnerup *et al.* (2008) reiterated the need for any assessments of chronological age that use the GP atlas to include an age range of 2 standard deviations (1 standard deviation = 1.1 years) as well as the more commonly reported variation of only 1 standard deviation.

It is of note that while all the named methods concentrate on the left side of the body, studies that have been completed on both living and deceased skeletal arrays all agree that there is little significant difference between age assessments performed on either side of the body (Schmeling *et al.*, 2006a; Rissech and Black, 2007).

In addition to secular changes and the differences that exist between populations, care should always be taken to remember that the hand–wrist, while useful in assessing skeletal maturity, is not necessarily representative of the whole skeleton as some areas can be in advance or lag behind others in maturity (Garn *et al.*, 1967). As already mentioned, other ossification centres in the body can also be utilized for age assessment. The risks posed by exposure of the body to ionizing radiation or their position on the body has meant that imaging difficulties have often restricted their use in the living (Webb and Suchey, 1985; Albert and Maples, 1995). The introduction of different imaging modalities, such as ultrasound and CT, means that these can be investigated and may in the future enable other, or even multiple areas, of the body to be used safely.

Efforts continue to try to find an alternative to radiographic imaging, in recognition of the need to reduce or minimize the X-ray burden on children (Malina *et al.*, 2007) and reduce the number of images in order to reduce the radiological burden (Alkhal *et al.*, 2008; Soegiharto, Moles and Cunningham, 2008b). CT utilizes X-rays but at a much lower dose than flat plate radiographs and investigation has shown no significant loss in accuracy with this approach (Aaron *et al.*, 1992). Magnetic resonance imaging (MRI) has also been investigated, especially for use in assessment of age for other than clinical reasons due to the greater pressure that exists in the use of X-rays in non-clinical situations (Malina, 1971; Varich, Laor and Jaramillo, 2000; Dvorak *et al.*, 2007; Malina *et al.*, 2007; Laor and Jaramillo, 2009). In the past ultrasound has been used mainly in imaging the fetus rather than in ageing juveniles but studies have shown that it can provide an image of sufficient clarity to identify the centres of ossification (e.g. hand–wrist or elbow), allowing age assessment to be performed (Barr and Babcock, 1991; Wagner, Diedrich and Schmitt, 1995; Castriota-Scanderbeg *et al.*, 1998; Bilgili *et al.*, 2003). Improved technology is likely to bring further benefits.

Borrowing again from the clinical arsenal of techniques, Risser's sign is used to assess skeletal maturity to identify the optimum time for clinical intervention for scoliosis of the vertebral column (Charles *et al.*, 2007; Reem *et al.*, 2009). This assesses the level of calcification of the iliac crest epiphysis of the pelvis. Despite limited investigation of the accuracy of this method, Reem *et al.* (2009) felt that this may be used with a reasonable degree of accuracy. It is therefore possible that the use of a non-ionizing imaging system could increase the areas of the body that could be assessed for age estimation (Nakahara *et al.*, 2006).

In 1972, Lamparski introduced a new approach that assesses change in the shape of the cervical vertebral bodies with increasing age and this has been investigated as a mechanism to determine skeletal maturity, particularly in relation to dentofacial orthopaedics (Lamparski, 1972; O'Reilly and Yanniello, 1988; Kucukkeles *et al.*, 1999; Hassel and Farman, 1995; García-Fernandez *et al.*, 1998). The method is based on assessment of the degree of concavity witnessed on the inferior border of cervical vertebrae 2–4 and the overall shape of the vertebral body, both of which are visible on lateral cephalometric radiographs being taken for the purposes of the original orthodontic assessment. Baccetti, Franchi and McNamara (2002) suggested that the peak pubertal growth spurt occurs between stages 2 and 3, when the concavity has started to develop on the inferior border of the C3 vertebra or is also commencing on the inferior border of the fourth cervical vertebra.

While clinically the use of skeletal maturation has a long history, the more recent increase in movement of individuals around the globe has elicited a demand for assessing the age of a living individual as accurately and safely as possible based on these older clinical studies. Much of the data that is relied on in the modern day is based on longitudinal studies from the early 1900s which would not be ethically acceptable today (Gindhart, 1973). Studies continue to shed light on the applicability of various methods for assessing the chronological age of the individual and corresponding work is also ongoing to limit observer error through the use of computerized methodology (Hadlock *et al.*, 1984; Hsieh *et al.*, 2007). Those working in the fields of forensic and immigrant ageing call for care to be taken when applying ageing techniques from the skeleton (Cameron, 1982). In addition, they recognize the need for continuing research as they recognize the limitations of ageing methods that were based on populations which are up to 80 years in the past and the ethical problems surrounding the use of X-ray imaging (Cameron, 1982; Schmeling *et al.*, 2003).

11.5   Age Estimation from the Skeleton in Living Adults

Once an individual has reached the end of puberty, the majority of the skeletal epiphyses have achieved complete fusion and dental development is also largely complete. As a consequence, the available diagnostic criteria for age evaluation become more restricted. The majority of age estimation studies have been carried out on *ex vivo* skeletal samples, which permit a degree of invasiveness not permissible in the living. Therefore, assessment of the traditional anatomical features used to determine age in skeletonized remains, such as the auricular surface of the ilium, is often severely limited or impossible in living individuals due to inaccessibility. For age evaluation from the skeleton of the living adult it is non-negotiable that the areas to be viewed must be imaged and in a manner that does not contravene health and safety concerns. The use of both X-rays and CT scanning for age assessment of the living individual limit which areas of the body can be used to those that are least likely to be adversely affected by radiation.

As the issue of age evaluation in the living continues to rise in prominence, a number of studies have compared *in vivo* radiographic and CT images with known dry bone age-related changes and the results so far are encouraging that direct comparisons are broadly comparable. However, as with juveniles, it is clear that as new ways of imaging of the skeleton are introduced, more work will be required to reconcile the traditional ageing standards with results from these emerging technologies.

11.6   Medial Clavicle

It is generally accepted that the epiphysis at the medial end of the clavicle is the last to fuse in the body (Stevenson, 1924; Todd and D'Errico, 1928; Scheuer and Black, 2004). The ossification commences in the epiphysis around 12–14 years and fusion first occurs in the central region of the articular surface around 16–18 years of age. The fusion extends posteriorly then superiorly or anteriorly before final union takes place in the inferior rim and this is usually always complete by the end of the third decade (McKern and Stewart, 1957; Scheuer and Black, 2004). The maturation rate appears to be relatively equal bilaterally (Schulze *et al.*, 2006).

There appears to be considerable variability in the correlation between age and the stages of union achieved but this seems to be linked to the method of investigation. Dry bone studies describe fusion as being complete by 30–35 years (McKern and Stewart, 1957; Webb and Suchey, 1985; Scheuer and Black, 2004) while others suggest that complete union is achieved by 25–28 years (Stevenson, 1924; Todd and D'Errico, 1928; Flecker, 1942; McKern and Stewart, 1957). More recent *in vivo* studies confirm a 26–27 years age range for complete fusion (Kreitner *et al.*, 1998; Schmeling *et al.*, 2003; Schulze *et al.*, 2006; Meijerman *et al.*, 2007). But it should be acknowledged that most investigations of the medial clavicle have been carried out on dry bone samples (Stevenson, 1924; Todd and D'Errico, 1928; McKern and Stewart, 1957; Webb and Suchey, 1985; Black and Scheuer, 1996). Radiographic and CT investigations of the medial clavicle tend to record younger ages for fusion (Flecker, 1942; Schmeling *et al.*, 2003, 2004; Schulze *et al.*, 2006; Meijerman *et al.*, 2007).

Meijerman *et al.* (2007) examined X-rays, CT scans and excised bone specimens for comparison purposes and found that the probability of a diagnosis of complete fusion was greater when more refined imaging modalities were employed, and one reason suggested for this is the effect of CT slice thickness (Meijerman *et al.*, 2007). CT slices with a resolution of more than 1 mm may be too coarse for accurate recording of fine features such as epiphyseal lines. Age ranges for fusion established from radiographic and CT images appear to be consistent (Meijerman *et al.*, 2007; Schulz *et al.*, 2008); however, X-ray images may be more susceptible to interference from surrounding anatomical structures (Schulz *et al.*, 2008).

As with most aspects of human development, females tend to mature earlier than males (Flecker, 1942). The medial clavicle is also influenced by sex, where females commence and complete fusion approximately one year in advance of males (Webb and Suchey, 1985; Meijerman *et al.*, 2007). The influence of ancestry on epiphyseal fusion times has also been studied and it has been concluded that genetic ancestry does not exert a significant influence in the maturation of the medial clavicle (Todd and D'Errico, 1928; Schmeling *et al.*, 2000; Meijerman *et al.*, 2007; Shirley, 2009).

The efficacy of the medial clavicle as an ageing feature in living individuals appears to be sound. Age ranges are well established, albeit with biological variation and *in vivo* images of the sternal end of the clavicle are, as a rule, visually uncomplicated. Radiographic and CT images appear to be reliable and consistent assessment tools.

11.7   Sternal Ribs and Costal Cartilages

A number of studies, both *ex vivo* and radiographic (McCormick, 1980; Iscan, Loth and Wright, 1984, 1985, 1987; McCormick and Stewart, 1988) have shown that there is a relationship between increasing age and the degree of costal cartilage ossification. This is particularly useful for *in vivo* age estimates as chest X-rays are common and not obscured by large amounts of overlying soft tissue although underlying soft tissue is an issue. The most anteriorly situated ends of the ribs articulate with the sternum via a series of cartilaginous bridges. In juveniles and adolescents this hyaline cartilage is flexible and rarely shows calcification/ossification. As maturation progresses the costal cartilage undergoes calcification and then ossification, which manifests as opaque regions on X-ray film and bony extensions from the anterior rib end (McCormick and Stewart, 1988; Barres, Durion and Paraire, 1989).

The ossification of the costal cartilage of the chest plate generally takes place as a consequence of the ageing process, although there is some evidence to suggest that it may be accelerated by physical activity, stress and certain drugs, particularly heroin (Iscan, Loth and Wright, 1987; Barchilon *et al.*, 1996). The main regions of ossification occur in the central and peri-sternal parts of the costal cartilage and tend to progress bilaterally in a largely homogenous fashion, with the exception of the first rib, which is known to ossify at a faster rate than the others. Studies have concluded that the ossification process observed in the first rib is too variable to be useful in medico-legal ageing (Barchilon *et al.*, 1996). Early ossification changes have been observed in the remaining costal cartilages in the second decade, and some change is usually observed by the middle of the fourth decade. The fourth rib has been subjected to extensive examination and found to exhibit ossification changes as early as 15 years of age and to continue to change into the sixth decade (Iscan, Loth and Wright, 1984, 1987; Yavuz, Iscan and Cologlu, 1998) but few studies have investigated the comparative age changes at each rib level.

Most studies have employed a visual assessment method, which scores features according to their morphological appearance (size of bony spurs, 'cupping' of the sternal rib) and physical properties (degree of calcification) (Iscan, Loth and Wright, 1984, 1985; McCormick and Stewart, 1988; Barres, Durion and Paraire, 1989; Barchilon *et al.*, 1996). These criteria are sex specific with different methods being developed for males and females (Rejtarová *et al.*, 2009) and it is recognized that the pattern of deposition is very different in the two sexes. Radiographic studies by McCormick and Stewart (1988) applied the developed criteria and recorded age estimates of within 5 years of chronological age in just over half (55%) of the bodies surveyed and within 25% of chronological age in 95% of bodies. This level of accuracy is not suitable for medico-legal purposes.

Ossification rates are affected by ethnicity (Semine and Damon, 1975) and Iscan, Loth and Wright (1987) demonstrated that Afro-Americans have a faster maturation rate than Caucasians. McCormick (1980) also reported earlier costal calcification in Americans of Mexican ancestry whereas Yavuz, Iscan and Cologlu (1998) found there was little variation within Caucasoid sub-groups (American and Turkish).

The usefulness of this method for ageing living adults in a medico-legal environment is questionable. Few, if any, previous studies have examined the ribs and associated costal cartilages *in vivo*. The majority of earlier studies used dry bone samples and most radiographic studies have utilized excised chest plates, thereby eliminating the effect of underlying organs and bony structures, as would be present in the chest X-ray of a living individual. It is not known how this three-dimensional aspect of an *in situ* chest plate would affect the ossification assessment.

11.8   Pelvis

In skeletonized remains, the sacrum (Belcastro, Rastelli and Mariotti, 2008; Rios, Weisensee and Rissech, 2008; Passalacqua, 2009), pubic symphysis (Hanihara and Suzuki, 1978; Jackes, 1985; Brooks and Suchey, 1990; Sinha and Gupta, 1995; Konigsberg *et al.*, 2008) and auricular surface (Lovejoy *et al.*, 1985) are all utilized in age assessment. In the living the positioning and anatomy of the auricular surface make it inaccessible for imaging. Using imaging modalities, such as radiographs, CT and MRI, it is possible to examine both the sacrum and the pubic symphysis and apply developed ageing criteria (Hanihara and Suzuki, 1978; Brooks and Suchey, 1990; Sinha and Gupta, 1995; Hens, Rastelli and Belcastro, 2008; Konigsberg *et al.*, 2008). Due to their positioning in the body, however, unless images of the pelvis have already been taken for diagnostic or therapeutic purposes then the ethics associated with exposing this area of the body to radiation should always be taken into account (Hall, 1991; Brenner *et al.*, 2003; Mazrani, Mchugh and Marsden, 2007; Ramsthaler *et al.*, 2009). Work is being undertaken into the value of ultrasound and MRI for imaging the skeletal system, especially in the sporting arena, where regular imaging of an individual can take place (Tuite and DeSmet, 1994; Lovell *et al.*, 2006; Allen and Wilson, 2007; Dvorak *et al.*, 2007; Schulz *et al.*, 2008). It will be interesting to see if this leads to safe imaging that is sufficiently sensitive to allow age assessment from areas such as the pubic symphysis.

11.9   Skull Sutural Closure

The closure of external skull sutures could arguably be utilized in ageing the living via the appropriate imaging techniques and the application of age assessment criteria such as those described by Meindl and Lovejoy (1985). Studies have been undertaken on the imaging of sutural closure using X-ray and CT scans, which indicate that if these images were available due to past imaging for therapeutic reasons then the application of this ageing methodology would be appropriate (Furuya *et al.*, 1984; Madeline and Elster, 1995; Nakahara *et al.*, 2006; Harth *et al.*, 2009) . As with the imaging of the pelvis, the radiation burden associated with many imaging techniques should be taken into consideration before this area is considered.

11.10   Laryngeal Cartilages

The largest of the laryngeal cartilages within the neck are the thyroid, cricoid and arytenoid cartilages. The thyroid cartilage is the largest and most superiorly located of the three. The next cartilages, in descending order, are the paired arytenoids, with the most inferiorly situated structure being the cricoid. The thyroid, cricoid and the largest portion of the arytenoids (and of course the cartilage rings of the trachea) are composed of hyaline cartilage, which is susceptible to calcification, and age-related patterns are detectable (Turk and Hogg, 1993; Scheuer and Black, 2004).

The patterns of ossification, particularly in the thyroid cartilage, appear to progress in a relatively predictable, albeit non-symmetrical, fashion (Yeager, Lawson and Archer, 1982). Turk and Hogg (1993) described up to five stages of ossification in the thyroid cartilage, four in the cricoid and three in the arytenoids. Ossification of the thyroid body commences in the margins, inferior then superior, before moving inwards to the main body (Garvin, 2008). A midline bridge often forms in the anterior body causing mostly un-ossified material to remain as 'windows' in the body of the cartilage (Scheuer and Black, 2004). Eventually, in most cases, the entire cartilage becomes ossified in old age. The cricoid follows a similar pattern of marginal ossification followed by the main body. The arytenoids commence ossification in the infero-anterior region and spread upwards across the body.

The majority of studies, while describing the ossification patterns in the neck cartilages, do not suggest there is a significant correlation with chronological age. It is generally accepted that some degree of ossification can begin in the mid- to late-teenage years, sometimes as early as 16.5 years (Hately, Evison and Samuel, 1965). Keen and Wainwright reported that 79% of males and 21% of females showed evidence of ossification below the age of 30 years (Keen and Wainwright, 1958). A stronger linkage between chronological age and ossification rates was suggested by Krogman and Iscan (1986), in which nine phases of ossification were correlated with age groups from 15 to 68 years, as support for the use of the laryngeal cartilages as a suitable forensic ageing feature. However, Scheuer and Black (2004) note that Cerný's (1983) sample numbers were small ($n = 5$) and no meaningful conclusions can be drawn from the study. In fact, later work by Garvin (2008) showed that the Cerný method was highly inaccurate when applied to a larger sample. When tested against material of known age at death, only 28.84% of individuals were assigned to the correct age group. This level of misclassification is clearly outside the acceptable boundaries of any medico-legal investigation.

11.11   Other General Ageing Features

Other skeletal elements have been cited in the literature as having potential as age estimators. One such is the hyoid bone which consists of five separate elements. Fusion of these hyoid elements often takes place sometime after middle age, but there is little evidence linking the timing of the fusion with chronological age (O'Halloran and Lundy, 1987).

The vertebral column has also been identified as a place where age-associated changes occur. Stewart (1958) suggested that the degree of osteophytic lipping observed on the margins of the vertebral bodies may be a useful age marker. He reported that osteophytes became more pronounced, particularly in the lumbar spine, after the age of 40 years, but cautioned that no further age groupings could be determined. Added complications include pathology and physical activity, which are known to exacerbate the development of vertebral osteophytes. Therefore, hyoid fusion and vertebral lipping are only useful as general indicators of post-middle age.

11.12   Summary

It is clear that a number of regions in the skeleton display age-related features. However, to be of use to the medico-legal system the features must change in a precise and predictable manner, with limited individual variation. Additionally, the assessment methodology must be reliable and reproducible, with small inter-observer errors. For living individuals the ageing features must be visible in radiographs and CT images and be relatively free of interference from imaging artefacts.

The skeletal feature that comes closest to satisfying the majority of these requirements is the medial clavicle. Low inter-observer error estimates, relatively discrete age groups and minimal interference from overlying soft tissue are all advantages. The fusion of the medial clavicle is also recommended by the Study Group on Forensic Age Diagnostics as the only skeletal feature useful for assessment of personal age in adults but not of course in elderly adults (Schmeling et al., 2006b). The other features described in this review are, from a medico-legal viewpoint, only useful as broad age indicators.

When undertaking age assessment of the adult skeleton, MRI and ultrasound imaging can be considered and work on the use of these imaging modalities, especially in the sports arena, is giving increasingly positive results.

It is clear, therefore, that age evaluation from the skeleton is one of the most reliable approaches for the approximation of chronological age. While the original research in this area may not have been undertaken specifically to serve this application, a resurgence in interest in this area to meet the increasing needs of immigration and asylum issues has resulted in new focused research being undertaken but there is clearly much more that requires to be achieved.

References

Aaron, A., Weinstein, D., Thickman, D. and Eilert, R. (1992) Comparison of orthoroentgenography and computed tomography in the measurement of limb-length discrepancy. *Journal of Bone and Joint Surgery*, **74A**, 897–902.

Acheson, R.M. (1954) A method of assessing skeletal maturity from radiographs. A report from the Oxford child health survey. *Journal of Anatomy*, 88, 498–508.

Albert, A.M. and Maples, W.R. (1995) Stages of epiphyseal union for thoracic and lumbar vertebral centra as a method of age determination for teenage and young adult skeletons. *Journal of Forensic Sciences*, 40, 623–633.

Alkhal, H.A., Wong, R.W.K., Bakr, A. and Rabie, M. (2008) Elimination of hand–wrist radiographs for maturity assessment in children needing orthodontic therapy. *Skeletal Radiology*, 37, 195–200.

Allen, G.M. and Wilson, D.J. (2007) Ultrasound in sports medicine – a critical evaluation. *European Journal of Radiology*, 62, 79–85.

Anderson, M., Green, W.T. and Messner, M. (1963) Growth and predictions of growth in the lower extremetries. *Journal of Bone and Joint Surgery*, 45A, 1–14.

Ashizawa, K., Kumakura, C., Zhou, X. *et al.* (2005) RUS skeletal maturity of children in Beijing. *Annals of Human Biology*, 32, 316–325.

Baccetti, T., Franchi, L. and McNamara, J.A. (2002) An improved version of the cervical vertebral maturation (CVM) method for the assessment of mandibular growth. *The Angle Orthodontist*, 72 (4), 316–323.

Barchilon, V., Hershkovitz, I., Rothschild, B. *et al.* (1996) Factors affecting the rate and pattern of the first costal cartilage ossification. *American Journal of Forensic Medicine and Pathology*, 17, 239–247.

Barr, L.L. and Babcock, D.S. (1991) Sonography of the normal elbow. *American Journal of Roentgenology*, 157, 793–798.

Barres, D.R., Durion, M. and Paraire, F. (1989) Age estimation from quantitation of features of 'chest plate' X-rays. *Journal of Forensic Sciences*, 34, 228–233.

Belcastro, M.G., Rastelli, E. and Mariotti, V. (2008) Variation of the degree of sacral vertebral body fusion in adulthood in two European modern skeletal collections. *American Journal of Physical Anthropology*, 135, 149–160.

Bertaina, C., Staslowska, B., Benso, A. and Vannelli, S. (2007) Is TW3 height prediction more accurate than TW2? *Hormone Research*, 67, 220–223.

Beunen, G., Malina, R.M., Ostyn, M. *et al.* (1982) Fatness and skeletal maturity of Belgian boys 12 through 17 years of age. *American Journal of Physical Anthropology*, 59, 387–392.

Bilgili, Y., Hizel, S., Kara, S.A. *et al.* (2003) Accuracy of skeletal age assessment on children from birth to 6 years of age with the ultrasonographic version of the Greulich–Pyle atlas. *Journal of Ultrasound Medicine*, 22, 683–390.

Black, S. and Scheuer, J.L. (1996) Age changes in the clavicle: from the early neonatal period to skeletal maturity. *International Journal of Osteoarchaeology*, 6, 425–434.

Bleich, A.R. (1960) *The Story of X-rays from Rontgen to Isotopes*, Dover, New York.

Bock, R.D. (2004) Multiple prepubertal growth spurts in children of the Fels Longitudinal Study: comparison with results from the Edinburgh Growth Study. *Annals of Human Biology*, 31, 59–74.

Bogin, B., Sullivan, T., Hauspie, R. and Macvean, R.B. (1989) Longitudinal growth in height, weight, and bone age of Guatemalan Latino and Indian schoolchildren. *American Journal of Human Biology*, 1, 103–113.

Brenner, D.J., Doll, R., Goodhead, D.T. *et al.* (2003) Cancer risks attributable to low doses of ionizing radiation: assessing what we really know. *Proceedings of the National Academy of Sciences of the United States of America*, 100, 13761–13766.

Brodeur, A.E., Silberstein, M.J. and Gravis, E.R. (1981) *Radiology of the Pediatric Elbow*, Hall, Boston, MA.

Brooks, S. and Suchey, J. (1990) Skeletal age determination based on the os pubis: a comparison of the Acsádi–Nemeskéri and Suchey–Brooks methods. *Human Evolution*, 5, 227–238.

Büken, B., Safak, A.A., Yazici, B. *et al.* (2007) Is the assessment of bone age by the

Greulich–Pyle method reliable at forensic age estimation for Turkish children? *Forensic Science International*, **173**, 146–153.

Büken, B., Büken, E., Safak, A.A. *et al.* (2008) Is the 'Gok Atlas' sufficiently reliable for forensic age determination of Turkish children? *Turkish Journal of Medical Sciences*, **38**, 319–327.

Büken, B., Erzengin, Ö.U., Büken, E. *et al.* (2009) Comparison of the three age estimation methods: which is more reliable for Turkish children? *Forensic Science International*, **183**, 103.e1–103.e7.

Cameriere, R., Ferrante, L., Mirtella, D. and Cingolani, M. (2006) Carpals and epiphyses of radius and ulna as age indicators. *International Journal of Legal Medicine*, **120**, 143–146.

Cameriere, R., Ferrante, L., Ermenc, B. *et al.* (2008) Age estimation using carpals: study of a Slovenian sample to test Cameriere's method. *Forensic Science International*, **174**, 178–181.

Cameron, N. (1982) Age estimation. Estimation of chronological age in children. *Science and Public Policy*, **9**, 20–27.

Castriota-Scanderbeg, A., Sacco, M.C., Emberti-Gialloreti, L. and Fraracci, L. (1998) Skeletal age assessment in children and young adults: comparison between a newly developed sonographic method and conventional methods. *Skeletal Radiology*, **27**, 271–277.

Cerný, M. (1983) Our experience with estimation of an individual's age from skeletal remains of the degree of thyroid cartilage ossification. *Acta Universitatis Plackianae Olomucensisi*, **3**, 121–144.

Charles, Y.P., Dimeglio, A., Canavese, F. and Daures, J.P. (2007) Skeletal age assessment from the olecranon for idiopathic scoliosis at Risser grade 0. *Journal of Bone and Joint Surgery. American Volume*, **89**, 2737–2744.

Chinn, D.H., Bolding, D.B., Callen, P.W. *et al.* (1983) Ultrasonographic identification of fetal lower extremity epiphyseal ossificiation centers. *Radiology*, **147**, 815–818.

Chumlea, C., Roche, A.F. and Thissen, D. (1989) The Fels method of assessing the skeletal maturity of the hand–wrist. *American Journal of Human Biology*, **35**, 385–386.

Cobb, W.M. (1971) Choice of area for assessment. *American Journal of Physical Anthropology*, **35**, 385–386.

Cole, A.J.L., Webb, L. and Cole, T.J. (1988) Bone age estimation: a comparison of methods. *British Journal of Radiology*, **61**, 683–686.

Coqueugniot, H. and Weaver, T.D. (2007) Brief communication: Infracranial maturation in the skeletal collection from Coimbra, Portugal: new aging standards for epiphyseal union. *American Journal of Physical Anthropology*, **134**, 424–437.

Davies, D.A. and Parsons, F.G. (1927) The age order of the appearance and union of the normal epiphyses as seen by X-rays. *Journal of Anatomy*, **62**, 58–71.

De Vasconcellos, H.A. and Ferreira, E. (1998) Metatarsal growth during the second trimester: a predictor of gestational age? *Journal of Anatomy*, **193**, 145–149.

Degani, S. (2001) Fetal biometry: clinical, pathological and technical considerations. *Obstetrics and Gynecological Survey*, **56**, 159–167.

Dvorak, J., George, J., Junge, A. and Hodler, J. (2007) Age determination by magnetic resonance imaging of the wrist in adolescent male football players. *British Journal of Sports Medicine*, **41**, 45–52.

Even, L., Bronstein, V. and Hochberg, Z.E. (1998) Bone maturation in girls with Turner's syndrome. *European Journal of Endocrinology*, **138**, 59–62.

Fazekas, I.G. and Kosa, F. (1978) *Forensic Fetal Osteology*, Akademiai Kiado, Budapest.

Fernandez, T.J.M., Santiago, R.F., Perez, C.A. *et al.* (2007) The influence of nutrition and social environment on the bone maturation of children. *Nutrición hospitalaria*, **22**, 417–424.

Filly, R.A., Golbus, M.S., Carey, J.C. and Hall, J.G. (1981) Short-limbed dwarfism: ultrasonographic diagnosis by mensuration of fetal femoral length. *Radiology*, **138**, 653–656.

Fishman, L.S. (1982) Radiographic evaluation of skeletal maturation. *The Angle Orthodontist*, **52**, 88–112.

Flecker, H. (1942) Time of appearance and fusion of ossification centers as observed by roentgenographic methods. *American Journal of Roentgenology and Radium Therapy*, **47**, 97–159.

Flores-Mir, C., Nebbe, B. and Major, P.W. (2004) Use of skeletal maturation based on hand–wrist radiographic analysis as a predictor of facial growth: a systematic review. *The Angle Orthodontist*, **74**, 118–124.

Furuya, Y., Edwards, M.S.B., Alpers, C.E. *et al.* (1984) Computerized tomography of cranial sutures. *Journal of Neurosurgery*, **61**, 53–58.

Garamendi, P.M., Landa, M.I., Ballesteros, J. and Solano, M.A. (2005) Reliability of the methods applied to assess age minority in living subjects around 18 years old. A survey on a Moroccan origin population. *Forensic Science International*, **154**, 3–12.

García-Fernández, P., Torre, H., Flores, L. and Rea, J. (1998) The Cervical Vertebrae and Maturational Indicators. *Journal of Clinical Orthodontics*, **32** (4), 221–225.

Garn, S.M. (1987) The secular trend in size and maturational timing and its implications for nutritional assessment. *Journal of Nutrition*, **117**, 817–823.

Garn, S.M., Rohmann, C.G. and Apfelbaum, B. (1961) Complete epiphyseal union of the hand. *American Journal of Physical Anthropology*, **19**, 365–372.

Garn, S.M., Rohmann, C.G. and Blumenthal, T. (1966) Ossification sequence polymorphism and sexual dimorphism in skeletal development. *American Journal of Physical Anthropology*, **24**, 101–115.

Garn, S.M., Rohmann, C.G., Blumenthal, T. and Silverman, F.N. (1967) Ossification communalities of the hand and other body parts: their implication to skeletal assessment. *American Journal of Physical Anthropology*, **27**, 75–82.

Garvin, H.M. (2008) Ossification of laryngeal structures as indicators of age. *Journal of Forensic Sciences*, **53**, 1023–1027.

Gindhart, P.S. (1973) Growth standards for the tibia and radius in children aged one month through eighteen years. *American Journal of Physical Anthropology*, **39**, 41–48.

Greulich, W.W. (1957) A comparison of the physical growth and development of American born and native Japanese children. *American Journal of Physical Anthropology*, **15**, 489–515.

Greulich, W.W. and Pyle, S.I. (1959) *Radiographic Atlas of Skeletal Development of the Hand and Wrist*, Stanford University Press, Stanford, CA.

Groell, R., Lindbichler, F., Riepl, T. *et al.* (1999) The reliability of bone age determination in central European children using the Greulich and Pyle method. *British Journal of Radiology*, **72**, 461–464.

Hadlock, F.P., Deter, R.L., Harrist, R.B. and Park, S.K. (1984) Estimating fetal age: computer assisted analysis of multiple fetal growth parameters. *Radiology*, **152**, 497–501.

Hadlock, F.P., Shah, Y.P., Kanon, D.J. and Lindsey, J.V. (1992) Fetal crown–rump length: reevaluation of relation to menstrual age (5–18 weeks) with high-resolution real-time US. *Radiology*, **182**, 501–505.

Hall, E.J. (1991) Scientific view of low-level radiation risks. *Radiographics*, **11**, 509–518.

Hanihara, K. and Suzuki, T. (1978) Estimation of age from the pubic symphysis by means of multiple regression analysis. *American Journal of Physical Anthropology*, **48**, 233–239.

Harth, S., Obert, M., Ramsthaler, F. *et al.* (2009) Estimating age by assessing the ossification degree of cranial sutures with the aid of flat-panel-CT. *Legal Medicine*, **11**, S186–S189.

Hassel, B. and Farman, A.G. (1995) Skeletal maturation evaluation using cervical vertebrae. *American Journal of Orthodontics and Dentofacial Orthopedics*, **107** (1), 58–66.

Hately, W., Evison, G. and Samuel, E. (1965) The pattern of ossification in the laryngeal cartilages: a radiological study. *British Journal of Radiology*, **38**, 585–591.

Henneberg, M. and Van Den Berg, E.R. (1990) Test of socioeconomic causation of secular trend: stature changes among favored and oppressed South Africans are parallel. *American Journal of Physical Anthropology*, **83**, 459–465.

Hens, S.M., Rastelli, E. and Belcastro, G. (2008) Age estimation from the human os coxa: a test on a documented Italian collection. *Journal of Forensic Sciences*, **53**, 1040–1043.

Children Act 2004 (c.31), HMSO, London.

Hoerr, N.L., Pyle, S.I. and Francis, C.C. (1962) *Radiographic Atlas of Skeletal Development of the Foot and Ankle*, Charles C. Thomas, Springfield, IL.

Hsieh, C.W., Jong, T.L., Chou, Y.H. and Tiu, C.M. (2007) Computerized geometric features of carpal bone for bone age estimation. *Chinese Medical Journal*, **120**, 767–770.

Hunter, C.J. (1966) The correlation of facial growth with body height and skeletal maturation at adolescence. *The Angle Orthodontist*, **36**, 44–54.

Iscan, M.Y., Loth, S.R. and Wright, R.K. (1984) Metamorphosis at the sternal rib end: a new method to estimate age at death in white males. *American Journal of Physical Anthropology*, **65**, 147–156.

Iscan, M.Y., Loth, S.R. and Wright, R.K. (1985) Age estimation from the rib by phase analysis: white females. *American Journal of Physical Anthropology*, **30**, 853–863.

Iscan, M.Y., Loth, S.R. and Wright, R.K. (1987) Racial variation in the sternal extremity of the rib and its effect on age determination. *Journal of Forensic Sciences*, **32**, 452–466.

Jackes, M.K. (1985) Pubic symphysis age distributions. *American Journal of Physical Anthropology*, **68**, 281–299.

Jeanty, P., Kirkpatrick, C., Dramaix-Wilmet, M. and Struyven, J. (1981) Ultrasonic evaluation of fetal limb growth. *Radiology*, **140**, 165–168.

Joseph, J. (1951) The sesamoid bones of the hand and the time of fusion of the epiphyses of the thumb. *Journal of Anatomy*, **85**, 230–241.

Kalichman, L., Malkin, I., Seibel, M.J. *et al.* (2008) Age-related changes and secular trends in hand bone size. *Homo*, **59**, 301–315.

Kant, S.G., Grote, F., De Ru, M.H. *et al.* (2007) Radiographic evaluation of children with growth disorders. *Hormone Research*, **68**, 310–315.

Keen, J.A. and Wainwright, J. (1958) Ossification of the thyroid, cricoid and arytenoids cartilages. *South African Journal of Laboratory and Clinical Medicine*, **4**, 83–108.

Kimura, K. (1976) Growth of the second metacarpal according to chronological age and skeletal maturation. *Anatomical Record*, **184**, 147–157.

Kimura, K. (1983) Skeletal maturity and bone growth in twins. *American Journal of Physical Anthropology*, **60**, 491–497.

Kimura, K. (1984) Studies on growth and development in Japan. *Yearbook of Physical Anthropology*, **27**, 179–214.

Koc, A., Karaoglanoglu, M., Erdogan, M. *et al.* (2001) Assessment of bone ages: is the Greulich–Pyle method sufficient for Turkish boys? *Pediatrics International*, **43**, 662–665.

Konigsberg, L.W., Herrmann, N.P., Wescott, D.J. and Kimmerle, E.H. (2008) Estimation and evidence in forensic anthropology: age-at-death. *Journal of Forensic Sciences*, **53**, 541–557.

Kreitner, K.F., Schweden, F.J., Riepert, T. *et al.* (1998) Bone age determination based on the study of the medial extremity of the clavicle. *European Radiology*, **8**, 1116–1122.

Krogman, W.M. and Iscan, M.Y. (1986) *The Human Skeleton in Forensic Medicine*, Charles C. Thomas, Springfield, IL.

Krook, P.M., Wawrukiewicz, A.S. and Hackethorn, J.C. (1985) Caveats in the sonographic determination of fetal femur length for estimation of gestational age. *Radiology*, **154**, 823–824.

Kucukkeles, N., Acar, A., Biren, S. and Arun, T. (1999) Comparisons between cervical vertebrae and hand–wrist maturation for the assessment of skeletal maturity. *Journal of Clinical Pediatric Dentistry*, **24** (1), 47–52.

Lamparski, D.G. (1972) Skeletal age assessment utilizing cervical vertebrae, Master of Science Thesis, University of Pittsburg, PA.

Laor, T. and Jaramillo, D. (2009) MR imaging insights into skeletal maturation: what is normal? *Radiology*, **250**, 29–38.

Lee, S.-H., Modi, H., Song, H.-R. *et al.* (2009) Deceleration in maturation of bone during adolescent age in achondroplasia – a retrospective study using RUS scoring system. *Skeletal Radiology*, **38**, 165–170.

Little, B.B. and Malina, R.M. (2007) Gene–environment interaction in skeletal maturity and body dimensions of urban Oaxaca Mestizo schoolchildren. *Annals of Human Biology*, **34**, 216–225.

Lovejoy, C.O., Meindl, R.S., Pryzbeck, T.R. and Mensforth, R.P. (1985) Chronological metamorphosis of the auricular surface of the ilium: a new method for the determination of age at death. *American Journal of Physical Anthropology*, **68**, 15–28.

Lovell, G., Galloway, H., Hopkins, W. and Harvey, A. (2006) Osteitis pubis and assessment of bone marrow edema at the pubic symphysis with MRI in an elite junior male soccer squad. *Clinical Journal of Sport Medicine*, **16**, 117–122.

Lynnerup, N., Belard, E., Buch-Olsen, K. *et al.* (2008) Intra- and interobserver error of the Greulich–Pyle method as used in a Danish forensic sample. *Forensic Science International*, **179**, 242.e1–242.e6.

Madeline, L.A. and Elster, A.D. (1995) Suture closure in the human chondrocranium: CT assessment. *Radiology*, **196**, 747–756.

Mahony, B.S., Callen, P.W. and Filly, R.A. (1985) The distal femoral epiphyseal ossification center in the assessment of third-trimester menstrual age: sonosgraphic identification and measurement. *Radiology*, **155**, 201–204.

Malina, R.M. (1971) A consideration of factors underlying the selection of methods in the assessment of skeletal maturity. *American Journal of Physical Anthropology*, **35**, 341–346.

Malina, R.M., Dompier, T.P., Powell, J.W. *et al.* (2007) Validation of a noninvasive maturity estimate relative to skeletal age in youth football players. *Clinical Journal of Sport Medicine*, **17**, 362–368.

Maresh, M.M. (1970) Measurements from roentgenograms. in *Human Growth and Development* (ed. R.W. McCammon), C.C. Thomas, Springfield, IL, pp. 157–200.

Maresh, M.M. (1971) Single versus serial assessment of skeletal age: either, both or neither. *American Journal of Physical Anthropology*, **35**, 387–392.

Maresh, M.M. (1972) A forty-five year investigation for secular changes in physical maturation. *American Journal of Physical Anthropology*, **36**, 103–109.

Maresh, M.M. and Deming, J. (1939) The growth of the long bones in 80 infants. Roentgenograms versus anthropometry. *Child Development*, **10**, 91–106.

Matsuoka, H., Sato, K., Sugihara, S. and Murata, M. (1999) Bone maturation reflects the secular trend in growth. *Hormone Research*, **52**, 125–130.

Mazrani, W., McHugh, K. and Marsden, P.J. (2007) The radiation burden of radiological investigations. *Archives of Disease in Childhood*, **92**, 1127–1131.

McCormick, W.F. (1980) Mineralisation of the costal cartilages as an indicator of age: preliminary observations. *Journal of Forensic Sciences*, **25**, 736–741.

McCormick, W.F. and Stewart, J.H. (1988) Age related changes in the human plastron:

a roetenogenographic and morphological study. *Journal of Forensic Sciences*, **33**, 100–120.

McKern, T.W. and Stewart, T.D. (1957) Skeletal age changes in young american males, analysed from the standpoint of age identification, technical report EP-45, Headquarters Quatermaster Research and Development Command, Natwick, MA.

Meijerman, L., Maat, G.J.R., Schulz, R. and Schmeling, A. (2007) Variables affecting the probability of complete fusion of the medial clavicular epiphysis. *International Journal of Legal Medicine*, **121**, 463–468.

Meindl, R.S. and Lovejoy, C.O. (1985) Ectocranial suture closure: a revised method for the determination of skeletal age at death based on the lateral-anterior sutures. *American Journal of Physical Anthropology*, **68**, 57–66.

Molinari, L., Gasser, T. and Largo, R.H. (2004) TW3 bone age: RUS/CB and gender differences of percentiles for score and score increments. *Annals of Human Biology*, **31**, 421–435.

Mora, S., Boechat, M., Pietka, E. *et al.* (2001) Skeletal age determinations in children of European and African descent: applicability of the Greulich and Pyle standards. *Pediatric Research*, **50**, 624–628.

Moss, M.L. and Noback, C.R. (1958) A longitudinal study of digital epiphyseal fusion in adolescence. *Anatomical Record*, **131**, 19–32.

Nakahara, K., Utsuki, S., Shimizu, S. *et al.* (2006) Age dependence of fusion of pimary occipital sutures: a radiographic study. *Child's Nervous System*, **22**, 1457–1459.

O'Connor, J.E., Bogue, C., Spence, L.D. and Last, J. (2008) A method to establish the relationship between chronological age and stage of union from radiographic assessment of epiphyseal fusion at the knee: an Irish population study. *Journal of Anatomy*, **212**, 198–209.

O'Halloran, R.L. and Lundy, J.K. (1987) Age and ossification of the hyoid bone: forenisc implications. *Journal of Forensic Sciences*, **32**, 1655–1659.

O'Reilly, M.T. and Yanniello, G.J. (1988) Mandibular growth changes and maturation of cervical vertebrae. *The Angle Orthodontist*, **58** (2), 179–184.

Ogden, J.A. (2000) Anatomy and physiology of skeletal development, in *Skeletal Injury in the Child*, 3rd edn, Springer, New York, pp. 1–37.

Ontell, F.K., Ivanovic, M., Ablin, D.S. and Barlow, T.W. (1996) Bone age in children of diverse ethnicity. *American Journal of Roentgenography*, **167**, 1395–1398.

Ott, W.J. (2006) Sonographic diagnosis of fetal growth restriction. *Clinical Obstetrics and Gynecology*, **49**, 295–307.

Özer, B.K. (2008) Secular trend in body height and weight of Turkish adults. *Anthropological Science*, **116**, 191–199.

Passalacqua, N.V. (2009) Forensic age-at-death estimation from the human sacrum. *Journal of Forensic Sciences*, **54**, 255–262.

Piercecchi-Marti, M.D., Adalian, P., Bourliere-Najean, B. *et al.* (2002) Validation of a radiographic method to establish new fetal growth standards: radio-anatomical correlation. *Journal of Forensic Sciences*, **47**, 328–331.

Pludowski, P., Lebiedowski, M. and Lorenc, R.S. (2004) Evaluation of the possibility to assess bone age on the basis of DXA derived hand scans – preliminary results. *Osteoporosis International*, **15**, 317–322.

Poland, J. (1898) *Skiagraphic Atlas Showing the Development of the Bones of the Wrist and Hand*, Smith, Elder & Co, London.

Pretorius, D.H., Nelson, T.R. and Manco-Johnson, M.L. (1984) Fetal age estimation by ultrasound: the impact of measurement errors. *Radiology*, **152**, 763–766.

Pyle, S.I. and Hoerr, N.L. (1969) *A Radiographic Standard of Reference for the Growing Knee*, Charles C. Thomas, Springfield, IL.

Pyle, S.I., Waterhouse, A.M. and Greulich, W.W. (1971) *Radiographic Standard of Skeletal Development of the Hand and Wrist*, Stanford University Press, Stanford, CA.

Ramsthaler, F., Proschek, P., Betz, W. and Verhoff, M. (2009) How reliable are the risk estimates for X-ray examinations in forensic age estimations? A safety update. *International Journal of Legal Medicine*, **123**, 199–204.

RCPCH (2007) X-rays and asylum seeking children: policy statement, Royal College of Paediatrics and Child Health.

Reem, J., Carney, J., Stanley, M. and Cassidy, J. (2009) Risser sign inter-rater and intra-rater agreement: is the Risser sign reliable? *Skeletal Radiology*, **38**, 371–378.

Rejtarová, O., Hejna, P., Soukup, T. and Kuchar, M. (2009) Age and sexually dimorphic changes in costal cartilages: a preliminary microscopic study. *Forensic Science International*, **193** (1–3), 72–78.

Richter, J. and Kern, G. (1987) Secular changes in the development of children born in Goerlitz, German Democratic Republic, 1956 to 1967. *Human Biology*, **59**, 345–355.

Rikhasor, R.M., Qureshi, A.M., Rathi, S.L. and Channa, N.A. (1999) Skeletal maturity in Pakistani children. *Journal of Anatomy*, **195**, 305–308.

Rios, L., Weisensee, K. and Rissech, C. (2008) Sacral fusion as an aid in age estimation. *Forensic Science International*, **180**, 111.e1–111.e7.

Rissech, C. and Black, S. (2007) Scapular development from the neonatal period to skeletal maturity: a preliminary study. *International Journal of Osteoarchaeology*, **17**, 451–464.

Rizzoli, R. (2008) Nutrition: its role in bone health. *Best Practice and Research. Clinical Endocrinology and Metabolism*, **22**, 813–829.

Roberts, D.F. (1994) Secular trends in growth and maturation in British girls. *American Journal of Human Biology*, **6**, 13–18.

Roche, A.F., Chumlea, C. and Thissen, D. (1988) *Assessing the Skeletal Maturity of the Hand–Wrist: Fels Method*, Charles C. Thomas, Springfield, IL.

Roche, A.F. and French, N.Y. (1970) Differences in skeletal maturity levels between the knee and hand. *American Journal of Roentgenology*, **109**, 307–312.

Sadler, T.W. (1985) *Langman's Medical Embryology*, Williams & Wilkins, Baltimore, MD.

Salpou, D., Kiserud, T., Rasmussen, S. and Johnsen, S.L. (2008) Fetal age assessment based in 2nd trimester ultrasound in Africa and the effect of ethnicity. *BMC Pregnancy and Childbirth*, **30** (8), 48.

Savaridas, S.L., Huntely, J.S., Porter, D.E. *et al.* (2007) The rate of skeletal maturation in the Scottish population. A comparison across 25 years (1980–2005). *Journal of Pediatric Orthopaedics*, **27**, 952–954.

Schaefer, M.C., Black, S. and Scheuer, J.L. (2009) *Juvenile Osteology: A Practitioner's Guide*, Elsevier, London.

Scheuer, J.L. and Black, S. (2004) *The Juvenile Skeleton*, Elsevier, London.

Scheuer, L. and Black, S. (2000) *Developmental Juvenile Osteology*, Academic Press, London.

Schmeling, A., Reisinger, W., Loreck, D. *et al.* (2000) Effects of ethnicity on skeletal maturation: consequences for forensic age estimations. *International Journal of Legal Medicine*, **113**, 253–258.

Schmeling, A., Olze, A., Reisinger, W. *et al.* (2003) Forensic age diagnostics of living individuals in criminal proceedings. *Homo*, **54**, 162–169.

Schmeling, A., Schulz, R., Reisinger, W. *et al.* (2004) Studies on the time frame for ossification of the medial clavicular epiphyseal cartilage in conventional radiography. *International Journal of Legal Medicine*, **118**, 5–8.

Schmeling, A., Baumann, U., Schmidt, S. *et al.* (2006a) Reference data for the Thiemann–Nitz method of assessing skeletal age for the purpose of forensic age estimation. *International Journal of Legal Medicine*, **120**, 1–4.

Schmeling, A., Reisinger, W., Geserick, G. and Olze, A. (2006b) Age estimation of unaccompanied minors. Part I. General considerations. *Forensic Science International*, **159S**, S61–S64.

Schmeling, A., Schulz, R., Danner, B. and Rosing, F.W. (2006c) The impact of economic progress and modernization in medicine on the ossification of hand and wrist. *International Journal of Legal Medicine*, **120**, 121–126.

Schmidt, S., Koch, B., Schulz, R. *et al.* (2007) Comparative analysis of the applicability of the skeletal age determination methods of Greulich–Pyle and Thiemann–Nitz for forensic age estimation in living subjects. *International Journal of Legal Medicine*, **121**, 293–296.

Schmidt, S., Nitz, I., Schulz, R. and Schmeling, A. (2008) Applicability of the skeletal age determination method of Tanner and Whitehouse for forensic age diagnostics. *International Journal of Legal Medicine*, **122**, 309–314.

Schulz, R., Zwiesigk, P., Schiborr, M. *et al.* (2008) Ultrasound studies on the time course of clavicular ossification. *International Journal of Legal Medicine*, **122**, 163–167.

Schulze, D., Rother, U., Fuhrmann, A. *et al.* (2006) Correlation of age and ossification of the medial clavicular epiphysis using computed tomography. *Forensic Science International*, **158**, 184–189.

Semine, A.A. and Damon, A. (1975) Costochondral ossification and aging in five populations. *Human Biology*, **47**, 101–116.

Shirley, N.R. (2009) Age and sex estimation from the human clavicle: an investigation of traditional and novel methods, thesis, University of Tennessee, Knoxville.

Sidhom, G. and Derry, D.E. (1931) The dates of union of some epiphyses in egyptians from X-ray photographs. *Journal of Anatomy*, **65**, 196–211.

Sinha, A. and Gupta, V. (1995) A study on estimation of age from pubic symphysis. *Forensic Science International*, **75**, 73–78.

Soegiharto, B.M., Cunningham, S.J. and Moles, S.R. (2008a) Skeletal maturation in Indonesia and white children assessed with hand–wrist and cervical vertebrae methods. *American Journal of Orthodontics and Dentofacial Orthopedics*, **134**, 217–226.

Soegiharto, B.M., Moles, S.R. and Cunningham, S.J. (2008b) Discriminatory ability of the skeletal maturation index and the cervical vertebrae maturation index in detecting peak pubertal growth in Indonesian and white subjects with receiver operating characteristics analysis. *American Journal of Orthodontics and Dentofacial Orthopedics*, **134**, 227–237.

Stevenson, P.H. (1924) Age order of epiphyseal union in man. *American Journal of Physical Anthropology*, **7**, 53–93.

Stewart, T.D. (1958) The rate and development of vertebral osteo-arthritis in American whites and its significance in skeletal age identification. *The Leech*, **28**, 144–152.

Taipale, P. and Hiilesmaa, V. (2001) Predicting delivery date by ultrasound and last menstrual period in early gestation. *Obstetrics and Gynecology*, **97**, 189–194.

Takai, S. and Akiyoshi, T. (1983) Skeletal maturity of Japanese children in western Kyushu. *American Journal of Physical Anthropology*, **62**, 199–204.

Tanner, J.M. (1962) *Growth at Adolescence*, Blackwell Scientific, Oxford.

Tanner, J.M., Healy, M.J.R., Goldstein, H. and Cameron, N. (2001) *Assessment of Skeletal Maturity and Prediction of Adult Height (TW3 Method)*, W.B. Saunders, London.

Tanner, J.M., Whitehouse, R.H. and Healy, M.J.R. (1962) *A New System for Estimating Skeletal Maturity from the Hand and Wrist with Standards Derived from a Study of 2600 Healthy British Children. Part II. The Scoring System*, International Child Centre, Paris.

Tanner, J.M., Whitehouse, R.H., Marshall, W.A. *et al.* (1975) *Assessment of Skeletal Maturity and Prediction of Adult Height*, Academic Press, London.

Todd, T.W. (1937) *Atlas of Skeletal Maturation*, C.V. Mosby, St Louis, MO.

Todd, T.W. and D'Errico, J. (1928) The clavicular epipyses. *American Journal of Anatomy*, **41**, 25–50.

Tuite, M.J. and Desmet, A.A. (1994) MRI of selected sports injuries: muscle tears, groin pain, and osteochondritis dissecans. *Seminars in Ultrasound, CT, and MRI*, **15**, 318–340.

Tupman, G.S. (1962) A study of bone growth in normal children and its relationship to skeletal maturation. *Journal of Bone and Joint Surgery*, **44B**, 42–67.

Turk, L.M. and Hogg, D.A. (1993) Age changes in the human laryngeal cartilages. *Clinical Anatomy*, **6**, 154–162.

Tyvalsky, F.A. (2004) Nutrition influences bone growth in children. *Journal of Nutrition*, **134**, 689S–690S.

Ulijaszek, S.L., Johnston, F.E. and Preece, M.A. (eds) (1998) *The Cambridge Encyclopedia of Human Growth and Development*, Cambridge University Press, Cambridge.

Van Lenthe, F.J., Kemper, H.C. and Van Mechelen, W. (1998) Skeletal maturation in adolescence: a comparison between the Tanner–Whitehouse II and the Fels method. *European Journal of Pediatrics*, **157**, 798–801.

Van Rijn, R.R. and Lequin, M.H. (2009) Automatic determination of Greulich and Pyle bone age in healthy Dutch children. *Pediatric Radiology*, **39**, 591–597.

Varich, L.J., Laor, T. and Jaramillo, D. (2000) Normal maturation of the distal femoral epiphyseal cartilage: age-related changes at MR imaging. *Radiology*, **214**, 705–709.

Vignolo, M., Naselli, A., Magliano, P. *et al.* (1999) Use of the new US90 standards for TW-RUS skeletal maturity scores in youths from the Italian population. *Hormone Research*, **51**, 168–172.

Wagner, U.A., Diedrich, V. and Schmitt, O. (1995) Determination of skeletal maturity by ultrasound: a preliminary report. *Skeletal Radiology*, **24**, 417–420.

Webb, P.A.O. and Suchey, J.M. (1985) Epiphyseal union of the anterior iliac crest and medial clavicle in a modern multiracial sample of American males and females. *American Journal of Physical Anthropology*, **68**, 457–466.

Whitaker, J.M., Rousseau, L., Williams, T. *et al.* (2002) Scoring system for estimating age in the foot skeleton. *American Journal of Physical Anthropology*, **118**, 385–392.

Yavuz, M.F., Iscan, M.Y. and Cologlu, A.S. (1998) Age assessment by rib phase analysis in Turks. *Forensic Science International*, **98**, 47–54.

Yeager, V.L., Lawson, C. and Archer, C. (1982) Ossification of the laryngeal cartilages as it relates to computed tomography. *Investigative Radiology*, **17**, 11–19.

Zhang, A., Sayre, J.W., Vachon, L. *et al.* (2009) Racial differences in growth patterns of children assessed on the basis of bone age. *Radiology*, **250**, 228–235.

Zhen-Wang, B. and Cheng-Ye, J. (2005) Secular growth changes in body height and weight in children and adolescents in Shandong, China between 1939 and 2000. *Annals of Human Biology*, **32**, 650–665.

12

Age Evaluation after Growth Cessation

Anil Aggrawal[1], Puneet Setia[2], Avneesh Gupta[3] and Anthony Busuttil[4]
[1]*Maulana Azad Medical College, New Delhi, 110002, India*
[2]*Department of Forensic Medicine, Vir Chandra Singh Garhwali Government Medical Sciences and Research Institute, Srinagar, Garhwal, Uttrakhand, India*
[3]*Cochise County Medical Examiner, 75 Colonia de Sauld, Suite 200D, Sierra Vista, AZ 85635, USA*
[4]*Forensic Medicine Unit, Medical School, University of Edinburgh, Edinburgh, EH 8 9 A G*

Previous chapters have explored methods of estimating age in a variety of settings. While it is possible to estimate an age range in younger individuals, problems arise when the person has attained maturity and there are no growth parameters that one can use. In such situations, one has to rely on the changes in the body that occur due to other ageing processes. This chapter discusses such changes.

12.1 Background

Age estimation has always been an important topic in medical, legal and anthropological settings. The majority of the work has been undertaken for younger individuals who have not reached adult status (Aggrawal and Busuttil, 1991; Aggrawal, 2000, 2003). In most of the Western world, birth records are officially and promptly issued, retained by the individual and stored in an efficient and retrievable means. Therefore, age estimation in the living is mainly required for those people who present as refugees or are not native of that country and their age is required for some legal purposes (Schmeling *et al.*, 2001). The situation is different in the developing world. Here, birth records may not be issued and are frequently not stored efficiently,

Age Estimation in the Living: The Practitioners Guide   Sue Black, Anil Aggrawal and Jason Payne-James
© 2010 John Wiley & Sons, Ltd

thereby necessitating age estimation at any given age (Aggrawal, 2009). Sometimes, there might be very peculiar situations that may warrant the need of such facilities (Chaturvedi, 2008; Prakash, 2009). A case that the authors (A.A., P.S., A.G.) encountered was where after the death of an individual, his widow was offered employment by the government, but there was no record of her age and simply by looking at her physical appearance, she seemed to be older than the maximum age of entry into service. Another such unusual case has been depicted in Figures 12.1 and 12.2.

Age, as determined by the examination of the living person, is always given in the form of a range. As has been seen in earlier chapters, in children the range usually varies from a few weeks (in infants) to about 1–5 years (until adulthood is achieved, which is usually in the early 20s). The situation in adults is very different. Once the developmental growth of the individual ceases, the variation in age determination increases substantially. In early adulthood it is in the range of a few years, which increases to more than a decade in the elderly (Rösing *et al.*, 2007; Wittwer-Backofen *et al.*, 2008). Therefore, it must be remembered that as the age of the individual increases, the probability of assigning a close match to chronological age decreases. Medico-legally there is therefore a balance to be struck. Accuracy of age prediction is of greater significance for the child, when the markers permit a closer relationship with chronological age, perhaps to within a few months or single figure years, whereas in the adult such specificity may not be so critical and therefore, and rather conveniently, a wider range is generally more acceptable.

12.2 Consent

This text considers age determination in the living. Whenever we are dealing with the examination of the living, consent is of paramount importance. Every country and every jurisdiction will have either implicit or explicit definitions of consent pertaining to its various practitioners (see Chapter 4). In Indian law, consent is defined in the Contract Act, which states that two or more persons are said to consent when they agree upon the same thing in the same sense. Though this provision is for the Contract Act, it is fairly reasonable to conclude that it can be applied to varied situations, most notably medical examination and treatment. Also, examination of a person without his/her consent can result in complaints to professional bodies or potential criminal charges of assault (see Chapter 4). If directed by a judge it may be appropriate for a practitioner to seek legal advice when faced with the need to undertake a process involving physical contact without consent. Since most of the time the request is from the law enforcement authorities, it is best for them to deal with the situation by simply informing them, in writing, that the person sent for examination has refused to give consent and thus could not be examined (Figure 12.3).

12.3 Radiology

Radiology is a vital investigative technique that can be utilized for establishing age in both the living and the deceased individual. The non-invasive nature of radiology,

इंडियन ऑयल कार्पोरेशन लिमिटेड
नार्दन रीजन :
इंडियन ऑयल भवन,
यूसुफ सराय, नई दिल्ली-110016

INDIAN OIL CORPORATION LTD.
Northern Region :
Indian Oil Bhawan, Yusuf Sarai, New Delhi-110016
Tel. : 2651 8080   Gram : INDIANOIL

मार्केटिंग डिविज़न
Marketing Division

Ref. : [_____]2007   Date : 31.3.2008

Dr. Anil Aggarwal.
Professor of Forensic Medicine Deptt.
Maulana Azad Medical College,
New Delhi.

Dear Sir,

Sub: <u>Verification of age of workmen</u>

We refer to our copy of memo ref. [_____] dated 28.2.08
from the Dean, Maulana Azad Medical College, New Delhi, nominating you as
Chairman, Faculty Members of the Forensic Medicine Department, constituted
for ascertaining the age of employees of Indian Oil Corporation, as per our
request vide letter of even ref. dated 06.02.2008. The other Faulty members are
[_____]

Accordingly, we would request you to kindly advise us the availability of the
Faculty Members to enable us to keep our all nine employees available for their
examination for ascertaining their age.

In view of urgency, we shall be grateful if you could kindly give your consent for
examination of the employees at the earliest. On receiving your confirmation, we
shall keep our employees informed to make sure their availability before the
Faculty Members on the date/time advised by you.   We may mention here that a
majority of the nine employees are posted outside Delhi and therefore, we shall
require a minimum of seven days for intimation/reporting here for their age
verification.

Thanking you,

Yours faithfully,
For INDIAN OIL CORPORATION LIMITED

रजि. ऑफिस : जी-9, अली यावर जंग मार्ग, बान्द्रा (पूर्वी) मुम्बई – 400 051
REGD. OFFICE G-9, ALI YAVAR JUNG MARG, BANDRA (EAST) MUMBAI - 400 051

Figure 12.1   An unusual case that was brought to the author (A.A.) in which there
was a merger of two corporate houses and in which the buying company disputed
the age of the employees of the other company, who had been recruited by that
company several years previously.

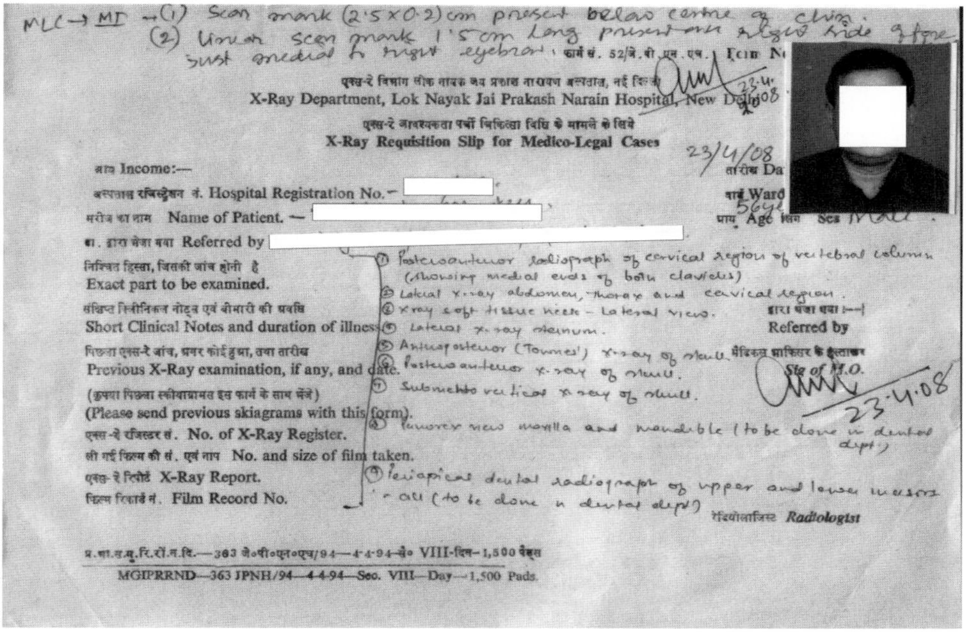

Figure 12.2 A typical X-ray form as used by the authors (A.A., P.S., A.G.). The present form was used for the case outlined in Figure 12.1 (by A.A.).

in addition to its economic benefits and ready availability, makes it an ideal and preferred investigative method for the estimation of age. It must be remembered that most of the studies quoted in the present chapter have been undertaken on the deceased.

12.3.1 Pubic Bones

The symphyseal surface of the pubic bone has long been recognized as a valuable area of the skeleton for age determination in adults. Ever since Todd first described the age-related changes seen on this joint surface (Todd, 1921), it has remained one of the most widely studied areas of the adult skeleton for age estimation. Over the years, many methods of age estimation have been developed using the pubic bone, including the pubic length and ischiopubic index (Rissech and Malgosa, 2007), acetabulum (Lovejoy et al., 1985; Buckberry and Chamberlain, 2002; Igarashi et al., 2005; Rissech et al., 2007; Rougé-Maillart et al., 2007, 2009), the symphyseal surfaces of the pubic bones (Hanihara and Suzuki, 1978; Meindl et al., 1985; Katz and Suchey, 1986), using digital images of pubic symphysis (Schmitt et al., 2002; Sitchon and Hoppa, 2005), auricular surface of the ilium (Buckberry and Chamberlain, 2002; Rougé-Maillart et al., 2004, 2009; Igarashi et al., 2005) and sacrum (Ríos, Weisensee and Rissech, 2008). However, almost all of these studies evaluated age estimation in the deceased after removal of the pubic bone during autopsy. With the advent of

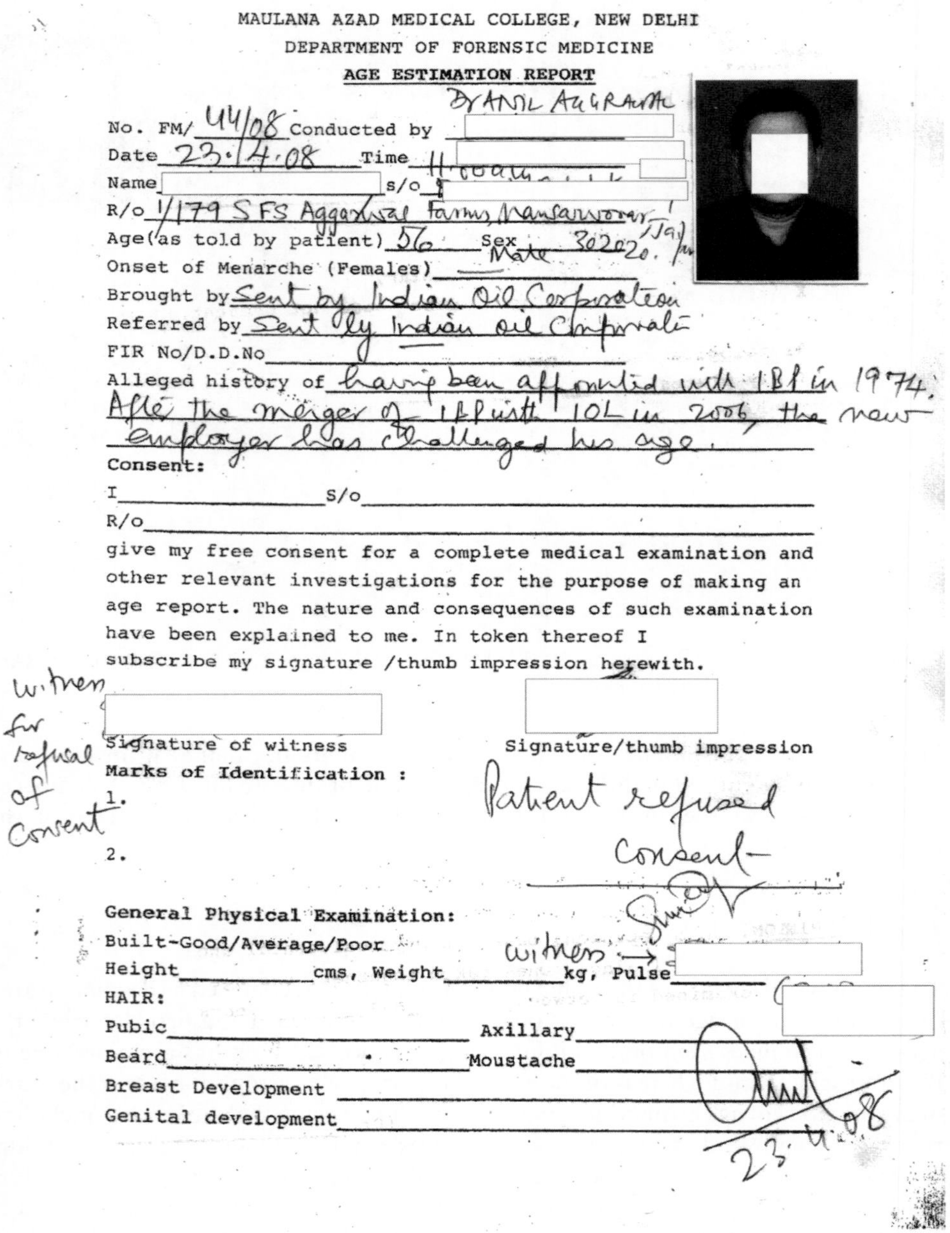

MAULANA AZAD MEDICAL COLLEGE, NEW DELHI
DEPARTMENT OF FORENSIC MEDICINE
AGE ESTIMATION REPORT

No. FM/ 44/08 Conducted by _DrANIL AGGRAWAL_
Date 23.4.08 Time 11.00am
Name _____ s/o _____
R/o 1/179 SFS Aggarwal farms, Mansarovar,
Age (as told by patient) 56   Sex Male 302020, 19/
Onset of Menarche (Females) _____
Brought by Sent by Indian Oil Corporation
Referred by Sent by Indian Oil Corporation
FIR No/D.D.No _____
Alleged history of having been appointed with IBP in 1974.
After the merger of IBP with IOL in 2006, the new
employer has challenged his age.
Consent:

I _____ S/o _____
R/o _____
give my free consent for a complete medical examination and
other relevant investigations for the purpose of making an
age report. The nature and consequences of such examination
have been explained to me. In token thereof I
subscribe my signature /thumb impression herewith.

witnen
for
refusal
of
consent

Signature of witness   Signature/thumb impression
Marks of Identification :
1.   Patient refused
2.   consent

General Physical Examination:
Built-Good/Average/Poor
Height_____ cms, Weight_____ kg, Pulse_____   witnen →
HAIR:
Pubic_____ Axillary_____
Beard_____ Moustache_____
Breast Development _____
Genital development_____

23.4.08

Figure 12.3 A case where the person refused to give consent for his examination and how the same was recorded.

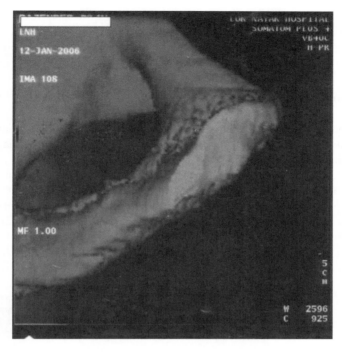

Figure 12.4 CT scan image of the pubic symphysis of a 52-year-old man (three-dimensional shaded surface display with slices of 1 mm).

modern technology, that handicap looks likely to be overcome, as is shown in Figure 12.4, where the computerized tomography (CT) scan of a person was used for age determination.

A preliminary study using CT images for estimation of age in the pubic bone has shown encouraging results (Ferrant *et al.*, 2009).[1] Although this study had many shortcomings, including a small sample size and limited matching characteristics, it showed that with further detailed study, this bone may be utilized effectively for age evaluation in the living in due course. Pasquier examined CT images of the pubic symphysis, albeit in the deceased, and found that it gave more reliable predictions of age when compared to direct observation of the bone surface (Pasquier *et al.*, 1999). This method gave a standard deviation of 7.3 years compared to the 10.18 years that is given by the Suchey–Brooks method (Katz and Suchey, 1986). Telmon compared direct observation with CT images for age estimation using the Suchey–Brooks method and found that there was little difference between the two (Telmon *et al.*, 2005), thereby implying that this method may be of value for age evaluation in the living with further work. An important point must always be remembered when using pubic bones for age estimation – in females, child bearing produces marked changes in the pubic bones, which can influence the accuracy of

---

[1] This study was undertaken on the individual bones after autopsy.

age evaluation (Stewart, 1957). Also, in older females, the progression of changes visualized on the bone surface may be different from those seen in males of the same age and some parameters cannot be used for age determination in both sexes with the same degree of reliability (Berg, 2008).

12.3.2   Long Bones

The long bones of the body are important age indicators in the growing child through the appearance and fusion of the epiphyses and the length of the diaphysis. It is considered that once the epiphyses have completed fusion, the long bones are of limited value for the purpose of age estimation. However, it has been shown that the trabecular pattern of the long bones can be highly individualistic and can be used for the purpose of positive identification (Mann, 1998). Utilizing this concept, some studies have evaluated the relationship between loss of trabecular bone in relation to age as witnessed via radiological means, as shown in Figure 12.5. Schranz undertook extensive work on the humerus and found that changes in the trabecular pattern at the proximal end correlated well with the age of the individual (Schranz,

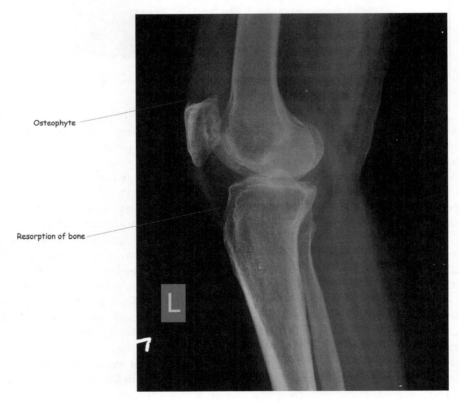

Figure 12.5   X-ray view of the knee joint, showing resorption of tibia and presence of osteophyte in patella.

1959). He divided these changes into various age cohorts, ranging from two years during puberty to a decade and a half during the sixth and seventh decades of life. With the advent of magnetic resonance imaging (MRI) and high resolution CT imaging techniques, the internal structure of the bones may now be better visualized in the living and used for age estimation. This work requires to be investigated and developed further.

One of the earlier studies designed to assess the age of adults from radiological images of the long bones utilized the proximal femur, proximal humerus, clavicle and calcaneus from individuals that comprise the Hamman–Todd collection (Walker and Lovejoy, 1985). The authors examined radiolucency of the trabecular framework and arranged the progressive changes in serial batches of five-year intervals. The radiographs were then examined using an optical densitometer and compared directly with the serially arranged radiographs to assess compatibility and evaluate the age of the individual. They found that the clavicle and the proximal femur showed the strongest correlation with age, with the clavicle being the most accurate. They divided the changes in both the bones into eight phases, starting from 18 years of age to more than 60 years of age.

The cortical thickness of the clavicle was used as a measure of age estimation by Kaur and Jit (1990), who investigated horizontal or parasagittal sections to measure the cortical thickness and consequently assess this in relation to the age of the individual. Similar results have been obtained on chest radiographs (Anton, 1969; Helela, 1969), showing that it is a possibility for further investigation.

A passing reference is made regarding age changes in the external dimensions of the long bones. In the single study of this type (Pfeiffer, 1980), it was found that various parameters, including maximum length, physiological length, maximum and minimum diameter and so on have a positive, although not strong, correlation with age. Although this aspect of human development has not been studied much for forensic purposes, it may also be a future source of investigation but currently has little value in age estimation procedures.

12.3.3 Skull Sutures

The pattern and progression of closure of the sutures of the skull have been studied quite extensively for more than 150 years. Although there were some pioneer researchers in the nineteenth century, including Gratiolet, Humphry, Welcker, Sauvage and so on, it was Todd who was the first to formalize the approach by providing formulae for age prediction from this feature (Todd and Lyon, 1924, 1925a,b,c). However, all of these early works were performed on individual skulls removed either during autopsies or as a result of anatomical dissection. A detailed description of this work has been summarized by Ashley-Montagu in his review article (Ashley-Montagu, 1938). It must be noted at this stage that the advancement in technology makes it possible to view virtually all aspects of the body, including skull sutures. So the methods that have been devised for age estimation in the deceased (Perizonius, 1984) may be considered of value for age evaluation in the living by exploiting present day imaging technologies, as shown in Figure 12.6.

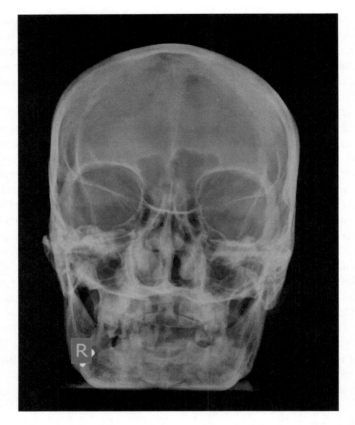

Figure 12.6   CT image of a 60-year-old man. The cranial sutures are obliterated.

Skull sutures commence closure endocranially in the late teens and early 20s and continue to do so progressively until completion when the individual is elderly (likely to be more than 60 years old; Meindl and Lovejoy, 1985; see Table 12.1). Indeed, Israel (1977) showed that the skull keeps growing even after the person reaches adult age. The overall effect of this on suture closure has yet to be investigated. However, it must be remembered that the relationship between progression of cranial suture closure and chronological age is not strong and therefore if used for age prediction it must be accompanied by a large range, which may vary from about 7 to 14 years or more (Meindl and Lovejoy, 1985). There is a general misconception that the skull sutures close earlier in females than in males and it is also described as an exception to the general rule that all parameters for age determination appear earlier in females. However, it has been shown that neither sex nor ethnicity appear to have any significant bearing on the age of closure of skull sutures (Meindl and Lovejoy, 1985).

Obliteration of the maxillary sutures can also be used for the estimation of age. The four sutures, that is the incisive, the anterior median palatine, the transverse palatine and the posterior median palatine, have been studied and have been

Table 12.1 Order in which the skull sutures commence and terminate closure.

Order of closure	Commencement		Termination	
	Lateral-anterior	*Vault*	*Lateral-anterior*	*Vault*
1	Pterion	Obelion	Pterion	Obelion
2	Midcoronal	Pterion	Sphenofrontal	Pterion
3	Sphenofrontal	Anterior sagittal	Midcoronal	Anterior sagittal
4	Inferior sphenotemporal	Lambda	Inferior sphenotemporal	Lambda
5	Superior sphenotemporal	Midlambdoid	Superior sphenotemporal	Bregma
6	—	Midcoronal	—	Midlambdoid
7	—	Bregma	—	Midcoronal

(Meindl and Lovejoy, 1985).

found to be positively correlated with age (Mann, Symes and Bass, 1987; Mann *et al.*, 1991). The ages for their obliteration have been recorded as shown in Table 12.2.

As a means of age estimation, the maxillary sutures have been reported to be both accurate (Ginter, 2005) and inaccurate (Gruspier and Mullen, 1991). Consequently, this feature has not been used widely for this purpose. The same is true for the frontosphenoidal sutures, which in autopsy specimens have given an age range of ±23 years, which is too wide to be used in routine practice (Dorandeu *et al.*, 2008).

It is pertinent to mention here that skull sutures are not necessarily of robust value for age estimation. Some authors have shown that the closure of skull sutures is largely independent of age and are in fact more heavily based on the sex of the individual or genetic factors (Hershkovitz *et al.*, 1997).

Table 12.2 Order in which the maxillary sutures obliterate (in females)[a].

Order of closure	Suture	Age of commencement of closure (years)	Age of termination of closure (years)
1	Incisive suture	16	20
2	Posterior median palatine	22	26
3	Transverse palatine	25	84
4	Anterior median palatine	27	67

(Mann *et al.*, 1991)
[a] Since females give a better estimate of age compared to males, only the values for females have been included.

12.3.4 Costal Cartilages

McCormick was one of the earliest researchers to utilize chest plate radiographs for age determination. He examined the mineralization of the costal cartilages in the specimens removed at the time of autopsy (McCormick, 1980) and found that the presence of any mineralization in the costal cartilage was a strong indicator that the person was likely to be at least in their third decade, and dense mineralization indicated that the individual was likely to be at least of middle age. This method was modified by adding four more criteria that improved the accuracy of this method (Barrès, Durigon and Paraire 1989). The five criteria are:

- Bone demineralization (BD)

- Fusion of the first costal cartilage to the manubrium (FM)

- Rib to cartilage attachment changes (RC)

- Cartilage mineralization (CM)

- Cartilage to sternum attachment changes (CS)

Each of these parameters is given a score from 1 to 5, with 1 being very light and 5 being very heavy. Whatever score is given to each parameter, it is multiplied by 15 and then the following equation is used for finding the age of the individual:

$$\text{Age} = \text{CS} \times 0.89 + \text{FM} \times 0.03 + \text{RC} \times 0.03 + \text{CM} \times 0.03 + \text{BD} \times 0.02$$

This regression equation is reported to give a root mean square deviation of ± 8.43 years and a 95% confidence interval of ± 17 years.

Figure 12.7 shows the CT of a 20-year-old woman with non-fused costal cartilages. It shows that all the parameters that have been mentioned in the preceding paragraph can be easily visualized in the living using CT scan.

12.3.4.1 Sternum The sternum has also been studied for the purpose of age estimation in both the living and the dead. Stewart studied the ossification of various parts of sternum in different age groups (Stewart, 1954). He gave a rough estimate of the ages of ossification of these parts, which has stood the test of time until now. In the dead, various features of the sternum have been used for the purpose of age determination. These features include (i) lateral projection of sternal manubrium; (ii) superciliary arch-shaped prominence on the ventral side of sternal manubrium; (iii) the second costal incisure of sternum and sternal synchondroses; (iv) radial stripes on the ventral side of the sternal body; (v) the other costal incisarae of sternum; and (vi) the lower part of the dorsal side of the sternum. It has been shown that these features have a strong correlation with age (correlation coefficient $R = 0.9774$ and standard deviation of ± 2.2 years (Sun, Zhao and Yan, 1995). In the living, the authors use the X-ray image of the sternum to determine the age of an individual on the basis of

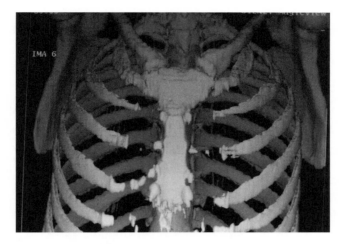

Figure 12.7 Spiral CT of a 20-year-old woman. It shows the non-fused costal cartilages. It shows that the modern imaging modalities can be used quite effectively in
the living for age determination.

the appearance and fusion of the various parts of the sternum as described in Figure
12.8, and an example of the same is shown in Figure 12.9 in the case of an adolescent
boy.

12.3.5   Vertebrae

Degenerative changes occur in the vertebral column with advancing age and they
can be used as indicators of age with some degree of caution. These changes include
epiphyseal union, osteophyte formation and ossification of longitudinal ligaments
(Gillett *et al.*, 1988; Nakai, 2001). Osteophytes usually begin to form after the age

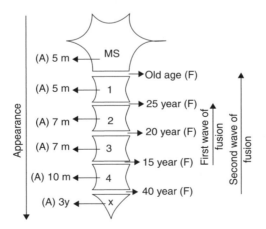

Figure 12.8   Order of appearance and fusion of various parts of the sternum.

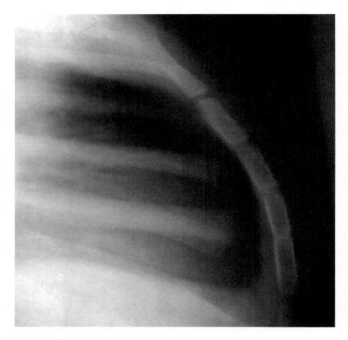

Figure 12.9   Chest radiograph showing the sternum. Only the third and the fourth sternebrae are fused with each other, indicating that the age of the person is between 15 and 20 years.

of 30 (shown in Figure 12.10) and may therefore be of value for age assessment in the adult, and have been used successfully in the elderly (Snodgrass, 2004). Osteophytes can be graded into four stages, 0 through 3, based on their height (Watanabe and Terazawa, 2006). However, this study was undertaken on autopsy samples and its validity on living individuals using radiological findings is still to be verified. The osteophytes are examined on each surface of the vertebral column and the maximum value at any of the surfaces in each vertebra is taken for the calculation. The average maximum values at the cervical, thoracic and lumbar regions can then be combined as an 'osteophyte formation index' and age can be estimated using the following regression equations:

Age = 37.90 + 12.07X (in males)
Age = 26.67 + 18.64X (in females)

where X = osteophyte formation index.

The confidence index of this method is reported to be 68% and the standard error for different parts of the vertebral column varies from 10.7 to 16.2, being greater in females than in males, and in both sexes, maximum in lumbar and thoracic regions and least in the cervical region.

In addition to osteophytes, the height of the body of lumbar vertebrae can also be used in age evaluation (Allbrook, 1956). This is achieved by measuring both the

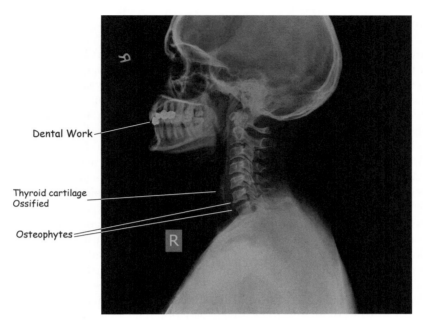

Figure 12.10 X-ray of the neck of a 55-year-old woman showing presence of osteophytes and calcification of thyroid cartilage.

posterior and anterior vertebral body height of all the five lumbar vertebrae. The mean of the posterior heights was found to be 133.67 mm at the age of 35 years, with an annual increment of 0.24 mm. For anterior heights, the mean was 131.0 mm at the age of 35 years with an annual increment of 0.20 mm. It should be borne in mind that these values are for both males and females and given the nature of sexual dimorphism this is not likely to be appropriate and sex-specific changes should be examined. With advancing age, the vertebral bodies eventually begin to decrease in height with loss of internal structural integrity and damage to end plates. Mosekilde (1990) reported a decrease in vertebral height with advancing age for both sexes. The height–breadth index (ratio of anterior height and transverse breadth), biconcavity index, average biconcavity index and the intervertebral disc height are some other parameters that have been assessed for the purpose of age determination using vertebrae (Ericksen, 1976, 1978a,b; Twomey and Taylor, 1985; Shao, Rompe and Schiltenwolf, 2002). But the findings need to be individualized for each ethnic group as each feature responds differently in each vertebra and in each ethnic group. These are promising findings but due to lack of extensive data, they are presently not being used.

Bone mineral content of the vertebrae is another feature that is well documented in the clinical literature as a characteristic that is age dependent. Although there is insufficient data to suggest that it has a predictive capacity, the little that is available suggests that this might also warrant further investigation (Sabatier *et al.*, 1999).

12.3.6   Laryngeal Cartilages

The laryngeal cartilages, principally the thyroid and cricoid cartilages, undergo calcification and/or ossification with advancing age (as shown in Figure 12.10), although it has been identified in individuals as young as 16 to 17 years (Hatley, Samuel and Evison, 1965; Curtis *et al.*, 1985) to about 30 years (Ajmani, Jain and Saxena, 1980). The pattern and volume of calcification/ossification can be utilized to indicate a probable age bracket for the individual for forensic purposes (Vastine and Vastine, 1952; Hatley, Samuel and Evison, 1965). De la Grandmaison, Banasr and Durigon (2003) removed laryngeal cartilages at autopsy and subjected them to a radiological analysis in an attempt to evaluate age-related change. Although the approach has been evaluated via radiological imaging and is therefore technically valid as a technique for application to the living, a greater deal of research is required in this regard. In this method, the thyroid, cricoid and arytenoid cartilages were scored on the basis of a scoring pattern devised by Keen and Wainwright (1958) using radiological and histological means and the sum of each score produced a total score. This method showed that there is a significant positive correlation (standard coefficient of 0.74 with a standard error of 12.7 years) between radiopacity and progressive build-up of calcifications within the cartilages and age. It has been suggested that this method is not sufficiently discriminative to be used in isolation but can be combined with other methods to result in a more reliable overall estimate of age. CT or MRI scans can be used instead of plain radiographs (Becker *et al.*, 1995; Fatterpekar *et al.*, 2004) and have the potential of achieving better results as they are routinely being used for the study of laryngeal carcinomas and the images may then be made available for age estimation in forensic practice. The relationship between laryngeal carcinomas and degree of cartilage calcification is not known. Low voltage radiology is another option that might be adopted as it is more efficient at detecting low levels of calcification compared to standard radiological approaches (Jurik, 1982). Turk and Hogg have postulated that radiology is an accurate method for the detection of calcification of the laryngeal cartilages when compared to direct observation by the eye (Turk and Hogg, 1993) and this is a valuable observation for utilizing laryngeal cartilages in age estimation in the living.

12.4   Odontology

Teeth are one of the most frequently utilized parts of the body for the estimation of age, starting from their eruption in infancy until their loss with old age. While in the early part of life, it is the mineralization and eruption of the teeth that are used for the determination of age, in the latter part, it is the changes that occur due to ageing which form the basis for age determination. For both processes, that is eruption and breakdown, teeth give estimates of age that are more accurate (Reppien, Sejrsen and Lynnerup, 2006) and easier to examine than any other method that can be used for such purposes. The major details about the various procedures and their descriptions are considered in depth in Chapter 10. Here it would suffice to state that the methods mentioned below are important, both in the dead and in the living.

Gustafson was one of the first to use teeth for age estimation in adults (Gustafson, 1950). Ever since his pioneering work on this subject, many authors have either used or modified his method or devised new methods for age estimation, though mainly in the dead (Dalitz, 1962; Bang and Ramm, 1970; Johanson, 1971; Lovejoy, 1985; Santini, Land and Raab, 1990; Lamendin *et al.*, 1992; Solheim, 1993; Li and Ji, 1995; Martin-de las Heras, Valenzuela and Overall, 2000; Prince and Ubelaker, 2002; Vasiliadis, Stavrianos and Kafas, 2009). It has also been suggested that the methodologies need to be individualized for the population for which they are being used for the best results (Gonzalez-Colmenares *et al.*, 2007), though some authors suggest that there is no effect of population variation on these results (Ubelaker and Parra, 2008).

Pulp/tooth ratio is one of the methods used quite commonly (Kvaal *et al.*, 1995; Cameriere, Ferrante and Cingolani, 2004; Paewinsky, Pfeiffer and Brinkmann, 2005; Cameriere *et al.*, 2007a,b). The advent of modern technology has offered alternative avenues for examination of teeth. CT is one such modality that is surpassing conventional methods of tooth examination (Vandevoort *et al.*, 2004; Aboshi *et al.*, 2005; Yang, Jacobs and Willems, 2006; Someda *et al.*, 2009). Other methods that have been used for age determination at various times include using tooth coronal index (Ikeda *et al.*, 1985; Drusini, Toso and Ranzato, 1997), measurement of occlusal tooth wear (Kim, Kho and Lee, 2000; Yun *et al.*, 2007) and others (Kolltveit, Solheim and Kvaal, 1998).

A comparison of various methods by Solheim and Sundness (1980) has shown that the method developed by Johanson (1971) and the visual examination of the teeth based on clinical experience give the best results. Put another way, it states that experience is the most important parameter for age estimation, at least while using teeth, and most scientific methods have some or other shortcoming that needs to be corrected with time.

12.5 Soft Tissues of Face

The soft tissues of the face, including the eyes, can also be used for the purpose of age estimation. As we have seen in Chapter 9, these factors may not be specifically accurate as indicators of age but they can augment the assessment made by more reliable features to improve results (Weale, 2001). These soft tissue markers have been studied in some detail (Stephan, 2002), although very rarely from the forensic perspective. In one such study on Italian individuals (Sforza *et al.*, 2009), three-dimensional measurements of the face were taken using an electromagnetic digitizer. It showed that most of the parameters that were studied, namely biorbital width, intercanthal width, height of orbit, length of eye fissure, inclination of eye fissure, external orbital surface area and so on, showed a correlation with age. However, the strongest correlation between these factors and age is to be found in the prepubertal individual and not in the ageing adult, as discussed in Chapter 9. Once adulthood is achieved, there is a gradual change in these parameters with advancing age, but it is variable and should not be used as an indicator of age in isolation.

12.6 Genetics in Age Estimation

In today's world, genetics plays a very important role in a medical professional's life. From the aetiology of diseases to their diagnosis and management, genetic markers have become predominant players. In such a scenario, it is to be expected that genetics would eventually invade forensic medicine and identification in particular. Apart from DNA matching, which is globally recognized as one of the most important functions of genetics in forensic medicine, it has, of late, been increasingly used in age estimation. The past two decades have surely been dominated by molecular biologists who have truly revolutionized the way age estimation can be achieved in both the living and the dead. Terminal restriction fragment (TRF) length, also called telomere length shortening, is the genetic marker used for this purpose. It has been observed that telomeres of cells shorten with every cell division due to the end replication problems, in both humans (Hastie *et al.*, 1990; Blackburn, 1991) and other animals (Lund, Grange and Lowe, 2007; Hatakeyama *et al.*, 2008). It has also been shown that people who live longer tend to have longer telomere lengths than people who live a shorter life (Hertzog, 2006). As a result, telomere length acts as a form of biological clock that marks the number of cell divisions that have taken place (Hastie *et al.*, 1990), and thus, indirectly, the age of the person.

Various tissues of human body have been used for the determination of age using telomere shortening. In the pancreas (Ishii *et al.*, 2006) telomere shortening has been recorded at a rate of 36 base pairs (bp) per year. In the epidermis, the rate of reduction has been found to be 9 bp/yr, while in the dermis it is 11 bp/yr (Sugimoto, Yamashita and Ueda, 2006) although various authors have given different ranges, up to as much as 75 bp/yr (Lindsey *et al.*, 1991; Friedrich *et al.*, 2000; Nakamura *et al.*, 2002). Blood is perhaps the most useful medium examined due to its ease of sampling (Harley, Futcher and Greider, 1990; Slagboom, Droog and Boomsma, 1994; Vaziri *et al.*, 1994; Kormann-Bortolotto, Borsatto and Smith, 1996; Halaschek-Wiener *et al.*, 2008).

One of the regression equations that have been given using blood is as follows (Tsuji *et al.*, 2002):

$$Age = -0.0095y + 148.9$$

where y = average TRF length.

This gives a standard error of ± 7.037 years and the correlation coefficient $R^2 = 0.6922$.

Ren *et al.*, on the other hand, have given the following regression equation using peripheral blood leucocytes in the Chinese population (Ren *et al.*, 2009):

$$Age = -16.539X + 236.287 \text{ where } X = \text{mean TRF length in kb.}$$

It has a regression coefficient $r = -0.913$ and $P < 0.01$.

Guan *et al.* (2007) reported an average telomere length reduction of 77 bp/year in the Japanese population using blood.

Ju and Rudolph (2006) used stem cells to assess telomere and telomerase activity and assess their relationship with ageing and disease. For the sake of completion, we may add that DNA from dental pulp can also be used for age determination, though only after removal of the tooth, and so this is not a practical option for age evaluation in the living (Takasaki *et al.*, 2003). The time is perhaps not far away when telomere length may become one of the most important parameters for age estimation in the living but, again, more research is required first to look at variation between the sexes and ethnic variation, among many other characteristics.

12.7 Physiological and Biochemical Parameters for Age Estimation

While teeth and bones have always formed the core for age estimation exercises, the various physiological and biochemical parameters that influence these changes cannot be overlooked, especially in relation to living people. These parameters, like many before, have not been studied with the intention of age estimation but there is still some reasonable data available to give us an insight into their utility for the present goal.

The mineralization of bones and their resultant alteration in density is one of the major criteria for this current section. It has been studied in great detail in orthopaedics, especially for osteoporosis and other age-related orthopaedic conditions (Ruff and Hayes, 1982; Marshall *et al.*, 2006). Only a few studies have been undertaken specifically for their role in age estimation and that too, only indirectly (Ruff and Hayes, 1984; Livshits, Karasik and Kobyliansky, 2002; Malkin *et al.*, 2002; Riggs *et al.*, 2004; Agarwal and Grynpas, 2009). These studies have shown significant correlation between the loss of mineral content of the bone and the age of the individual, and require to be investigated in more detail.

Hormones play an important role in the normal metabolic functions of the body. Their variations can also be used as a marker for age estimation. Some of the studies undertaken to relate the level of testosterone to age have shown promising results (Nahoul and Roger, 1990; Gray *et al.*, 1991; Harman *et al.*, 2001; Ellison *et al.*, 2002; Lapauw *et al.*, 2008). One basic problem with this parameter is that the results have to be individualized for each ethnic group as they are not found to be reproducible in different ethnic groups, and of course clinical conditions and drug prescriptions are major influences on this relationship.

Menopause is another aspect of human physiology that can be utilized for the determination of age. Although the age of menopause has not been studied in a forensic perspective, it has been studied for its relationship to clinical conditions and to diseases. It is this relationship that we can extrapolate for our use. In normal gynaecological practice, menopause occurring before the age of 40 years is referred to as premature menopause while that between 40 and 45 years is referred to as early menopause, the range being 45–55 years with the median being about 48–51 years, depending on the socio-demographic profile of the population (Treloar, 1981; Sievert, 2001; Kok *et al.*, 2005; Shuster *et al.*, 2009). Among the various factors that are postulated for the age of menopause, hormones and genetics are the two most common ones (Snieder, MacGregor and Spector, 1998; de Bruin *et al.*, 2001; Moron, Ruiz and Galan, 2009). Because of the many factors that can modify its occurrence, the age of menopause cannot be used as a reliable marker for age but can definitely be an adjunct to other methods for the purpose of age confirmation.

12.8   Areas of Future Research

While this chapter has shown that there are many areas of potential for future research in relation to age prediction in the adult and the elderly, there is clearly a significant amount of research still required to be undertaken. However, there are some areas that deserve special mention.

12.8.1   Small Long Bones

Small long bones of the hand and foot that are morphologically similar to the long bones of the limbs and comprise the metacarpals, metatarsals and phalanges. While long bones can and have been used for the determination of age, the small bones have not been fully investigated for this purpose on a large scale. One of the studies that has been conducted on these bones has shown encouraging results and has indicated that these bones may be used for age determination (Kalichman *et al.*, 2008). In this study, radiological examination of the bones of the hand showed that there was a significant correlation between the length and/or width of the bones and age, although the correlation was neither linear for all ages nor the same for males and females. Although this was a qualitative study, it did show that these bones offer promise for the purpose of determination of age.

12.8.2   Scapula

The value of the scapula as a means of determining age has not been studied in great detail. The first account of its utility was given by Graves almost a century ago (Graves, 1922). He described various changes in the scapula that occurred with advancing years. However, most of those changes were very general and at that time, could be observed only in the scapula removed after dissection. With the advancement of the technology, today, we can visualize the three-dimensional structure of the bones in the living. This has opened the possibility of visualizing the scapula in a totally different modality as far as age determination is concerned with many features, like lipping of the glenoid fossa, atrophic spots, and superficial and deep vascularity. These and other such changes may then be utilized for age determination.

12.8.3   Others

Age and sex differences in the size of the lacrimal duct of the skulls (Post, 1969) have been examined. Although the study was undertaken on the skeletonized remains and the method used was crude compared to today's standards, it did give a suggestion that age differences do occur in the tear duct in both males and females, which may reach a level of significance.

Changes to the chondral surfaces of the ribs has gained prominence as a means of age evaluation during later decades of life. However, the problem remains common to many other techniques in that it was devised to assist with age evaluation in the deceased and can currently only be examined in post-mortem samples after removal of the bones during autopsy (Iscan, Loth and Wright, 1984; Kunos et al., 1999; Oettle and Steyn, 2000; DiGangi et al., 2009). With the advancement of technology, this shortcoming may be overcome and calcification of the costal cartilages through alteration to the costochondral junction may gain importance in the future as a more accurate method of age determination in the living.

The ratio of central to peripheral vertebral arteries and the amount of coiling of the vertebral arteries have also been studied for age determination and have been found to have a statistically significant relationship with age (Ratcliffe, 1986). However, at present these can be utilized only in the deceased and we need to wait for the development of appropriate technology for them to be utilized in the living.

Quantitative ultrasound has been used as a method to measure age-related changes in a Lebanese population (Maalouf et al., 2007). In this study an ultrasound examination of the phalanges of the hands was undertaken. Although this study was undertaken to develop standard data to assist with the diagnosis of osteoporosis, it has shown that it has potential to be extrapolated for age estimation.

The human auricular cartilage (external ear) is another part of the body that has been studied for age determination (Ito et al., 2001) and it has been established that the various dimensions of the cartilage continue to increase with advancing age at a level that is statistically significant. Again, with appropriate clinical imaging this may prove to be a valuable potential tool for the future.

The frontal sinus can be added to the list of lesser markers of age estimation. Although not studied in much detail for the determination of age, it has potential to be used for this purpose as it has been shown that the frontal sinus increases in size with age, both due to pneumatization as well as bone resorption (Harris et al., 1987; Nambiar, Naidu and Subramaniam, 1999; Fatu et al., 2006).

Pelvic phleboliths are the calcified thrombi present in the peri-vesical venous plexuses (Clark, 1909; Dovey, 1966; see Figure 12.11). Their appearance and number have been studied by various authors for their relationship to age and these have shown that there is a positive correlation (Greenberg, 1949; Steinbach, 1960). While Dovey analysed phleboliths on the basis of age and sex without statistical analysis, Green and Thomas did undertake some statistical analysis for the same (Green and Thomas, 1972). They found a statistically significant rise in the number of phleboliths with age with a correlation coefficient (r) of 0.956 and $p < 0.01$. Mattsson has also shown similar results (Mattsson, 1980). This has shown that phleboliths may form a useful corroborator to the more established methods of age determination.

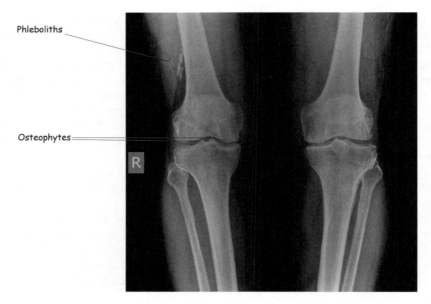

Phleboliths

Osteophytes

Figure 12.11   Phleboliths in the thigh region of a 55-year-old man. Although commonly they are seen in the pelvic region, they can be seen in other parts of the body too, as is visible in the present case.

12.8.4   Histology

There are various histological indicators of age that are utilized for identification in the deceased. These methods involve destruction of the bones and so are not appropriate for evaluation in the living. A further problem with histological analysis is that the results vary with the eyepiece that is used for the examination of the slides under the microscope (Kerley and Ubelaker, 1978; Stout and Gehlert, 1982). Not all histological methods give equal results (Keough, L'Abbé and Steyn, 2009) and so one has to decide which method to use for which bone. Singh and Gunberg estimated age from the mandible, femur and tibia (Singh and Gunberg, 1970) and these methods have been developed by various researchers for age estimation using bones including the femur (Crane *et al.*, 1990; Watanabe *et al.*, 1998; Wang *et al.*, 2003; Lynnerup, Frohlich and Thomsen, 2006; Chan, Crowder and Rogers, 2007; Britz *et al.*, 2009), ribs (Takahashi and Frost, 1966; Kim *et al.*, 2007), iliac crest (Boel, Boldsen and Melsen, 2007) and the occipital bone (Cool, Hendrikz and Wood, 1995). Colour changes in various tissues of the body including the tendocalcaneus, costal cartilage and so on have also been used for evaluating age (Pilin, Pudil and Bencko, 2007a,b,c). The histological alteration to the cranial sutures has also been utilized (Dorandeu *et al.*, 2009), although it would seem prudent to add that there is still significant research required to be undertaken before it can be adopted for evaluation in the living.

Analysis of mitochondrial DNA from biopsy samples of skeletal muscle is both a histological and a genetic form of evaluation (Meissner *et al.*, 1999). In this method the deletion at 4977-bp is detected as this deletion has been found to accumulate with age. A regression equation with correlation coefficient of $r = 0.83$ ($R^2 = 0.63$) has been achieved and this shows promise for the future.

12.9 Conclusion

The most reliable way to confirm age is to have documentary proof of birth. However, this is not always available, and when the individual is adult or indeed elderly, then whichever method is employed, the results can only ever be considered to be an approximation of chronological age and will never be accurate. This variation increases with advancing years when the person passes from a young adult into middle years and then into an elderly category (Cattaneo *et al.*, 2008). There is also a strong ethnicity factor that must be recognized as cultural and genetic influences will have a strong effect on the ageing process. Although most of the studies on ethic variation have been undertaken on younger individuals (Olze *et al.*, 2004), it is reasonable to assume that the results can be extrapolated to the older population. As age determination is unquestionably a sex- and ethnicity-dependent variable, one must use the appropriate group statistics when an evaluation is being attempted to ensure that as reliable a prediction as possible is achieved. There is very little data that is specific to individual ethnic groups and the likelihood of one being available for a specific case regarding immigration or asylum purposes is highly unlikely.

Most of the topics and findings that have been discussed in this chapter are based on research undertaken on the deceased, whether through clinical, forensic or anthropological means. Assessment via visualization techniques through a 'virtual' examination (Grabherr *et al.*, 2009) gives hope that much of what has been discussed in the present chapter will become the reality of the future.

References

Aboshi, H., Takahashi, T., Komuro, T. and Fukase, Y. (2005) A method of age estimation based on the morph metric analysis of dental pulp in mandible first premolars by means of three-dimensional measurements taken by micro CT. *Nihon University Dental Journal*, **79**, 195–203.

Agarwal, S.C. and Grynpas, M.D. (2009) Measuring and interpreting age-related loss of vertebral bone mineral density in a medieval population. *American Journal of Physical Anthropology*, **139** (2), 244–252.

Aggrawal, A. (2009) Estimation of age in the living: in matters civil and criminal. *Journal of Anatomy*, 11 May [Epub ahead of print].

Aggrawal, A. and Busuttil, A. (1991) Age estimation in the living. *The Police Surgeon (Journal of the Association of Police Surgeons)*, **38** (Jan), 33–36.

Aggrawal, A. (2000) Age estimation in the living – some medicolegal considerations. *Anil Aggrawal's Internet Journal of Forensic Medicine and Toxicology*, serial online, **1** (2), 23.

Aggrawal, A. (2003) Age estimation in the living, in *Forensic Medicine: Clinical and Pathological Aspects* (eds J. Payne-James, A. Busuttil and W. Smock), Greenwich Medical Media, San Francisco, CA, pp. 391–408.

Ajmani, M.L., Jain, S.P. and Saxena, S.K. (1980) A metrical study of laryngeal cartilages and their ossification. *Anat Anz*, **148** (1), 42–48.

Allbrook, D.B. (1956) Changes in lumbar verterbral body height with age. *American Journal of Physical Anthropology*, **14** (1), 35–39.

Anton, H.C. (1969) Width of clavicular cortex in osteoporosis. *British Medical Journal*, **1** (5641), 409–411.

Ashley-Montagu, M.F. (1938) Aging of the skull. *American Journal of Physical Anthropology*, **23** (3), 355–375.

Bang, G. and Ramm, E. (1970) Determination of age in humans from root dentin transparency. *Acta Odontologica Scandinavica*, **28** (1), 3–35.

Barrès, D.R., Durigon, M. and Paraire, F. (1989) Age estimation from quantitation of features of "chest plate" X-rays. *Journal of Forensic Sciences*, **34** (1), 228–233.

Becker, M., Zbaren, P., Laeng, H. *et al.* (1995) Neoplastic invasion of the laryngeal cartilage: comparison of MR imaging and CT with histopathologic correlation. *Radiology*, **194** (3), 661–669.

Berg, G.E. (2008) Pubic bone age estimation in adult women. *Journal of Forensic Sciences*, **53** (3), 569–577.

Blackburn, E.H. (1991) Structure and function of telomeres. *Nature*, **350** (6319), 569–573.

Boel, L.W., Boldsen, J.L. and Melsen, F. (2007) Double lamellae in trabecular osteons: towards a new method for age estimation by bone microscopy. *Homo*, **58** (4), 269–277.

Britz, H.M., Thomas, C.D., Clement, J.G. and Cooper, D.M. (2009) The relation of femoral osteon geometry to age, sex, height and weight. *Bone*, **45** (1), 77–83.

Buckberry, J.L. and Chamberlain, A.T. (2002) Age estimation from the auricular surface of the ilium: a revised method. *American Journal of Physical Anthropology*, **119** (3), 231–239.

Cattaneo, C., De Angelis, D., Ruspa, M. *et al.* (2008) How old am I? Age estimation in living adults: a case report. *Journal of Forensic Odonto-Stomatology*, **27** (2), 39–43.

Cameriere, R., Ferrante, L. and Cingolani, M. (2004) Variations in pulp/tooth area ratio as an indicator of age: a preliminary study. *Journal of Forensic Sciences*, **49** (2), 317–319.

Cameriere, R., Ferrante, L., Belcastro, M.G. *et al.* (2007a) Age estimation by pulp/tooth ratio in canines by mesial and vestibular peri-apical X-rays. *Journal of Forensic Sciences*, **52** (5), 1151–1155.

Cameriere, R., Ferrante, L., Belcastro, M.G. *et al.* (2007b) Age estimation by pulp/tooth ratio in canines by peri-apical X-rays. *Journal of Forensic Sciences*, **52** (1), 166–170.

Chan, A.H., Crowder, C.M. and Rogers, T.L. (2007) Variation in cortical bone histology within the human femur and its impact on estimating age at death. *American Journal of Physical Anthropology*, **132** (1), 80–88.

Chaturvedi, M. (2008) Girl flees 'sale' by stepdad, husband accused of kidnap. *Times of India*, 4 May, p. 7.

Clark, G.O. (1909) XI. Peri-ureteral pelvic phleboliths. *Annals of Surgery*, **50** (5), 913–921.

Cool, S.M., Hendrikz, J.K. and Wood, W.B. (1995) Microscopic age changes in the human occipital bone. *Journal of Forensic Sciences*, **40** (5), 789–96.

Crane, G.J., Fazzalari, N.L., Parkinson, I.H. and Vernon-Roberts, B. (1990) Age-related changes in femoral trabecular bone in arthrosis. *Acta Orthopaedica Scandinavica*, **61** (5), 421–426.

Curtis, D.J., Allman, R.M., Brion, J. *et al.* (1985) Calcification and ossification in the arytenoid cartilage: incidence and patterns. *Journal of Forensic Sciences*, **30** (4), 1113–1118.

Dalitz, G.D. (1962) Age determination of adult human remains by teeth examination. *Journal of the Forensic Science Society*, **3**, 11–21.

de Bruin, J.P., Bovenhuis, H., van Noord, P.A. *et al.* (2001) The role of genetic factors in age at natural menopause. *Human Reproduction*, **16** (9), 2014–2018.

de la Grandmaison, G.L., Banasr, A. and Durigon, M. (2003) Age estimation using radiographic analysis of laryngeal cartilage. *American Journal of Forensic Medicine and Pathology*, **24** (1), 96–99.

DiGangi, E.A., Bethard, J.D., Kimmerle, E.H. and Konigsberg, L.W. (2009) A new method for estimating age-at-death from the first rib. *American Journal of Physical Anthropology*, **138** (2), 164–176.

Dorandeu, A., Coulibaly, B., Piercecchi-Marti, M.D., Bartoli, C. *et al.* (2008) Age-at-death estimation based on the study of frontosphenoidal sutures. *Forensic Science International*, **177** (1), 47–51.

Dorandeu, A., de la Grandmaison, G.L., Coulibaly, B. *et al.* (2009) Value of histological study in the fronto-sphenoidal suture for the age estimation at the time of death. *Forensic Science International*, **191** (1–3), 64–69.

Dovey, P. (1966) Pelvic phleboliths. *Clinical Radiology*, **17** (2), 121–125.

Drusini, A.G., Toso, O. and Ranzato, C. (1997) The coronal pulp cavity index: a biomarker for age determination in human adults. *American Journal of Physical Anthropology*, **103** (3), 353–363.

Ellison, P.T., Bribiescas, R.G., Bentley, G.R. *et al.* (2002) Population variation in age-related decline in male salivary testosterone. *Human Reproduction*, **17** (12), 3251–3253.

Ericksen, M.F. (1976) Some aspects of aging in the lumbar spine. *American Journal of Physical Anthropology*, **45** (3 pt. 2), 575–580.

Ericksen, M.F. (1978a) Aging in the lumbar spine. II. L1 and L2. *American Journal of Physical Anthropology*, **48** (2), 241–245.

Ericksen, M.F. (1978b) Aging in the lumber spine. III. L5. *American Journal of Physical Anthropology*, **48** (2), 247–250.

Fatterpekar, G.M., Mukherji, S.K., Rajgopalan, P. *et al.* (2004) Normal age-related signal change in the laryngeal cartilages. *Neuroradiology*, **46** (8), 678–681.

Fatu, C., Puisoru, M., Rotaru, M. and Truta, A.M. (2006) Morphometric evaluation of the frontal sinus in relation to age. *Annals of Anatomy*, **188** (3), 275–280.

Ferrant, O., Rougé-Maillart, C., Guittet, L. *et al.* (2009) Age at death estimation of adult males using coxal bone and CT scan: a preliminary study. *Forensic Science International*, **186** (1–3), 14–21.

Friedrich, U., Griese, E., Schwab, M. *et al.* (2000) Telomere length in different tissues of elderly patients. *Mechanisms of Ageing and Development*, **119** (3), 89–99.

Gillett, N.A., Gerlach, R., Cassidy, J.J. and Brown, S.A. (1988) Age-related changes in the beagle spine. *Acta Orthopaedica Scandinavica*, **59** (5), 503–507.

Ginter, J.K. (2005) A test of the effectiveness of the revised maxillary suture obliteration method in estimating adult age at death. *Journal of Forensic Sciences*, **50** (6), 1303–1309.

Gonzalez-Colmenares, G., Botella-Lopez, M.C., Moreno-Rueda, G. and Fernández-Cardenete, J.R. (2007) Age estimation by a dental method: a comparison of Lamendin's and Prince & Ubelaker's technique. *Journal of Forensic Sciences*, **52** (5), 1156–1160.

Grabherr, S., Cooper, C., Ulrich-Bochsler, S. *et al.* (2009) Estimation of sex and age of 'virtual skeletons' – a feasibility study. *European Radiology*, **19** (2), 419–429.

Graves, W.W. (1922) Observation on age changes in the scapula. *American Journal of Physical Anthropology*, **5** (1), 21–33.

Gray, A., Feldman, H.A., McKinlay, J.B. and Longcope, C. (1991) Age, disease, and changing sex hormone levels in middle-aged men: results of the Massachusetts Male Aging Study. *Journal of Clinical Endocrinology and Metabolism*, **73** (5), 1016–1025.

Green, M. and Thomas, M.L. (1972) The prevalence of pelvic phleboliths in relation to age, sex and urinary tract infections. *Clinical Radiology*, **23** (4), 492–494.

Greenberg, G. (1949) Post-operative complications and sequelae with special reference to embolism following prostatectomy and a historical review. *Urologic and Cutaneous Review*, **53** (12), 726–731.

Gruspier, K.L. and Mullen, G.J. (1991) Maxillary suture obliteration: a test of the Mann method. *Journal of Forensic Sciences*, **36** (2), 512–519.

Guan, J.Z., Maeda, T., Sugano, M. *et al.* (2007) Change in the telomere length distribution with age in the Japanese population. *Molecular and Cellular Biochemistry*, **304** (1–2), 353–360.

Gustafson, G. (1950) Age determinations on teeth. *Journal of the American Dental Association*, **41**, 45–54.

Halaschek-Wiener, J., Vulto, I., Fornika, D. *et al.* (2008) Reduced telomere length variation in healthy oldest old. *Mechanisms of Ageing and Development*, **129** (11), 638–641.

Hanihara, K. and Suzuki, T. (1978) Estimation of age from the pubic symphysis by means of multiple regression analysis. *American Journal of Physical Anthropology*, **48** (2), 233–239.

Harley, C.B., Futcher, A.B. and Greider, C.W. (1990) Telomeres shorten during ageing of human fibroblasts. *Nature*, **345** (6274), 458–460.

Harman, S.M., Metter, E.J., Tobin, J.D. *et al.* (2001) Longitudinal effects of aging on serum total and free testosterone levels in healthy men. Baltimore Longitudinal Study of Aging. *Journal of Clinical Endocrinology and Metabolism*, **86** (2), 724–731.

Harris, A.M., Wood, R.E., Nortjé, C.J. and Thomas, C.J. (1987) The frontal sinus: forensic fingerprint? A pilot study. *Journal of Forensic Odonto-Stomatology*, **5** (1), 9–15.

Hastie, N.D., Dempster, M., Dunlop, M.G. *et al.* (1990) Telomere reduction in human colorectal carcinoma and with ageing. *Nature*, **346** (6287), 866–868.

Hatakeyama, H., Nakamura, K., Izumiyama-Shimomura, N. *et al.* (2008) The teleost *Oryzias latipes* shows telomere shortening with age despite considerable telomerase activity throughout life. *Mechanisms of Ageing and Development*, **129** (9), 550–557.

Hatley, W., Samuel, E. and Evison, G. (1965) The pattern of ossification in the laryngeal cartilages: a radiological study. *British Journal of Radiology*, **38**, 585–591.

Helela, T. (1969) Age-dependent variations of the cortical thickness of the clavicle. *Annals of Clinical Research*, **1** (2), 140–143.

Hershkovitz, I., Latimer, B., Dutour, O. *et al.* (1997) Why do we fail in aging the skull from the sagittal suture? *American Journal of Physical Anthropology*, **103** (3), 393–399.

Hertzog, R.G. (2006) Ancestral telomere shortening: a countdown that will increase mean life span? *Medical Hypotheses*, **67** (1), 157–160.

Igarashi, Y., Uesu, K., Wakebe, T. and Kanazawa, E. (2005) New method for estimation of adult skeletal age at death from the morphology of the auricular surface of the ilium. *American Journal of Physical Anthropology*, **128** (2), 324–339.

Ikeda, N., Umetsu, K., Kashimura, S. *et al.* (1985) [Estimation of age from teeth with their soft X-ray findings]. *Nihon Hoigaku Zasshi*, **9** (3), 244–250 [in Japanese].

Iscan, M.Y., Loth, S.R. and Wright, R.K. (1984) Metamorphosis at the sternal rib end: a new method to estimate age at death in white males. *American Journal of Physical Anthropology*, **65** (2), 147–156.

Ishii, A., Nakamura, K., Kishimoto, H. *et al.* (2006) Telomere shortening with aging in the human pancreas. *Experimental Gerontology*, **41** (9), 882–886.

Ito, I., Imada, M., Ikeda, M. *et al.* (2001) A morphological study of age changes in adult human auricular cartilage with special emphasis on elastic fibers. *Laryngoscope*, **111** (5), 881–886.

Israel, H. (1977) The dichotomous pattern of craniofacial expansion during aging. *American Journal of Physical Anthropology*, **47** (1), 47–51.

Johanson, G. (1971) Age determination from teeth. *Odontologisk revy*, **22**, 121–126.

Ju, Z. and Rudolph, K.L. (2006) Telomeres and telomerase in stem cells during aging and disease. *Genome Dynamics*, **1**, 84–103.

Jurik, A.G. (1982) Visualisation of the intralaryngeal joints: a low voltage radiological study. *Clinical Radiology*, **33** (6), 687–690.

Kalichman, L., Malkin, I., Seibel, M.J. *et al.* (2008) Age-related changes and secular trends in hand bone size. *Homo*, **59** (4), 301–315.

Katz, D. and Suchey, J.M. (1986) Age determination of the male os pubis. *American Journal of Physical Anthropology*, **69** (4), 427–435.

Kaur, H. and Jit, I. (1990) Age estimation from cortical index of the human clavicle in northwest Indians. *American Journal of Physical Anthropology*, **83** (3), 297–305.

Keen, J.A. and Wainwright, J. (1958) Ossification of the thyroid, cricoid and arytenoid cartilages. *South African Journal of Laboratory and Clinical Medicine*, **4**, 85–103.

Keough, N., L'Abbé, E.N. and Steyn, M. (2009) The evaluation of age-related histomorphometric variables in a cadaver sample of lower socioeconomic status: implications for estimating age at death. *Forensic Science International*, **191** (1–3), 114.e1–114.e6.

Kerley, E.R. and Ubelaker, D.H. (1978) Revisions in the microscopic method of estimating age at death in human cortical bone. *American Journal of Physical Anthropology*, **49** (4), 545–546.

Kim, Y.K., Kho, H.S. and Lee, K.H. (2000) Age estimation by occlusal tooth wear. *Journal of Forensic Sciences*, **45** (2), 303–309.

Kim, Y.S., Kim, D.I., Park, D.K. *et al.* (2007) Assessment of histomorphological features of the sternal end of the fourth rib for age estimation in Koreans. *Journal of Forensic Sciences*, **52** (6), 1237–1242.

Kok, H.S., van Asselt, K.M., van der Schouw, Y.T. *et al.* (2005) Genetic studies to identify genes underlying menopausal age. *Human Reproduction Update*, **11** (5), 483–493.

Kolltveit, K.M., Solheim, T. and Kvaal, S.I. (1998) Methods of measuring morphological parameters in dental radiographs. Comparison between image analysis and manual measurements. *Forensic Science International*, **94** (1–2), 87–95.

Kormann-Bortolotto, M.H., Borsatto, B. and Smith, M. (1996) Telomere shortening, ageing, and chromosome damage. *Mechanisms of Ageing and Development*, **89** (1), 45–49.

Kunos, C.A., Simpson, S.W., Russell, K.F. and Hershkovitz, I. (1999) First rib metamorphosis: its possible utility for human age-at-death estimation. *American Journal of Physical Anthropology*, **110** (3), 303–323.

Kvaal, S.I., Kolltveit, K.M., Thomsen, I.O. and Solheim, T. (1995) Age estimation of adults from dental radiographs. *Forensic Science International*, **74** (3), 175–185.

Lamendin, H., Baccino, E., Humbert, J.F. *et al.* (1992) A simple technique for age estimation in adult corpses: the two criteria dental method. *Journal of Forensic Sciences*, **37** (5), 1373–1379.

Lapauw, B., Goemaere, S., Zmierczak, H. *et al.* (2008) The decline of serum testosterone levels in community-dwelling men over 70 years of age: descriptive data and predictors of longitudinal changes. *European Journal of Endocrinology*, **159** (4), 459–468.

Li, C. and Ji, G. (1995) Age estimation from the permanent molar in northeast China by the method of average stage of attrition. *Forensic Science International*, **75** (2–3), 189–196.

Lindsey, J., McGill, N.I., Lindsey, L.A. *et al.* (1991) In vivo loss of telomeric repeats with age in humans. *Mutation Research*, **256** (1), 45–48.

Livshits, G., Karasik, D. and Kobyliansky, E. (2002) Complex segregation analysis of the radiographic phalanges bone mineral density and their age-related changes. *Journal of Bone and Mineral Research*, **17** (1), 152–161.

Lovejoy, C.O. (1985) Dental wear in the Libben population: its functional pattern and role in the determination of adult skeletal age at death. *American Journal of Physical Anthropology*, **68** (1), 47–56.

Lovejoy, C.O., Meindl, R.S., Pryzbeck, T.R. and Mensforth, R.P. (1985) Chronological metamorphosis of the auricular surface of the ilium: a new method for the determination of adult skeletal age at death. *American Journal of Physical Anthropology*, **68** (1), 15–28.

Lund, T.C., Grange, R.W. and Lowe, D.A. (2007) Telomere shortening in diaphragm and tibialis anterior muscles of aged mdx mice. *Muscle Nerve*, **36** (3), 387–390.

Lynnerup, N., Frohlich, B. and Thomsen, J.L. (2006) Assessment of age at death by microscopy: unbiased quantification of secondary osteons in femoral cross sections. *Forensic Science International*, **159** (Suppl 1), S100–S103.

Maalouf, G., Wehbe, J., Farah, G. *et al.* (2007) Phalangeal osteosonogrammetry age-related changes and assessment of a Lebanese reference population. *Bone*, **40** (6), 1650–1654.

Malkin, I., Karasik, D., Livshits, G. and Kobyliansky, E. (2002) Modelling of age-related bone loss using cross-sectional data. *Annals of Human Biology*, **29** (3), 256–270.

Mann, R.W. (1998) Use of bone trabeculae to establish positive identification. *Forensic Science International*, **98** (1–2), 91–99.

Mann, R.W., Symes, S.A. and Bass, W.M. (1987) Maxillary suture obliteration: aging the human skeleton based on intact or fragmentary maxilla. *Journal of Forensic Sciences*, **32** (1), 148–157.

Mann, R.W., Jantz, R.L., Bass, W.M. and Willey, P.S. (1991) Maxillary suture obliteration: a visual method for estimating skeletal age. *Journal of Forensic Sciences*, **36** (3), 781–791.

Marshall, L.M., Lang, T.F., Lambert, L.C. *et al.* (2006) Dimensions and volumetric BMD of the proximal femur and their relation to age among older US men. *Journal of Bone and Mineral Research*, **21** (8), 1197–1206.

Martin-de las Heras, S., Valenzuela, A. and Overall, C.M. (2000) Gelatinase A in human dentin as a new biochemical marker for age estimation. *Journal of Forensic Sciences*, **45** (4), 807–811.

Mattsson, T. (1980) Frequency and location of pelvic phleboliths. *Clinical Radiology*, **31** (1), 115–118.

McCormick, W.F. (1980) Mineralization of the costal cartilages as an indicator of age: preliminary observations. *Journal of Forensic Sciences*, **25** (4), 736–741.

Meindl, R.S. and Lovejoy, C.O. (1985) Ectocranial suture closure: a revised method for the determination of skeletal age at death based on the lateral-anterior sutures. *American Journal of Physical Anthropology*, **68** (1), 57–66.

Meindl, R.S., Lovejoy, C.O., Mensforth, R.P., Walker, R.A. (1985) A revised method of age determination using the os pubis, with a review and tests of accuracy of other current methods of pubic symphyseal aging. *American Journal of Physical Anthropology*, **68** (1), 29–45.

Meissner, C., von Wurmb, N., Schimansky, B. and Oehmichen, M. (1999) Estimation of age at death based on quantitation of the 4977-bp deletion of human mitochondrial DNA in skeletal muscle. *Forensic Science International*, **105** (2), 115–124.

Moron, F.J., Ruiz, A. and Galan, J.J. (2009) Genetic and genomic insights into age at natural menopause. *Genome Medicine*, **1** (8), 76.

Mosekilde, L. (1990) Sex differences in age-related changes in vertebral body size, density and biomechanical competence in normal individuals. *Bone*, **11** (2), 67–73.

Nahoul, K. and Roger, M. (1990) Age-related decline of plasma bioavailable testosterone in adult men. *Journal of Steroid Biochemistry*, **35** (2), 293–299.

Nakai, M. (2001) Vertebral age changes in Japanese macaques. *American Journal of Physical Anthropology*, **116** (1), 59–65.

Nakamura, K., Izumiyama-Shimomura, N., Sawabe, M. *et al.* (2002) Comparative analysis of telomere lengths and erosion with age in human epidermis and lingual epithelium. **119** (5), 1014–1019.

Nambiar, P., Naidu, M.D. and Subramaniam, K. (1999) Anatomical variability of the frontal sinuses and their application in forensic identification. *Clinical Anatomy*, **12** (1), 16–19.

Oettle, A.C. and Steyn, M. (2000) Age estimation from sternal ends of ribs by phase analysis in South African Blacks. *Journal of Forensic Sciences*, **45** (5), 1071–1079.

Olze, A., Schmeling, A., Taniguchi, M. *et al.* (2004) Forensic age estimation in living subjects: the ethnic factor in wisdom tooth mineralization. *International Journal of Legal Medicine*, **118** (3), 170–173.

Paewinsky, E., Pfeiffer, H. and Brinkmann, B. (2005) Quantification of secondary dentine formation from orthopantomograms – a contribution to forensic age estimation methods in adults. *International Journal of Legal Medicine*, **119** (1), 27–30.

Pasquier, E., De Saint Martin Pernot, L., Pernot, L. *et al.* (1999) Determination of age at death: assessment of an algorithm of age prediction using numerical three-dimensional CT data from pubic bones. *American Journal of Physical Anthropology*, **108** (3), 261–268.

Perizonius, W.R. K. (1984) Closing and non-closing sutures in 256 crania of known age and sex from Amsterdam. *Journal of Human Evolution*, **13**, 201–216.

Pfeiffer, S. (1980) Age changes in the external dimensions of adult bone. *American Journal of Physical Anthropology*, **52** (4), 529–532.

Pilin, A., Pudil, F. and Bencko, V. (2007a) Changes in colour of different human tissues as a marker of age. *International Journal of Legal Medicine*, **121** (2), 158–162.

Pilin, A., Pudil, F. and Bencko, V. (2007b) The image analysis of colour changes of different human tissues in the relation to the age. Part 1. Methodological approach. *Soudní lékarství*, **52** (2), 26–30.

Pilin, A., Pudil, F. and Bencko, V. (2007c) The image analysis of colour changes of different human tissues in the relation to the age. Part 2: Practical applicability. *Soudní lékarství*, **52** (3), 36–42.

Post, R.H. (1969) Tear duct size differences of age, sex and race. *American Journal of Physical Anthropology*, **30** (1), 85–88.

Prakash, N. (2009) 27 years on, still struggling to get birth date corrected. *Hindustan Times*, 23 March, p. 9.

Prince, D.A. and Ubelaker, D.H. (2002) Application of Lamendin's adult dental aging technique to a diverse skeletal sample. *Journal of Forensic Sciences*, **47** (1), 107–116.

Puh, U. (2009) Age-related and sex-related differences in hand and pinch grip strength in adults. *International Journal of Rehabilitation Research*, **33** (1), 4–11.

Ratcliffe, J.F. (1986) Arterial changes in the human vertebral body associated with aging. The ratios of peripheral to central arteries and arterial coiling. *Spine*, **11** (3), 235–240.

Ren, F., Li, C., Xi, H. *et al.* (2009) Estimation of human age according to telomere shortening in peripheral blood leukocytes of Tibetan. *American Journal of Forensic Medicine and Pathology*, **30** (3), 252–255.

Reppien, K., Sejrsen, B. and Lynnerup, N. (2006) Evaluation of post-mortem estimated dental age versus real age: a retrospective 21-year survey. *Forensic Science International*, **159** (Suppl 1), S84–S88.

Riggs, B.L., Melton, L.J. III (3rd), Robb, R.A. *et al.* (2004) Population-based study of age and sex differences in bone volumetric density, size, geometry, and structure at different skeletal sites. *Journal of Bone and Mineral Research*, **19** (12), 1945–1954.

Ríos, L., Weisensee, K. and Rissech, C. (2008) Sacral fusion as an aid in age estimation. *Forensic Science International*, **180** (2–3), 111.e1–111.e7.

Rissech, C. and Malgosa, A. (2007) Pubis growth study: applicability in sexual and age diagnostic. *Forensic Science International*, **173** (2–3), 137–145.

Rissech, C., Estabrook, G.F., Cunha, E. and Malgosa, A. (2007) Estimation of age-at-death for adult males using the acetabulum, applied to four Western European populations. *Journal of Forensic Sciences*, **52** (4), 774–778.

Rösing, F.W., Graw, M., Marré, B. *et al.* (2007) Recommendations for the forensic diagnosis of sex and age from skeletons. *Homo*, **58** (1), 75–89.

Rougé-Maillart, C., Telmon, N., Rissech, C. *et al.* (2004) The determination of male adult age at death by central and posterior coxal analysis – a preliminary study. *Journal of Forensic Sciences*, **49** (2), 208–214.

Rougé-Maillart, C., Jousset, N., Vielle, B. *et al.* (2007) Contribution of the study of acetabulum for the estimation of adult subjects. *Forensic Science International*, **171** (2–3), 103–110.

Rougé-Maillart, C., Vielle, B., Jousset, N. *et al.* (2009) Development of a method to estimate skeletal age at death in adults using the acetabulum and the auricular surface on a Portuguese population. *Forensic Science International*, **188** (1–3), 91–95.

Ruff, C.B. and Hayes, W.C. (1982) Subperiosteal expansion and cortical remodeling of the human femur and tibia with aging. *Science*, **217** (4563), 945–948.

Ruff, C.B. and Hayes, W.C. (1984) Age changes in geometry and mineral content of the lower limb bones. *Annals of Biomedical Engineering*, **12** (6), 573–584.

Sabatier, J.P., Guaydier-Souquières, G., Benmalek, A. *et al.* (1999) Evolution of lumbar bone mineral content during adolescence and adulthood: a longitudinal study in 395 healthy females 10–24 years of age and 206 premenopausal women. *Osteoporosis International*, **9** (6), 476–482.

Santini, A., Land, M. and Raab, G.M. (1990) The accuracy of simple ordinal scoring of tooth attrition in age assessment. *Forensic Science International*, **48** (2), 175–184.

Schmeling, A., Olze, A., Reisinger, W. and Geserick, G. (2001) Age estimation of living people undergoing criminal proceedings. *Lancet*, **358** (9276), 89–90.

Schmitt, A., Murail, P., Cunha, E. and Rougé, D. (2002) Variability of the pattern of aging on the human skeleton: evidence from bone indicators and implications on age at death estimation. *Journal of Forensic Sciences*, **47** (6), 1203–1209.

Schranz, D. (1959) Age determination from the internal structure of the humerus. *American Journal of Physical Anthropology*, **17**, 273–277.

Sforza, C., Grandi, G., Catti, F. *et al.* (2009) Age- and sex-related changes in the soft tissues of the orbital region. *Forensic Science International*, **185** (1–3), 115.e1–115.e8.

Shao, Z., Rompe, G. and Schiltenwolf, M. (2002) Radiographic changes in the lumbar intervertebral discs and lumbar vertebrae with age. *Spine*, **27** (3), 263–268.

Shuster, L.T., Rhodes, D.J., Gostout, B.S. *et al.* (2009) Premature menopause or early menopause: long-term health consequences. *Maturitas*, **65** (2), 161–166.

Sievert, L.L. (2001) Menopause as a measure of population health: an overview. *American Journal of Human Biology*, **13** (4), 429–433.

Singh, I.J. and Gunberg, D.L. (1970) Estimation of age at death in human males from quantitative histology of bone fragments. *American Journal of Physical Anthropology*, **33** (3), 373–381.

Sitchon, M.L. and Hoppa, R.D. (2005) Assessing age-related morphology of the pubic symphysis from digital images versus direct observation. *Journal of Forensic Sciences*, **50** (4), 791–795.

Slagboom, P.E., Droog, S. and Boomsma, D.I. (1994) Genetic determination of telomere size in humans: a twin study of three age groups. *American Journal of Human Genetics*, **55** (5), 876–882.

Snieder, H., MacGregor, A.J. and Spector, T.D. (1998) Genes control the cessation of a woman's reproductive life: a twin study of hysterectomy and age at menopause. *Journal of Clinical Endocrinology and Metabolism*, **83** (6), 1875–1880.

Snodgrass, J.J. (2004) Sex differences and aging of the vertebral column. *Journal of Forensic Sciences*, **49** (3), 458–463.

Solheim, T. (1993) A new method for dental age estimation in adults. *Forensic Science International*, **59** (2), 137–147.

Solheim, T. and Sundnes, P.K. (1980) Dental age estimation of Norwegian adults – a comparison of different methods. *Forensic Science International*, **16** (1), 7–17.

Someda, H., Saka, H., Matsunaga, S. *et al.* (2009) Age estimation based on three-dimensional measurement of mandibular central incisors in Japanese. *Forensic Science International*, **185** (1–3), 110–114.

Steinbach, H.L. (1960) Identification of pelvic masses by phlebolith displacement. *American Journal of Roentgenology, Radium Therapy, and Nuclear Medicine*, **83**, 1063–1066.

Stephan, C.N. (2002) Position of superciliare in relation to the lateral iris: testing a suggested facial approximation guideline. *Forensic Science International*, **130** (1), 29–33.

Stewart, T.D. (1954) Metamorphosis of the joints of the sternum in relation to age changes in other bones. *American Journal of Physical Anthropology*, **12** (4), 519–535.

Stewart, T.D. (1957) Distortion of the pubic symphyseal surface in females and its effect of age determination. *American Journal of Physical Anthropology*, **15** (1), 9–18.

Stout, S.D. and Gehlert, S.J. (1982) Effects of field size when using Kerley's histological method for determination of age at death. *American Journal of Physical Anthropology*, **58** (2), 123–125.

Sugimoto, M., Yamashita, R. and Ueda, M. (2006) Telomere length of the skin in association with chronological aging and photoaging. *Journal of Dermatological Science*, **43** (1), 43–47.

Sun, Y.X., Zhao, G.C. and Yan, W. (1995) Age estimation on the female sternum by quantification theory I and stepwise regression analysis. *Forensic Science International*, **74** (1–2), 57–62.

Takahashi, H. and Frost, H.M. (1966) Age and sex related changes in the amount of cortex of normal human ribs. *Acta Orthopaedica Scandinavica*, **37** (2), 122–130.

Takasaki, T., Tsuji, A., Ikeda, N. and Ohishi, M. (2003) Age estimation in dental pulp DNA based on human telomere shortening. *International Journal of Legal Medicine*, **117** (4), 232–234.

Telmon, N., Gaston, A., Chemia, P. *et al.* (2005) Application of the Suchey–Brooks method to three-dimensional imaging of the pubic symphysis. *Journal of Forensic Sciences*, **50** (3), 507–512.

Todd, T. (1921) Age changes in the pubic bone. *American Journal of Physical Anthropology*, **4** (1), 1–77.

Todd, T. and Lyon, D.W. Jr. (1924) Endocranial suture closure. Its progress and age relationship, Part I: Adult males of white stock. *American Journal of Physical Anthropology*, **7** (3), 325–384.

Todd, T. and Lyon, D.W. Jr. (1925a) Cranial suture closure. Its progress and age relationship, Part II: Ectocranial suture closure in adult males of white stock. *American Journal of Physical Anthropology*, **8** (1), 23–43.

Todd, T. and Lyon, D.W. Jr. (1925b) Cranial suture closure. Its progress and age relationship, Part III: Endocranial closure in adult males of Negro stock. *American Journal of Physical Anthropology*, **8** (1), 44–71.

Todd, T. and Lyon, D.W. Jr. (1925c) Suture closure. Its progress and age relationship, Part IV: Ectocranial closure in adult males of Negro stock. *American Journal of Physical Anthropology.*, **8** (2), 149–168.

Treloar, A.E. (1981) Menstrual cyclicity and the pre-menopause. *Maturitas*, **3** (3–4), 249–264.

Tsuji, A., Ishiko, A., Takasaki, T. and Ikeda, N. (2002) Estimating age of humans based on telomere shortening. *Forensic Science International*, **126** (3), 197–199.

Turk, L.M. and Hogg, D.A. (1993) Age changes in the human laryngeal cartilages. *Clinical Anatomy*, **6**, 154–162.

Twomey, L. and Taylor, J. (1985) Age changes in lumbar intervertebral discs. *Acta Orthopaedica Scandinavica*, **56** (6), 496–499.

Ubelaker, D.H. and Parra, R.C. (2008) Application of three dental methods of adult age estimation from intact single rooted teeth to a Peruvian sample. *Journal of Forensic Sciences*, **53** (3), 608–611.

Vandevoort, F.M., Bergmans, L., Van Cleynenbreugel, J. *et al.* (2004) Age calculation using X-ray microfocus computed tomographical scanning of teeth: a pilot study. *Journal of Forensic Sciences*, **49** (4), 787–790.

Vasiliadis, L., Stavrianos, C. and Kafas, P. (2009) A forensic aspect of age characteristics of dentine using transversal microradiography: a case report. *Cases Journal*, **2** (1), 4.

Vastine, J.H. 2nd and Vastine, M.F. (1952) Calcification in the laryngeal cartilages. *AMA Archives of Otolaryngology*, **55** (1), 1–7.

Vaziri, H., Dragowska, W., Allsopp, R.C. *et al.* (1994) Evidence for a mitotic clock in human hematopoietic stem cells: loss of telomeric DNA with age. *Proceedings of the National Academy of Science of the United States of America*, **91** (21), 9857–9860.

Walker, R.A. and Lovejoy, C.O. (1985) Radiographic changes in the clavicle and proximal femur and their use in the determination of skeletal age at death. *American Journal of Physical Anthropology*, **68** (1), 67–78.

Wang, X., Li, X., Shen, X. and Agrawal, C.M. (2003) Age-related changes of noncalcified collagen in human cortical bone. *Annals of Biomedical Engineering*, **31** (11), 1365–1371.

Watanabe, S. and Terazawa, K. (2006) Age estimation from the degree of osteophyte formation of vertebral columns in Japanese. *Legal Medicine (Tokyo)*, **8** (3), 156–160.

Watanabe, Y., Konishi, M., Shimada, M. *et al.* (1998) Estimation of age from the femur of Japanese cadavers. *Forensic Science International*, **98** (1–2), 55–65.

Weale, R. (2001) Age, eyes, and crime. *Lancet*, **358** (9293), 1644–1645.

Wittwer-Backofen, U., Buckberry, J., Czarnetzki, A. *et al.* (2008) Basics in paleodemography: a comparison of age indicators applied to the early medieval skeletal sample of Lauchheim. *American Journal of Physical Anthropology*, **137** (4), 384–396.

Yang, F., Jacobs, R. and Willems, G. (2006) Dental age estimation through volume matching of teeth imaged by cone-beam CT. *Forensic Science International*, **159** (Suppl 1), S78–S83.

Yun, J.I., Lee, J.Y., Chung, J.W. *et al.* (2007) Age estimation of Korean adults by occlusal tooth wear. *Journal of Forensic Sciences*, **52** (3), 678–683.

13

The Presentation of Results and Statistics for Legal Purposes

David Lucy
Department of Mathematics and Statistics, Lancaster University, Lancaster LAI 4YF, UK

13.1 Introduction

In January of 2003 a young Turkish immigrant to Germany made his way into a women's fitness centre in Telgte, Germany and shot three members of that centre's cleaning staff. The offender in this instance was a young man named Timucin 'O'. He alleged he had been paid the equivalent sum of £3250 to kill the spouse of an associate. He also claimed he had killed the other two women in an attempt to cover his tracks by obscuring the motive for this particularly vindictive attack (Boyes 2003).

Timucin 'O' was soon in custody, the trial being held in Munster in July of 2003. He was originally to be tried as a full adult, but during the course of the trial it emerged that he might have been under 21 years of age at the time the offence was committed. German law precludes trial as an adult for those under 21 years of age, and consequently a maximum sentence of 10 years for an offence of this nature. However, Timucin 'O"s documents stated that he had been born on 26 January 1981, which would have made him over 21 at the time of the offence. Timucin 'O"s legal representatives claimed he had in fact been born on 26 January 1982 and that he was under 21 years at the time of the offence. The defence claimed that it is common for migrants to Germany to mislead the authorities about their age, and that records kept in Turkey would be too poor to establish age reliably.

To establish Timucin 'O"s age the defence took the unusual step of requesting a medical examination to see whether age-related observations could be used to

Age Estimation in the Living: The Practitioners Guide   Sue Black, Anil Aggrawal and Jason Payne-James
© 2010 John Wiley & Sons, Ltd

establish his age, thus determining whether he was under 21 years, 21 years or over 21 years, at the time of the offence.

This particular case is a specific instance where the pathologists' skills, expertise and judgement will be challenged in ways that may be initially unforeseen to them. Uncertainty in the age-related features imply that any judgement as to the age of Timucin 'O' will likewise be shrouded in uncertainty, and it is the quantification of that uncertainty with which statistical science concerns itself.

The question, in the case of Timucin 'O', revolved around whether he was under 21 years of age, at the time of the offence. This is a peculiarly precise question to which the pathologists must address themselves, but it is by no means the only question asked of pathologists and other investigators who are concerned with estimating the age of an individual from the physical manifestations of age. The question of the chronological age of an immigrant to a sovereign state upon entry to that state is of interest to authorities, as indeed it was in the case of Timucin 'O', and in previous chapters in this volume we have seen other similar critical uses for human age estimation. Participation in the correct age classes in junior sport, validation of age in adopted children, and the falsification of age for preferential educational treatment are some examples. More upsetting are cases involving the sexual abuse of children, the legal obligations of sovereign states to abandoned children, forced child labour, and the use of young men and women as soldiers.

The need for accurate and precise age estimates for individuals with no believable documented age is obvious; however, the importance of how accurate and how finely resolved an age estimate must be to fulfil its purpose depends upon that purpose and requires some consideration.

In the case of Timucin 'O', a finely resolved, and accurate, age is of utmost importance. In other instances this may not be the case. If an individual is claiming a pension, and for the UK the pensionable age for men is 65 years of age, then a 60-year-old claiming they are 65 in order to claim their pension some 5 years early will not be of such great importance. This is because the size of the pension will depend upon the number of years of contribution to the pension fund. If, by claiming a premature age, they claim their pension early any net financial advantage they may gain will be offset to a certain degree through the reduction in their final pension through the lower payouts. The same is true, to a lesser degree, for the component of their income provided by the state pension.

The same questions as to the accuracy and fine resolution can be asked of many of the social processes associated with immigration of individuals to any sovereign state that may be new to them. So long as an individual can be clearly placed into some category, or can not claim membership of some age-related category they are obviously not members of, then some fairly large-grained, inaccurate estimate of an individual's age will suffice for most purposes.

Even in fairly extreme cases of identity of living individuals, an accurate, and narrowly defined knowledge of chronological age, may be desirable but is not as critical to know as in the case of Timucin 'O'. On 7 April 2005, officers from Kent constabulary found a young man in a soaking wet suit wandering around the streets of Sheerness in England. He was named 'Piano Man' after playing said instrument for staff at the chapel at Medway Maritime Hospital. The quality of the recital was debatable (BBC News, 2005a,b; Moyes and Kaila, 2005). After some four months of baffling the British authorities, and a strenuous search by police and public throughout Europe, the young man was confirmed by the German authorities as 20-year-old Andreas Grassl from Prosdorf in Eastern Bavaria. At no point did the fact that Grassl was 20 years of age become critical; however, the knowledge that he was a young man was important to his eventual identification.

13.2   Evidence and Intelligence

Undoubtedly the quickest and most accurate method of age estimation is the location of some documentary evidence upon the individual for whom it is desired that chronological age be known. Unfortunately, a small portion of those for whom age needs to be known have concealed their true age and identity, so documentary methods tend to be prone to fraud and deception. A universal adoption of biometric-based records may help to combat this in the medium to distant future, but in the short term, accurate documentation that can be relied upon in all situations will not be available for all individuals.

In the absence of reliable documentary evidence, physicians, dentists and other health workers can, on the whole, make extremely appropriate estimates of age, particularly if those persons for which age needs to be known are from a population with which the dentist or health professional happens to be familiar. A health professional using their expertise will make finely balanced judgements based upon experience with many hundreds, or even thousands, of individuals for which they do know the chronological age, and with whom they have intimate day to day contact. These experts will use many age-related observables, some of which may be used only by that particular expert, and the expert may combine these observations to make some estimate for an age in a way that their experience best dictates. Anecdotal evidence suggests that an expert making a well-informed estimate will often, within a large sample, outperform even the best of anthropological measures.

However, what may be the most accurate estimate is not by necessity the best estimate to use in a legal context. In most jurisdictions the criminal and civil laws impose a burden of proof based upon evidence. Evidence is a form of information, but a very special form in that it is a public knowledge, or one that can be used to bear upon the truth, or otherwise, of some specific proposition in a very public way. This is still knowledge, but of a type that is distinct from a knowledge based upon instinct and unquantified experience, which can be a form of private knowledge known only to the mind that apprehends it. Evidence must be fully explicable, that is it must be based upon observations that are open so that all may make those same observations. The years and years worth of accumulated observations that exist in the mind of an expert do not, as a rule, constitute a set of data that is open to the sort of examination which would satisfy others as to its veracity. So, despite potentially being a more accurate estimate, estimates made by the experience and intuition of experts do not satisfy the criterion of being publicly demonstrable.

So it is for the expert to somehow make an estimate based upon observations, and using a method that can be used so others can come to the same, or very similar, conclusions as to an individual's chronological age. When seen with this light it is not so much a wonder that commonly used age estimation methods are imprecise, but that they manage to produce any estimates at all given they are based upon small, carefully measured, highly controlled training sets, and a very limited number of observables, which are at best poorly related to the chronological age of the individual.

13.3   Statistical Methods in Age Estimation

To satisfy the public nature of evidence, some method by which a set of observations that are age related can be turned into an estimate of age is required, and because any estimate of age will have associated with it a level of uncertainty, those methods will inevitably be statistical, or statistically based, methods.

There are broadly two classes of approach to using more formal quantitative methods for the estimation of the age of a human from the observation of their physical characteristics. From a statistical point of view, there is nothing special about the case where an individual is alive, or whether only the mortal remains of the individual are open to inspection by the pathologist or anthropologist. The only vital requirement is that there is some feature that can be observed which is related to age, and that for a given state of the feature the observations made by investigators will be the same, or different in some known way. The process of observation and inference is not, in principle, different between the deceased individuals seen by pathologists and physical anthropologists, and live individuals, although the actual features observed may be different.

The two sets of approaches, for want of better terminology, are:

1. Classical approaches, sometimes termed frequentist approaches, in which, among other tenets, a probability is seen as some function of ratios of frequencies. For frequentists the emphasis for inference tends to be on long runs of repeatable experiments (Efron, 2005).

2. Bayesian approaches, by contrast, tend to think of parameters as random variables in the same way that data are random variables. The emphasis for Bayesians is the estimation of probabilities, and probabilities tend to be expressions of degrees of belief.

Few applied statisticians would consider themselves as working exclusively in either of the two paradigms briefly characterized above. Most would tend to think in whatever manner best suited the nature of the immediate problem with which they were faced. There is a theorem called Bayes' theorem, which is the basis of any Bayesian approach. However, rather confusingly, frequentists may also use Bayes' theorem. This is because what is called Bayes' theorem is a small extension of the third law of probability, and, given the axioms of statistics, is equally true for both frequentist and Bayesian schools of thought.

Both approaches have been used by pathologists and forensic scientists for making estimates of age for humans for whom age was unknown.

13.4 Classical, or Frequentist, Approaches

If it has been observed that for a sample of individuals some specific feature changes in some systematic manner with age, then by appealing to induction, one can say that due to some inherent biological similarity the wider population of humans will respond in a similar fashion. If that change happens to be on a continuous scale of variation – that is, can, in principle at least, take on any value – and is not confined to groups, or to integer, or whole number, values, then some form of model may be considered an appropriate device by which to make estimates of the age for an individual of unknown age.

This process, at its simplest, assumes a linear relationship between age and the observable quantity, and the parameters for the model itself can be calculated by the minimization of errors in one, or the other. In which dimension errors should be minimized is a subject of debate (Aykroyd *et al.*, 1997; Samworth and Gowland, 2007), but what is less contentious is the form of any estimate of age made from such a model. Usually an estimate takes the form of a point, which represents the most likely age for the individual of unknown age, and an associated 'confidence interval', which is some measure of the uncertainty associated with the estimate. However, it is the nature of the confidence interval, which has a strict interpretation, that makes such estimates, in many circumstances, unsuited to forensic contexts.

A confidence interval involves some level, usually denoted α, as being equal to some percentage, or proportion, score. For instance, such an estimate, in the case of an age, may cite 'an $\alpha = 0.95$ confidence interval of 30 to 50 years', a strict interpretation of which means that *in the long run, were the same experiment repeated many times, on 95% of those occasions the quantity of interest would fall within the confidence interval.*

To interpret a confidence interval as somehow standing in for a distribution representing uncertainty about the point estimate would be incorrect. It would, for instance, be a misinterpretation to take the 68% confidence interval and treat it as one of the parameters of a corresponding normal distribution, then use that normal to calculate arbitrary percentile probabilities for other quantities of interest. A confidence interval should not really be treated in that manner, although many scientists do so.

13.5 Bayesian Approaches

An alternative to ordinary least squares regression and frequentist-based methods is Bayesian methods. These have been explicitly developed for population age profile estimation (Konigsberg and Frankenberg, 1992), and for giving estimates of age for an individual (Lucy, Aykroyd and Pollard, 2002).

Bayesian methods calculate a posterior distribution for the quantity of interest given the particular states for some set of quantities that may be observed. Some workers feel uneasy about using Bayesian approaches as, to calculate the posterior distribution, some prior distribution is required. The notion of a prior distribution for some scientists can be seen as a weakness in the Bayesian approach, although few statisticians will regard it as such.

A Bayesian approach will take some prior distribution for the age of an individual for whom age is unknown, using observations of that individual and other individuals who are of known age and thought to have some underlying biological similarity with the individual for whom age is unknown. Then the application of Bayes' theorem turns the observations and the prior distribution into a posterior distribution. It is the posterior distribution that is a probability distribution, and can be regarded in the Bayesian paradigm as the degree of belief for the age for the unknown individual given the observations and prior belief.

The key to Bayesian approaches is the production of a posterior probability distribution for the age of interest. This is in fact what many scientists think they are calculating when they conduct some form of regression analysis and calculate confidence intervals. Interpreting a posterior probability distribution is unproblematic. If the probability density function can be defined simply, say for instance it is normal, then any percentile range can be expressed as an age range.

13.6 The Relevance to Age Estimation

The discussion above should make it clear why statisticians have, especially in the past few years, been making many inroads into producing more and more Bayesian approaches to the various problems with which they are presented. If one's purpose is to calculate the value for a parameter of a model involving some natural process, and one is basing the estimate upon data from a repeatable experiment, then a 95% confidence interval is a perfectly reasonable way to couch the uncertainty of the estimate. A trivial example might be human height with age in the prepubescent phase of life. Overall stature of the individual will increase with age at a given rate, and that rate would be a parameter which one could calculate from some least squares fit of height to age, where height for any given age for a cross-section of the developing population may be considered to vary with some known random function. From this model the gradient would be known with some confidence interval, and the researcher would know that when, for other samples from this same population, 95% of the point estimates for the gradient would fall within the 95% confidence interval calculated in the first instance, for that is what a 95% confidence interval is.

It is this feature of frequentist statistics that can make the paradigm simply unsuited to answering questions of evidence. The notion of a 'long run' of identical, or nearly identical, experiments, has an appeal in sciences such as physics, where there are infinite potential observations to be made, or in chemistry, where an experiment can be repeated as many times as the experimenter has patience to do so, but in the forensic sciences the idea of a class of similar events has a more difficult meaning. In the context of an estimate made of age for an unknown individual there is precisely that, an individual. The experiment is not open to replication in the same way that the observation of the force of gravity is, or the products from a certain chemical reaction are. Even though upon each occasion an observation in a physical science is made, there is a univocity, or ontological singularity (Deleuze, 1990, p. 177) in a very technical sense, the instances have sufficient similarities that for practical purposes they can be regarded as a class of events. The singularities between forensic events are much more difficult, if not impossible, to regard as classes. For instance, criminal courts are concerned with the specific and particularistic, not the general. This manifests itself in a disinterest in whether a particular suspect has been found to commit offences of a certain nature in previous instances, and in fact any such evidence would be dismissed as prejudicial; instead, any criminal court would focus on *this* suspect and *this* offence on *this* particular occasion.

A confidence interval may be appropriate for any intelligence role of age estimation, where for instance an investigator may simply need a rough idea of the age of an individual, but in a case such as that of Timucin 'O' an answer involving a 'long run of similar observations' is no answer to the question of whether Timucin 'O' was over or under 21 years of age as the question is highly specific and repeated experiments are out of the question.

Does a Bayesian estimate offer a better solution to the problem? The answer is a rather ambivalent 'yes' and 'no'. Yes, because a posterior probability distribution given the observables, and the prior distribution, is a measure of belief to the specific question as to the age of the individual whose age is otherwise unknown. It has none of the baggage of repeatability of the confidence interval; however, it does carry the requirement for a prior belief. A prior belief should not be seen as an insurmountable obstacle to the calculation of Bayesian estimates for age. It is relatively easy to show that in the case of some linear models, the posterior estimate for the distribution for the age of an individual is normal, with parameters the same as the point estimate and confidence interval. The restriction is that the prior for the age distribution is the same as the age distribution for the training set from which the parameters for the model were calculated. There are many instances in which frequentist estimates, and confidence intervals, can be given a Bayesian interpretation with certain strong assumptions about the prior distribution, and age estimates can usually be restated along these lines.

To show a Bayesian estimate has certain properties that may be more suited to making any specific age estimate for forensic purposes rather than an equivalent estimate made from a frequentist tradition is not the same as answering whether Bayesian solutions are appropriate solutions as this depends very much on the nature of the individual estimates.

Returning to the case of Timucin 'O', if one were requested to make an estimate for age in which all the probability was so confined that it fell between 19 and 20 years of age, then the estimate would answer the question as to whether Timucin 'O' was under 21 years of age at the time the offence was committed, and would be affirmative. Similarly, were the posterior probability for age to be all above 25, then the question would be equally adequately answered, this time in the negative. However, an estimate of a 95% probability for Timucin 'O' of between 20 and 30 years of age doesn't really answer the question. One might use the posterior density function to calculate the relative posterior probabilities of him being under, and over, 21 years, then use that to calculate the posterior odds of him being under, or over, 21. This would be a form of answer that would encompass all the uncertainties within a publicly demonstrable form, the only disadvantage being that the prior distribution for age has to be agreed and stated.

Whether an age estimate answers the question or not can be seen to be dependent on the precision and accuracy of that age estimate. If, by some chance, the age estimates were highly precise and accurate, then from a practical point of view the exact nature of the treatment of the observations is immaterial. However, until some pathologist, or forensic anthropologist, makes some new discovery of an age marker that is highly correlated with chronological age, then forensic science will have to make the best of the somewhat vague age estimates that can be calculated from the current set of age-related features.

13.7 Likelihood Ratio Approaches

Part of the problem with the provision of an age estimate as an answer to some questions that might be posed in the course of a forensic investigation is that the age estimate itself verges, in some cases, on being a *non sequitur*. The legal question in the case of Timucin 'O' was 'was this individual 21 years of age, or greater, or under 21 years of age at the time he committed the offence?'. In some senses to answer, 'he was 20 to 30 years of age' fails to answer the legal question. If, as suggested above, one could answer 'he was precisely 20 years of age', or 'he was above 30', then the legal question would, by implication, be unambiguously settled. The salient point is that an extra inference is necessary to answer the legal question, but, in the case of an accurate and precise age estimate, this would be an unproblematic inference.

The estimate of age given as some range, or point estimate with some indication of uncertainty, is an attempt to answer any universal question pertinent to the age of the individual, and, if precise enough for the purpose in hand, will do so without the fact finder making a fairly solid inference from the information presented by the expert. However, for certain forms of question, it is possible to give an answer to the legal question in a more direct way without having to provide an age estimate, or make any attempt to provide some universal answer to the question.

In recent years statisticians who work in forensic science have been looking closely at a quantity called a 'likelihood ratio' as a measure of evidential value in forensic contexts (Aitken and Taroini, 2004). Although likelihood ratios are not new quantities, the uptake in their use over the past decade has been rapid. Likelihood ratios are, at the moment, seen as the measure of choice for evidential interpretation in DNA (Buckleton, Triggs and Walsh, 2005), glass (Curran, Hicks and Buckleton, 2000), handwriting (Bozza *et al.*, 2008), human identification (Steadman, Adams and Konigsberg, 2006), and more general multivariate matching problems (Aitken and Lucy, 2004; Aitken, Zadora and Lucy, 2007).

Likelihood ratios, in a simple form, are relatively easy to calculate, do not necessitate many prior assumptions, and answer questions involving dichotomous propositions in a direct way. The derivation and mathematical justification is usually approached from a Bayesian viewpoint; however, the use of a likelihood ratio, and its interpretation, are neither specifically Bayesian nor frequentist. A likelihood ratio is:

$$\text{likelihood ratio} = \frac{\text{probability of the evidence given one proposition}}{\text{probability of the evidence given the other proposition}} \quad (13.1)$$

and it is probably better to explain what it is, and how to calculate and interpret it, by example. Chapter 10 refers to a pioneering paper in age estimation (Gustafson, 1950), and the Appendix to this chapter has a table with a subset of two of the variables observed by Gustafson in that paper.

The terms in Equation 13.1 refer to probabilities given the truth of some propositions. In the case of Timucin 'O' the legal questions revolved around whether he was 21 years, or under, or over 21 years of age, so the propositions could be stated:

- Timucin 'O' was younger than 21 years at the time of the offence.

- Timucin 'O' was 21 years, or older, at the time of the offence.

These two propositions are exclusive and exhaustive in that they cover all possibilities for the age status of Timucin 'O', and they cannot both be true together. These propositions can be fitted into Equation 13.1, so that it becomes:

$$\text{likelihood ratio} = \frac{\text{probability of the evidence given Timucin 'O'} \geq 21 \text{ years}}{\text{probability of the evidence given Timucin 'O'} < 21 \text{ years}} \quad (13.2)$$

Which proposition appears on the numerator and which the denominator is a matter of personal preference. It is customary to have propositions that suggest the prosecution case as the numerator; here that is Timucin 'O' was 21 years, or greater, at the time of the offence and thus can be tried as an adult. Consequently propositions that suggest the defence case form the denominator, which here is that Timucin 'O' was under 21, and imply that he cannot be tried as an adult.

Next we need some evidence. Evidence can be, and in this case would be, a matter of simple observation, so suppose that an appropriate tooth was examined from Timucin 'O', and found to have a root dentine score, on the Gustafson scale, of zero. So the evidence, at the moment, could be said to comprise the observation that Timucin 'O''s root dentine translucency score was zero.

This new information can be inserted into Equation 13.2:

$$\text{likelihood ratio} = \frac{\text{translucency score} = 0 \text{ given Timucin 'O'} \geq 21 \text{ years}}{\text{translucency score} = 0 \text{ given Timucin 'O'} < 21 \text{ years}} \quad (13.3)$$

To put numbers into Equation 13.3 we need to appeal to data. Any appropriate database should suffice; for the purposes of the examples presented here those data come from Gustafson (1950). Here we do need two assumptions about the nature of the sample, and those individuals that comprise the sample:

1. The sample has observations made upon individuals who, using a form of the uniformitarian assumption, have some underlying biological similarity to the individual from whom the evidence has been extracted.

2. The sample has sufficient observations so the population frequency of the evidence can be estimated with sufficient accuracy from the data.

In this particular instance there may well be all sorts of reasons for doubting whether these two assumptions are true. The Scandinavian population upon which Gustafson made the original observations may have some fundamentally different rates of biological change with age in the dental organs, and Gustafson's sample was based upon only 41 teeth. However, as this example is purely illustrative we shall continue without addressing these potential shortcomings in the database.

Estimation of the two probabilities in Equation 13.3 from Gustafson's data can be made from the frequency table. Table 13.1 gives the numbers of individuals in each age category from Gustafson's sample, with each stage of root dentine translucency. The numerator from Equation 13.3 calls for the probability of observing Timucin 'O''s root dentine translucency score as zero, were it true that Timucin 'O' was 21 years, or of an age greater than 21 years. To find this from Table 13.1 we focus upon those who are at least 21 – that is, the bottom row of data – and see that there are $8 + 19 + 7 = 34$ individuals who were 21 or over. Of these 8 had a root dentine translucency score of 0. Were the requirements for the sample met – that is, Timucin 'O' has some form of underlying biological similarity to the sample, and that the observations from the sample were sufficient in both quality, and quantity, to estimate the relevant probability – then the probability of making the observation of Timucin 'O''s tooth having a root dentine translucency score of 0 could be said to be 8/34.

Table 13.1 Tabulation of root dentine translucency score from Gustafson (1950), the data for which are given in the Appendix.

	Transparency score		
Age group	0	1	2
Age < 21	7	0	0
Age ≥ 21	8	19	7

Here the rows represent those individuals who, in Gustafson's sample, were under 21, and 21 years and over, respectively. The columns correspond to the root dentine transparency scores. The numbers in the cells are the numbers of individuals from the age category with the given root dentine translucency state, so, for example, there are 7 individuals from Gustafson's sample who were under 21 years of age and who had a root dentine translucency score of 0, and 7 individuals who were 21 or over, and who had a root dentine score of 2.

The denominator in Equation 13.3 requires the probability of observing Timucin 'O''s root dentine translucency score of 0 were it true that Timucin 'O' were truly less than 21 years. Making the same assumptions about the relevance of Gustafson's observations as for the numerator, we can say that, of 7 individuals from the data who were under 21, 7 had root dentine translucency scores of zero. An estimate for the probability of observing a root dentine translucency score of zero were it true that Timucin 'O' were truly under 21 years of age could be said to be $7/7 = 1$.

Inserting these two probabilities into Equation 13.3:

$$\text{likelihood ratio} = \frac{8/34}{1} = \frac{8}{34} \tag{13.4}$$

which, in this instance, gives a likelihood ratio of 8/34, or, $\approx 1/4$. The interpretation of this figure is quite straightforward and uncomplicated, and could be stated: 'the observation of the root dentine translucency is 1/4 times as likely were Timucin 'O' 21 years of age, or over, than were Timucin 'O' under 21 years'. It is quite legitimate to invert this statement to: 'the observation of the root dentine translucency is 4 times as likely were Timucin 'O' under 21 years of age, than were he 21 years, or over, thus these observations offer limited support for the proposition that Timucin 'O' is under 21'.

Many observations that can be made of the human to establish chronological age occur in a multivariate case, and Gustafson's (1950) observations were no different.[1] Table 13.2 has data from Gustafson (1950) for the joint occurrences of attrition *and* root dentine translucency for those under 21, and those 21 or over.

Were the evidence from Timucin 'O' to consist of a root dentine translucency score of 0 *and* an attrition score of 1, then Equation 13.3 can be rewritten to take account of the additional information:

$$\text{likelihood ratio}$$
$$= \frac{\text{translucency} = 0 \text{ and attrition} = 1 \text{ given Timucin 'O'} > 21 \text{ years}}{\text{translucency} = 0 \text{ and attrition} = 1 \text{ given Timucin 'O'} < 21 \text{ years}} \tag{13.5}$$

Making the same assumptions, and working in the same way as in the univariate case, the numerator can be estimated by observing that there are 4 individuals who had a translucency score of 0 *and* attrition score of 1, of the 34 individuals who were over 21 years of age. The numerator can therefore be written as 4/34. The denominator in the likelihood ratio can be estimated by observing that there is only a single individual who has a translucency score of 0 and attrition score of 1, from

---

[1] Gustafson (1950) handled the multivariate nature of the observations by using an unweighted sum to reduce six observations from each tooth to a single observation. This made a great deal of sense in the light of Gustafson's subsequent use of a linear model, and produced a simplification that led to a highly manageable method of age estimation.

Table 13.2 Tabulation of root dentine translucency score and attrition score from Gustafson (1950), the data for which are given in the Appendix.

	Age < 21			Age ≥ 21		
	Translucency			Translucency		
Attrition	0	1	2	0	1	2
0	6	0	0	3	1	1
1	1	0	0	4	7	3
2	0	0	0	1	10	3
3	0	0	0	0	1	0

Here the left-hand side of the table represents those individuals who, in Gustafson's sample, were under 21 years, and the right-hand side those 21 years or over. The columns correspond to the root dentine transparency scores and the rows to the attrition scores. The numbers in the cells are the numbers of individuals from the age category with the given root dentine translucency state and the given attrition score. So, for example, there are 6 individuals from Gustafson's sample who were under 21 years of age, and who had a root dentine translucency score of 0 and attrition score of 0. There were 7 individuals who were 21 years of age or over, and who had a root dentine translucency score of 1 and an attrition score of 1.

the 7 individuals from the sample who were under 21 years. This gives an estimate for the denominator of 1/7. The likelihood ratio is the quotient of these, so:

$$\text{likelihood ratio} = \frac{4/34}{1/7} = \frac{28}{34} \tag{13.6}$$

and can be stated: 'the observation of an attrition score of 1 *and* a translucency score of 0 is ~7/9 times as likely were Timucin 'O' 21, or greater than 21, as were Timucin 'O' less than 21 years of age'. Or, again, it is perfectly legitimate to restate the inverse to frame the likelihood ratio in support of the defence case, which would read: 'the observations of a translucency score of 0 *and* an attrition score of 1 offer about 1.25 as much support for Timucin 'O' being under 21, than 21, or older than 21, thus these observations offer very limited support for the proposition that Timucin 'O' is under 21'.

The advantages for the forensic scientist of employing this sort of statement of the evidential worth, or value, of the observations, are not immediately apparent, but:

1. The scientist can confine their statements quite specifically to their observations, and the support those observations give to the various propositions, rather than being forced to make a comment upon the relative merits of the propositions. The truth, or otherwise, of a proposition is usually the province of the fact finders – juries, judges and the like – in most jurisdictions. A case may comprise of many elements, and much evidence. The scientist examines only the evidence in which they have some special expertise, and it is inappropriate, and premature, to comment upon the whole case from a single piece of evidence.

2. It allows the scientist to approach the question in hand directly, rather than giving an answer that requires further inference on the part of the fact finder to make the information provided by the scientist relevant to the question asked by the court.

3. Each and every assumption is clear and explicit. In this way a likelihood ratio easily satisfies every criteria for a 'publicly demonstrable' knowledge, making it a way in which a forensic scientist can safely provide a court with the full facts in as compact a form as possible.

4. The framework is simple, and can act as a template within which many problems of forensic evidence may be hung. However complicated any single probability calculation may be, the framework requires the calculation of only two conditional probabilities, which may be estimated by any legitimate means.

Chapter 1 highlights the sorts of questions with which the medical examiner or forensic scientist may be faced when approached to comment on the age of an individual. Many of these questions revolve around the ages of legal maturity, and can best be answered in any specific case by a likelihood ratio. However, not all questions of age can be addressed this way. Those questions tend to be where, for some form of record keeping, the age itself is required. So for passports an age estimate may be the best solution; however, for some document that is age dependent, such as a driving licence, the question may be 'is the individual qualified by age to hold some licence?', then the report of a likelihood ratio may be the best solution.

13.8   Errors of Interpretation

It would be all too easy to use some table such as Table 13.1 to find a posterior probability for the age group of any individual given the age-related observations. So, for the first example Timucin 'O' was said to have a root dentine translucency score of 0. From Table 13.1 there are $7 + 8 = 15$ individuals who have a root dentine translucency score of 0, 7 of whom were under 21 years. A statement that could be made might be, given the same assumptions about the sample as before, is 'the probability that some individual is under 21 years, given the observation of a root dentine translucency score of 0, is 7/15, or just under half'. A consequence is that the probability that Timucin 'O' is 21 years, or over, given the observation of root dentine translucency, is just over half. These two would, on the face of it, offer support for the proposition that Timucin 'O' was 21, or over 21; however, the forensic scientist should be on their guard for this sort of evaluation of the evidence.

The probability of 7/15 for Timucin 'O' being under 21 years is the posterior probability of age *given* the observations. It is a Bayesian estimate for the posterior probability for him being under 21 years, but it is easy to show that this Bayesian estimate has within it an implied prior probability for Timucin 'O' being under 21 years, which is equal to the probability of observing an individual from the sample who is under 21 years. As there are 41 teeth in the sample, 7 of which came from individuals who were under 21, this would make the prior probability of Timucin 'O' 7/41, which is quite a strong prior, and would require quite a lot of data in favour of the younger age group to make the posterior probability support that case.

It is this sort of confusion which modern statistical evaluation of forensic evidence hopes to avoid by using likelihood ratio based measures of evidential value.

Another error that scientists can be all too tempted by is to confuse the likelihood ratio for a posterior probability ratio, so some statement such as: 'the observations of a translucency score of 0, *and* an attrition score of 1 offer about 1.25 as much support for Timucin 'O' being under 21, than 21 or older' gets confused for a comment such as: 'it is 1.25 times as probable that Timucin 'O' was under 21, than 21 or over'. This statement has left out the important clause about the ratio being about observations, rather than propositions. This sort of error is called a 'transposed conditional', and is where the probability of observations given propositions is mistaken for the probabilities of propositions given observations. It is also sometimes referred to as 'the prosecutor's fallacy' because often it takes the form of a low probability for some evidence given the innocence of some suspect being mistaken for a low probability of innocence.

Evett (1995) suggests that all statements of probability should include the terms 'were', or 'given' to indicate precisely what the conditioning is for any probability, and forensic scientists can thus avoid making fundamental, and sometimes danger-ously so, errors of interpretation and evaluation.

13.9   Concluding Comments

Were it the case that pathologists, physical anthropologists and forensic scientists could assign an accurate and highly precise chronological age on the basis of some physical or other feature for human beings, then statistical calibration could largely be neglected. Unfortunately, this is not the case, and until some near miraculous set of age-related features is discovered, age estimates will always have some degree of uncertainty associated with them, and that uncertainty will, for the foreseeable future, be large.

Traditional frequentist methods of calibration have a precise interpretation involv-ing repeatability and samples from 'long runs' of identical events, which, although appropriate in many areas of science, can conflict with the ontological singularities that exist at a fundamental level in the forensic sciences. To circumvent these diffi-culties it is recommended that Bayesian estimates are used whenever possible, which have an interpretation that invokes a 'degree of belief' given the observations.

An estimate for age, followed by some interval that describes the uncertainty for that estimate, can be seen as a universal solution for questions surrounding age; however, it is not always the best solution in any given case and specific question within a legal framework. Many of the more critical questions set by case work can be dichotomised into sets of mutually exclusive and exhaustive propositions. Questions such as how old a young female found working in a brothel in London really is, from the legal view, more questions whether the young female is younger than, or older than, some arbitrarily defined chronological age stated in law. These questions can best be answered, and presented in court, as a likelihood ratio gives a measure of the strength of support of evidence for any given proposition without the forensic scientist having to comment upon their opinions upon the propositions themselves. Steadman *et al.*, although more interested in human identification, age being part of identification, point to how likelihood ratios can be used with continuous data, rather than the ordinal data illustrated in this chapter.

Age estimation will always require data upon which to base estimates of probabilities and/or parameters. These data should be conditioned correctly for the exact circumstances for the questions under consideration. For instance, any calibrated value of Timucin 'O''s chronological age, or estimate of a likelihood ratio for age class, should be based in so far as possible upon samples of humans drawn from those individuals of known age thought to somehow resemble him at some basic biological level. Many of the critical ages with which the law in various jurisdictions operates are at the younger end of the spectrum of human age, and it is this end that, from Chapter 7, is most prone to systematic change through secular trends in the way in which humans mature. This will be a significant factor in human age estimation regardless of the way in which an age is represented to the fact finder, and the purpose to which the age estimate is to be put. However, it is unlikely to prove a major problem so long as pathologists and forensic scientists are aware of the magnitude of the secular trends and account for them by either modelling them or using data from a temporally relevant sample.

Timucin 'O' was found to be guilty by a count in Munster, and was given a life sentence.

Appendix 13.A Age-Related Data from Gustafson (1950)

These observations were made from extracted teeth and are stages, or points, awarded to predefined stages in the development of quantities whose underlying distribution is continuous. As such, despite being from extracted organs, the discretized nature of these observations are similar to many of the age-related features used by pathologists and forensic scientists to make estimates of chronological age. Gustafson originally looked at six features from these data; here, for the purposes of illustration, we will only examine occlusal attrition and root dentine translucency.

Age	Attrition	Translucency	Age	Attrition	Translucency
11	0	0	48	1	1
12	0	0	48	0	1
12	0	0	49	1	2
13	0	0	49	1	2
15	0	0	50	2	2

(Continued)

(Continued)

Age	Attrition	Translucency	Age	Attrition	Translucency
16	0	1	51	2	2
17	0	0	51	2	1
23	0	0	51	1	2
23	0	1	52	1	2
25	0	0	52	1	1
28	0	1	52	2	1
35	1	2	53	2	0
37	0	1	55	1	1
37	0	0	55	2	2
38	1	2	59	1	2
38	1	1	64	1	2
39	1	1	64	1	0
39	0	2	65	1	2
45	1	2	69	1	3
45	1	1	69	1	1
48	2	1			

From Gustafson (1950).

References

Aitken, C.G.G. and Lucy, D. (2004) Evaluation of trace evidence in the form of multivariate data. *Applied Statistics*, 53, 109–122.

Aitken, C.G.G. and Taroni, F. (2004) *Statistics and the Evaluation of Evidence for Forensic Scientists*, John Wiley & Sons, Ltd, Chichester.

Aitken, C.G.G., Zadora, G. and Lucy, D. (2007) A two-level model for evidence evaluation. *Journal of Forensic Sciences*, 52 (3), 412–419.

Aykroyd, R.G., Lucy, D., Pollard, A.M. and Solheim, T. (1997) Technical note: Regression analysis in adult age estimation. *American Journal of Physical Anthropology*, 104 (2), 259–265.

BBC News (2005a) Fantastic response to 'Piano Man', 16 May, http://news.bbc.co.uk/1/hi/4550069.stm (accessed 13 May 2010).

BBC News (2005b) 'Piano Man' flies back to Germany, 22 August, http://news.bbc.co.uk/1/hi/england/kent/4172662.stm (accessed 13 May 2010).

Boyes, R. (2003) Murderer says he is too young to grow old in jail, *The Times*, 8 July.

Bozza, S. Taroni, F., Marquis, R. and Schmittbuhl, M. (2008) Probabilistic evaluation of handwriting evidence: likelihood ratio for authorship. *Applied Statistics*, 57, 329–341.

Buckleton, J., Triggs, C.M. and Walsh, S.J. (eds) (2005) *Forensic DNA Evidence Interpretation*, CRC Press, Boca Raton, FL.

Curran, J.M., Hicks, T.N. and Buckleton, J.S. (2000) *Forensic Interpretation of Glass Evidence*, CRC Press, Boca Raton, FL.

Deleuze, G. (1990) *The Logic of Sense*, Continuum, London.

Efron, B. (2005) Bayesians, frequentists, and scientists. *Journal of the American Statistical Association*, **100** (464), 15.

Evett, I.W. (1995) Avoiding the transposed conditional. *Science and Justice*, **35** (2), 127–131.

Gustafson, G. (1950) Age determination on teeth. *Journal of the American Dental Association*, **41**, 45–54.

Konigsberg, L.W. and Frankenberg, S.R. (1992). Estimation of age structure in anthropological demography. *American Journal of Physical Anthropology*, **89**, 235–256.

Lucy, D., Aykroyd, R.G. and Pollard, A.M. (2002) Nonparametric calibration for age estimation. *Applied Statistics*, **51** (2), 183–196.

Moyes, S. and Kaila, J. (2005) Exclusive: Piano Man sham, *The Mirror*, 22 August.

Samworth, R.J. and Gowland, R. L. (2007) Estimation of adult skeletal age-at-death: statistical assumptions and applications. *International Journal of Osteoarchaeology*, **17**, 174–188.

Steadman, D.W., Adams, B.J. and Konigsberg, L.W. (2006) Statistical basis for positive identification in forensic anthropology. *American Journal of Physical Anthropology*, **131** (1), 15–26.

14

Key Practical Elements for Age Estimation in the Living

Sue Black[1], Jason Payne-James[2] and Anil Aggrawal[3]
[1] *Centre for Anatomy and Human Identification, University of Dundee, Dundee, DD1 5EH, UK*
[2] *Cameron Forensic Medical Sciences, Barts and London School of Medicine and Dentistry, London EC1M 6BQ, UK*
[3] *Maulana Azad Medical College, New Delhi, 110002, India*

The most important element of any age estimation procedure is to ensure that it complies with, and fulfils, all local and/or national legal, jurisdictional, professional and ethical requirements. If any practitioner is in doubt with regards to the legality of any of the procedures, then it is paramount that this is addressed prior to commencement of any investigation. Recourse to this text as a legal guideline is not advised as the following protocols are based on the prime assumption that within the country of operation, approval for these procedures has already been given by both the judicial and investigative authorities and more importantly through non-coercive consent by the subject of the age estimation. Examples that have been given are jurisdiction specific. All practitioners, clinical or forensic, must take full responsibility for their actions in relation to the human rights of the subject undergoing investigation.

It is essential that the practitioner, clinical or forensic, undertaking the estimation is experienced in the interpretation and presentation of data emanating from the investigation. They must have a current and extensive understanding of the limitations of their investigation both in relation to the physical technology available to them and to the nature of the database to which they will refer, for comparison purposes. This also requires that the practitioner have a realistic understanding of the variation expressed by the human form and the extrinsic and intrinsic factors that may affect any age estimation process.

Age Estimation in the Living: The Practitioners Guide   Sue Black, Anil Aggrawal and Jason Payne-James
© 2010 John Wiley & Sons, Ltd

There are four fundamental pillars for age estimation investigation, and the greater the number of pillars that can be involved in the final evaluation, the more likely the result of the examination will correlate well with the actual chronological age of the individual. Each pillar will provide a potential range for the age estimation, and utilizing realistic overlap principles, the most likely age may become more focused following inter-pillar interpretation. However, it must always be borne in mind that while an underestimation of age is unlikely to raise any issue in relation to an infringement of human rights, an overestimation of age can have devastating effects. Therefore, while the lowest aspect of an age range may be considered to have a lesser impact on human rights, it is the upper extent of the range that is most important as the majority of age estimations will be undertaken for the purposes of ascertaining adult or juvenile status. It is essential that the final estimation is robust and conveys a realistic range within which the chronological age is most likely to occur. Any element of doubt must result in an increased range of possibilities for the age of the individual. It is also essential to remember that a legal boundary – for example, 21 years, which may determine whether an individual will be housed in a young offender institution or an adult prison – is an artificial judicial milestone and does not reflect any genetic or biological milestone that will be represented in the individual. Therefore, it is not possible in any circumstance to ascertain with certainty whether an individual is 20 or 21 years of age and it must be realized that an assessment of 20 years ranges from a specific calendar date (birthday) to a date that is 364 days beyond that date and only one day short of the assessment of an age of 21 years. Therefore, a chronological age is not a single point in time but a period that spans close to a full calendar year, which is a periodicity equivalent to the decision being asked regarding the age of the individual; that is, whether the person is 21 years of age or younger.

As research continues and technology advances, it is possible that in the future our estimations of age will become more accurate and reliable but at present our practices are based on fundamentally flawed procedures that were not developed for the purposes for which they are being used in this regard, and there is heavy reliance by courts, tribunals, and legal and medical professionals on data that are outdated and that may be inappropriate. All of these taken into account, should ring significant professional warning bells with practitioners and will ensure that any estimation undertaken will be, and should be, heavily scrutinized by opposing legal counsel. Any evaluative opinion is simply an informed opinion that should be based on a likelihood ratio.

The guiding principles of balance of probability, logic, robustness of methodology and transparency of procedures are core to the degree of reliability that can be attributed to the final result. The practitioner, clinical or forensic, must not attempt to give evidence that is outwith either their field of expertise or their level of experience. Professional self-awareness is critical to the judicial component of the investigation and to the human rights of the subject.

Therefore, before the practitioner commences their investigation, there are a number of questions that must be asked:

- Is the investigation legal?

- Do you have all the necessary consent? This includes from legal authorities, health authorities, clinicians and practitioners and particularly from the subject under investigation.

- Is the age estimation being based on a biological or a legal boundary for age? For example, a question that asks the likely chronological age of the individual is fundamentally different to the question that asks if the person is 21 years of age or younger.

- Do you have the necessary level of experience and expertise to undertake this investigation and on what is this based?

- Have you access to colleagues with other expertise that may reinforce your findings?

- Do you have appropriate reference data for comparison purposes?

- Do you understand the implications of using data that is not directly relevant to the individual under investigation?

- Do you have the level of experience and expertise to interpret the findings of this investigation in a realistic manner?

14.1   The Four Pillars of Age Estimation

14.1.1   Pillar 1: Social and Psychological Evaluation

This requires evaluation by a properly trained clinician or social work practitioner. The aim of this process is to assess the mental, and not the physical, maturation of the subject. The practitioner will interrogate areas of the person's life history in relation to recall of events and form an opinion as to the nature of the response both at the time of the events under discussion and the current attitude towards pivotal episodes in their past. Given the often traumatized nature of the individual being interviewed, it is essential that this is a slow process that builds trust and forges a bond between the individual being investigated and their assessor so that as objective a view as possible is achieved. It may be that on completion of this process there is deemed no need to progress to a physical estimation of age. This may be the preferred course of action as any further investigation will be physically intrusive and may be deemed objectionable and contrary to certain core human rights in some cultural groups.

14.1.2   Pillar 2: External Estimation of Age

This evaluation must be undertaken by a qualified medical practitioner (which may be a paediatrician for the child and geriatrician for the elderly). It is unlikely that a primary care physician will have the level of experience and expertise to undertake this investigation and interpret the findings appropriately. Some forensic physicians and some forensic pathologists will have such skills. It is essential that this examination is undertaken with the full consent of the individual being investigated as it requires that the clinician visually assess private areas of the individual's anatomy, and therefore sensitivity and discretion are paramount, particularly in relation to certain cultures.

In the prepubescent child, such an assessment of maturity may include some standard anthropometric parameters, including height, weight, chest circumference and so on. Recourse to population-appropriate growth charts will be essential and the practitioner must have access to current and relevant comparable data.

However, assessment of the presence or indeed absence of secondary sexual characteristics is most likely to be of value in the estimation of age in the sub-adult. There is no more advanced or appropriate system of grading pubertal status of external anatomical features than that of the Tanner stages, which have been referenced throughout this text. Therefore, in summary, assessment will be made on:

Hair

- Pubic

- Axillary

- Facial

- Chest.

Soft tissue characteristics

- Penile development

- Scrotal development

- Breast development.

Other features

- Date of menstruation

- Voice breaking

- Scars

- Tattoos and so on.

Of these, it must be borne in mind that hair is a transient feature that can be removed very efficiently through chemical means, and recall of the date of commencement of menstruation can be both subjective and fraudulently relayed. Written documentation of findings must address all of these issues, recording both positive and negative findings.

14.1.3   Pillar 3: Skeletal Estimation of Age

This investigation cannot be undertaken through external viewing of the individual and therefore relies on technology to assist the process. Exposure to much of the relevant technology carries a health warning with regards to ionizing radiation and therefore this pillar should only be undertaken when informed consent is secured from a series of parties to the investigation and professional guidelines are followed. The parties from whom consent should be sought include:

- The participant under investigation.

- The clinical premises which will be responsible for the imaging.

- The individual practitioner who will be responsible for operating the equipment.

This consent is essential for the practitioner and the clinical premises within which the investigation will be undertaken to ensure that they have not contravened any rules and regulations, and that the application of radiation for non-diagnostic or non-therapeutic purposes does not contravene their professional code of ethics. Consent from the individual to be examined should be in writing and obtained with the assistance of an interpreter or relevant adult if appropriate.

There is no doubt that the most cost effective and efficacious means of skeletal imaging that is most readily available in all clinical premises is standard flat plate radiographs. The technology is used to identify elements of continued growth or to confirm cessation of growth in certain regions of the skeleton. It is therefore imperative that the practitioner, whether clinical or forensic, select a region of the skeleton that:

- Ensures the safety of the patient in terms of protecting sensitive soft tissue from the side effects of ionizing radiation.

- Maximizes the likelihood of a relevant estimation of age.

Preference is therefore given to regions of the body that are outwith the central trunk to limit soft tissue exposure, particularly in relation to the proximity of the ovaries or testes and of course the uterus in case the patient should be pregnant. Therefore, the appendicular skeleton tends to be selected and bone growth at major joints is targeted. These will include in order of preference:

- Hand/wrist (usually left)

- Shoulder or knee

- Ankle

- Elbow.

The hip radiograph is not advocated, first because of the potential for radiation exposure to the pelvic region, and second as no reliable comparison atlas is available. The practitioner must accept that only one flat plate radiograph may be permitted and therefore it is essential that they choose a joint that is appropriate for the proposed age (or judicial area of interest) of the individual.

If CT capabilities are available then a scan that includes the following may prove to be of considerable assistance:

- Medial clavicle

- Acromion process

- Upper costal cartilages

- Upper sternal notches

- Laryngeal region.

CT cannot be utilized in individuals who may have any form of a metal implant (e.g. pacemaker, metallic implants).

MRI and ultrasound will likely increase in value as comparative data becomes available and as research continues in this area of investigation. These techniques ensure that the patient is not exposed to ionizing radiation and therefore comply more closely with health and safety requirements and form a potential solution to many of the issues on which objections may be based.

14.1.4   Pillar 4: Dental Estimation of Age

The dental investigation can occur following two processes:

- Visual intra-oral inspection

- Radiographic imaging.

A visual intra-oral inspection will inform the practitioner as to the stage of emergence and loss of the dentition and is particularly useful for age evaluation in the pre pubertal years. Pubertal and post-pubertal individuals will, however, require a radiographic investigation to be able to inspect areas such as root closure. While there is no doubt that greater image clarity is achieved via bitewing images, it is not appropriate to subject the individual to a series of radiographic procedures and therefore an orthopantomogram is currently the preferred process. This permits all dentition to be viewed following only one exposure although it is accepted that the definition is not as clear as for bitewing radiographs.

Removal of a tooth for analysis may be a possibility but in most countries this is unlikely to be considered an appropriate ethical option except in very rare circumstances and with the informed consent of the individual. It may be that teeth harvesting is undertaken at the time of dental treatment and extraction for health reasons. The practitioner must seek advice if such a request is made from their local/national ethics profiles to ascertain whether this is an accepted procedure. CT scans may be of value but if there has been any restorative work undertaken then this can cause artefacts in the final image, which will largely render them useless.

14.2 Conclusion

It is essential that the information obtained within any one pillar is assessed in relation to the age ranges provided within the other pillars. While no pillar carries precedence, greater reliability will be paid to information that is not dependent upon recall or that cannot be substantiated.

At the end of this process, the clinician or the forensic practitioner will provide the investigative authority with a potential age range for the individual. To ensure that this is achieved in the most objective way possible, it is imperative that the practitioner pay due respect to all information available from as many pillars as possible. Equally, it is essential that throughout the process the individual is accorded the highest level of dignity and respect as the procedures to be undertaken will undoubtedly cause some degree of discomfort. It is vital that the practitioner realizes and accepts that they are simply in possession of a tool box that is fundamentally flawed and not designed for the purpose for which they will use it. The outcome can only approximate to a chronological age and therefore a realistic evaluation with a comfortable age range is the best possible outcome for both justice and human rights. An analysis that provides a single age estimation or a very narrow range may indicate a practitioner who does not understand the limitations of their subject.

Index

Note: page numbers in *italics* refer to figures; page numbers in **bold** refer to tables.

Age Estimation in the Living: The Practitioners Guide Sue Black, Anil Aggrawal and Jason Payne-James
© 2010 John Wiley & Sons, Ltd